RADICAL
SUFFICIENCY

Selected Titles from the Moral Traditions Series

David Cloutier, Andrea Vicini, SJ, and Darlene Weaver, editors

RADICAL
SUFFICIENCY

WORK,
LIVELIHOOD,
and a
US CATHOLIC
ECONOMIC ETHIC

CHRISTINE FIRER HINZE

GEORGETOWN UNIVERSITY PRESS/WASHINGTON, DC

The publisher is not responsible for third-party websites or their content. URL links were active at time of publication.

Library of Congress Cataloging-in-Publication Data

Names: Hinze, Christine Firer, author.
Title: Radical sufficiency : the Catholic livelihood agenda / Christine Firer Hinze.
Other titles: Moral traditions series.
Description: Washington : Georgetown University Press, 2021. | Series: Moral traditions | Includes bibliographical references and index.
Identifiers: LCCN 2020008217 | ISBN 9781647120252 (hardcover) | ISBN 9781647120269 (paperback) | ISBN 9781647120276 (ebook)
Subjects: LCSH: Ryan, John A. (John Augustine), 1869-1945. | Economics—Religious aspects—Catholic Church. | Economics—Moral and ethical aspects—United States. | Social justice—United States. | Christian sociology—Catholic Church. | Christian sociology—United States. | United States—Economic conditions—21st century.
Classification: LCC BX1795.E27 H56 2021 | DDC 261.8/5088282—dc23
LC record available at https://lccn.loc.gov/2020008217

22 21   9 8 7 6 5 4 3 2 First printing

Cover design by Jeremy John Parker

For Brad, with thanks and love beyond all telling

CONTENTS

ACKNOWLEDGMENTS

Reflecting on one's debts of gratitude at the close of a twenty-plus-year project is humbling, heartening, and awe-inspiring. Throughout this long journey, I have been sustained by the kindness, support, care, and encouragement of many remarkable people. Some of these people have accompanied me continually, some at key junctures. Some are friends and family, some are colleagues; others professionals and medical, care, and service providers. Many know well how they've helped, others have helped in ways cherished by me but likely unknown to them.

Of this vast roster, I can mention just a few of you by name. But to all of you, my own "communion of saints" near and far, living and dead: I am profoundly grateful. I could not have done it without you. I pray that this moment of completion for me is a moment of grace for you as well.

I thank the Louisville Institute for the Christian Faith and Life Sabbatical Grant that enabled me to embark on this project. Great thanks are also due to past and current editors and staff at Georgetown University Press, especially Richard Brown; James Keenan, SJ; David Cloutier; and Al Bertrand. I am most grateful for your patience and for your confidence in this work.

Thanks to Marquette and Fordham University deans, theology departments, and staff for generous writing, collegial, and administrative support. I thank artist Mark Thomas for granting permission to use the image of his 2011 painting *Distribution* on the book's cover. And warm thanks to the Dominican Sisters of Hope and staff at Mariandale Retreat Center in Ossining, New York, especially Linda Rivers, OP, for gifts of hospitality and quiet space to think and write.

Heartfelt thanks go to my wonderful mentors and colleagues over the years, many of whom I am privileged to also call friends, including Charlie Curran, Elizabeth A. Johnson, James M. Gustafson, Robin W. Lovin, and fellow faculty at St. Norbert College, Marquette University, and Fordham University.

For exemplary research and editing assistance, thanks to Kari-Shane Davis Zimmerman, Krista Stevens, Mary Kate Holman, Vanessa Williams, Paul Schutz, Jim Robinson, Meg Stapleton-Smith, and in particular, the stellar Catherine Osborne. For their support and encouragement I thank Maria

Terzulli and Angela Alaimo O'Donnell of Fordham's Curran Center and my department chairs Phil Rossi, SJ; Patrick Carey; Terry Tilley; and J. Patrick Hornbeck.

I am grateful for the friendship of many, but in special ways to Marcie Paul, M. Shawn Copeland, Deirdre Dempsey, Judi Longdin, Steve Goldzwig, Lee Coppernoll, and the Mustard Seed and Faber CLC communities; to Brenna Moore and John Seitz, Michael Lee and Natalia Imperatori-Lee; and especially to my best friend of over a half century, the irreplaceable M. Beth Hendershot.

I am deeply grateful for the support and love of my late parents, Donald and Rosemary, my remarkable siblings, Donna, Jane, Paul, and Peggy, and their families, as well as my Hinze family relatives. Finally, my greatest thanks and unending love go to my spouse, Brad, and to our beloved sons, Paul Thomas and Karl Joseph, and partners Gabrielle and Jeff.

The American Dream and the Dream of Livelihood

Over the past century and more, the US experience has been shaped by a widely shared narrative of civic and economic success, encapsulated in a discourse of "the American dream." Deeply etched into the national consciousness, this common dream is variously conceived and expressed.[1] At its civic and political heart is a vision of "liberty and justice for all," accompanied by the freedom to engage in "the pursuit of happiness." And whatever else it has meant, this sought-for happiness has included, prominently and unabashedly, economic well-being.

The millions who have pursued this dream have judged success using varied standards and criteria. For some, attaining the American dream has required great wealth and a conspicuously consumptive lifestyle. Abetted by popular tales of rags-to-riches successes possible "only in America," faith in this grandiose goal has assuaged the consciences of the rich and fueled the fantasies of many poor and working-class families, especially new and prospective immigrants.[2] Many others have measured success in more modest terms: acquiring and keeping a decent-paying job, being able to support one's family and pay one's bills, and perhaps buying and maintaining a home of one's own. Still others among the poor and working poor have grasped at just a tiny corner of that dream, devoting themselves to educating and securing upward mobility for children whose lives, they hoped, would be better than their own. At its heart, American dream rhetoric has celebrated people's desire to make and enjoy a "good living" through work whose conditions and rewards make possible dignified material and social circumstances for oneself and one's household. And at least in this basic sense, most have agreed, this dream ought to be within the reach of every citizen and family.

As workers and families pursue their dreams of a good living, their activities also carry moral, even spiritual import. Beneath the surface of Americans' efforts to achieve a better economic life lie moral landscapes shaped by groups' culturally embedded identities and histories, and by crisscrossing patterns of social power. And percolating in the daily labors that command our energies and attention are spiritual dynamics—questions, yearnings, hopes, and fears that orient persons in relation to meaning, transcendence, and ultimacy.

True, labor's toil and trouble can lead people to minimize their expectations concerning work and its rewards—as when we shrug and sigh, "It's a living." But most people, most of the time, seek more from economic activity than simply a paycheck, a full stomach, or a pile of consumer goods. Through their labor in households and in paid workplaces, people seek material sufficiency and security, but they also seek to foster capabilities and exercise creativity and to participate in and contribute to their communities. Seen in this fuller way, our aspirations for a *good* living disclose vital features of a life lived with wholeness and dignity in the company of loved ones, neighbors, and fellow citizens. Together with other essential human activities such as leisure and reflection, across arenas including the familial, political, and religious, the economic flourishing that "a good living" connotes plays a foundational role in making possible the larger, multifaceted good of a whole and happy life.

Over the past century, people have attained this American dream of a good living to sharply varying degrees. Yet this undeniable fact has not dispelled the dream's influence. Distilling a powerful and resilient set of beliefs, aspirations, and expectations, the American dream's formative ideology conveys a set of criteria for measuring success, failure, and worth. President Bill Clinton, for example, invoked this ideology in a 1993 speech, declaring, "The American dream that we were all raised on is a simple but powerful one—if you work hard and play by the rules you should be given a chance to go as far as your God-given ability will take you." In this single sentence, sociologist Jennifer Hochschild comments, Clinton "captured the bundle of shared, even unconsciously presumed, tenets about achieving success that make up the ideology of the American dream. Those tenets answer the questions: Who may pursue the American dream? In what does the pursuit consist? How does one successfully pursue the dream? Why is the pursuit worthy of our deepest commitment?"[3] Hochschild articulates four of these shared tenets. First, every American can pursue the dream, and even if one falters, one can always start again. Second, while nothing is guaranteed, everyone has a reasonable chance to realize success. Third, "success results from actions and traits under one's control." Finally, virtue—especially honesty, responsibility, and hard work—begets success, and success, in turn, demonstrates a person's virtue.

This belief set packs a potent psychic punch, not least by blurring the differences between success's realistic anticipation and its certain expectation.

Linking these two, Hochschild writes, "presents little problem so long as there are enough resources and opportunities that everyone has a reasonable chance of having some expectations met." But the fact of failure "challenges the blurring between anticipation and promise that is the emotional heart of the American dream." And because, as the third tenet posits, success is largely of one's own making, those who fail most likely "lack talent or will." The American dream ideology's fourth tenet, "the association of success with virtue," compounds failure's shamefulness, for "if success implies virtue, failure implies sin," or at least personal or moral inadequacy.[4] These powerful beliefs help explain why persons facing underemployment, unemployment, or financial insecurity often feel betrayed, guilty ashamed, or stigmatized to degrees that far transcend their lost wages or diminished material circumstances.[5]

Into the early twenty-first century, Americans of all classes clung to the belief that those who work hard and play by the rules can expect to attain reasonable economic success.[6] Yet over the course of US history, powerful structural dynamics have smoothed the path to economic success for members of some groups (primarily white male elites), while obstructing or blocking the way for others. For non-elites—the lower-middle and working classes, the working poor, and the poor—roadblocks to dignified livelihood have been numerous and persistent, "working hard and playing by the rules" notwithstanding. In times of economic downturn, the obstacles to livelihood faced by these groups further multiply.

This book concerns non-elite American families' quest for economic well-being through the work women and men perform daily, in homes, in communities, and at paid jobs. I also explore larger impulses and patterns—economic, cultural, political, moral, and spiritual—that surround and undergird these ordinary activities. As I investigate US work justice in the early twentieth and the early twenty-first centuries, US Catholic families' stories provide my focus. Along the way I will consider livelihood's many dimensions, ambiguities, and struggles surrounding its pursuit and its prospects in the present century. Drawing on elements of both the American dream and modern social Catholicism's dreams of justice and flourishing, I will describe and advocate for a twenty-first-century economic ethic that situates the pursuit of livelihood within a larger vision of sustainable "radical sufficiency" for each person, and for all.

US CATHOLICS AND LIVELIHOOD

The story of US Catholic families' quest for work justice and dignified livelihood over the past century-plus is entwined in the larger plot of American working people's dreams and struggles to make it, by making a good living. Though not always explicitly aware of this, Catholic working families have also been heirs to a different dream about livelihood, grounded in a tradition of Catholic moral thought that has been officially articulated as "modern Catholic social teaching." Since the late nineteenth century, Catholic leaders seeking to respond to the problems facing working people and their families in modern industrialized economies have engaged this teaching's evolving moral vision, whose centerpiece is the right of workers to a decent livelihood by way of a family supporting, living wage.

Over the course of the nineteenth and early twentieth centuries, waves of Catholic immigrants from Ireland, Germany, and later Italy, Eastern Europe, and Latin America, flocked to working-class jobs in US urban centers. In the early decades of the twentieth century, the fight for a "family living wage" crystallized a broad economic and cultural agenda that animated social justice efforts joined by Progressive Era political, labor, and religious leaders. For Catholic leaders, their church's advocacy for economic justice and the large number of Catholics among the working classes made support for the living-wage and union movements a natural fit.

Easily the most prominent and influential of these Catholic leaders was the priest-economist Monsignor John A. Ryan (1869–1945). In his 1906 treatise *A Living Wage* and his 1916 text *Distributive Justice*, and through wide-ranging publications, activism, teaching, and policy work, Ryan interpreted for the US setting the nascent modern tradition of official papal teaching on work, family, and economy initiated by Pope Leo XIII's groundbreaking 1891 social encyclical on the condition of labor, *Rerum novarum*.[7] As a priest, scholar, activist, and public intellectual, Ryan engaged vigorously in Progressive Era policy debates, helped draft several pieces of labor-friendly legislation, and became a well-known and articulate supporter of the legislative and economic initiatives of Franklin D. Roosevelt's New Deal. Ryan's Catholic economic ethics infused an influential form of US social Catholicism that left a strong mark on both subsequent episcopal teaching and lay thought and action.[8]

Ryan, following the lead of Popes Leo XIII and Pius XI, focused his work justice agenda on practical reforms to benefit vulnerable working families in the waged economy. Yet both Ryan and the popes situated economic practicalities within a broader, Catholic understanding of personal and common flourishing fostered within families, local communities, civil society and state, and church. In Catholic social thought, economic institutions and activities are organically connected within, and serve, a moral-spiritual vision of reality that integrates the spiritual and the material, the temporal and the eternal. The specific shapes of social institutions differ with changing circumstances, but their fundamental concern and goal remains the same: the *totum bonum* of a dignified life for each and all, whose parts fit together in a coherent fabric of meaning and value. Part of the appeal of the family living wage agenda was its ability to capture, for its day, an economic version of this integrative ideal.

By the time of Ryan's death in 1945, twentieth-century American families had experienced two world wars, punctuated by the Great Depression. The prosperous post–World War II era was also a period of unprecedented development for the US Catholic community. Large Catholic families contributed to a postwar "baby boom." Catholic schools and religious institutions burgeoned, and many Catholics migrated from the working into the middle classes. Although still somewhat set apart by their religious allegiances and practices, by the late 1950s most Euro-American white Catholics were more settled than ever in the American mainstream. Many were moving away from their parents' working-class jobs and urban, parish-bounded neighborhoods into the world of white-collar professionalism and suburbia.[9] As they later grappled with dramatic shifts in the Church wrought by the Second Vatican Council (1962–65; also known as Vatican II), US Catholics were also buffeted by the waves of cultural, social, and economic change that swept through the 1960s and 1970s, and their repercussions in the 1980s and 1990s. Over this period, the majority Euro-American Catholic population and its leaders engaged questions and conflicts pertaining to gender, class, and race in ways that often differed little from the responses of white America as a whole.[10]

ETHICAL AND THEOLOGICAL APPROACH

Radical Sufficiency probes the narrative of US Catholics' pursuit of economic livelihood in search of a more complete understanding of the dynamics of work and livelihood over the last century. Building this more comprehensive picture will equip us to better evaluate trends surrounding livelihood in our current century, and to propose directions for the future. I argue that our twenty-first-century circumstances demand a US Catholic ethics of work and livelihood that is critical, comprehensive, and radical. By *critical*, I mean relentlessly dedicated to uncovering and acknowledging reality, truth, and value wherever they may be found. This is in line with modern Catholic social teaching's insistence on the relationship between truth and ethics.[11] Being *comprehensive* requires attending to livelihood's larger context and multiple dimensions. And an approach that is *radical*, as the word's etymology suggests, interrogates the roots and underlying meanings of ideas and events, in all their complexity and including their structural and ideological and dimensions.

This challenging project requires a stance and method adequate to the task. To this end, I engage the US work-justice problem from a theological-ethical perspective influenced by social-critical, progressive-liberationist, and feminist strands in contemporary Catholic and secular thought. My theological-ethical lens refracts modern social Catholicism's emphasis on sacramentality, solidarity, and transformation. *Sacramentality* refers to the Catholic affirmation that any dimension of created reality can be a mediator of or site for encountering the sacred, ultimately, God's presence and trans-forming grace.[12] Seeing the world sacramentally reveals its beauty and inter-connectedness but also its brokenness. Such seeing invites a moral and spiritual response: *solidarity.* As the recognition, acceptance, and respon-sible engagement of our interdependencies with neighbors near and far, solidarity combats falsely atomistic or fatalistic understandings of person-hood, work, and economy. Finally, opposing an economic status quo where subtle forms of sloth or cultured despair reinforce a creed of "me and mine," Catholicism's sacramental and solidary emphases underwrite avenues for work and economy that are concretely *transformative.*[13] Inspired by Ryan's hope, expressed a century ago, that his Catholic economic ethics was both publicly persuasive and "sufficiently radical," I propose *radical sufficiency* as the linchpin of a fresh, compelling agenda for work justice and good liveli-hood in the present day.

Because a Catholic ethic seeks truth and value wherever it may be found, what follows draws on diverse sources of knowledge and wisdom, including political and social theory, the social sciences (especially history and eco-nomics), and observations of concrete circumstances and particular expe-riences. Critical social analysis will be facilitated by sources that illumine dynamics of power, conflicts of interest, and the workings of ideology in the arenas of economy and work. And to steady a multifaceted investigation, I employ Ryan's succinct formula for worker justice—sufficiency, security, and status—augmented by a fourth aim developed for the twenty-first-century world: sustainability.

Like other religious traditions, Catholic Christianity is grounded in the affirmation, intuition, or gamble that life is about something more than the daily struggle for material survival. Simultaneously, Catholicism's incarna-tional sensibilities affirm and celebrate the fact that life's deeper registers sound within and through the material, the particular, the local, the small, and the passing. As embodied, reflective, spiritual beings, we are enmeshed simultaneously in the deep and the daily. Household, local community, work-place, or public square: the gaze of faith recognizes in each of these arenas a spiritual depth that furnishes the soil and roots whereby human persons exist, survive, and thrive in the medium of the mundane. Always present, this depth is available for notice by the rightly attuned eye, ear, mind, and heart.[14]

Work and economy, even when seen in this contemplative light, do not lose their everydayness. A Catholic perspective does not catapult working for a living into some angelic or idealized spiritual zone. But incorporating this spiritual lens has several important consequences. First, it helps us situate economy and work within a broader and deeper narrative about life's interconnectivity and meaning. Second, seeing the tethering of our economic strivings and material delights to deeper meanings, hopes, and desires illuminates our daily labors as both fully human and redolent of the holy. Third, while honoring the everyday, this spiritual lens challenges our tendencies to seek total security, complete sufficiency, and ultimate power or status by way of economic—or any other—activity or achievement. As Ryan puts it, we are led to love our work and the rewards it brings "in proportion to [their] likeness to God." This study keeps its eye, then, on the intermeshing material and moral, quotidian and transcendent dimensions of economic life, as from Leo XIII forward, modern Catholic social teaching and its interpreters have consistently tried to do.

TWO FOCI FOR CRITICAL INQUIRY

Aided by social sciences and critical social theory, I give special attention to two lines of questioning; each illumines consequential subtexts that thread through the historical narrative of US Americans' pursuit of livelihood. First, I will be asking how the relation between household and public economies has been understood and enacted. Ryan's Catholic living wage agenda depicted the household/public economy relationship in ways that reflected the industrialized and urbanized conditions of US political economy in his day. Since the mid-nineteenth century, the domestic household had receded as the primary site of work and production for most people. The arenas of household and waged work had become increasingly separate, and increasingly gendered. Once a center of economic production, the household was reconstructed as a locale of unpaid domestic labor and consumption activities. As we shall see, the story of family and work over the past century has enfolded shifting relations and tensions between gendered ideas and practices surrounding feminized "care work" and masculinized "providing work." Gendered expectations about breadwinning and homemaking influenced policy and popular consciousness, while marginalizing or subtly disgracing those who, like the millions of women who were "out to work" even in Ryan's day, could or would not conform to the cultural norm.[15] Mindful of shifting household and workplace dynamics over the latter decades of the twentieth century, a twenty-first-century agenda for inclusive livelihood must address and reconceive key aspects of this domestic-public economy relationship.

A second line of inquiry will focus on how relations of power, negotiated along lines of socially interpreted difference—sexual, racial-ethnic, and class—shape pursuit of livelihood in public and domestic economic arenas and influence how these arenas are related and distinguished. "Power," observes Catholic economic ethicist Daniel Finn, "is part of the software of organizational life, of relational life. And ignoring it in any view of human life—especially in a theological view—can only handicap the attempt at understanding and undercut any attempt at transformation. Attempting to understand human life while avoiding any analysis of power is like trying to play ping-pong while ignoring a strong crosswind."[16]

This study will attend to these crosswinds in twentieth-century US labor history by analyzing the ways power gets distributed and exercised along shifting lines of asymmetrically valued difference. Specifically, we will study influential, morally ambiguous power dynamics at work in our modern economy's treatment of gender, women, and "women's work"; in links between evolving standards of livelihood and class-based values and inequalities; and in the United States' ugly history of racism and nativism, one effect of which has been to limit full access to civic rights and a good livelihood to the "white" working man and his family. In the economic narrative of the last century, gender, racial-ethnic, and class subplots are tightly intertwined. Within them lie complex stories of opposition and coalition, of pride and shame, of submission and resistance, and of inflicting and enduring suffering and oppression, which my account will only be able to suggest.

Though rarely highlighted in official social teaching, Catholic commitments to justice and solidarity warrant—indeed, require—this kind of power analysis. To this end, subsequent chapters probe what Pope Benedict XVI calls "logics of power" in US economic life, and the ways power disparities have been reinforced by distorted, deeply ingrained valuations and practices surrounding group identities and differences.[17] At the heart of what theologian Bernard Lonergan, SJ, calls collective bias, and what Pope John Paul II and Pope Francis call structures of sin, these warped valuations and practices help generate, legitimate, and entrench socio-economic inequality, exploitation and exclusion. And by fostering a false consciousness that occludes structural dynamics, they impede well-intentioned people from recognizing, understanding, or effectively combating economic injustices.[18] Because pernicious historical patterns, valuations, and practices surrounding class, race, and gender form a particularly ugly snarl in the fabric of US economic and social life, sorting through and addressing them is an essential task for any project that seeks to enact "intelligent love" in the economic sphere today.[19]

RETRIEVING AND RADICALIZING RYAN

One way to capture the intersections between the profound and the mundane in a Catholic ethic of livelihood is through Ryan's summary vision of worker justice. Ryan held that complete justice for workers and their families comprised three essential elements: sufficiency, security, and status. Ryan's plain meaning here is sufficiency through a living wage; security against old age, illness, or calamity through benefits and pensions; and status at work, through opportunities to creatively participate and share appropriately in the business's running and profits. Yet we can also glimpse in this formula the larger moral and religious vision that grounds and animates Catholic economic thought.

Ryan regarded economic sufficiency, security, and status as fundamental prerequisites that, once attained, create the conditions for people to cultivate and exercise their "higher faculties" for knowledge and love. On this view, economic sustenance and well-being provide a sturdy ground or platform from which we can "look up" to engage higher, immaterial things. While not the supreme good, however, economic engagement and its fruits are not merely stepping-stones to what is truly important. As part of what Thomas Aquinas called the *bonum honestum* of our temporal lives, economic life, work, and livelihood are genuine human goods, valuable in themselves.

Ryan was no mystic; the very suggestion would likely have elicited laughter from those who knew him; and his public-facing writings tended to relegate God language to the background. Yet his economic ethics is firmly anchored in a theological worldview that cherishes the dignity of persons as *imago dei*, beings made in God's image whose authentic flourishing—in a freely embraced life of love and communion—glorifies God; beings whose sin and immorality are real and pernicious but who are also susceptible to the healing powers of redemptive grace; and beings whose ultimate and complete blessedness rests in a final destiny of union with God and neighbors.

Ryan and the Catholic social tradition, then, approach work and economic well-being as genuine human goods that also provide conditions for seeking and attaining supervening, noneconomic human and spiritual goods. To fulfill its purposes, a decent livelihood must entail not just "bare subsistence" but rather access to the range of things a person needs "to live in a manner worthy of a human being." For Ryan, these include "food, clothing and housing sufficient in quantity and quality to maintain the worker in normal health, in elementary comfort, and in an environment suitable to the protection of morality and religion; sufficient provision for the future to bring elementary contentment, and security against sickness ... and sufficient opportunities of recreation, social interaction, education and church membership to conserve health and strength and to render possible the exercise of one's higher faculties"—that is, one's ability to "know the best there is to be known, and love the best there is to be loved, namely, God, and his creatures in proportion to their likeness to Him."[20]

In short, the modern Catholic labor-justice agenda reflects and connects to deeper emotional, psychological, and spiritual realities that anchor and form human life in ways beyond the material. Though I doubt he explicitly intended this, Ryan's "three-S" formulation—sufficiency, security, and status—also points to human needs and aspirations for wholeness and freedom in their existential and spiritual aspects. We yearn for sufficiency, for enough, to be freed from consuming hunger and crippling lack. Security connotes freedom from bondage to fear and anxiety about the future. Status points to the importance of being liberated from the invisibility, humiliation, impotence, and harm that come with being oppressed, excluded, marginalized, or treated as of no account. In every sector of our existence, it turns out, we need and seek these three; when, despite our efforts, they elude us, we fear, mourn, languish, or lash out. In both our personal and collective lives, conflict and violence frequently arise from threats—real or perceived—to one or more of these three.

For Christians, ultimately, only a loving, sustaining, and forgiving God can fully and completely meet humanity's very deepest needs and desires for deliverance from want in the present; from fear and anxiety about the future; and from marginalization, shame, and worthlessness. In the scriptures, the profundity of these basic human needs and yearnings comes through strikingly in the Psalms, perhaps quintessentially in Psalm 23. In this beloved text, which begins "The Lord is my shepherd, I shall not want," sufficiency beyond one's own effort or desert, security amid and beyond one's fears, and one's status as loved, cared for, and significant are all trustingly anticipated as the gifts of a provident, shepherding God, who in the New Testament becomes identified with Jesus.[21]

Across the last century, labor justice advocates have focused on the practical sufficiency, security, and status that people seek in work and economic life. For the Catholic social tradition these mundane aims connect to, and invite integration with, our deeper identities and longings as human beings.

Doing this does not mean ignoring economic facts or vitiating fruitful economic action. Cultivating awareness of the ways our economic lives connect to our larger longings, and, ultimately, our desire for the supremely Radical Sufficiency Christians call God, can enrich our understanding of economy and work and impel effective action to assure access to livelihood to all God's children. Clear-eyed socioeconomic analysis based on a robust understanding of humanity, wed to a sturdy, religiously grounded commitment to justice: this is precisely what modern Catholic social teaching has sought to promote.[22] This is what animated Monsignor Ryan's economic analysis and advocacy and what animates the analysis and arguments offered here.

FROM "SUFFICIENTLY RADICAL" TO RADICAL SUFFICIENCY

In the papal social teaching of his day, Ryan found warrants for a labor justice agenda that entailed neither violent revolution nor overthrow of the market system. Yet he regarded his US iteration of this Catholic agenda to be "sufficiently radical" and believed that achieving it would demand "greatly, even radically" amending the present economic system.[23] Over a century later, an agenda committed to ensuring dignified work and a good livelihood to every family and household without exception remains more than sufficiently radical. This agenda evokes an economic vision that transcends the standard, individually focused American dream: a radical and catholic (concretely and universally inclusive) dream of good work, economic sufficiency, security and status, and a dignified living for all. In plying this work-justice agenda, modern social Catholicism has sought to articulate directions toward an economy that better reflects, however imperfectly, the scriptural dream of radical kinship and inclusive flourishing under God's reign.

For Christians, complete liberation from want and perfectly sustainable sufficiency for all can never be fully secured in this finite and fallen world, nor by human effort alone. In the tradition of Augustine's famous dictum that "our hearts are restless till they rest in Thee," and cognizant of sin's persistent effects, Catholic approaches to economy thus maintain a realistic recognition of the flaws and limits that will beset any program for inclusive livelihood. Yet today as in the past, social Catholicism's transformative impulse, animated by a continually struggled-for solidary love, impels practical efforts to bring American work and economy into closer alignment with God's dreams for radically inclusive sufficiency and flourishing. Heated struggles over economic inclusion and gritty fights for decent wages may serve, in their way, the reign of peace and justice that Christians pray will come to be, "on earth as it is in heaven."

CONCLUSION

Reframing the American dream as a dream of ample sufficiency for all through a dignified economic livelihood is the radical, catholic, and Catholic agenda that propels this study. In the stories of ordinary US Catholic working families and their neighbors I will seek resources and guidance for advancing a twenty-first-century work-justice agenda that is critical, comprehensive, and radically inclusive. In 2020, as millions of vulnerable working families are pummeled by the initial waves of economic devastation that a global pandemic is wreaking, the need to reorient our economic vision and policies around this simple touchstone—that everyone, without exception, deserves access to a sustainable, dignified livelihood—is as great and urgent as it has ever been.

The book proceeds as follows. Chapter 1 lifts up the story of Catholic advocacy for workers' right to a decent livelihood, focusing on the work and leadership of Monsignor John A. Ryan. The contributions and limitations of this influential priest-economist provide a window into US Catholic social thought and its connections to the Catholic, largely working-class community and the economic scene of the times. As we will see, Ryan's advocacy for a family living wage and his program for "economic reform through legislation" instantiated, in the United States context of his day, the integral understanding of a good living that social Catholicism intended to advance.

Chapters 2 through 6 reconsider US working families' quest for livelihood between the early twentieth and the early twenty-first centuries from a perspective attuned to ideology and to dynamics of power. Chapter 2 proposes a theological, social-scientific, and practical radicalization of Ryan's Catholic economic agenda; a radicalization that, I argue, addressing livelihood in our day requires. Chapters 3 through 6 treat gender and the household economy; race; class; and ecology/consumption, highlighting people, groups, and structural patterns that standard Catholic discourse on economy and wage justice has tended to underacknowledge or ignore.

The concluding chapter draws on the aforementioned analyses to address US families' struggle for a living in a twenty-first-century economy that is globalized, unequal, and ecologically endangered. The challenges facing workers and their families today are many: difficulties in relating home work and waged work; an unsettled culture of gender and controversies concerning gender-related divisions of labor; the chronic intersection between racial injustice and economic exploitation that continues to deny many persons of color the essentials of livelihood; the effects on working households of a globalized capitalist system that asymmetrically distributes labor, products, and wages among peoples (all with rights to decent livelihood) of different cultures, nations, or class locations; and recent permutations of the perennial temptations to idolize or repress the embodied and material aspects of living as these play themselves out in household and wage-earning economies.

In the face of these challenges, I attempt to sketch what Catholic philosopher Jacques Maritain (1882–1973) called a "concrete historical ideal" of economic livelihood appropriate to today's "historical climate."[24] Like the early twentieth-century Catholic livelihood agenda, this new concrete historical ideal will direct persons and communities toward economic sustenance and security and toward participation and achievement through their labor, work, and action. It will articulate practical and policy proposals within a normative picture of economy that encompasses household, informal, and wage-earning dimensions; that recognizes and values the work of women and of men; that insists on economic and civil arrangements that enable workers and their households to enjoy dignified and sustainable livelihoods; and that is both aspirational and concretely approachable through strategic political and cultural action.

Like Ryan, most twenty-first-century Catholic livelihood advocates will pursue practical, reformist objectives. But their goal—economic sufficiency for every one of God's children—bespeaks an agenda that is radical. Pursuing it seriously requires cultivating a solidarity that fuses our personal economic aspirations with willingness to act and sacrifice for the common good. To advance a practicable agenda for inclusive economic sufficiency, critical masses of people must be willing to undergo conversion to the twin solidary convictions often repeated in recent Catholic teaching, that every person is "precious, and that the human self cannot find itself except through the sincere gift of self."[25]

Finally, if it is not to be all talk and no walk, a twenty-first-century Catholic ethic of economic justice for workers and families must be enfleshed in specific, inclusive practices, communities, and social arrangements. Collaborating with like-minded neighbors, people of faith can help their communities imagine, articulate, and enact concrete strategies for exposing and overcoming the material, cultural, and institutional obstacles that presently block the path to inclusive livelihood. Taking to heart Ryan's claim that "obviously we shall make mistakes in the process, but until the attempt is made, and a certain (and very large) number of mistakes are made, there will be no progress," dedicated livelihood advocates will need creativity and fortitude as they experiment with transformative initiatives, fail at many, and learn to do better.[26] In this effort, we each have a part to play in advancing the new attitudes, relations, practices, and institutions necessary to ensure that our economy fulfills its central purpose: to make a dignified, sustainable, livelihood accessible to every person and family.

My hope in this project is to open ways for addressing work and economy that are intellectually rigorous and practically illuminating, as well as morally and spiritually energizing. The measure of its success will be the extent to which it offers a better grasp of the complex human and socioeconomic contexts in which we and our work are enmeshed and assists the efforts of citizens and believers "to think what we are doing" so that, in this historical moment, we may more clearly envisage and more effectively act to build a political economy that ensures a dignified livelihood for all.[27]

NOTES

1. See Adams, *Epic of America*; David Kamp, "Rethinking the American Dream," *Vanity Fair*, April 2009, https://www.vanityfair.com/culture/2009/04/american-dream200904.
2. Popular rags-to-riches stories by Horatio Alger (1832–99) are the classic example, although interestingly, Alger's protagonists rarely became sumptuously rich. See Weiss, *American Myth of Success*.
3. Hochschild, *Facing Up to the American Dream*, 18.
4. Hochschild, 19–29, 30.
5. Hochschild, 34, adumbrates my argument in chapter 2, observing that the fourth tenet "can be taken a further, most dangerous step. For some Americans always, and for many Americans in some periods of our history, virtuous success has been defined as the dominance of some groups over others."
6. Hochschild, 34.
7. Social encyclicals are publicly and ecclesiastically circulated long-form "letters" issued by popes on matters of concern. The first in this genre, *Rerum novarum*—"Of new things"—addressed the human impacts of the new economic realities of modern industrial capitalism.
8. See Ryan, *Living Wage*; Ryan, *Distributive Justice*. Cf. Firer Hinze, "John A. Ryan"; "Bridge Discourse on Wage Justice"; Coleman, *American Strategic Theology*, ch. 4.
9. E.g., Dolan, *American Catholic Experience*, chs. 13, 14; Greeley, *Church and the Suburbs*; O'Brien, *Public Catholicism*, ch. 8. Cf. McCarraher, "Saint in the Gray Flannel Suit."
10. E.g., Jacobson, *Whiteness of a Different Color*; Roediger, *Wages of Whiteness*; West, *Prophesy Deliverance!*; Davis, *History of Black Catholics*; McGreevy, *Parish Boundaries*; Massingale, *Racial Justice and the Catholic Church*.
11. This connection is underscored in John Paul II, *Veritatis splendor*, and Benedict XVI, *Caritas in veritate*. All references to papal encyclicals, speeches, or official documents of the Pontifical Council for Justice and Peace are from the vatican.va website unless otherwise noted.

12. Roman Catholicism's "sacramental imagination" is most immediately recognized in the church's seven sacraments, "but the seven are both a result and a reinforcement of a much broader Catholic view of reality." Greeley cites Catholic fiction writer Andre Dubus's description of this sacramental sensibility: "'A sacrament is physical and within it is God's love; as a sandwich is physical, and nutritious, and pleasurable, and within it is love, if someone makes it for you and gives it to you with love; even harried or tired or impatient love, but with love's direction and concern, love's again and again wavering focus on goodness, then God's love too is in the sandwich.'" Greeley adds, "The sandwich becomes enchanted because it is permeated by, dense in, awash with the two loves—human and divine." Greeley, *Catholic Imagination*, 1.

13. See Welch, *Feminist Ethics of Risk*, part I (cultured despair); Jones and Kelly, "Sloth."

14. Cf. Latina theologians' foregrounding of *lo cotidiano*, the milieu of the everyday or ordinary life, as a privileged *locus theologicus* for Catholic living and reflection. See, for example, Isasi-Díaz, *En la Lucha*, 176–94; Aquino, *Our Cry for Life*, 26–41, 38–39; Imperatori-Lee, *Cuentamé*, ch. 1.

15. See Kessler-Harris, *Out to Work*.

16. Finn, "Power and Public Presence," 72.

17. Benedict XVI, *Caritas in veritate*, §5.

18. See Pope John Paul II on structures of sin in *Sollicitudo rei socialis*; Bernard J. F. Lonergan on bias as the flight from understanding and its social consequences in *Insight*, and in Copeland, *Genetic Study*, ch. 3. See also Ford, *Sins of Omission*, on "myths of indifference" that enable people to ignore or rationalize situations of injustice. For sociological analyses of ideology and practice, see Bourdieu, *Outline of a Theory of Practice*; Balkin, *Cultural Software*.

19. Benedict XVI, *Caritas in veritate*, §30.

20. Ryan, *Distributive Justice* (1942 ed.), 270–73.

21. John 10:11–15. Cf. Firer Hinze, *Glass Ceilings, Dirt Floors*, ch. 1. The fact that girls and women commonly labored as shepherds in ancient Israel further enriches the imagery of YHWH as caring and protecting shepherd employed in Psalm 23. Borowski, *Every Living Thing*, 43–48.

22. Kasper, *Power of Christian Love*, ch. 6, for instance, draws theological, epistemological, and practical links between Christian love and truth-seeking, ideology-shattering ways of perceiving and acting in the world.

23. Hillquit and Ryan, *Socialism*, 13.

24. See Maritain, *Integral Humanism*, 127–28, 132.

25. *Gaudium et spes*, §24.

26. Ryan, *Distributive Justice* (1927), 355–56; Arendt, *Human Condition*, 236–47.

27. "To think what we are doing": with this phrase Hannah Arendt described the enterprise of political philosophy. *Human Condition*, 5. To her mind, the hard work of thinking well is distinct from action but crucially linked to it. Arendt, *Life of the Mind*, 4. Cf. Lonergan, *Insight*, 609–17, cited in Copeland, *Genetic Study*, 95. Elsewhere Lonergan writes, "It is quite true that objective knowing is not yet authentic human living; but without objective knowing there is not authentic living; for one knows objectively just in so far as one is neither unperceptive, nor stupid, nor silly; and one does not live authentically inasmuch as one is either unperceptive or stupid or silly." In Crowe, *Collection*, 238–39.

CHAPTER 1

John A. Ryan's US Catholic Case for Worker Justice

In what does economic livelihood consist? How can a decent living be secured? As the twentieth century dawned, most US working people addressed these questions practically, amid whatever circumstances and choices their daily labors afforded. Meanwhile, religious and political leaders, and some scholars, sought to give public voice to the concerns and hopes these workers' struggles bespoke. The most effective among them managed to wed a sturdy vision of economic livelihood to specific strategies for moving from vision to reality.

Turn-of-the-century US Catholics' efforts to understand and to promote economic justice took multiple routes: theoretical and practical, informal and organized, official and popular. The resulting concatenation of thought and teaching, activism and everyday life bred a distinctive US Catholic contribution to working people's quest for a good living in modern market economies. US social Catholicism situated economy's role within a complex picture of personal and communal flourishing, making its vision remarkably comprehensive. At the same time, its concern to realize worker justice in the concrete led to be specific and strategic.

Twentieth-century Catholic economic thought and activism were inspired and shaped by a series of modern papal social teachings, beginning with Pope Leo XIII's 1891 social encyclical, *Rerum novarum*. Leo and his successors sought to address the moral and practical challenges posed to workers and citizens by modern industrialized market economies. Official teachings gave special attention to the plights of the poor and working-class families most vulnerable to market vagaries. In the United States, this emergent body of official Catholic social teaching found its most influential US interpreter and spokesperson in Monsignor John Augustine Ryan (1869–1945), a Minnesota-born priest, Catholic University professor of industrial ethics, and director of the Social Action Department of the US bishops' National Catholic Welfare Council.

Through copious writings and tireless public advocacy, Ryan gained a wide hearing for a US Catholic vision of justice for working families that was impressive for its detail and scope. His widely collaborative legislative and policy efforts were instrumental in passing early minimum wage legislation in Oregon and Minnesota (1913); and his economic writings influenced Franklin Delano Roosevelt's policies.[1] Through scholarly books and essays, pamphlets, journalistic articles, and public speeches, Ryan articulated the normative purposes of the modern market economy and laid out a case for social-economic reform whose centerpiece was access to a decent livelihood that would ensure all families the minimum material conditions for a good life. Justly remunerated work in humane conditions was the way most people could expect to procure these benefits. At the same time, Ryan's social Catholic perspective led him to regard work as but one part of the well-lived life that economic institutions and activities are meant to support.

A priest trained in economics and an academic engaged in the public arena, Ryan seized every available venue to champion the cause of workers and their families. His political-economic vision had its limits and flaws, and his moral and theological vocabulary and perspective bear marks of his social and ecclesial context. Yet through his teaching and writing, his indefatigable advocacy for work justice, and his political engagement, Ryan achieved a creative fusion of US and Catholic social economics unparalleled before or since. In the particularities of his biography, Ryan also embodies and symbolizes the center of gravity (white, male, clerically led, son of immigrants from working-class roots) around which most twentieth-century US American Catholic Church polity and leadership revolved. Ryan's contributions provide rich historical antecedents and resources from which a twenty-first-century Catholic economic ethic can profitably learn and draw. In fact, for hammering out a contemporary US Catholic livelihood agenda, we will find no better dialogue partner—and at times, foil—than the man whom critics nicknamed, in the aftermath of the Great Depression, the "Right Reverend New Dealer." This chapter examines how US Catholics addressed the economic well-being of working families during the period between 1900 and 1950, giving special attention to the work and legacy of the inimitable monsignor.

CATHOLIC WORKING-CLASS FAMILIES AND NEIGHBORS, CIRCA 1900

Over a public career spanning more than four decades, John A. Ryan's multifaceted engagements were united by a passionate concern for US working families and the economic difficulties that beset them. While never forgetting farming families in rural communities like his own northern Minnesota hometown, Ryan's energies centered on the plight of working-class families in the industrialized cities where Catholic populations were largest. By the later nineteenth century, a modernizing market economy was decisively reshaping the lives of most working Americans. As Ryan's first book, *A Living Wage*, went to press in 1905, the realities of industrialization, urbanization, and new waves of immigration and internal migration continued to powerfully influence the fortunes of ordinary participants in the nation's economic life.[2]

Working-class families seeking a good living had long tended to concentrate in populous urban centers. With ample supplies of entry-level jobs and cheap (if inadequate) housing, large northeastern and midwestern cities attracted throngs of immigrants who included large numbers of Catholics.[3] Between 1890 and 1945, these urban Catholic families formed a shifting patchwork of communities of relatively recent immigrant background, mostly—albeit not completely—of European extraction. By 1900 the most established Catholic communities in these urban centers were among the faithful of Irish and German descent.[4] The predominance of Irish and German Americans in church leadership testified to the influence of these groups within ecclesial ranks. Simultaneously, the active involvement of Irish American and other Catholics in urban politics and in the labor union movement bespoke the civic status that many had attained.[5]

The turn of the century witnessed a fresh surge of immigration from nations in southern and Eastern Europe, including Poland, Italy, and the Balkans, countries with large numbers of Catholics.[6] Like their coreligionists before them, Catholic "new immigrants" congregated in urban enclaves, speedily establishing parish communities where worship and religious instruction often took place in their native tongues. In "national" parishes and ethnically homogeneous Catholic neighborhoods, often coexisting—more or less peacefully—within blocks of one another, members sought to preserve in the new world their distinctive cultural identities and practices.[7] Parishes served both as spiritual centers and as focal points for neighborhood life.

Working-class Catholics' experiences during these years varied depending on their cultural and racial-ethnic backgrounds. After 1900, as nativist sentiments sharpened, Eastern and southern European immigrants became the frequent targets of public intolerance, including by their English-speaking Irish and prosperous German fellow Catholics. American-born Hispanic and African American Catholics, emigrating from the rural South and Southwest into large cities in increasing numbers, encountered especially severe discrimination at the hands of their white Catholic neighbors. Meanwhile, US

Catholics as a whole continued to be affected by a sense of being "other" in relation to the convictions and culture of the Protestant mainstream.[8] In different ways and to varying degrees, most Catholics during this period experienced the tensions between participation and marginalization, and between assimilation into a new culture and preservation of the old, that marked the experiences of immigrants and migrants generally.

Urban Working Families in the Crucible of Economic Modernization

Fueling all this were the epochal changes that accompanied the rise of the modern industrial market economy. In the United States as elsewhere, working-class families grappled with the challenges this economy posed to their material survival and the opportunities it held for material betterment. Amid tensions and differences, more established "white" Catholics, newly arriving Eastern and southern European Catholics, urbanizing Hispanic Catholics, and Catholics (and Catholic converts) among African Americans migrating from the South into northern cities like Detroit and Chicago, together formed a large, though disunified, de facto Catholic working class. For recent immigrants, the literal move from old country to new world telescoped and intensified what for others had been a more gradual process of encounter and adaptation to the changed living and working conditions of the industrialized and urbanized economy. Whatever the differences that separated them, working- and lower-middle-class Catholics and their neighbors had all found themselves compelled to accommodate to the new world of economic modernity.

Early twentieth-century working families contended with city life at a time when distinctions between rural-agricultural and urban-industrial cultures had grown increasingly sharp.[9] Families who had left rural, agricultural communities—whether in the US South, the Southwest, or Europe—to seek their fortunes in urban centers found themselves negotiating unfamiliar geographical, cultural, and economic terrain. Most obvious were the sheer physical differences between the spacious and land-connected environment of the farm or village and the crowded, artificial, and frequently unhealthy living conditions that obtained for non-elites in the cities. Repugnant and unsanitary aspects of life in places like turn-of-the-century New York and Chicago fueled demand by the middle classes for public works projects, including sanitation systems, parks, and paved streets. For those who could afford to escape city noise and squalor, new trends toward suburbanization and rising demand for cheap and fast means of transport between outlying areas and downtown business and cultural centers were already well under way.

But few urban poor or working-class families could indulge in this popular American practice of picking up and moving on—or out—to purportedly greener suburban pastures. Many 1900s working-class families lived a virtually proletarian city existence, depending for survival on unreliable work that offered paltry pay, little security, and few or no benefits. The shift from the meager self-sufficiency attainable by farming to dependence on wages and purchased commodities in the cities left the working poor particularly vulnerable. Whether one remained on the farm or not, whether one was native-born or newly arrived, "industrialization and urbanization so transformed the United States [by] the late nineteenth and early twentieth century that all Americans . . . had to confront changing life patterns."[10] In the economic sphere, these changes had fundamentally dislocated traditional markers of order, space, and time. David M. Katzman and William M. Tuttle describe this shift: "As producers and consumers, Americans became interdependent on each other and on regional and national markets. Subsistence farming, for example, gave way to the staple agricultural system where farmers grew crops for market and entered the money economy. Railroads brought their farm produce to market and returned with manufactured and consumer goods for farmers to purchase. Simultaneously, the craftsmen's workshops and the apprentice-journeyman-master system gave way to structured factories and assigned work tasks."[11]

Experiences of time in relation to work were also altered by the industrial-urban economy as "the discipline of the clock replaced seasonal and cultural rhythms." New habits were imposed as workers were required to conform to factory routines in which their efforts formed part of "a complex machine which required harmony, unity, and subservience to function." Workers hoping to benefit from this "new American industrial order" had to adapt and comply. Not to do so threatened the work of "building modern America."[12] But evading industrial discipline carried a more immediate price: to resist endangered not only one's chances for economic success but possibly one's very survival.

Immigrants and rural Americans migrating to cities thus faced sometimes severe tensions and jarring transitions between their traditional worldviews and practices and new ways of life.[13] The firsthand account of Antanas Kaztauskis, who left his Lithuanian village around 1900 for a job in Chicago's stockyards, reflects these. As he traveled from his peasant community across the Atlantic and into the States, Kaztauskis recalls, "I felt everything get bigger and go quicker every day."[14] The young man finally reached Chicago after a grueling journey during which he felt acutely his disorientation and vulnerability, falling prey more than once to "grafters." His new roommates, fellow Lithuanians, were swift to disabuse him of his rose-colored visions of life in America:

That first night we sat around the house and they asked me, "Well, why did you come?" I told them about . . . "life, liberty, and the getting of happiness." They all leaned back and laughed. "What you need is money," they said. It was all right at home. You wanted nothing. You ate your own meat . . . on the farm. You made your own clothes and had your own leather. . . . But here you want a hundred things. Whenever you walk out you see new things you want, and you must have money to buy everything.[15]

Within days, Kaztauskis had exhausted his meager savings and lay awake at night sick with anxiety. The stark realities of working-class survival in the modern economy hit home with full force: "I knew then that money was everything I needed. My money was almost gone and I knew that I would soon die unless I got a job, for this was not like home. Here money was everything and a man without money must die."[16]

In the city and industry graphically depicted in journalist Upton Sinclair's 1906 fictionalized exposé *The Jungle*, Kaztauskis and multitudes of unskilled newcomers like him were easy prey for foremen in Chicago's stockyards, who hired day laborers from crowds desperate for work and willing to accept any rate of pay.[17] Low wages, poor treatment, and job insecurity were routine. His own experiences led Kaztauskis to conclude that everywhere in America, there were "sharp men beating out slow men like me." Everything was done as cheaply and quickly as possible "so as to save everything and make money." As a fellow Lithuanian working twelve-to-fourteen-hour shifts in the cattle-killing room put it: "They get all the blood out of those cattle and all the work out of us men."[18] In subsequent decades, the rising union movement, in which Catholic wage earners became significant participants, would play a key role in alleviating the worst of these abuses.

Immigrant and urbanizing Catholics negotiated the gulf between traditional and modern economic cultures in light of, or in tension with, their religious backgrounds and sensibilities. Some, like Kaztauskis and his family, became impatient with the old country religiosity that national parishes strove to maintain and shed them as impediments to the faster-paced, more secular attitudes and habits they associated with being successfully Americanized. Kaztauskis confesses that now, "We do not go much to church, because the church seems to be too slow." Nor does he plan to send his young son to the Lithuanian Catholic school, which has only "two bad rooms and two priests who teach only in Lithuanian from prayer books. I will send him to the American school, which is very big and good."[19] But a great many working-class Catholics embraced the rich and redolent piety, structured ecclesial organization and authority, and tightly knit communities in the parochial schools and parish neighborhoods that marked urban Catholicism during these years.[20] Together these defined a familiar Catholic world that buffered some of industrial capitalist culture's harshest effects. And as we shall see, this milieu also shaped US Catholicism's interpretation of working-class families' struggles, needs, and aspirations.

The Separation of Domestic and Public Economies

Modern urban-industrial economy clashed in crucial ways with traditional family and kin ties, social customs, and religious codes. As the impersonal, mechanized, large-scale workings of this new economy displaced local household (*oikos*)-centered production over the course of the nineteenth century, millions of workers and families underwent painful transitions as "urbanizing peasants."[21] Increasingly relegated to the margins of the economy, the domestic household came to be regarded as a largely extraeconomic, "private sphere." The familial household's nonmonetary functions and contributions to livelihood continued but were no longer seen or valued as economic.

Sociologist Anthony Giddens emphasizes "the knowledgeability of lay actors," arguing that the behavior and choices of everyday people reflect implicit, frequently canny, practical understandings of their social situations and its requirements.[22] In precisely such nontheoretical yet knowledgeable ways, modernizing workers and families perceived, and sought strategies to cope with, the threats that the market economy posed to longstanding, *oikos*-based values and practices. In modern circumstances no less than in traditional, the familial household, and the socially reproductive labor performed there, remained essential for survival and for maintaining people's lives in minimally healthy and happy circumstances. By locating household-based labor under the broad aegis of *oikonomia*, traditional societies acknowledged such work's economic and social, as well as its personal and familial, value. The dissolution of this ethos removed cultural and economic supports for a whole sector of necessary, labor-intensive work. If economic value in the modern market economy was now purely money-related, what would become of the personal and use values that household-based labor was still needed to produce?[23]

One way to address this challenge involved reconceiving adult roles and relationships within the household and waged economic spheres. Household and marketplace became distinguished, and reunited, by way of a gendered ideology of "separate spheres." Originating in the late eighteenth century, the separate spheres ideology became a key support for a female homemaker/male breadwinner division of labor between household and waged workplaces. Laden with constraints and marred by patriarchal power relations though it was, this dual-spheres norm was also an ingenious strategy for coping with the threats to traditional family economic functions that industrial capitalism posed.[24] The division of spheres supplied a badly needed template for responding to complicated questions about how, in modern circumstances, economic survival and integrated livelihood for men, women, and their families could be imagined and pursued.

By the later nineteenth century the framing of household and marketplace as separate, gendered spheres with asymmetrical functions was rarely questioned. "Economy" had become primarily identified with the public machinations of the labor, commodity, and financial markets. Households, demoted from their traditional positions as productive centers, were relegated to the economic backstage. All non-wage-earning family members were depicted as economic dependents and households as units of consumption.[25] Meanwhile, home and family—with woman at its heart—were popularly romanticized as a private haven sealed off from the commodification, impersonality, and competition of the public marketplace.

In modern capitalist economy, "stable working-class households participate(d) in relations of production, reproduction, and consumption by *sending out* their labor power in exchange for wages" and purchasing power.[26] Wage dependency became the defining characteristic of the modern working and middle classes. In this context, the family living wage ideal valorized the breadwinning, male family head as the primary economic provider, upon whose wages and support all other household members relied. Even as most working-class households in fact depended for survival on the combined wages of two or more members, labor-market participation was widely regarded as the special prerogative of family-supporting men. As chapter 3 will address in more detail, late twentieth-century feminist critics would subject this gendered ideology to vigorous and deserved critique. Yet with all its flaws and pitfalls, it has wielded tremendous and enduring influence over Americans' cultural imaginations and work-family practices.

Catholic families, too, embraced the homemaker/breadwinner ideal as a way to reconcile cherished values with economic necessity. We hear the genuine appreciation for this arrangement in the voices of people like Antanas Kaztauskis, who praises his wife's domestic skill and economic good sense and revels in the dignity and opportunities his decent-paying and secure job eventually afforded him and his young family.[27] Official papal teaching at the time echoed and further legitimated Catholics' assumptions concerning the gendered separation of spheres. Yet the experiences of Catholic immigrant families like that of Joe Podles, who recounts his Polish mother's and young

siblings' extensive engagement in toilsome, poorly paid agricultural and factory labor during the 1910s, belie the myth of the nonworking, "dependent
homemaker" for most poor and working-class households.[28]

For US working families at the turn of the twentieth century, then, good
work at a decent wage for the household's head held out the hope of not only
survival but a better life. Catholic working people and their neighbors shared
a vision of a good living that connected successful wage earning for men with
the preservation of hearth and home as the domain of women and family. Even
in highly dissonant and unpromising economic circumstances, working-class
families sought out ways to inch this dream of a good living closer to reality.

CATHOLICISM ENGAGES THE
MODERN "SOCIAL QUESTION"

A decade earlier, Pope Leo XIII (1878–1903) had stepped into an unprecedented public confrontation and dialogue with the panoply of "new things"
wrought by modern industrialized economy by issuing *Rerum novarum*,
the first papal encyclical to address "the social question"—the common
parlance of the day for problems and issues concerning labor and capital in
the ascendant industrialized economy. Leo's effort to systematically address
this social question, and especially the plight of wage laborers in the capitalist order, was the climax of nearly a century of percolation among a con-
geries of largely European academic and activist efforts that had formed a
loosely defined movement identifiable as "social Catholicism."[29] With *Rerum
novarum*, Leo propelled the institutional church into the thick of the day's
economic debates; he also poised the papacy and church leadership to continue this engagement over the subsequent century. The encyclical, directed
to bishops and pastors who were then to instruct the laity, was primarily
intended to guide and persuade the powerful and affluent. But its central
focus of concern—one that would continue in subsequent official social
teaching—was justice for those who are the least economically powerful
and most easily exploited: the poor and poor wage workers.[30]

The bedrock on which *Rerum novarum* built its interpretation of economy and justice for working people, and the criterion against which it judged
competing economic theories and practices, was its affirmation of the irre-
vocable, divinely bestowed dignity of each human being. Persons in their
God-given dignity tend toward and require society in order that their needs
might be met and capabilities developed. Leo and his successors drew upon
a neoscholastic theological and moral vision that identifies family, economy,

and political community as naturally grounded, communal arenas wherein various aspects of human personhood and dignity are to be nurtured. Persons and community are regarded as interdependent, an interdependence understood in terms of a normative interplay between hierarchical and (sometimes more egalitarian) organic relations.[31]

Rerum novarum condemned the evils of both unfettered economic liberalism and communistic socialism. Leo was careful to distance the church from allegiance to any single economic theory or program. Then and since, popes and bishops have framed Catholic teaching on the economy as moral, rather than "technical" in its authority, as wed to no single economic theory, and as generally limited to offering principles and guidance rather than concrete economic policy directives.

Yet while this framing holds some truth, it understates and even obscures the significant degree to which *Rerum novarum* and official Catholic social teaching since *has* operated with a particular constellation of judgments and claims about economics, drawn from and aligning with specific streams of classical and modern economic thought. Alternatively called "corporatist," "solidarist," "communitarian," or, most broadly, "social" economics, the sorts of economic theory on which Catholic thought has relied contrast with predominant, neoclassical economics at three fundamental points. First, as opposed to the atomistic, rational self-maximizers assumed by neoclassical economic theory, social economics understands economic actors as whole and multiply motivated persons embedded in complex communities and relationships.[32] Second, against mainstream economics' value-neutral commitments, social economics maintains a classical, normative definition of economy and its raison d'être—to serve the material survival and well-being of all members. If the economy is by definition such a normative enterprise, the criterion for assessing its well-functioning is the degree to which it is succeeding in its productive, provisioning, and distributional purposes. Third, against mainstream economic theory's strict separation of market from state and strong bias against governmental interference in market exchange, Catholic social thought retained classic political economy's regard for government's role in actively securing the common good, including by acting to ensure that the economy fulfills its normative purposes.

Leo rejected work's commodification and defended labor's worth on human and religious grounds. He decried the treatment of workers as tools or animals and insisted on workers' rights to what is necessary in order that their human dignity be respected and preserved.[33] This included rights to decent working conditions and treatment and to a wage sufficient to modestly support self and family. In a just economic order, Leo further averred, every household head should be able to secure some small property, house, or land, for private ownership was a way of promoting security, lessening the gap between haves and have-nots, and encouraging conditions for virtue and industriousness on the part of laborers. Against the isolation and atomization of individuals typical of liberal capitalism on the one hand, and persons' absorption into the masses by atheistic socialist movements on the other, Leo's Catholic social vision regarded sociality and personhood as distinct and interpenetrating realities. Labor and management, state and citizenry, workers and their fellows—all were exhorted to exercise virtues of justice and charity in a framework of solidarity and cooperation. *Rerum novarum* thus presented a robust Catholic economic vision that stressed access to modest but genuine material livelihood for all, through decent work in dignified conditions, and the obligations of economic agents and institutions to play their parts in securing a political economy that made this possible.

For the century-plus to follow, reverence for human dignity and its requirements would continue to anchor the Catholic economic vision guided by official papal teaching. Catholic leaders affirmed the value of honest labor but insisted that the laborer was due a just return. This meant remuneration enough to fulfill working families' basic material needs and to provide opportunities for members to cultivate their "higher faculties" both for their own good and for their communities. Catholic teaching identified rights and responsibilities for all economic agents but emphasized the rights of more vulnerable workers to economic sustenance and participation, and the responsibilities of more advantaged parties to enable the less powerful to attain those rights. Underpinning this Catholic economic vision was a social anthropology that gave it a deep appreciation for solidarity, understood as both the de facto organic interconnections among people and groups, and the de jure obligations of individuals and groups to respect and advance in the economic sphere the complex common good of a whole society. In the United States, as Progressive Era intellectuals and organizers took up the cause of worker justice, a dynamic brand of economic thought grounded in this Catholic social vision found its most talented architect and effective spokesman in professor and monsignor John A. Ryan.

RYAN, PUBLIC INTELLECTUAL AND CATHOLIC ADVOCATE FOR WORKER JUSTICE

Ryan drew on neoscholastic philosophy, church social teachings, the data of the social sciences, and common experience to craft an influential US

Catholic social ethics that combined appeals to religious and moral princi-
ples with realistic attention to "economic facts" and concrete circumstances.
An academic, priest, economist, public intellectual, and policy wonk, Ryan's
long tenure as director of the Social Action Department of the US Bishops'
National Catholic Welfare Council (forerunner to the US Catholic Bishops'
Conference) enabled him to establish a form of public involvement by the US
Catholic Church that continues today.

From his seminary days, Ryan's conviction that religious concerns directly
interfaced with the plight of poor workers impelled him to see his vocation
in terms of economic and political engagement. Looking back, he made this
link plain:

> With each succeeding year of my theological studies, my desire and
> determination increased to devote as much time and labor to the
> study of economic conditions, institutions and problems as would
> be possible and permitted after my ordination. I wanted to examine
> economic life in the light of Christian principles, with a view to mak-
> ing them operative in the realm of industry. It seemed to me that the
> salvation of millions of souls depended largely upon the economic
> opportunity to live decently, to live as human beings in the image and
> likeness of God.[34]

Ryan first encountered the text of *Rerum novarum* in an 1894 English class
at the Saint Paul, Minnesota, theologate. Ryan was thrilled to find vindicated
in nascent papal social teaching his own heartfelt attraction to a priestly career
dedicated to grappling with social issues and advancing justice. Noticed early
for his academic promise, Ryan was sent for further studies to Catholic University in Washington, DC, where he undertook training in economics and
moral theology. With the help of distinguished University of Wisconsin
economist Richard Ely, Ryan's doctoral dissertation was published in 1906
under the title *A Living Wage*. Ryan became professor of moral theology
and industrial ethics at Catholic University in 1916, a post he occupied, in
addition to directing the bishops' Social Action Department, until retiring in
1939. In the latter capacity he penned a stream of US church statements on
economic and social matters, most famously the Bishops' Program for Social
Reconstruction, issued in 1919 in the wake of World War I.[35]

Highly unusual for a Catholic cleric in his day, Ryan moved between his
academic, ecclesial, and public worlds with skill and ease. He became an
influential spokesperson and policy consultant for progressive social and
economic reformers, playing an active role in significant labor legislation and

helping forward policies that President Franklin Roosevelt would later incorporate into his New Deal.[36] Widely respected as an ecumenically minded and articulate Catholic supporter of labor justice, his articles and editorials appeared regularly in widely circulated publications like *Commonweal*, the *Nation*, the *New Republic*, and the *Harvard Business Review.*

If the patrician Pope Leo XIII embodied the aristocratic tone and posture of late nineteenth-century papal social teaching, Ryan, smart yet down-to-earth, the citified son of Irish-born Minnesota farmers, quintessentially reflected the immigrant, urbanizing background of many Euro-American Catholics of his day.[37] His economic ethics translated the Eurocentric core of Leonine thought into a distinctly American Catholic idiom—scientifically informed, ecumenical, more democratic than paternalistic, more pragmatic than theoretical, but with a passion for worker and family justice that more than matched Leo's own. Though he moved in elite circles, Ryan's primary constituency remained "plain folk" like Kaztauskis, average working people dependent on wages for daily bread who, on their own, lacked the resources or the power to defend themselves against the vicissitudes of a profit-driven capitalist marketplace.

Ryan's zeal for the cause of working-class laborers and their families prompted one later observer to describe him as a kind of "theologian of liberation *avant la lettre.*"[38] His social activism also modeled a Catholic analogue to Protestant social gospel impulses of the day. While he supported charitable efforts and the rising field of social work, Ryan was convinced that helping could never be limited to relieving individual suffering caused by economic conditions. His fervent desire was to diagnose and seek ways to cure the institutional and structural deficiencies that prevented so many from enjoying access to economic well-being.[39]

As a youth, Ryan worked on his family's farm. But he never labored in a factory, earned wages, or provided for a family. Living a cleric's life a step removed from mundane household cares, Ryan also remained a step removed from direct grassroots activism, unlike, for instance, his contemporary Peter Dietz, the German American priest of New York City.[40] While energetically involved in public advocacy and legislative reform efforts, Ryan presided over pre-1950s US social Catholicism as its chief intellectual and spokesperson but not its primary organizer.[41]

Yet through his policy work and by helping his fellow citizens "think what we are doing," Ryan succeeded as both a thinker and doer. This practical intellectual developed the century's most comprehensive American Catholic reception of papal social thought on economy, family, work, and wages. And Ryan's ability to enunciate his moral vision in terms that crossed parochial boundaries contributed to twentieth-century Catholicism's evolving role in public dialogue and civic advocacy.[42] Examining what he had to say on these matters reveals both strengths and limitations of a substantive legacy to which twenty-first-century social Catholics are heir.

RYAN'S THEOLOGICALLY GROUNDED US CATHOLIC ECONOMIC ETHIC

Ryan's vision of economic justice is anchored in his Catholic faith and articulated primarily by way of the natural-law moral philosophy then commonly taught in seminaries. More an ethicist than a theologian, Ryan was accused by influential contemporaries like Virgil Michel, OSB, of paying little more than lip service to the importance of spirituality and the need for religious conversion. Indeed, Ryan's ethics show little direct engagement with scripture or with dogmatic themes like God, sin, or redemption. He downplayed papal exhortations concerning the Christianizing of the social order or the critical need for a return to true (Catholic) religion by the masses. Explicit references to the links between economic reform and religious conversion tend to occur only briefly in Ryan's work, and in closing paragraphs.[43] Moral and social issues in the temporal order, rather than nuanced theological reflection concerning the supernatural order, were the primary focus of his attention.[44]

Yet he understood the principles and priorities that oriented his economic ethics, especially the God-given sacredness and dignity of every person, to be thoroughly theological. At times he reminded his readers of this:

> The principles which underlie the teaching of the Church on industrial relations are found in the Gospel of Christ and in the moral law of nature. One of these is the principle of justice. Its basis is Christ's teaching on personality. Every human being has intrinsic worth, has been redeemed by Christ, and is destined for everlasting union with God. In the eyes of God all persons are of equal importance. Neither in industry nor in any other department of life may one man be used as a mere instrument to the advantage of other men. Industrial, no less than other relations, must be so conducted as to safeguard personality and afford to all persons the means and conditions of life as children of God.[45]

Arguing for the right of workers to a decent livelihood, Ryan appealed to church teachings and to theological paragons such as Thomas Aquinas, who,

Ryan noted, regarded a certain amount of material goods as a prerequisite for fostering the practice of virtue. And he adduced biblical warrants for both his critique of materialism and his depiction of livelihood's ultimate aim as the pursuit of higher values: "For a man's life doth not consist in the abundance of things which he possesseth."[46]

A NATURAL-LAW PHILOSOPHICAL FRAMEWORK

As a Catholic moral theologian, Ryan's *lingua franca* was a natural theology and philosophy that assumed that moral norms could be discovered by reflecting on rational human nature. By way of such reflection, one could discover a "natural law" that pointed out basic directions for reaching one's divinely given purpose: authentic human flourishing in relations with God, self, and others. In his 1944 essay "the norm of morality," Ryan, paraphrasing Thomas Aquinas, defines the natural law as "a necessary rule of action, determined by rational nature, imposed by God as the Author of nature and perceived intuitively."[47] Moral knowledge concerning humanity's *telos* and how to fulfill it is inscribed within rational nature and available for discovery by all reasonable and good-willed people, which means that authentic ethical claims are knowable by and binding on all, not just Catholics or Christians. These guiding assumptions led Ryan to craft economic-ethical arguments that were publicly directed and meant to be broadly persuasive. The conviction that the Creator makes His intent known through nature and its designs also warranted Ryan's consistent attention to all available sources for knowledge. For him, plumbing these sources required both meticulously observing common experience and rigorously engaging with data and scholarship, especially modern economic science.

Ryan cites an additional reason for careful and ongoing analysis of all available sources of information: in any given time or place, sinful, finite humans' inability to grasp fully or perfectly the contours of reality and the moral responsibilities to which nature points. Natural-law-based morality holds that an act is morally good or evil insofar as it conforms to or deviates from the dictates of "man's rational nature, adequately considered." But popular or scholarly apprehensions of human nature and flourishing are always to some degree partial or inaccurate, whether due to ignorance, error, or sinful self-deception. This recognition informed Ryan's persistent quest for the best, most up-to-date knowledge of economic and social facts, and his efforts to align moral principles with that knowledge in diverse and changing circumstances.[48]

RYAN, SOCIAL ECONOMIST

Ryan's training and thought located him within the broad stream of economic scholarship today known as "heterodox" or "social economics."[49] Social economists share a critical stance toward laissez-faire and neoclassical economics, especially in the positivistic and value-free forms that predominated in Ryan's day and after. Prominent social economists on whom Ryan relied included Richard Ely, Sidney and Beatrice Webb, and John Hobson. Ryan was also conversant with the work of European solidarist political economists like Matteo Liberatore, Heinrich Pesch, and Oswald von Nell-Breuning, whose thought informed Leo XIII's *Rerum novarum* and Pius XI's subsequent *Quadragesimo anno*. All these scholars criticized neoclassical economics for its tendencies toward deductive abstraction, its narrow depiction of human agency, and its separation of economic analysis from normative considerations.[50] Without sacrificing scholarly rigor and technically accurate analysis, Ryan and other social economists sought to articulate a fuller anthropological basis and normative contextualization for economics. They "share[d] a strong conviction that a meaningful economics capable of addressing social problems needs to be value-directed or normative and guided by such basic ideals as community, . . . human fulfillment, and meaningful work."[51] In the United States, Ryan was one of the founders of "Catholic social economics," whose professional society, the Association of Catholic Economists (established in 1941), was reorganized in 1970 to become the present-day Association for Social Economics.[52]

Both heterodox economics and modern Catholic social thought carried forward the normative understanding of the economy's participative and provisioning purposes that characterized premodern economics, and which continued to be assumed by early modern political economists, including Adam Smith.[53] Both a moral philosopher and political economist, Smith presumed connections between ethics and economics, between market workings and economy's normative, provisioning purposes, and between economy and government. In his view, when markets distributed wealth in highly unequal ways or failed to provide workers with a decent living, government had a responsibility to redress those outcomes. With Smith, modern Catholic social thought considers work and livelihood within the larger ambit of "political economy," pursuing economic analysis in the context of "social change and history, the social totality, moral philosophy, and praxis" and their varied intellectual, cultural, and material settings.[54] The Catholic livelihood agenda that Ryan championed reflected this way of thinking, especially in its assumptions that markets should serve the material well-being of all citizens, including the working poor, and that government had an obligation to ensure this end.

A PRACTICAL-EXPERIMENTAL STANCE

Ryan's distinctive approach to economic questions fused social Catholicism with an American brand of reformist, experimental, and practical thought and activism. His neoscholastic, natural-law training was tempered by a degree of historical consciousness: because, he saw, circumstances in the modern period have changed, our apprehensions of economic and social justice must also change. Simultaneously, while he did not use terms like *ideology* or *false consciousness*, Ryan was aware of the distortion that culture could exert on the beliefs and values of even the wisest and holiest. Our human susceptibility to delusion, he argued, made it all the more imperative that ethicists stay close, and accountable, to the facts of situations. Inevitably we grasp facts fallibly, but by remaining alert to realities on the ground, and seeking out and hewing to the most accurate estimations available, we can guard against being trapped in reigning cultural illusions.[55]

Ryan's method of attacking economic problems thus wedded basic moral principles, research, and action. He advocated economic reforms that were ethically and empirically informed, pragmatic, experimental, strategic, and revisable. At the end of his second and most important major work, *Distributive Justice*, Ryan expresses this call to intelligent, experimental engagement: "If there exist moral rules and rational principles applicable to the problem of wage justice, it is our duty to state and apply them as fully as we can. Obviously we shall make mistakes in the process, but until the attempt is made, and a certain (and very large) number of mistakes are made, there will be no progress."[56]

Though he employs deductive language here, in fact Ryan's method synthesized inductive and deductive elements.[57] In analyzing economic conditions, he brought to bear a set of premises concerning human nature and flourishing in its individual and communal dimensions. At the same time he recognized that to draw credible ethical conclusions or identify effective plans of action required careful study and ongoing adjustment in light of the actual economic, cultural, and historical conditions in which people struggle to survive and flourish.[58]

A GOOD LIFE AND ITS ECONOMIC SETTING

Ryan's program for worker justice was part of a larger vision of what it meant to lead a good life, and of economy's role in facilitating or impeding that. By providing for the material sustenance and well-being of its members, a good economy makes essential contributions to a "good living" that is humanly integrated and edifying. Ryan articulated the specifics of an integrated, humanly edifying "good life" in the teleological, Thomistic-Aristotelian idiom of Catholic moralists of his generation. Like his justification for why persons are due the opportunity to live a good life, his description of that life begins from Christianity's affirmation of the dignity of the human person made in the image of God. The person is conceived as a complex unity composed of materiality, senses, emotions, will, and reason (intellect understood broadly, as the capacity to discover and appreciate meaning). These interrelated components are all significant, but they possess an ascending order of value that runs from the material to the rational and spiritual. As a primary means to fulfill people's material needs, a decent economic livelihood secures the sustaining conditions needed for full human development, most importantly for development in regard to life's deeper purposes, to know and to love.

This lofty anthropology underpinned Ryan's largely instrumental view of economy, and especially of the material acquisition it enables.[59] He frequently criticized modern market economy's tendency to portray human fulfillment reductively, as the unending satisfaction of ever-expanding material "needs." Ryan judged this "working creed of materialism" illegitimate on both Christian and human grounds. The Gospel clearly relativizes the worth of material goods. And reason too "informs us that neither our faculties nor the goods that satisfy them are of equal moral worth or importance. The intellectual and spiritual faculties are essentially and intrinsically higher than the sense faculties." In fact, "only in so far as they promote, either negatively or positively, the development of the mind and soul have the senses any reasonable claim to satisfaction."[60] This view measures "good living" not primarily quantitatively but qualitatively. An authentically good life centers on "thinking, communing, loving, serving, and giving, rather than having and enjoying."[61] It consists "not in the indefinite satisfaction of material wants, but in the progressive endeavor to know the best that is to be known, and to love the best that is to be loved," that is, "God and his creatures in the order of their importance."[62]

In this Catholic vision of a good life, each person and family deserves access to and the chance to participate in "a hierarchy of humanly valuable things" that culminates in spiritual union with God.[63] Government, economy, and civil institutions exist, ultimately, to support this. With Pope Leo, Ryan assumed that a basic task of modern political economy was to make provisions for material welfare of all members, primarily by assuring people decent work that yields wages sufficient to support a life of "reasonable and frugal comfort." Modest material security freed persons and families to attend to higher human potentials, including developing the mind through learning and intellectual activities, and enriching and expanding human and neighborly contacts through marriage, children, and wider associations in family, community, and polis. These values were supported by and also to some degree realizable in the context of economic activity. The highest human purpose, communion with Ultimate Truth and Goodness, germinated in the soil of temporal communities and undertakings but supremely transcended them. In its light, the relatively subordinate value of work and economy, and the importance of access to noneconomic time spent in activities such as social relationships, religion, contemplation, and leisure, are brought into clear relief.

This vision of human nature and destiny orients Ryan's entire economic analysis. Within the waged labor force, he insists that flourishing for workers depends on decent pay but also upon decent work quality, participation, conditions, and benefits. And like his contemporaries, Ryan pictured the proper interaction and relationship between waged and household economies in gendered terms. However, unlike more severe versions of the separate spheres ideology, his Catholic social approach precluded any sharp divorce between economy and home that would treat the household as a purely private, noneconomic realm.

I will probe further this broader setting for Ryan's economic vision, and examine what he has to say about women in relation to public and domestic economy, in a later chapter. Here, I turn to Ryan's best-known and perhaps most influential achievement: his articulation of a rationale and concrete agenda for economic justice for the "average working man."

A PROGRAM OF JUSTICE
FOR THE WORKINGMAN

Ryan anchors his case for workers' right to a decent economic livelihood, first, in Catholic social teaching's bedrock claim about the inviolable dignity of each human person.

> Like every other human being, the wage-earner is a person, not a thing, nor a mere animal. Because he is a person, he has certain needs that are not felt by animals, and his needs and his welfare have a certain sacredness that does not belong to any other species of creatures. . . . [The human person] has intrinsic worth and dignity. He is made in the image and likeness of God. He is an end in himself . . . he is worthwhile for his own sake.[64]

Ryan further grounds the right to livelihood in three claims "regarding man's position in the universe." First: God created the earth for the sustenance of all His children; therefore all persons are equal in their inherent claims upon the bounty of nature. Second: the inherent right of access to the earth is conditioned upon, and becomes actually valid through, the expenditure of useful labor. With the exception of the very young, the infirm, and the landed wealthy (though more ambiguously), people must and ought to work in order to live. "For those who refuse to comply with this condition the inherent right of access to the earth remains suspended." Third: "The men who are in present control of the opportunities of the earth are obliged to permit reasonable access to these opportunities on reasonable terms." Every person willing to work has an inborn right to sustenance from the earth on reasonable terms and conditions. Further, every worker is entitled to "a certain minimum of goods," comprising "at least a *decent* livelihood, that is . . . so much of the requisites of sustenance as will enable him to live in a manner worthy of a human being."[65] And because, in modern market economies, most people will access a decent livelihood by way of wage earning, Ryan and Catholic social thought more generally deem the first requirement for economic justice to be securing the worker's right to a "living wage."

Economic Sufficiency through a (Family) Living Wage

Despite Ryan's occasional intimations, Catholics did not invent the living wage agenda.[66] The injustice of the laissez-faire capitalist wage contract, and a need for a wage based on the worker's personal and familial needs, had been rallying points for workers and labor leaders since the early nineteenth century. Martha May observes that the living wage agenda first emerged as a way to address the threats industrialization posed to working men: "The family wage, as a solution to the threats the workingman perceived to himself and to his family in the new industrial order, appeared first as a class demand for industrial justice, and a defense of traditional work and family arrangements."[67] Advocacy for a living wage and a decent livelihood took a variety of forms at the time, but by the late nineteenth century had acquired a specific emphasis on gender.[68] By the time Ryan published *A Living Wage* in 1906, the breadwinner/homemaker rationale for a *family* living wage had been embraced across classes, functioning, May argues, as a way to stabilize a social order founded on male rights and responsibilities as family head and provider. Ryan's family living wage agenda, an early and perduring element of his program for economic justice, reflects both earlier working-class-focused and the later gender-focused appeals.[69]

Ryan defines a living wage as monetary remuneration for labor sufficient to provide an individual workingman with a "decent livelihood." The "workingman" Ryan has in mind is "the adult male of average physical ability who is exclusively dependent upon the remuneration that he is paid in return for his labor."[70] A decent livelihood, as we have seen, is "that amount of the necessaries and comforts of life that is in keeping with the dignity of a human being . . . that minimum of conditions which the average person of a given age or sex must enjoy in order to live as a human being should live."[71] More than simply keeping body and soul together, a living wage should enable workers to access at least the minimum of the material conditions of "reasonable" living. In keeping with Ryan's understanding of human flourishing, "this implies the power to exercise one's primary faculties, supply one's essential needs, and develop one's personality."[72] Living wages should enable workers and their families to live in "reasonable comfort," the minimum measure of which can be determined by "the judgment of competent and fair-minded men," and more fundamentally, "in the light of man's nature and essential needs."[73] In sum: "food, clothing, shelter, insurance, and mental and spiritual culture—all in a reasonable degree—are, therefore, the essential conditions of a decent livelihood. Remuneration inadequate to secure all of these things to the laborer and his family falls below the level of a Living Wage."[74]

Ryan contended that the dollar amount of a living wage could be determined with reasonable accuracy, in light of the general standard of living and economic conditions of a particular time and geographical region. Relying on his own observations and on cost-of-living estimates he gathered from economists, government analyses, and the accounts of working-class families, Ryan composed fairly detailed lists of the material goods requisite to decent livelihood for workers and families of "average" size.[75] He judged, for instance, that US families in 1906 needed a minimum of $601.03 per year (the equivalent of about $17,132 in 2019 dollars) to purchase adequate goods and services; though in larger cities, different regions, and subsequent years, he noted, this figure would likely need to be raised to meet higher costs.[76] Though difficult and inevitably approximate, to calculate a specific dollar amount was necessary for setting a target at which efforts to secure better wages could aim. And because living wage calculations indicated a required *minimum* that the majority of workers were denied, these calculations also served a prophetic function, placing the current economic system and its leaders under moral judgment and making plain the need for change.

In line with both papal teaching and Progressive Era thought, Ryan further championed the workingman's right—that is, the adult male worker's right—to a *family* living wage. Strikingly, Ryan's justification for this right centers on the well-being not of the family but of the individual working man. First, he argues, just remuneration for work is a right derived from the worker's essential and intrinsic worth; its primary end is the worker's own welfare. Accordingly, the primary end of the right to a family living wage is also the welfare of the male worker: "The right to the means of maintaining a family . . . is not finally derived from the *duty* of maintaining it—from the needs of the family—but from the laborer's *dignity*, from *his* own essential needs."[77]

On this view, the adult male worker holds the right to a family living wage by virtue of his own, patriarchal destiny in the social and familial order. Ryan suggests the tiniest of openings to different alternatives when he acknowledges that "if the support of wife and children did not in the normal order of things fall upon the husband and father, he would not have a right to the additional remuneration required for this purpose." But to him, the need and right of adult males to the material conditions for successfully founding and heading a family seemed self-evident. And "because nature and reason have decreed that the family should be supported by its head," this implies the head's further right to a family-supporting wage.[78]

Nature and reason, Ryan was convinced, had also decreed a role for women, and was not in the public workplace: women were by nature best suited to the tasks of the non-wage-earning domestic sphere. Ryan was fully aware that many women *were* wage earners; as historian Alice Kessler-Harris notes, "at the time Ryan wrote, women constituted close to 25 percent of the industrial work force."[79] Though he regarded "working women," especially working wives and mothers, to be in an "abnormal" circumstance, his characteristic honesty and practicality in the face of the facts led him to support female employees' right to an individual living wage. At times he also seems to advocate some form of family allowance to assist women who become the sole economic support of their children due to calamities like widowhood or husband desertion. Yet he consistently depicts domestic homemaking as women's normal, and normative, economic role. Given this, a single working woman has the right to remuneration sufficient to support herself but not to a family living wage. The male worker, even if single, retains the right to the higher family wage, for saving against the day when he may exercise his family rights.[80]

Complete Worker Justice through Sufficiency, Security, and Status

Chapter 3 will more thoroughly examine Ryan's understanding of economic activities that lie outside the purview of paid labor, especially the domestic sphere and the work of women within it. But first I must highlight two further agendas that complete Ryan's program for economic justice for the working-man.[81] Though the living wage is an indispensable prerequisite to worker jus-tice, workingmen's dignity, needs, and capabilities as human beings call for more than simply cash remuneration that ensures material *sufficiency* in the present. Workers also require, Ryan contends, access to *security* for the future, in two forms. First, security against sickness, disability, and old age requires either a high enough wage to allow the worker to put up savings for this purpose or benefits such as medical insurance and pensions. Second, Ryan advocated for profit-sharing programs whereby workers could actively build a secure future through both savings and, ideally, modest property owner-ship.[82] Combined, these better enable people to realize work's capacity not just to sustain biological survival but to help build a temporally stable human world that endures into the future.

Finally, the capstone of wage-earner justice envisaged by Ryan was a new, vastly improved, *status* for labor in a form of "industrial democracy," where workers would have a reasonable share not only in profits but in manage-ment and ownership. Since most participants in the modern market will remain employees rather than owners, Ryan reasons, it is imperative for "the development of human faculties and the maintenance of human dignity" that workers have opportunities in their jobs to practice and develop their "creative or directive capacities."[83] To realize this goal would require develop-ing avenues for employee profit sharing, for sharing in business ownership, and for workers' active participation in the running of business concerns.[84] Other vehicles to improved status were associations such as labor unions or occupational groups, through which, Ryan argued, workers could collectively address conflicts and advance mutually beneficial cooperation among labor, management, and capital.

DISTRIBUTIVE JUSTICE FOR ALL

Ryan expounded his agenda for worker justice in the context of a theory of distributive justice whose goal is inclusive human welfare and that identifies need as the primary warrant for people's rights to economic access. As Harlan Beckley notes, Ryan prized both liberty (the signature value of liberal cap-italism) and equality (the great goal of socialism) but saw each as a means to a larger goal: the perfection, well-being, or flourishing of each person in community.[85] This God-given destiny of every person means, first, that any good economy must ensure first that human needs are met. Because humans are "beings endowed with the dignity and potencies of personality," meeting needs requires institutions capable of ensuring what people require for reasonable personal development. In this regard the distributive canon of need calls for an allocation of resources that is proportional to peoples'—inevitably unequal—desires and capacities. Here Ryan recognizes claims based on the higher levels (and different sorts) of excellence of which some are capable. This leads him to prioritize distributing economic resources based on what persons "need" in order to develop and perfect their higher capacities (rather than what they may deserve for contributions that this self-development may allow them to make). So, the needs that a living wage ought to meet may include, for one family, piano lessons for a musically gifted child; for another, special training for members talented in carpentry or computers. While *need* is the primary canon of distributive justice, it is not its sole criterion. Varying forms of *desert* can also warrant distributing more or different resources among parties. Desert may arise, for instance, from the superior development of talents by some, or superior contributions to the economy or general common good.[86] Together, in Ryan's ethic, need and desert are the two most basic principles of economic justice.

By what means, finally, is economic justice for all to be attained? In this chapter I have focused on the public face of livelihood and wage-worker justice. As noted, the centerpiece of Ryan's agenda for justice in this sphere is the family living wage, ideally delivered to all adult male workers who in turn will support themselves and their wives and children. In the forefront of public debates and advocacy for minimum wage laws, Ryan nonetheless considered other, nonlegislative avenues for attaining a universal living wage on a number of occasions.[87] A living wage, he conjectured, might be attained solely through the natural workings of the market, or through "the benevolence of employers" who might be persuaded to pay it. In the end, though, Ryan dismissed both as highly improbable, and naïve, expectations on which to pin hopes for wage justice. Instead, he aligned himself with two other means he regarded as more effective: the organization of labor and the legislation of universal minimums that would actually approximate a living wage. Ryan saw unionization as a necessary and to some degree effective means for exerting countervailing power to press employers to pay just salaries.[88] Yet he believed that to secure worker justice would require social reform legislation, and was an outspoken public supporter of such legislation, especially during the New Deal years.[89]

In the first half of the twentieth century, US Catholic economic ethics dovetailed considerably with broader societal movements for worker justice that focused on family living wages and breadwinner/homemaker gender roles. Yet Ryan's Catholic agenda for worker sufficiency, security, and status was distinctive in subtle but important ways.[90] First and most significantly,

Catholicism's theological, nonmaterialistic (though decidedly incarnational) understanding of human nature and destiny provided a religious foundation for the universal right to a decent material livelihood. Economic rights were warranted by the sacred dignity bestowed by God on each human personality. This same religious warrant underlay Ryan's holistic sense of what a good living entailed. An authentic, but in the end limited, good, economic livelihood's purpose was ultimately to serve human beings' temporal and spiritual destinies.[91] Christian faith and "right reason" also proscribed untrammeled material gain seeking or consumerism. Economic life as God intended dictated honesty, industriousness, and concern for the commonweal in production and wage earning and moderation in spending and consumption. As I will discuss further in chapter 6, this moral and spiritual vantage point inclined—or at least should have prodded—Catholics to challenge and resist major premises and features of the mass-consumerist ideal of livelihood that predominated after 1920.

A second distinctive feature of social Catholicism's living-wage teaching was its integrated and normative understanding of the social order and the economy's role within it. Laws and institutions exist to protect and foster the members' dignity within related social arenas: the familial, the civil, the economic, and the political. Economy, civil society, and polis exist for the well-being of their members; in a real sense all are servants of the family, which is regarded as the foundational community and unit of society. Catholics' integrated economic vision sees the household sector and the public waged sectors as interdependent and complementary rather than divorced or opposed. It also refuses to identify productive work only with paid work and expects domestic and formal waged economies to cooperate in serving personal and social welfare. And despite US Catholics' embrace of then-dominant gender roles, this vision also preserved potential space, at least in theory, for a variety of arrangements under which adult family members might participate in and contribute to domestic and waged economies.

CONCLUSION

US working people in the early twentieth century faced an uphill battle to wrest their livelihoods from a complex, impersonal, industrialized marketplace. While Catholic families daily labored to earn a decent living, Catholic pastors and intellectuals strove to aid the workingman's cause through social teaching, ethical analysis, and advocacy for change. John Ryan's thought and work combined all three in what became the twentieth century's most influential US Catholic economic ethics and livelihood agenda. And his efforts to advance economic justice reflected his tradition's larger vision of humanity and the human good. A practical-ethical form of Catholic *sacramentality* abides in Ryan's reverence for the human person's dignity and potentials, and in his appreciation of the value and significance of the temporal-material arenas of work and family, economy and *polis*. Ryan also personified *solidarity* in his alliances with everyday working people, his unshakable commitment to economically vulnerable workers and families, and his dedication to promoting reforms that would uphold workers' dignity, fairly remunerate honest work, and ensure families' access to the minimum material requirements for a good life. Finally, his *transformative* orientation led him to press for practically attainable reforms, while recognizing the need for more profound changes on both personal-local and institutional-structural fronts.[92]

Biographers and historians tend to judge Ryan as not quite a genius, nor a prophet, nor a hero. Yet this teacher and reformer did model a kind of practical heroism impelled by zeal for justice and expressed in dedication, diligent work, and active public engagement in service of an inclusive vision of dignified livelihood. Ryan, not immune to wondering about his legacy, would likely appreciate knowing that his work was being seriously considered more than a century after *A Living Wage* and *Distributive Justice* were first published. Yet his realism and respect for the changing facts of economy and history would lead him to caution against applying his analyses and proposals uncritically to today's altered circumstances. On the contrary, Ryan would insist that we undertake the hard work of discerning the facts, judging how Catholic social teaching might illumine them, and crafting, then evaluating and adjusting, strategies fitted to the exigencies of the present. Any agenda for work and family justice sufficient to twenty-first-century circumstances will need to be at least as practical and at least as "sufficiently radical" for our day as Ryan's was for his own.

The twentieth-century Catholic livelihood agenda had much to recommend it. But as I have already suggested, it also harbored ambiguous elements that worked at cross-purposes to the positive ends it aimed to serve. As corporate tycoons like Henry Ford recognized early on, the wage-dependent, breadwinner-supported household could serve the interests of business, in particular by promoting a stable labor force consisting of acquiescent workers who could not afford to rock the boat.[93] Later in the century, stagnant wages combined with steeply rising levels of household debt further cemented the advantages of employers over their wage-dependent workers. And in key respects, the US campaign for family living wages reflected and reinforced patterns of distributing power, status, and resources that favored some and disadvantaged others on the basis of class, gender, and racial-ethnic differences. As I will argue next, reviewing Catholic economic thought and US workers' quest for livelihood with a focus on these power-inflected differences exposes their significant, interacting influences and can help equip us for a contemporary agenda that more effectively takes these dynamics and differentials into account.

NOTES

1. See, e.g., Murphy, "Indestructible Right."
2. Ryan, *Living Wage.*
3. Between 1865 and 1918 the US Catholic church underwent "enormous growth." After 1890 Catholic immigrants no longer came primarily from Germany and Ireland. "In 1907, 81 percent of newcomers came from eastern and southern Europe." In 1916 approximately 47 percent of all Catholic parishes were foreign-language speaking. O'Brien, *Public Catholicism,* 77.
4. In 1882, 87 percent of immigrants came from the British Isles, Germany, Scandinavia, Switzerland, and Holland; in 1907, 81 percent were "new immigrants" from Italy, Russia, Austria-Hungary, Greece, Romania, and Turkey. Katzman and Tuttle, *Plain Folk,* xiii. By 1916, Irish, German, Italian, Polish, French-Canadian, and Mexicans constituted the largest Catholic communities in the United States, accounting for at least 75 percent of sixteen million American Catholics. Most first- and second-generation Catholics were Eastern Europeans from countries like Slovakia, Czechoslovakia, Lithuania. Dolan, *American Catholic,* ch. 5, esp. 134–36.
5. With the sense of belonging as Americans that some Irish American and German American Catholics enjoyed by 1920, however, came accommodation to religiously problematic cultural values like possessive individualism and racist self-aggrandizement. See esp. Roediger, *Wages of Whiteness;* Jacobson, *Whiteness of a Different Color.*
6. A 2006 Catholic Charities policy paper draws parallels between earlier and contemporary waves of immigration to the United States, and anti-immigrant backlash. Donald Kerwin, "Immigration Reform and the Catholic Church," *Migration Information Source: The Online Journal of the Migration Policy Institute,* May 1, 2006, https://www.migration policy.org/article/immigration-reform-and-catholic-church.
7. Euro-American Catholics of differing ethnicities and nationalities frequently engaged in mutual stigmatization and exclusion. So-called mixed marriages (for example, between Italian American and Irish American Catholics) were actively discouraged and could occasion the shunning of the "interracial" couple by both families. Dolan, *American Catholic,* ch. 5.
8. To immigrant Catholics, Protestantism also seemed foreign. Rocco Corresca, who arrived in New York from Italy about 1904, remembers, "At first we did not know much of this country, but by and by we learned. There are here plenty of Protestants who are heretics, but they have a religion, too. Many of the finest churches are Protestant, but they have no saints and no altars, which seems strange." Katzman and Tuttle, *Plain Folk,* 37.
9. See Duis, *Challenging Chicago.* A similarly intimidating clash of small-town and urban cultures, exacerbated by extreme economic vulnerability, was experienced by working-class women when the loss of underpaid and poorly conditioned industrial work in

their hometowns forced them to seek usually even more poorly paid, domestic work in larger cities. See, e.g., Gertrude Barnum, "Story of a Fall River Mill Girl," *Independent* 58 (1905): 241–43.

10. Katzman and Tuttle, *Plain Folk*, xviii.

11. Katzman and Tuttle, xviii.

12. Katzman and Tuttle, xix.

13. Young, unmarried "girls" employed in industrial sweatshops withstood horrendous conditions: long hours, grueling paces of work, low pay, injuries that at times led to amputations, and personal and sexual mistreatment, as described by Sadie Frowne, a sixteen-year-old Polish immigrant, around 1910. Yet Sadie dwells on the small savings and consumer pleasures that frugal management of her puny salary have afforded her. She speaks glowingly of trips to Coney Island, picnics, frequenting the cinema, buying nice clothes, and especially, dancing. Katzman and Tuttle, *Plain Folk*, 49–57. Cf. Peiss, "Gender Relations and Working-Class Leisure."

14. Kaztauskis, "Life Story," 13.

15. Kaztauskis, 13–14.

16. Kaztauskis, 15.

17. *The Jungle*, whose protagonist is a Lithuanian immigrant stockyard worker, depicted the poverty, isolation, squalid living, and oppressive working conditions endured by laborers in Chicago's meatpacking industry. A review by the writer Jack London called it "the *Uncle Tom's Cabin* of wage slavery." Wikipedia, s.v., "*The Jungle*," August 11, 2017, https://en.wikipedia.org/wiki/The_Jungle.

18. Kaztauskis, "Life Story," 16.

19. Kaztauskis, 18.

20. See, e.g., O'Brien, *Public Catholicism*, 77–81, 94. By contrast, in 1902, Corresca speaks with enthusiasm of his own church involvement. Katzman and Tuttle, *Plain Folk*, 3–13.

21. On "urbanizing peasant," see Hochschild, *Second Shift*, ch. 16.

22. See Giddens, *Central Problems in Social Theory*, 58, 71; also King, "Accidental Derogation of the Lay Actor."

23. Historian Allan Carlson offers a socially conservative account of these developments in *From Cottage to Work Station*.

24. On origins of separate spheres ideology see Cott, *Bonds of Womanhood*; also Kerber, "Separate Spheres, Female Worlds"; Wright, "Theorizing History."

25. Economist Nancy Folbre exposes the historical evolution of the "dependent house-wife," a term adopted as an official US census designation circa 1900, in "Unproductive Housewife."

26. Rapp, "Family and Class in America," 187.

27. Kaztauskis proudly describes his wife Alexandria's immigration to the United States after Antanas had procured a union job. Alexandria quickly mastered English and schooled herself in gendered domesticity, "so now she looks the finest of any woman in the district. We have four nice rooms, which she keeps very clean, and she has flowers growing in boxes in the two front windows." "Life Story," 19.

28. Joe Podles, interview by Michael Tiranoff, August 9, 1979, archives, Mullen Library, Catholic University of America, Washington, DC, https://cuomeka.wrlc.org/exhibits/show/howmuch/documents/hm-doc1.

29. On *Rerum novarum*'s historical and movement background, see Misner, *Social Catholicism in Europe*; Molony, *Worker Question*; Schuck, *That They May Be One*, chs. 1, 2.

30. As a young priest, the well-born and well-educated Vincenzo Gioacchino Pecci actively sought out struggling workers, developing understanding and genuine compassion for their plight. Later, as Pope Leo XIII, he embodied the posture of papal social Catholicism at the time: paternalist solicitude for the socially and economically vulnerable, and a "double-pulsed" approach that condemned social ills and injustices, and made substantive recommendations for their redress, addressed primarily to those with power to effect change. Schuck, *That They May Be One*, 31; Molony, *Worker Question*, 11–15, 46–48.

31. On organic and hierarchical thinking, see, e.g., Charles E. Curran, *Modern Catholic Social Teaching*, 86–87; also Matthew Shadle's analysis and proposed retrieval of CST's organicist communitarian vision in *Interrupting Capitalism*.

32. Counterfactual to the law of supply and demand, e.g., a laborer who needs a certain amount of money to survive, finding his wages reduced, "will not reduce his supply of labor [and thereby stimulate a return of higher wages]; on the contrary, he has to increase his supply of labor in order to achieve his target income. This increases labor supply and reduces the wage rate again: What results is 'an abnormal supply reaction' which then requires government action 'in order to stop results which are not in line with the ethical values of a society and to keep the market process working in a fair way.'" Lachmann, "Just Trade and Social Markets," 104–5.

33. On the evolution of Catholic discourse on human rights, which took a different course than the individual-based rights discourse common to political and economic liberalism, see Hollenbach, *Claims in Conflict*.

34. Ryan, *Social Doctrine in Action*, 59. Cited in McShane, "*Sufficiently Radical*," 29.

35. McShane, "*Sufficiently Radical*," insightfully analyzes Ryan's contributions to the NCWC and the 1919 Bishops' Program for Social Reconstruction.

36. Ryan was a charter member of the American Civil Liberties Union and a political appointment to the Industrial Appeals Board of the National Recovery Administration, 1934–35. Ryan offered the benediction at Roosevelt's second inaugural ceremony, the first Catholic priest to be invited to do so. See Beckley, *Passion for Justice*, 230n2; Gearty, *Economic Thought of Monsignor John A. Ryan*, 264–65; also, correspondence between Franklin Roosevelt and Ryan from September 24, 1935, visible at American Catholic History Classroom, American Catholic History Research Center and University Archives, https://cuomeka.wrlc.org/files/original/ed8e9ec6961fa0513772fd26e64e3107.pdf.

37. Molony, *Worker Question*, 49–50. Ryan, who was sent into seminary and then university teaching early in his career, was atypical for his lack of parish experience.

38. Arts, "Spirituality of John A. Ryan," 333.

39. Arts, 5.

40. See Cronin and Flannery, *Church and the Workingman*, 141–46; O'Brien, *Public Catholicism*, 143ff. "Father Ryan urged industrial democracy; Father Dietz was a fighter for trade unionism. Ryan enunciated the principles of social justice; Dietz battled in the arena. . . . Ryan was the academician and Peter Dietz the organizer. . . . Both men sought to rouse others into affirmative action." Cronin and Flannery, *Church and the Workingman*, 141. Cf. Curran, *American Catholic Social Ethics*, ch. 1.

41. The tension between elitism and populism in Ryan's work reflected liberal Progressive intellectuals generally. See Kazin, *Populist Persuasion*, ch. 5; cf. Firer Hinze, "John A. Ryan," 186–88.

42. O'Brien writes, "What distinguished Ryan from every major figure in American Catholic life until the 1950s was that . . . he enlisted in the larger public debate, making a case for

a particular reform in light of American conditions and with reference to values shared
with other Americans." He thus "became a bridge between the church and the larger
world of reform politics." *Public Catholicism*, 148–49. Cf. Beckley, *Passion for Justice*, 113;
Calo, "'True Economic Liberalism.'"

43. Ryan, *Distributive Justice* (1942), 347–48; Ryan, *Living Wage*, 331–32; Ryan, *Social
Reconstruction*, 216.

44. Ryan once told a friend: "Of course I do not regard the supernatural order as a kind of second
story, built as if by afterthought on top of the natural order, but I confess that the assumption
of no connection between the two except by elevator has always seemed to me rather logical and involving fewer difficulties than the opposite assumption." Letter to Russell Wilber,
October 14, 1935, cited in O'Brien, *American Catholics and Social Reform*, 216–17.

45. Ryan, *Declining Liberty*, 185.

46. Luke 12:15, quoted by Ryan in *Declining Liberty*, 323. Also, e.g., Ryan, baccalaureate ser-
mon, Catholic University of America, June 12, 1927, published in *Catholic University
Bulletin*, 33, no. 3 (1927): 22, found in box 37, file: "Commencement Addresses," John A.
Ryan Archives, Mullen Library, Catholic University of America, Washington, DC; Ryan,
Church and Socialism, 200.

47. Ryan, *Norm of Morality*, 27.

48. Ryan, "Two Objectives for Catholic Economists."

49. See Frederic S. Lee, "Heterodox Economics."

50. Emil B. Berendt discusses Ryan's disagreements with neoclassical economics in "Mathematical Note," 461.

51. Lutz, "Nature and Significance of Social Economics," in Lutz, ed., *Social Economics*, 423.
See also essays by Edward O'Boyle, Thomas O. Nitsch, and Lutz in the same volume; and
Davis and O'Boyle, eds., *Social Economics of Human Material Need*.

52. Lutz, "Social Economics in the Humanistic Tradition," 262. Cf. O'Boyle, "Origins of the
Association," 104–6. The development and breadth of the field today are represented in
the two scholarly journals published by the ASE, *Review of Social Economy* and *Forum for
Social Economics*; cf. also, *Feminist Economics*.

53. Here see recent contributions by ethicist Christina McRorie, including "Adam Smith,
Ethicist," and "Heterodox Economics."

54. Mosco, *Political Economy of Communication*, 36.

55. If, Ryan reasoned, luminaries like Aquinas and Aristotle could fall prey to false doctrines
such as that of the natural inferiority of slaves—an error upheld for centuries by a combination of longstanding custom, false information, and economic interests—we today are
at least equally susceptible. Ryan, *Questions of the Day*, 218–20.

56. Ryan, *Distributive Justice* (1927), 355–56.

57. On Ryan's deductive methodology, see, e.g., Curran, *American Catholic Social Ethics*,
ch. 6, esp. 84–91; Beckley, *Passion for Justice*. On Ryan as an inductive protorevisionist,
see Gaillardetz, "John A. Ryan."

58. John A. Ryan, "Attitude of the Catholic Church towards Radical Social Reforms," 18,
John A. Ryan Archives, Mullen Library, Catholic University of America, Washington, DC.

59. This "instrumental" understanding of economy, money, and wealth, studies suggest,
remained prominent among US Catholics over most of the twentieth century. See Keister, "Upward Wealth Mobility," 6, 19.

60. Ryan, *Distributive Justice* (1942), 244.

61. Ryan, *Declining Liberty*, 323.

62. Ryan, *Distributive Justice* (1942), 244.

63. This summary is indebted to Hunnicutt, "Ryan and the Shorter Hours of Labor," 398–99. Harlan Beckley echoes that "the good Ryan seeks to promote is "the development of the whole person toward the end constitutive in his or her created rational nature." "Legacy of John A. Ryan's Theory of Justice," 62. Cf. Beckley, "Love, Human Dignity, and Justice."

64. Ryan, *Church and Socialism*, 59. Today, ecological theologians question such uncritically anthropocentric claims.

65. Ryan, *Distributive Justice* (1942), 270–73; cf. *Church and Socialism*, 64–66.

66. Ryan credits Catholicism with providing the anthropological and economic foundations for the modern living wage agenda, suggesting that its "interpretation of the human dignity of the laborer as demanding a living wage . . . has proved the most revolutionary idea that has been injected into modern economic life." Ryan, *Declining Liberty*, 197–98. Daniel K. Finn analyzes Aquinas's treatment of just price in *Christian Economic Ethics*, ch. 9.

67. May, "Bread before Roses."

68. Labor leader Samuel Gompers argued that a living wage should enable a worker "to sustain himself and those dependent upon him in a manner sufficient to maintain his self-respect, to educate his children, and supply his household with literature, with opportunities to spend a portion of his life with his family." Gompers, "A Minimum Living Wage," cited in Kessler-Harris, *Woman's Wage*, 131n14. Cf. May, "Bread before Roses," 3–6.

69. Parts of the following description appeared originally in Firer Hinze, "Bridge Discourse on Wage Justice."

70. Ryan, *Living Wage*, 81–82.

71. Ryan, 72–73.

72. Ryan, 117.

73. Ryan, *Church and Socialism*, 59, 60.

74. Ryan, *Living Wage*, 136.

75. Ryan, ch.7. Ryan offers a detailed rationale for a list that includes the basics of food and clothing (together accounting for over 50 percent of costs), shelter and insurance, expenditures for "labor and other organizations," "religion and charity," "books and newspapers," "amusements and vacations," "intoxicating liquors," and "tobacco."

76. Ryan, 148–50.

77. Ryan, 119, emphasis in original.

78. Ryan, 118, 119. Ryan was a stalwart champion of marriage and childbearing, even for the poor, and an opponent of birth control and family limitation. Cf. Ryan, *Family Limitation*; also Tentler, *Catholics and Contraception*, 40–42, 50.

79. Kessler-Harris, *Woman's Wage*, 10.

80. Ryan argues that unmarried working women ought to be paid a personal living wage equivalent to that paid to unmarried men doing the same job in *Living Wage*, 107–9; cf. *Distributive Justice* (1927), 333–35. On single male workers' right to the higher, family wage, see *Distributive Justice*, 395; *Living Wage*, 109n1. On wives' and mothers' duty to work only in the home, see *Living Wage*, 133. On family allowances (which Ryan believed should be paid by employers, not the government) see *Living Wage*, 335, also, "The Family and Wages Policy," unpublished typescript, n.d. [early 1930s], John A. Ryan Archives, Catholic University of America, Washington, DC.

81. Detailed in several places, a good summary of Ryan's depiction of "complete economic justice" in terms of workers' "sufficiency, security, and status" is Ryan, *Better Economic Order*, ch. 7.

82. Ryan, 157ff. Here Ryan echoes Leo's statements about property ownership in *Rerum novarum*, §46.
83. Ryan, *Questions of the Day*, 226–27. "The men and women who compose our industrial population have not been sharply divided by their Creator into two utterly different classes, one possessing all the managerial ability and the other having no capacity except to do what they are told." Ryan, 226–27.
84. Workers' participation, however, was to be appropriately limited; Ryan never completely eschewed the labor-management hierarchy.
85. Beckley, "Legacy of John A. Ryan's Theory of Justice," 61.
86. Beckley, 90, 91. Ryan frequently asserted that "the equal dignity of persons means they have an equal right to what they need for self-perfection, but inequalities of need and desert justify an unequal distribution of goods." Beckley, 90, 91. Cf. Ryan, *Distributive Justice* (1942), 180–90.
87. Ryan, *Church and Socialism*, 74–75, is a helpful summary treatment. Cf. Laura Murphy's informative "'Indestructible Right.'"
88. See, e.g., Ryan, *Questions of the Day*, 229–31. Ryan's Catholic sensibilities led him to favor cooperation over brute conflict with owners and management. Yet, he acknowledged, "effective labor unions are . . . by far the most powerful force in society for the protection of the laborer's rights and the improvement of his condition. No amount of employer benevolence, no increase of beneficial legislation, can adequately supply for the lack or organization among the workers themselves. . . . Always and everywhere the salvation of the working classes has been collective action; and while the wage system remains, their progress will continue to be dependent upon collective action." Ryan, 230.
89. While Catholic leaders supported it, "the New Deal was passionately opposed by a coalition of Christian ministers and businessmen who theologically defended the free market and the rights of private property. . . . Christian sermons decried welfare, the national debt, corporate taxation, Social Security, and the growth of government employment. In the 1950s a young charismatic preacher, Billy Graham, told a rally that in the Garden of Eden, there were 'no union dues, no labor leaders, no snakes, no disease.'" He added that a Christian worker "would not stoop to take unfair advantage" of an employer by joining a union and going on strike." Albrecht, "Forget Your Right to Work," 126, citing Kruse, *One Nation under God*, 33–34, 37.
90. Ryan, *Better Economic Order*, 157–74; Ryan, *Distributive Justice* (1942), 333–42.
91. Ryan, *Church and Socialism*, 198; also John A. Ryan, baccalaureate sermon, Trinity College, Washington, DC, June 3, 1923, 5, box 37, file "Commencement Addresses," John A. Ryan Archives, Mullen Library, Catholic University of America, Washington, DC; Ryan, baccalaureate sermon, Catholic University of America, June 12, 1927, 25.
92. Hillquit and Ryan, *Socialism*, 13. Speaking in 1917 on Catholicism and "radical social reforms," Ryan described the church as "old enough to know that not everything that is new is good, though some things that are new are good. . . . She realizes that progress means modification, substitution, addition, but in very few instances in so-called social matters does it mean a complete abolition of all the institutions we already have." Still, his biographer Francis L. Broderick concludes, "In scope and daring, Ryan's program probably went beyond what any other prominent Catholic had offered. Radical and detailed, it set a standard by which the proposals of others could be measured." Broderick, *Right Reverend New Dealer*, 61, citing Ryan, "Church and Radical Social Reforms."
93. See Snow, *"I Invented the Modern Age"*, ch. 13.

CHAPTER 2

Radicalizing Ryan

As we consider the contours of a twenty-first-century livelihood agenda, Ryan's contributions offer an enduring prototype. But today we must press beyond Ryan's vision, toward a critically grounded Catholic agenda that advances *radical sufficiency*—the embodied welfare of all workers and families amid the exigencies of our ecologically, economically, and globally interdependent era. Drawing on interdisciplinary sources including critical social theory and alternative streams in economics, the next several chapters aim to contribute to social Catholicism's mission to enact what Pope Benedict XVI calls "intelligent love" in our contemporary economy.[1] To do this requires carefully attending to, in Benedict's words, the "logics of power" that mark collective life, logics that are codetermined by deeply ingrained, consequential valuations and practices surrounding group difference. Across history and cultures, social narratives that grow up around group differences have often operated to uphold and conceal unjust systems and dynamics, making it difficult for even well-intentioned people to recognize or combat them. By contributing to what Bernard Lonergan, SJ, calls collective bias, and helping to legitimate and reproduce economic inequities and oppression, difference-focused valuations and practices play crucial roles in what recent Catholic social teaching describes as "structures of sin."[2] Distorted beliefs and practices surrounding class, race, and gender differences are tightly interwoven in patterns of economic inequity that thread through US history, including US Catholic history. Investigating these threads, therefore, is essential to this book's effort to illuminate the obstacles to livelihood faced by so many today, and to propose ways to surmount them.

IS CATHOLIC ECONOMIC THOUGHT REFORMIST OR RADICAL?

How radical is the vision of economic transformation that modern Catholic social thought intimates? To what degree does it cohere or conflict with mainstream economics and business-as-usual in the United States? What sorts and degrees of change to the status quo does it imply?

The early twentieth-century Catholic Church had little reputation for social progressivism, much less radicalism.[3] Still, Pope Leo XIII's 1891 brief on the condition of labor had ushered the Church into a new type of public engagement, in which its criticisms of the economic status quo were clear and prominent. Leo's letter, which garnered wide ecclesial and public attention, would later be credited with inaugurating a modern papal social tradition that continues to evolve. Few Catholics have regarded these official social teachings as lockstep marching orders; critics have questioned their rigor and their coherence; and a range of Catholic thinkers and activists have claimed them as warrants for their own, often conflicting, positions and programs. For all that, these papal interventions helped to stake out modern Catholic social thought as a contested, but fertile, discursive and practical field whose theological and moral vision, principles, and vocabulary have continued to inform and engage socially concerned believers and citizens. Between 1891 and the 1950s this social teaching was invoked by an array of US Catholic leaders and initiatives—from Dorothy Day and her Catholic Worker Houses of Hospitality to the small-scale agrarianism of the National Catholic Rural Life Conference to defenders of free-market capitalism like Father Edwin Keller—and by non-Catholic labor and political leaders as well. Among US bishops, clergy, and wide swaths of Catholics in the pews, Ryan's iteration of Catholic social teaching's program for economic and work justice drew especially wide support, and it remained influential in the US Bishops' conference for the remainder of the century.

A number of factors contributed to the appeal of Ryan's Catholic economic ethics in the US setting. As we've seen, with his Irish immigrant, working-class background, his ability to speak to and for everyday working people, and his unassuming "average Joe" persona, Ryan aptly represented the white ethnic "working-class-but-moving-up" demographic that dominated US Catholicism through the better part of the twentieth century. Moreover, in contrast with the abstract deductivism of much Catholic moral thought at the time, Ryan's inductive, historically attentive method gave his economic and policy analyses an attractive practicality and relevance. His commitment to correlating Catholic social principles with the facts and workings of modern industrial society, and his engagement with the concrete circumstances and problems facing working families, earned Ryan credibility both among fellow Catholics and in the public arena.[4]

Finally, Ryan managed to thread an ideological needle by articulating a potentially radical Catholic livelihood agenda within a politically moderate and recognizably American rhetorical frame. In an era when nativism and anti-Catholicism remained influential, proving themselves fully American continued to be a palpable priority for US Catholics.[5] Among Catholic leaders of his era, Ryan excelled in connecting a Catholic reform agenda with mainstream, patriotic US progressivism. Joining the popes in both criticizing capitalist excesses and distancing himself from socialism or revolutionary Marxism, Ryan focused on "social reform through legislation," aligning himself with Progressive Era and, later, New Deal initiatives for enhancing worker justice within the existing market economy.[6] At the same time, he recognized that achieving the truly inclusive economy envisaged by social Catholics would require much deeper and more thoroughgoing change.

An illuminating example of this strategy is the US bishops' 1919 Program of Social Reconstruction, largely written by Ryan. In it, the bishops recommend moderate political and economic reforms, but they acknowledge that their moderation is pragmatically motivated. In the postwar United States, they (and Ryan) observe, "superior natural advantages and resources, [and] the better industrial and social condition of our working classes still constitute an obstacle to anything like revolutionary changes." Given this,

> No attempt will be made in these pages to formulate a comprehensive scheme of reconstruction. Such an undertaking would be a waste of time as regards immediate needs and purposes, for no important group or section of the American people is ready to consider a program of this magnitude. Attention will, therefore, be confined to those reforms that seem to be desirable and also obtainable within a reasonable time, and to a few general principles which should become a guide to more distant developments.[7]

By advocating moderation and gradualism, and campaigning for practical reforms that built on already existing government and grassroots initiatives, Ryan and the 1919 bishops modeled a tack that would be taken by most official Catholic leadership over the next century.[8]

In truth, however, Ryan's agenda for worker and distributive justice, like the bishops' plan for social and economic reconstruction he penned, balanced on a razor's edge between ameliorative reform and radical transformation. Ryan had earlier acknowledged this radical-reformist tension during a 1913 series of public debates with socialist Morris Hillquit under the title "Socialism: Promise or Menace?" After vigorously presenting a Catholic case against socialism, Ryan concluded by stating that while church economic teaching does not demand the revolutionary overturn of the market system, from a Catholic perspective, a just economy would entail "the present system, greatly, even radically, amended."[9] And as I have noted, Ryan, following the 1919 program's publication, expressed satisfaction that he had helped produce a document that was, he hoped, "sufficiently radical."[10] All of this hints at a more revolutionary Catholic social agenda than initial impressions might suggest.

Some interpreters link Ryan's reformist-radicalism to his neo-Thomist natural law ethics, which distinguished universal, immutable moral principles from their prudential application to concrete, messy, and changing circumstances. This method enabled Ryan to maintain a principled commitment to a vision of universal economic justice whose full implementation would require major systemic changes, while in practice promoting strategic, reformist initiatives to improve conditions for working families within extant economic circumstances. Ryan's tendency, common in pre–Vatican II Catholic thought, to firmly separate the supernatural and temporal realms also contributed to the distinction yet relation between lofty, religiously inspired ethical ideals and what Joseph McShane, SJ, calls Ryan's pragmatic, "possibilist" political ethics:

> Roman Catholic social thought did not envision the full realization of the kingdom of God on earth. Instead ardently believing that grace cooperated with nature, Ryan believed that social amelioration was achieved through the advocacy of specific and practical measures that established an incremental approximation of full justice. Thus, as Ryan understood it, Leonine social thought possessed an elasticity that worked two ways: it enshrined the ideals of full justice as the transcendent goal that judged and directed human social behavior and it was patient of imperfection on the practical level at which measures were advocated to bring about approximations of justice.[11]

Ryan engaged the economic problems of his day on multiple fronts: ecclesial, public opinion, policy, and legislative. Skilled in navigating complex interactions among principles, policies, and politics, he was also unafraid to speak out against institutional and cultural trends that he deemed corrosive to justice and social virtue. And in championing rights to a decent livelihood for all workers and families, Ryan mirrored Catholic social teaching's—also natural-law-based—inclusivity. Taken seriously, Ryan's Catholic claims about universal economic rights constituted a radical challenge to the US economic and political status quo. A twenty-first-century Catholic livelihood agenda, I argue, must be more explicit about this radicality, even as it continues to find ways to connect radical vision with concrete, transformative social and political initiatives.[12]

Since Ryan's death in 1945 this radical-reformist tension in US Catholic economic teaching and action has persisted, taking on different tonalities in different times and political and social climates. Broadly speaking, US Catholics' economic-reformist zeal waned over the 1920s, waxed during the New Deal years, then morphed into ardently anticommunist Cold War conservatism following World War II.[13] In the later twentieth century, popes, bishops, and US Catholics continued to debate the implications of their church's teachings for economic and labor policies.

Twenty-first-century advocates for a Catholic livelihood agenda must attend carefully to this history, to our changed contemporary circumstances, and to the light that theological, ethical and social analysis can shed. In attempting to do this over the next several chapters, I seek to emulate Ryan by consulting current scholarship, policy analyses, and economic and social data—for example, on children's poverty rates, racial disparities in family wealth, or pay differences between men and women. Additionally, in ways that Ryan and most official Catholic teaching have not, I will undertake critical analysis of deeply formative background beliefs, and enabling and constraining social dynamics—ideologies and power relations—that underlie economic facts and statistics.

Sustained, critical-theoretical analysis of ideologies and power dynamics most probably would not have been the practical Monsignor Ryan's cup of tea. But becoming more attuned to the workings and effects of ideology and power can strengthen our assessments of the economic status quo, and help us hone intelligent strategies for change. So without disregarding the attention to on-the-ground facts, practicality, and strategic thinking that Ryan's work exemplifies, the chapters that follow undertake critical analyses intended to contribute to a contemporary Catholic social ethics better equipped to advance the goal of inclusive economic livelihood. To this end, we will explore both recent social-scientific data and the deeper architectures of power that, in varying historical manifestations, have continuously shaped US work and economy.

CRITICAL SOCIAL ANALYSIS AND CATHOLIC SOCIAL THOUGHT

Modern Catholic social teaching embraces understandings of humanity and of society that have influenced US advocates for economic justice from Ryan's day to our own. Shunning both atomistic individualism and homogenizing collectivism, this Catholic social imaginary pictures an organically related, multiassociational polity marked by widely dispersed power among interdependent groups, all of whom participate in a shared, common good that it is government's role to oversee and protect.[14] Particularly before the 1960s, this social vision tended to leave political and class hierarchies unquestioned and to underplay conflicting group interests, power struggles, and the ideological false consciousness that can mask them. Insufficient attention to ideology, to power dynamics, and to social conflict are weaknesses that have also beset liberal universalisms, including the forms of US political liberalism with which Ryan and likeminded US bishops and laity tended to align.[15]

But since the later twentieth century, numerous US scholars and activists—most secular, some religious—have employed critical methods of social analysis to examine economy and work through ideologically and structurally focused lenses. Amid heightened awareness of the systemic and interstructured effects of race, gender, and socioeconomic status on human experience, intellectuals and justice advocates have endeavored to better understand how power dynamics surrounding group identities and differences have shaped and constrained Americans' pursuit of livelihood in the past and how they continue to do so today.

Social Identity and Social Groups

These critical-theoretical approaches focus attention on ways social groups orient how we see the world, including by shaping our identities as members of particular "we's" in contradistinction to those who are deemed "other." Political theorist Iris Marion Young elaborates: "While groups do not exist apart from individuals, they are socially prior to individuals, because people's identities are partly constituted by their group affinities. Social groups reflect ways that people identify themselves and others, which lead them to associate with some people more than others, and to treat others as different. Groups are identified in relation to one another. Their existence is fluid and often shifting, but nevertheless real."[16]

Group identities cluster around context-specific cultural expressions and actions, which then act as symbolic carriers of communal values, memories, and hopes. With an emotional intensity that can seem irrational to outsiders, members invest in these identity-bearing symbols and practices, at times to the point where perceived threats to either can arouse existential fears about security or even survival.[17] Conflicts in the late 2010s over dismantling Confederate war memorials in the US South offer one recent example of these dynamics.[18] Economic aspirations and anxieties frequently fuel group-identity concerns, especially in contexts where economic opportunity, security, or prestige are (or feel) threatened or scarce. Group members who fear for their own sufficiency, security, and status tend to turn inward, protectively circling the wagons. And some seek to bolster group advantage and morale by ginning up competitive, hostile, or superior attitudes toward outsiders.

The story of twentieth-century US working families, Catholics among them, is punctuated by several social facts concerning group identity, power, and difference. First, group identities have significantly defined lines of social inclusion, exclusion, and conflict, as well as asymmetries of power and status. In this regard, racial-ethnic categories, class, and gender get attached to socially designated differences that are often framed in binary ways: male versus female, Anglo versus Hispanic, Black versus white, working versus middle class, poor versus rich. Whether natural or constructed, these differences lead to varying social experiences, different degrees of access to resources and opportunities, and distinctive group perspectives and interests. Whether freely accepted or imposed, attributed to nature or nurture, racial-ethnic-, gender-, or class-based group identities have perennially influenced Americans' pursuit of and prospects for economic livelihood.

Markers of group belonging are formed and carried in shared practices, meanings, and memories that are nurtured, celebrated, and passed down across generations. Being Italian, Greek, working class, a woman, or a man in a particular historical and geographical setting connects one to stories, values, and sensibilities that help form each person and group's distinctive, incarnational beauty. Multilayered and often overlapping, group identities are sources of shared dignity and vehicles for strengths that contribute to the multifaceted mosaic of the United States' national identity and common good. Yet group differences are also consistently entangled in competitions and conflicts over material and social resources, power, and status. Wending through such cross-group tensions one finds all-too-common dynamics, as members seek to build themselves up by dehumanizing nonmembers as inferior, detestable, or dangerous.

No adequate approach to work justice can afford to take these social facts lightly. Given their ubiquity and psychosocial salience, group attachments can thwart economic reform campaigns or programs that ignore or seek to erase them. Change advocates must find ways to honor and protect group belongings while also fostering intergroup connections and participation in common and public goods. But as a glance at history and at the contemporary US landscape—crisscrossed with conflict and finger pointing among groups across the racial, class, and ideological spectrum—readily demonstrates, this is a notoriously difficult task. For its part, modern social Catholicism has striven to articulate, but struggled to enact, a social vision capable of combating both facile universalisms and terminal fragmentation among groups. One shortcoming that has dogged Catholic efforts in this area is an underdeveloped analysis of power.

Power, Domination, and Oppression

Catholic social thought, Daniel Finn has noted, would benefit from a better grasp of power and its workings, and this holds especially true for Catholic economic thought.[19] Labor economist Michael Zweig argues that to gain an accurate understanding of power in contemporary political economies, one must recognize, first, that even in highly unequal situations everyone has some kinds of power. Second, one must become aware of the multifarious power relations that permeate daily life. "Some power is obvious," he writes, "and some is invisible. The power that we can see we tend to identify with individuals. . . . I have power, and you do, too, in the aspects of our lives that we can control our influence. Most of us are acutely aware of power in its visible, individual forms."[20]

But other kinds of power are located less in individual agency than in background systems and structures, making them less apparent and easy to miss. So, for example:

> The power of inertia tends to perpetuate existing ways of doing things and existing relationships. We aren't necessarily aware, day to day, of the power that limits alternatives, the power of a kind of social automatic pilot, invisible as long as everyone goes along with the program. Invisible force fields of power are built into the structures that hold society together, giving it shape, setting the paths for our opportunity, and setting the limits as well. We tend to take these contours for granted, internalize them, think of them as the natural order.[21]

Becoming aware of power's structural manifestations can help people pose better questions about power's functions and distribution. But doing so carries with it certain risks. In any social or economic arrangement, structural power relations shape and steady a status quo that inevitably benefits some more than others. Questioning or even drawing attention to extant power arrangements reminds people of the asymmetric ways power is distributed and suggests that the current setup is subject to change. None of this serves power holders. In many historical instances, therefore, when "some group of people seriously challenges this kind of power, in politics, in the culture, in assertions of new ways to organize the economy, what had been invisible roars into full view," and "'the powers that be' step out to demolish the threat."[22]

As we begin to notice and analyze power's operations in our worldviews and social structures, writes Young, we find our notion of justice pressed beyond equal exchange, or even a fair distribution of goods and opportunities. Fair exchange and distribution are important, but to approach economic justice only in these terms misconstrues power by treating it as a kind of stuff or possession that needs only to be spread around differently. This, Young argues, is problematic for several reasons.

First, to regard power (economic or otherwise) as a possession or attribute obscures the fact that power is a relationship, a process rather than a thing. As Michel Foucault puts it, power "exists only in action."[23] Second, commutative and distributive notions of justice overemphasize individualist, direct relationships of authority or exchange, while missing "the larger structure of [third-party] agents and actions that mediate between two agents in a power relation," and thereby obscure the dynamics of domination; that is, the "structured or systemic phenomena which exclude people from participating in determining their actions or the conditions of their actions."[24] Foucault writes that power, being complexly relational and structured, "must be analyzed as something that circulates, rather than something which only functions in the form of a chain. . . . Power is employed and exercised through a net-like organization. And not only do individuals circulate between its threads; they are always in the position of simultaneously undergoing and exercising their power."[25]

Finally, to think of power as a possession makes it easy to imagine that the answer to economic injustice is taking power away from some and giving it to others. Redistributive schemes are indeed important steps toward redressing economic inequities. Yet in many late-modern corporate economies and states, as Young elaborates memorably, formal political power is widely distributed, but institutionalized patterns of social and economic domination (structured constraints on self-determination), oppression (structured constraints on human development), and exploitation (structured economic constraints on some to the benefit of others) remain in place, reinforced by corresponding ideological beliefs, institutions, and practices.[26] In light of this, critical theorists like Young and Foucault insist that to properly understand and address social and economic inequities, agent-focused or "actionist" power discourses that highlight visible forms of domination must be complemented by structural analyses capable of surfacing more complicated, often less obvious, patterns of oppression.

Oppression in this context designates "disadvantage and injustice" that some people undergo, but not only when some despotic ruler or boss coerces them. The term also refers to systemic constraints on groups that are structural, rather than the result of a few people's choices or policies. Oppression, then, names "an enclosing structure of forces and barriers which tends to the immobilization and reduction of a group or category of people" and gets "embedded in the unquestioned norms, habits, and symbols, in the assumptions underlying institutional rules and the collective consequences of following those rules." Understood in this larger sense, writes Young, oppression refers to "the vast and deep injustices some groups suffer as a consequence of . . . the normal processes of everyday life."[27]

Sociologists like Anthony Giddens emphasize that power- and oppression-carrying social structures are properly understood not as fixed edifices we inhabit but as dynamic processes in which we participate and are shaped.[28] J. R. Balkin explains how socially structured power relationships reproduce themselves using the metaphor of "cultural software" that is replicated and passed from group to group and generation to generation, continually adapting, updating, and occasionally mutating. Community members unthinkingly take on cultural assumptions and practices that circulate in what Balkin calls *memetic patterns* or *memes*. Together, the meanings and valuations carried in these cultural memes form the "software" that defines and operationalizes a community's social bonds, boundaries, and oppressions.[29]

Given all this, one cannot combat structural oppression just by eliminating bad rulers, bureaucrats, or laws and installing new ones. If oppression is "systematically reproduced in major economic, political and cultural institutions," entire underlying patterns of thought and action, not simply personnel and rules, will have to change.[30] But like the air we breathe or the water fish swim in, structured power inequities can be simultaneously pervasive and hard to see, especially for those who have a vested interest in not seeing them. The fact that "the systemic character of oppression implies that an oppressed group need not have a correlate oppressing group" exacerbates the difficulty of identifying, much less effectively dismantling, oppressive social structures.[31]

To be effective, a twenty-first-century livelihood agenda must take structural analysis seriously. This means approaching economic matters attentive to relations of power that get embedded in group identities, reproduced in social practices, and legitimated by ideologies, giving particular attention to the impacts that asymmetrically valued group identities have had on people's competition for and acquisition of economic resources and power. In the United States, gender, racial-ethnic, and class identifications and differences have shaped working families' economic fortunes and access to livelihood in highly significant and overlapping ways.

CRITICAL DEVELOPMENTS IN POST-1965 CATHOLIC SOCIAL THOUGHT

Early twentieth-century Catholic leaders were aware of connections among group identities, group differences, power, and conflict. Yet official social teaching was slow to acknowledge or to explicitly address power- and difference-based ideologies, structures, and the struggle and conflict that surround these. Several factors help explain this hesitation. Popes have associated ideology criticism and class struggle with Marxist, atheistic communism, which the church vehemently rejected. Catholic moralists have shied away from structural and ideological power analyses that appeared to supplant personal responsibility. Its traditional, hierarchical worldview and ecclesial organization have also fostered Catholicism's conflict aversion and investment in maintaining social order.[32]

More recent official teaching has slowly but increasingly acknowledged larger social forces and patterns of conflict—ideological, cultural, and institutional—that legitimate and compound injustices, making them difficult to eradicate. Vatican II's 1965 Pastoral Constitution on the Church in the Modern World (*Gaudium et spes*), for instance, laments the conflictual divisions between nation and nation, racial and ethnic groups, rich and poor that riddle our increasingly interdependent contemporary world. When greed and ambition drive groups to seek to dominate or exploit one another, "what results is mutual distrust, enmities, conflicts and hardship," of which humanity "is at once the cause and the victim."[33]

Vatican II's call for a socially engaged church responsive to the "joys and hopes, needs and anxieties" of everyday people; a rapidly changing postcolonial and globalizing political and economic order; greater opportunities for ecumenical and interdisciplinary collaboration; and an upsurge of new political and liberation theologies from amid on-the-ground struggles against mass injustice and massive human suffering—these were among the factors that led post-1960s Catholics to more explicitly attend to the complex social structures and conflictual power dynamics underpinning labor and economic life. They did so against the backdrop of Catholicism's rich theological and moral imaginary, which affirms universal human dignity and siblinghood, but also values created and cultural diversities. On this Catholic view, these diversities do not necessitate conflict and separation but may be sources of beauty, interdependence, and mutual benefit.[34] Divinely created and intended, human differences, and cultural differences arising from them, are meant to contribute to and enrich the common good; to exclude, mistreat, or exploit others based on such differences is unjust and sinful.

This theological perspective also recognizes, however, that under the limiting conditions of creaturehood, personal and group differences can and often do evoke ambivalence, fear, or misunderstanding. When faced with the unfamiliar, we humans seem evolutionarily hardwired to hesitate. Difference evokes in us curiosity and interest but also caution and fear; the "other" both attracts and threatens.[35] In Christian parlance, sin—the willful warping and breaking of right-relations with God and neighbor—enters when people, abandoning efforts at mutual respect, communication, and solidarity, employ violence or oppression to resolve the tensions and anxieties that encounters with different others evoke. In these cases, we may alienate or marginalize, treating others as foreign and dangerous and taking action to isolate or push them away. We may dominate, relegating others to subordinate positions and/or exploiting their labor or resources to benefit the in-group. Or we may seek to obliterate the "otherness" itself, neutralizing it either through violent destruction, or—as is more often true in modern liberal societies—by denying, appropriating, or underplaying others' differences in order to tame or erase them.

Behind these common responses, social theorist Young detects a dialectic between a false "logic of difference" and an equally false "logic of sameness." Taking different forms in different times and circumstances, these binary logics press some people to absolutize otherness and differences, and some to deny them. Both logics contribute to abuses and disrespect of neighbors that thwart solidarity, and which the Catholic catechism regards as major causes of "the '*sinful inequalities* that affect millions of men and women ... in open contradiction of the Gospel.'" The "equal dignity as persons" of hundreds of millions of people lacking a decent livelihood across the globe today "demands that we strive for fairer and more humane conditions." To this end, modern Catholic social thought has condemned "excessive" social and economic disparities as "a source of scandal" that "militates against social justice, equity, human dignity, [and] social and international peace."[36] In papal social teaching since 1965, critiques of extreme inequality have gone hand-in-hand with heightened attention to structural injustice and transformative social struggle. Official Catholicism's slow shift in these directions is reflected in church social documents' evolving treatments of concepts such as ideology, social sin, solidarity, and the "preferential option" for the poor and vulnerable.

Ideology

In modern papal teaching, "ideology" is understood as a skewed interpretation of reality, often imposed on others by force or manipulation, which undermines the good of persons and communities by distorting relationships, limiting freedom, poisoning public discourse, and hobbling virtue.[37] Echoing Marxist interpretations, Catholic social teaching has portrayed ideologies negatively, as totalizing belief systems or worldviews that reify, legitimate, and seek to impose or stabilize an incomplete or misshapen picture of reality, thereby betraying humans' capacity and responsibility to freely seek and discover what is authentically true. Ideologies also function to support and conceal social injustice, thereby undermining the human vocation to love and seek what is genuinely of value.

But is ideology always, or only, a perniciously distorting lens on social reality? Posing this question to the influential "Puebla document" that emerged from the Latin American bishops' 1979 meeting in Brazil, Canadian theologian Gregory Baum points out inconsistencies in the treatment of ideology by those bishops, and by modern Catholic social teaching as a whole. The bishops at Puebla criticized a number of dangerous and destructive ideologies ascendant at the time. But they went on to offer a distinctive definition of ideology that, Baum underscores, "reveals that ideologies can be both oppressive and liberating and that they are in fact indispensable for political life." In their 1979 document, the Latin American bishops use "ideology" to refer to "a set of ideas representing a vision of social life promoted by a particular group or movement in society. Ideologies are associated with political parties and trends. In fact, ideologies are necessary to translate ideals and values into political reality. Ideologies gather people in the same movement, inspire them to common action, direct their thoughts, legitimate their efforts and sacrifices and involve them in the transformation of the social order."[38]

The Latin American bishops offer two principles for evaluating ideologies: First, "they must be in accordance with the image of the human that respects human dignity," and, second, because ideologies inevitably embody the vision of a particular segment of a society, "they must protect pluralism and leave room for the rights of others."[39] Providing it meets these two criteria, "ideology has an essential function in the transformation of society." But at the same time, the bishops insist that Christian faith is nonideological, emphasizing that while "Catholic social teaching is meant to inspire Christians in their political life and guide them in the formulation of policies," that social teaching is not an ideology.[40]

At Puebla, official Catholic teachers provided, for the first time, a wide and positive definition of ideology, even insisting on its necessity for social change. But, Baum laments, the bishops then declined to describe for Catholics what, in the concrete, a transformative ideology may entail: "Nothing is said that points to the creation of an ideology adequate to people's political and human needs." Baum argues (correctly, in my view) that this failure to articulate a positive Catholic understanding of ideology as a tool for social transformation "enormously weakens" the bishops'—and Catholic social teaching's—"moral exhortation in favor of justice and human liberation." For if, as the Puebla bishops aver, enacting the positive change the gospel calls for requires an accompanying ideology, then "unrelated to a specific ideology these moral aspirations [will] remain powerless."[41]

Pope John Paul II's 1991 encyclical celebrating the centenary of Leo XIII's *Rerum novarum* reinscribes modern papal social teaching's generally negative understanding of ideology, and its description of Christian truth and faith as nonideological. Christianity, the pope explains, is not an ideology; nor does it presume to "imprison" changing temporal realities within any rigid, ideological scheme. While recognizing that humans live their lives in historical conditions that are "diverse and imperfect," the church affirms each person's "transcendent dignity" and respects their freedom.[42] Popes Benedict XVI and Francis have spoken of ideology in similar terms, arguing that Christian faith and social thought are liberating realities that neither impose nor can be contained in any ideology.

This quite constricted understanding of ideology in modern Catholic teaching merits critique. A broader understanding of ideology as a coherent set of beliefs and values about people and the social order that adherents have naturalized (that is, they take for granted as being, in fact, true and valuable) enables us to recognize, as theologian Craig Prentiss persuasively argues, that articulating, advancing, and adapting a potent ideology in the face of changing circumstances is exactly what modern Catholic social teaching has been attempting to do.[43] Recognizing this more capacious meaning of ideology is important for at least two reasons. First, it helps to dereify modern Catholic social documents and tradition, enabling us to analyze them more critically, and accurately. Second, recognizing the modern Catholic social tradition, its livelihood agenda included, as at least in part an ideological project will enable us to better articulate and advance that agenda in the face of other, currently dominant economic ideologies that obstruct or oppose it. A critical grasp of ideologies and their workings is also crucial for comprehending and combating the social structures and systemic dynamics that undermine the economic well-being of vulnerable workers and families.

Social Structures and Social Sin

Modern Catholic social teaching has consistently held that social groups, institutions, or structures cannot, in themselves, be morally good or evil, righteous or sinful; only particular human agents can be held morally or spiritually accountable for their actions and their consequences. Without denying this position, post–Vatican II popes have sought to acknowledge ways that institutions and systems may in fact operate in some sense beyond the explicit intentions of participants.[44] These two insights about social structures—an actionist emphasis on human agents' responsibility and a structurist recognition of systemic dynamics—are combined in the terminology of "social sin" or "sinful social structures," first used in papal social teaching by Pope John Paul II.[45] John Paul was also the first to speak explicitly of the antidote to structural sin as the virtue and practice of solidarity, guided by a "love of preference for the poor" and vulnerable. Significantly, each of these themes has trickled up into official parlance from movements and reflection in sites across the globe where poor or marginalized peoples have engaged in gospel-inspired struggles for justice.[46]

Writing in 1984, Pope John Paul described a world "shattered to its very foundations" by social evils including the squelching of basic human rights; religious, cultural, and racial discrimination; violence and terrorism; torture and repression; stockpiling of arms; and an "unfair distribution of the world's resources and of the assets of civilization" that aggravates the gap between the rich and poor.[47] He identifies sin—deliberate choices and actions that break or distort right-relations with God, self, and neighbor—as the original wound and root of all these evils.[48] As Genesis 3–11 illumines, through sin, the self's "internal balance is destroyed" and is replaced by contradictions and conflicts.[49] Inevitably, distorted relationships ensue.[50] Whatever its social effects, sin in this Catholic view is irreducibly personal: "There is nothing so personal and untransferable in each individual as merit for virtue or responsibility for sin."[51]

What, then, might "social sin" signify? John Paul considers four different meanings of the term. In the first place, social sin connotes the innumerable ripple effects of every individual sin that occur "by virtue of human solidarity [one could call this our de facto, connectedness and common lot] which is as mysterious and intangible as it is real and concrete." This mystery of "a communion of sin" betrays and abuses the God-given interdependencies among humans, which, at their apogee, create the spiritual solidarity of the communion of saints. Our inescapable interrelatedness, the pope writes, leads every soul that lowers itself through sin to also drag down, in some way, the whole world. In this sense, "every sin can undoubtedly be considered as social sin."[52]

Second, sin is social insofar as it entails the direct mistreatment of others, in opposition to Jesus's command to love one's neighbors. Here, social sin applies to "every sin against justice in interpersonal relationships, committed by the individual against the community or by the community against the individual." Economic activities or policies that contravene the rights, dignity, or legitimate freedom of persons are socially sinful in this sense; so are sins of omission or commission against the common good by leaders, citizens, workers, or family members.

Third, social sin may refer to unjust relationships between groups and communities. These situations involve collective dynamics that, when entrenched, are often experienced as anonymous forces. When negative social dynamics become experienced as impersonal forces, inscrutable in their causes, operations, and effects, they can be called "structures of sin."[53] Echoing the wider Catholic moral tradition, John Paul cautions that here the term *sin* is used strictly analogically. To forget this risks occluding the moral accountability of individuals who cooperate with, or benefit from, these sinful patterns, and the responsibility of all to ameliorate or transform them.

Catholic ethicist Cristina Traina's description of "structural evil" captures this impersonal yet agential character of structural sin and evil: "Structural evil," she writes, "is the comprehensive complex of interdependent, overlapping systems that, by distributing risks, benefits, and harms unequally generates an oversupply of violence, insecurity and disadvantages for some and relative immunity from them for others. Because systems involve institutions and institutions have actors, participation in structural evil is inescapable. . . . It implicates everyone, if to radically different degrees." Analogous to some descriptions of original sin, structural evil shapes our visions of reality and forms our attitudes and behavior by creating implicit and explicit biases. This structured evil arises from "an amalgam of practices that mutually reinforce their collective power": ill intention, "unintention," neglect, and preservation of privilege. Though structured, this form of evil is never wholly detached from human agency. Structural evil "has actors: *people* do this intending and unintending, neglecting, and preserving."[54]

Here Traina affirms Catholic thought's rejection of a fourth, purely structural interpretation of social evil that divorces sinful structures from participants' decisions or intentions. On the contrary, as John Paul insists, every situation of social sin is "the result of the accumulation and concentration of many personal sins."[55] Over time, as collective patterns become ingrained, we may participate in them largely without conscious thought or choice. But the moral responsibility of those who participate in, benefit from, or perpetuate these patterns is never fully abrogated. Accordingly, changing sinful structures requires illuminating sufficient numbers of individual minds, and converting sufficient numbers of individual hearts.[56]

In 1996 the Pontifical Council for Human and Christian Development used the nascent papal vocabulary of structural sin in its document concerning world hunger.[57] The council's analysis of hunger's causes highlights the intertwining of finitude and sin in unjust economic and political structures.[58] Culpable ignorance concerning the common good, combined with abuse of the commonweal through the idolatrous pursuit of profit and power, conspire to breed "structures of sin," which the council defines as "those places and circumstances in which habits are perverse" and end up sustaining vicious social patterns that become extremely difficult to resist.[59] Specifically, economic structures of sin "deliberately steer the goods of the earth away from their true purpose, that of serving the good of all, toward private and sterile ends in a process which spreads contagiously." There is a vicious, reciprocal relationship between these sinful structures and the sinful acquiescence of persons who participate in them: "Greed, pride, and vanity blind those who fall prey" to sinful structures, and these structures reinforce "the limitations of their perceptions and the self-destructive nature of their actions."[60] The resulting, entrenched "lack of will and ability to freely serve humanity" is a primary driver of nondevelopment or "mis-development" in both impoverished and advantaged nations.[61]

Solidarity and the Option for the Poor and the Vulnerable

In the face of structural sin's intransigence, how can the personal, ideological, and institutional dynamics that support social and economic injustice be resisted or dismantled? Developing a theme central to liberation theology, later twentieth-century Catholic teaching responded to this question by sounding the theme of solidarity, described variously as a fact, a social principle or norm, a human virtue, and a Christian calling.

In this discourse, solidarity denotes, first, the fact of human relatedness, which for Christians is theologically rooted but manifest in experience. De facto human interdependence is the condition for the possibility of social sin and sinful structures, but also for what we might call social "grace" and redemptive structures.[62] Second, solidarity considered as a norm bespeaks individuals' and communities' duties to take appropriate responsibility for the micro- and macrorelations and interdependencies that enmesh them. In late modern circumstances, discerning and responding to these normative implications of de facto solidarity are complicated and demanding tasks.[63]

Third, enacting solidarity as a social principle that orders institutions to the common good requires solidary practices and patterns of action—that is, cultivating solidarity as a moral virtue.[64] This virtue's heart is a habituated disposition to acknowledge and to take active responsibility for the common good.[65] For Christians, solidary virtue further encompasses a way of love that, in the social arena, gets expressed in actions for the neighbor and the common good.[66] *Gaudium et spes*'s claim that human persons can fully discover themselves only "through a sincere gift of self" affirms an inextricable bond between personal flourishing and neighbor love; it is this bond that grounds solidarity as both fact and norm. Finally, in all the circumstances of daily life, solidarity's chief concern is to be with and for those most in need: the poor, the afflicted, and the marginalized: what recent popes have called "the love of preference for the poor." Solidarity's prioritizing of the vulnerable, however, is neither do-goodism nor noblesse oblige; rather, solidarity entails a disciplined, risky praxis of humble presence, listening, and collaboration. And as Jesus's example teaches, traveling the path of solidarity will inevitably require sacrifice and suffering, carrying the crosses "which flesh and the world inflict on the shoulders of any who seek after peace and justice."[67]

As with structural sin, solidarity's more detailed treatment in official papal teaching was first undertaken by Pope John Paul II.[68] It has since been affirmed and further developed by Pope Benedict XVI, and especially by Pope Francis.[69] Solidarity, John Paul writes, is not simply a compassionate feeling but "a firm and persevering determination to commit oneself to the common good . . . to the good of all and of each individual, because we all really are responsible for all."[70] "The social face of Christian love," solidarity impels Christians to stand beside the poor and victims of injustice and to work with these and other neighbors to redress unjust structures.[71] "Love for others, and in the first place love for the poor, in whom the Church sees Christ himself, is made concrete in the *promotion of justice*."[72] Christians today, therefore, must "become a church of and for the poor . . . while keeping in mind the common good."[73]

As noted, John Paul also draws into official doctrine liberation theology's theme of the preferential option for the poor.[74] But true to previous papal social teaching, he seeks to mute this theme's conflictual potentials, stressing collaboration both between rich and poor and among the poor themselves.[75] Pope Francis has offered sharper, more prophetic, critiques of economic disparities that shut out the poor, frequently adverting to structural injustice and the conflicts of interest that divide more and less powerful groups. While continuing to stress conversion of minds and hearts and small acts of encounter and neighborly love, Francis also more explicitly connects solidarity to work for structural change. "Solidarity with the poor is thinking and acting in terms of community, of the priority of the life of all over the appropriation of goods by the few. It is also fighting the structural causes of poverty: inequality, unemployment and homelessness, the denial of social and labor rights. Solidarity is a way of making history with the poor, avoiding the allegedly altruistic works that reduce the other to indifference."[76]

Affirming with John Paul that solidarity is not primarily a feeling, Francis further stresses *embodied* solidarity, expressed in concrete encounters with the poor and collaborative work to end systemic injustice, as integral to the church's mission of evangelization and a responsibility incumbent on every Christian. Taking up this responsibility means "working to eliminate the structural causes of poverty and to promote the integral development of the poor, as well as small daily acts of solidarity in meeting the real needs which we encounter."[77]

All recent popes emphasize that to seriously undertake neighborly love as social solidarity demands major changes of perspective and commitment, or in traditional Christian terms, conversion of hearts, minds, and lives.[78] For advantaged persons and communities in particular, solidarity requires a risky easing of one's clenched grip on a privileged place in the status quo. To walk the path of solidarity, the better-off must be willing to pay a personal and a social price for the sake of the common good: "It is not merely a matter of 'giving from one's surplus,' but of helping entire peoples which are presently excluded or marginalized to enter into the sphere of economic and human development. *For this to happen . . . requires above all a change of life-styles, of models of production and consumption, and of the established structures of power which today govern societies.*"[79]

In recent Catholic teaching, then, solidarity emerges as a key weapon in the fight against attitudes, practices, and arrangements that deny economic well-being and even survival to so many today.[80] People, policies, and institutions oriented by solidarity, including "structures of solidarity," or "structures of common good," are the keys to counteracting and repairing harms and divisions that social sin wreaks.[81] To put it more positively, for a twenty-first-century ethic of livelihood, solidarity is an energizing ideal and a promising—and demanding—virtue. Its practice entails continuously striving to *see* one's fellow human beings, lovingly and truthfully. It refers to *judgments* about economic value and the *actions* those judgments require to advance a common good in which all are invited to participate and to contribute.[82]

For US working families and their communities, the Great Depression of the 1930s, the 2008 financial crisis and recession, and the COVID-19 pandemic in 2020 all brought home the inescapable connectedness—the *de facto solidarity*—of household, national, and global economies.[83] But the daunting task of infusing this simultaneously global and localized web with the *intentional solidarity* needed to build ecologically sustainable, inclusive livelihood economies bespeaks a radical change agenda, superseding anything attempted to date either in the United States or internationally. In the face of this enormous challenge, people across the country and the globe are courageously lifting up their voices and dedicating efforts to this vast, transformative work. During the Global Climate Strike of fall 2019, for instance, the need for a radical change agenda reverberated in the voices of advocates like Greta Thunberg and in young people's vocal demands for economic and political action adequate to the impending crises of global climate change. In 2020 the unprecedented economic turmoil wrought by the COVID-19 pandemic further underscored humans' interdependence and the need to radically recenter the country's political-economic axis on the goal of ensuring dignified work and a decent livelihood for every US worker and family.

Though differing in contour and substance at some points, modern social Catholicism, too, points toward this sort of radically transformative social agenda. Pope Francis's 2015 encyclical *Laudato si'* demonstrates this, highlighting the inextricable connections among the ecological, economic, and political challenges facing humanity, and the radically solidary local and institutional responses that these call for in contemporary Catholic thought and action: "In the present condition of global society, where injustices abound and growing numbers of people are deprived of basic human rights and considered expendable, the principle of the common good immediately becomes, logically and inevitably, a summons to solidarity and a preferential option for the poorest of our brothers and sisters" and for our increasingly vulnerable planet.[84]

TOWARD A CRITICAL CATHOLIC ECONOMIC ETHIC

Trusting that good action may be served, though never replaced, by good scholarship, the next chapters revisit the twentieth-century US Catholic livelihood agenda, employing a critical lens intended to illuminate the structural and ideological dynamics that shape and constrain ordinary people's efforts to earn their daily bread. Doing so will help to surface and more clearly articulate the radicality and promise of Catholic social teaching's vision of sustainable, economic sufficiency for all. I hope it will also help us identify the contours of a livelihood agenda for today centered on a "concrete histori-cal ideal" of *radical sufficiency,* an agenda capable of generating strategies and energizing action toward a political economy that makes livelihood accessi-ble for every worker and every family.[85]

This renewed Catholic livelihood agenda must join intelligent critique of the economic status quo with a constructive agenda for inclusive economic sufficiency, anchored in an ethical and theological vision in which each per-son and community counts. Speaking beyond its own faith communities but no longer hewing solely to the traditional vocabulary of natural law, contem-porary Catholic social discourse emphasizes God's presence and action in all sectors of life. This *sacramental seeing* helps disclose and evokes compassion for the tangled web of interdependencies that constitute our world. Seeing aright becomes the foundation for *solidary* judging and valuing, whereby in our spe-cific circumstances we take responsibility for the relationships that enmesh us. Solidarity, in turn, becomes the impetus for *transformative action* on behalf of justice and the common good. The upshot is an economic ethic keenly atten-tive to data and experience, structurally critical, practically astute, and explic-itly rooted in spiritually attuned habits of perceiving, valuing, and living.

Pressing forward developments in recent teaching and thought, a con-temporary Catholic economic ethic will incorporate critical analyses of power, ideology, and structures, will acknowledge and address social conflict, and will side with the poor and vulnerable. Engaging in struggle and con-flict for the sake of justice, Christians remain responsible to their tradition's commitment to universal human dignity and solidarity and to serving a larger common good from which, ultimately, no one is to be excluded. Struggle that reflects this solidary ethic will give primacy to nonviolent action motivated by concern for opponents and aimed at reaching wide consensus, for this has the best chance of preserving the love of neighbor that Christians are required to extend even to enemies.[86] All of this is much easier said than done.

The arduous work of advancing a sustainable, inclusive-livelihood econ-omy in our day, I contend, is best served by an ethic of *radical sufficiency.* This ethic is radical in its inclusivity: dedicated to economic sufficiency, security, and status for all. It is committed to radically comprehensive analysis: employ-ing critical, evidence-based disciplines and analysis to understand material, ideological, and structural obstacles to inclusive livelihood, especially in asymmetries of power and in intersecting, difference-based inequities and oppression. At the same time, a radical sufficiency ethic is practically trans-formative: dedicated to undertaking smart, solidary action to combat those obstacles and to move its inclusive vision closer to on-the-ground reality by linking its critical diagnosis and radically inclusive aims to strategic steps to improve life for ordinary people in their actual contexts. Absent such a critically grounded, practice-focused ethic, social Catholicism's sacramental, solidary, and transformative impulses too easily succumb to dilution, cooptation, or defeat. Sacramentality becomes reduced to sentimentality. Solidarity remains at the level of safe and fairly painless talk or token gestures. And well-intentioned efforts at transformation stay caught in the well-worn grooves of business as usual.

Fighting to avoid these pitfalls, a radical-sufficiency livelihood agenda pushes people in every social situation to connect their economic hopes and ideals (which themselves must be continually clarified and discerned) to intelligent practices and adaptable strategies for advancing change. To be successful, change seekers must also build and maintain communities and coalitions that can help sustain their work for economic justice amid the ambiguities, frustrations, and setbacks that long-haul transformative work inevitably entails.

These practical and strategic commitments distinguish a critical Catholic economic ethics from other Christian stances that urge withdrawal from public engagement, whether for the sake of preserving one's ideals unsullied, or because, in this vale of tears, no real change is deemed possible. Practical radicality is also an antidote to superficial, parasitic, or "virtual" consumerist responses to social injustice that amount to cheap, counterfeit forms of solidarity.[87] A critical Catholic livelihood ethic instead encourages individuals and communities to reflect realistically, judge astutely, and act courageously in the tensive space between what is and what ought to be, motivated by a faith-based conviction that "sometimes the world as it should be can have limited, positive impact on the world as it is. It is likely to happen only when love enjoins power in the interests of justice, and this assumes a willingness to study critically and to engage the rough and tumble public arena of the world as it is."[88]

In this spirit, the next several chapters revisit twentieth-century working families' struggles for livelihood, concentrating on intersecting, power- and difference-related dynamics that Ryan's earlier brief for worker justice tended to ignore or obscure.[89] Ryan envisaged the worker as the male head of household; chapter 3 will look more carefully at women and the intersection between economy and gender. Ryan assumed the primary constituency for Catholicism's economic advocacy to be Euro-American white men and their families, but chapter 4 examines how dynamics surrounding race and ethnicity have marked the story of Catholic working people and their neighbors since the nation's beginnings, in ways with which US citizens today, including Catholics, have yet to come fully to terms. Ryan's focus was on a largely working-class US Catholic audience, and he followed Popes Leo XIII and Pius XI in critiquing gross economic inequalities. Chapter 5 takes a careful look at how class and inequality have figured into socioeconomic and work relations both then and now. Ryan considered wage earning within a holistic Catholic vision that valued moderation in consumption and a balance between work and rest, leisure, contemplation, and worship. Chapter 6 examines the changes that have taken place in American work-life culture over the course of the last century, as well as the new urgency for retrieving and articulating boundaries around work and material sufficiency in an era of looming ecological crises. Along the way we will gather further resources for articulating a contemporary Catholic livelihood agenda whose foundation and lodestar is what I am calling *radical sufficiency*, a task to which the final chapter returns.

NOTES

1. Benedict XVI, *Caritas in veritate*, §30, §5.
2. E.g., John Paul II, *Sollicitudo rei socialis*, §36; Copeland, *Genetic Study*, ch. 3.
3. A vigorous, if flawed case for the antiradicalism of US Catholic social thought, especially after 1937, is Seaton, *Catholics and Radicals*.
4. Ryan's stress on attending to economic "facts" and people's concrete needs transcended manualist theology's focus on abstract first principles of natural law as the starting point for ethics. Cf. Firer Hinze, "John A. Ryan," 189.
5. See, e.g., McGreevy, *Catholicism and American Freedom*.
6. To conservatives' claims that *Rerum novarum* fomented worker radicalism and unrest, Ryan responded that ensuring economic justice would prevent radicalism and revolutions. Prentiss, *Debating God's Economy*, 171.
7. US Catholic Bishops, *Program of Social Reconstruction*, §12–13. "A statement thus circumscribed . . . will also serve as an imperative call to action. It will keep before our minds the necessity for translating our faith into works." The program sought to be "practical and persuasive."
8. See, e.g., McShane, "Sufficiently Radical," 231ff.
9. Hillquit and Ryan, *Socialism*, 13. See also US Catholic Bishops, *Program of Social Reconstruction*, §36. By the 1950s "Catholic leaders' appeals for radical transformation became significantly less frequent," yet Catholics concerned with social justice continued to believe "that some substantive structural changes were necessary if the American social order was to be authentically Christian." Prentiss, *Debating God's Economy*, 143–44.
10. Ryan, in a 1919 letter to his sister, Sister Mary John. Broderick, *Right Reverend New Dealer*, 108.
11. McShane, "Sufficiently Radical," 230–31. Prentiss, *Debating God's Economy*, challenges Seaton's claim that post-1937 US Catholics' union involvement was dominated by interests in purging radical (socialistic and communistic) elements. Cf. Seaton, *Catholics and Radicals*, 27n44.

12. I call this a "radically transformative" social ethics. See ch. 7; also, Firer Hinze, "Response to Michael Baxter," 46–49.

13. Seaton, *Catholics and Radicals*, and Prentiss, *Debating God's Economy*, trace this historical pattern.

14. See Pontifical Commission for Justice and Peace, *Compendium of the Social Doctrine of the Catholic Church*, esp. chs. 4, 8; also, Taylor, "Modern Social Imaginaries."

15. Cf. Calo, "'True Economic Liberalism.'"

16. Young, *Justice and the Politics of Difference*, 9.

17. Ross, *Cultural Contestation*, chs. 1, 2.

18. E.g., "Confederate Monuments Are Coming Down across the United States," *New York Times*, August 28, 2017, https://www.nytimes.com/interactive/2017/08/16/us/confederate-monuments-removed.html.

19. See Finn, "Power and Public Presence," 62–77.

20. Michael Zweig, "Six Points on Class," *Monthly Review*, July 1, 2006, https://monthlyreview.org/2006/07/01/six-points-on-class/.

21. Zweig, *Working Class Majority*, 12.

22. Zweig, 10.

23. Young, *Justice and the Politics of Difference*, 31–32. Similar points about power are made by Christian thinkers like Paul Tillich, social theorists like Anthony Giddens, and political philosophers like Hannah Arendt. See Firer Hinze, *Comprehending Power*.

24. Young, *Justice and the Politics of Difference*, 31–32. Young's insight is echoed in later twentieth-century Catholic teaching; e.g., John Paul II's treatment of the "indirect employer" (*Laborem exercens*, §17) and of "structures of sin" (*Sollicitudo rei socialis*, §§36–37).

25. Foucault, *Power/Knowledge*, 32.

26. Young, *Justice and the Politics of Difference*, 32–33.

27. Young, 41, citing Frye, *Politics of Reality*, 11.

28. Cf. Giddens's theory of structuration; see, for example, *Central Problems in Social Theory*, ch. 2.

29. Balkin, *Cultural Software*.

30. Young, *Justice and the Politics of Difference*, 41.

31. Young, 41.

32. See, e.g., Curran, *Catholic Social Teaching*, 85–90; Shadle, *Interrupting Capitalism*, esp. chs. 7, 11.

33. Vatican II, *Gaudium et spes*, §§4, 82, 85.

34. *Catechism of the Catholic Church*, §1936, states: "On coming into the world, man is not equipped with everything he needs for developing his bodily and spiritual life. He needs others. Differences appear.... The 'talents' are not distributed equally. These differences belong to God's plan, who wills that each receive what he needs from others, and that those endowed with particular 'talents' share the benefits with those who need them."

35. See, e.g., Memmi, *Dominated Man*, 185–205; see also Memmi, *Racism*.

36. *Catechism of the Catholic Church*, §1938, quoting *Gaudium et spes*, §29.

37. *Gaudium et spes*, §8. In *Caritas in veritate*, §14, Benedict XVI recalls Paul VI's warnings about "the danger constituted by utopian and ideological visions that place its ethical and human dimensions in jeopardy." John Paul II praised the twentieth-century workers' movement for its justice-motivated, "widespread campaign for reform, *far removed from vague ideology and closer to the daily needs of workers.*" John Paul II, *Centesimus annus*, §16.

Post-1989, he warned that "a *radical capitalistic ideology* could spread . . . which blindly entrusts [the solutions of all social problems] to the free development of market forces" (§42. Cf. §§18, 22, 42, 46).

38. Baum, "Meaning of Ideology," 172.

39. Baum, 172.

40. Baum, 172, 173.

41. Baum, 173.

42. John Paul II, *Centesimus annus*, §46. Benedict XVI's *Caritas in veritate* eschews the language of structural sin that John Paul had employed. Amid the 2008 Great Recession, Benedict stressed markets' neutral, instrumental nature; the problem, he contends, is ultimately not markets but actors in markets who succumb to selfishness, distorting "cultural configurations," and "ideologies." Benedict XVI, *Caritas in veritate*, §36.

43. Prentiss, *Debating God's Economy*, frames and critiques Catholic social teaching as ideology in this broader sense. See esp. chs. 1 and 2.

44. See, e.g., Kelly, "Nature and Operation of Structural Sin"; Finn, "What Is a Sinful Social Structure?"; Baum, "Structures of Sin."

45. Cf. Wrong, *Power*, ch. 1, also 251–55.

46. Some argue that in migrating into official teachings, these themes have been deradicalized and domesticated. See Curran, *Catholic Social Teaching*, 181–88.

47. John Paul II, *Reconciliatio et paenitentia*, 1984, §2. Cf. *Compendium*, §§115–19. Parts of what follows are drawn from Firer Hinze, "Drama of Social Sin."

48. John Paul II, *Reconciliatio et paenitentia*, §3.

49. John Paul II, §15.

50. John Paul II, §15.

51. John Paul II, §16.

52. John Paul II, §16.

53. John Paul II, *Sollicitudo rei socialis*, §36.

54. Traina, "'This is the Year,'" 4, 5.

55. John Paul II, *Reconciliatio et paenitentia*, §16. Cf. John Paul II, *Sollicitudo rei socialis*, §36n65. Undergirding this discussion of social sin is a Catholic anthropology that locates moral responsibility in persons, and a social theory that, despite a penchant for images of organic unity, remains "actionist" rather than structurist: communities never exert agency completely detached from the intentions and decisions of members. Firer Hinze, *Comprehending Power*, 15–17, esp. 16n5.

56. John Paul II, *Reconciliatio et paenitentia*, §16.

57. Pontifical Council "Cor Unum," "World Hunger: A Challenge for All: Development in Solidarity," Vatican City, 1996, http://www.vatican.va/roman_curia/pontifical_councils /corunum/documents/rc_pc_corunum_doc_04101996_world-hunger_en.html.

58. Pontifical Council "Cor Unum," §10.

59. Pontifical Council "Cor Unum," §25.

60. Pontifical Council "Cor Unum," §25.

61. Pontifical Council "Cor Unum," §10.

62. Vatican II, *Gaudium et spes*, §§40–45. Cf. Pontifical Council "Cor Unum," "World Hunger," §27.

63. Pontifical Council "Cor Unum," "World Hunger," §4, §5.

64. Bilgrien, *Solidarity*, ch. 6, describes solidarity as a particular form of general justice.

65. Vatican II, *Gaudium et spes*, §30.

66. Vatican II, §24.
67. Vatican II, §38, see also §30, §32.
68. John Paul II, *Sollicitudo rei socialis*, §§37–40.
69. "Solidarity . . . is a structural value of the social doctrine. . . . [We need] to rethink solidarity no longer as simply assistance for the poorest, but as a global rethinking of the whole system, as a quest for ways to reform it and correct it in a way consistent with the fundamental human rights of all human beings." Francis, address to the *Centesimus Annus* Pro Pontifice Foundation, Vatican City, May 25, 2013, http://w2.vatican.va/content/francesco/en/speeches/2013/may/documents/papa-francesco_20130525_centesimus-annus-pro-pontifice.html.
70. John Paul II, *Sollicitudo rei socialis*, §39; cf. Pontifical Commission for Justice and Peace, *Compendium*, §193. Since the 1990s Catholic teaching and in particular Catholic theologians have connected solidarity with ecological concerns. See, e.g., Elizabeth Johnson, "An Earthy Christology: 'For God so loved the cosmos,'" *America: The Jesuit Review*, April 13, 2009, https://www.americamagazine.org/issue/693/article/earthy-christology; Johnson, *Ask the Beasts*, esp. ch. 10.
71. John Paul II, *Sollicitudo rei socialis*, §40.
72. John Paul II, *Centesimus annus*, §58.
73. Cf. Bilgrien, *Solidarity*, 149.
74. See Gerald S. Twomey's thorough "John Paul II and the 'Preferential Option.'"
75. Donal Dorr judges John Paul II's account of solidarity insufficiently prophetic, and "somewhat bland, since he offers no strong social analysis and less theological emphasis than liberationists do on the role of the poor in God's liberation." "Solidarity and Integral Human Development," 149.
76. Francis, address to the Federation of Christian Organizations for International Volunteer Service, December 4, 2014, http://www.vatican.va/content/francesco/en/speeches/2014/december/documents/papa-francesco_20141204_focsiv.html.
77. Francis, *Evangelii gaudium*, §188.
78. John Paul II, *Centesimus annus*, §58. Cf. Pontifical Council "Cor Unum," §25.
79. John Paul II, *Centesimus annus*, §58. Hollenbach, *Claims in Conflict*, 204, captures the radical implications of commitment to the common good in three "strategic moral priorities": "1) The needs of the poor take priority over the wants of the rich; 2) The freedom of the dominated takes priority over the liberty of the powerful; 3) the participation of marginalized groups takes priority over the preservation of an order which excludes them." Cf. Hollenbach, "Globalization, Solidarity, and Justice."
80. John Paul II, *Sollicitudo rei socialis*, §40.
81. On "structures of the common good," see Pontifical Commission for Justice and Peace, *Compendium*, §193, also Pontifical Council "Cor Unum," "World Hunger," §25: "Conversely, as soon as groups of men and women begin working together in order to take due account of the need to serve the whole community, and each individual member of it . . . a positive effect gradually improves the material, psychological and moral conditions of their lives. This is really the 'obverse' of the 'structures of sin.' One might call them the 'structures of the common good.'" Cf. US senator Robert F. Kennedy's earlier, memorable invoking of "ripples of hope," in "Day of Affirmation"; and Pope Francis's frequent affirmation that "everything is connected." Kennedy, "Day of Affirmation Address," University of Capetown, South Africa, June 6, 1966, https://www.jfklibrary.org/learn

/about-jfk/the-kennedy-family/robert-f-kennedy/robert-f-kennedy-speeches/day-of
-affirmation-address-university-of-capetown-capetown-south-africa-june-6-1966.

82. Joseph Cardijn developed the method of "see, judge, act" in 1925, for the Catholic Action
movement in Belgium. Atkin and Tallett, *Priests, Prelates and People*, 236. Cf. John XXIII,
Mater et magistra, §236; Maria Teresa Dávila, "Role of the Social Sciences in Catholic
Social Thought."

83. For intertwining global and local effects in the 2008 financial crisis see, e.g., Charles
Duhigg and Carter Dougherty, "From Midwest to M.T.A., Pain from Global Gamble,"
New York Times, November 1, 2008, https://www.nytimes.com/2008/11/02/business
/02global.html.

84. Francis, *Laudato si'*, §§156, 158.

85. On concrete historical ideal, see Maritain, *Integral Humanism*, 127–28, 132.

86. Pope Francis frequently acknowledges conflict's reality, even its necessity, but he sees its
function as surfacing obstacles on the path to common ground and unity. See, e.g., *Evangelii gaudium*, §227; Francis, address to Eucharistic Youth Movement, August 7, 2015,
https://w2.vatican.va/content/francesco/en/speeches/2015/august/documents/papa
-francesco_20150807_meg.html.

87. On parasitic solidarity, see Scholz, *Political Solidarity*. On superficial, virtual solidarity, see Miller, *Consuming Religion*, 75–76. Cf. Firer Hinze, "Over, Under, Around, and
Through."

88. Jacobsen, *Doing Justice*, 12.

89. My analysis in upcoming chapters, while focusing in turn on varying dimensions of
group-difference based injustice and oppression, aims to keep in mind what Black feminist legal scholar Kimberlé Crenshaw has called the intersectionality—the complicating,
overlapping impacts—of power dynamics relating to, e.g., sex/gender, race/ethnicity, or
socioeconomic class on people in varied social locations. On this view, the struggle for
livelihood for poor women of color differs in distinct ways from the struggles of poor
white women or working-class white men. See Crenshaw, "Demarginalizing the Intersection of Race and Sex." Cf. Harris, "Whiteness as Property," 1719n34; Carbado and
Gulati, "Law and Economics of Critical Race Theory," 1775.

CHAPTER 3

Gender and Economic Livelihood

The vision of economic well-being for US workers and their families championed by reformers in John A. Ryan's era had many merits. Pay and working conditions that provided sufficiency, security, and status for workers, and a decent livelihood for their families—this work justice agenda, shared by a wide swath of US citizens, bespoke a larger dream of a society where dignified work and basic economic well-being are available to all. Sounding within the American dream's dominant tropes of economic opportunity and potential for social mobility, this dream of livelihood as inclusive "radical sufficiency" has been a continuous, contrapuntal theme, whose resonances have been felt especially by the economically precarious and vulnerable.

Gender, our focus in this chapter, denotes "the socially constructed roles, behaviors, activities, and attributes that a given society considers appropriate for men and women."[1] Often purporting to reflect innate differences between males and females, gender is deeply intertwined with the history of economy and work. Examining that history with gender-attuned eyes uncovers fundamental issues concerning difference, power, and justice that an effective work justice agenda needs to take into account. This chapter, then, asks how the American dream of livelihood has carried and been carried by gender, and what this might augur for a twenty-first-century re-visioning of livelihood as radical sufficiency.[2]

EARLY-TWENTIETH CENTURY WORKING FAMILIES, GENDER, AND LIVELIHOOD

We have seen that in modern industrialized economies, a new type of gendered division of labor arose in response to households' increased reliance on wage earning. Gendered work roles, however, are by no means a modern invention.[3] In preindustrial economies, husband and housewife jointly performed distinct, but interdependent and geographically proximate, roles in household production and provision.[4]

The modern breadwinner/homemaker division of labor reflected a dual-spheres gender ideology that linked public value to paid labor, and male economic success, earlier centered on self-sufficiency, with a man's ability to support a wife and family through his wages.[5] The homemaker—or "dependent housewife," as she became known by 1900—was charged with upholding the household by performing unpaid labor, including caring for home, spouse, children, and the sick and frail, as well as tending to kin and community relations.[6] Girls and women learned to interiorize these obligations as constitutive to their identities and roles as wives, mothers, and daughters. These expectations of women were also "incorporated into law and social policy."[7]

Perceived as occurring in a "private," noneconomic realm, women's household labors were to be recompensed indirectly; their material sufficiency and security conferred on them through family wages earned by male breadwinners.[8] Status was also bestowed on homemakers in nonwaged ways. According moral and emotional value to her work as a "priceless labor of love" helped make the wife-mother-homemaker a cultural icon, and the subject of public sentimentality (Mother's Day was declared a national holiday in 1914). In both law and popular understanding, writes Evelyn Nakano Glenn, women's "unpaid responsibilities were stripped of economic significance and instead viewed as moral and spiritual vocations. In contrast to men's paid labor, women's unpaid caring was simultaneously priceless and worthless—that is, not monetized."[9] Meanwhile households, economically productive for most of history, were reinscribed as unproductive "units of consumption": dependent, along with the women and children who inhabited them.[10]

Two deep contradictions confronted women striving to live up to dual-spheres standards of domesticity, which played out differently for women of different classes and races/ethnicities. The first was a contradiction "between the elevation of [women's] caring labor in spiritual, moral, and altruistic terms on the one hand and the devaluation of that same labor in economic and political terms on the other." In "an economic system that counted only monetized labor and a political system that made earning the basis for entitlements of citizenship," unpaid care work was discounted in wage markets, and its practitioners rendered economically invisible and politically voiceless.[11]

Another set of contradictions emerged between "the valorization of spiritual labor" performed by homemakers, such as nurturing, moral and religious formation, and relationship tending, and a cultural tendency to denigrate "bodily labor as an expression of baseness." The ideal wife-homemaker-mother was clean, pure, and soft, but caring for a 1900s household also required toilsome and dirty bodily tending and physical labor. Those who could afford it resolved this tension by distributing the "clean" and "dirty" aspects of care work among different classes of women: the spiritual work to family, and the dirty work to servants, often recent immigrants or women of color.[12] Less privileged women who had to earn wages to make ends meet—often by engaging in domestic labor in richer women's homes—were still influenced by middle-class ideals of domesticity, but deprived of the practical opportunity to fully enact them.[13]

By the turn of the twentieth century, the breadwinner/homemaker division of labor had become the culturally dominant revision of the nineteenth-century separate-spheres ideology. By linking wage earning with successful manhood and homemaking with womanly virtue, the breadwinner/homemaker norm acquired powerful emotional resonances that helped ensure that these socially necessary activities would be performed.[14] This gendered ideology informed Progressive Era family living wage advocates' assumption that wives' unpaid household labor would be remunerated by way of husbands' paychecks. In the waged labor force, jobs in areas regarded as women's work held less status and commanded lower salaries.[15] And the fact that these gendered discrepancies went largely unchallenged suggests how taken for granted the feminized household's secondary public and economic status had become. These discrepancies, however, did not go completely unchallenged; over this same period there arose successive movements dedicated to advancing women's civil rights, equal status, and full participation in both the political and economic arenas.[16]

Manhood, Womanhood, and the Living Wage Agenda

Male "provider" roles were not original to modern market economies. But prior to the industrial revolution, non-elite US men's aspirations for economic success centered on agricultural or artisanal self-sufficiency that would enable them to avoid having to work for wages. Well into the nineteenth century, US labor advocates contrasted the degradation suffered by workers subjected to "wage slavery" with the dignity of the independent entrepreneur or artisan who worked for no one but himself. This ideal of manly "free labor" was widely admired and pursued.[17] As it became clear that wage earning would be the lot of the majority in both working and middle classes in modern markets, a new ideal overwrote the earlier masculine script; now, a steady job and family-supporting wage became markers of adult male identity and achievement.[18] Men's economic aspirations became focused on earning income sufficient to support a stay-at-home wife and children, and to pass on to children modest savings or purchased opportunities (such as education) that would increase their future chances of realizing a better standard of living.

While deeply influential as a social ideology, in practice the male bread-winner/female homemaker arrangement was never fully realized by more than a minority of US families, not even at its post–World War II apex.[19] Frequently, especially for working-class families, gendered ideals foundered on the shoals of economic reality; making even modest ends meet usually required the combined wages of two or more family members. The ideal's normative weight, however, lay heavy on wage-earning wives or mothers who experienced social disapproval or felt guilt for deviating from a gender script that most wished to perform. And as the family living wage normalized female economic dependency, wage-earning women who eschewed that dependency "impugned male roles and male egos."[20] In periods of high unemployment, wage-earning women were criticized for stealing jobs to which men were assumed to have a prior claim. In this climate, pay and other disparities between men and women workers appeared logical and were accepted, even as millions of women, both married and unmarried, depended on waged work to support themselves and their households.

The gap between gendered norms and working-class economic realities is reflected poignantly in the story of Sarah, a single, thirty-four-year-old mill worker from Fall River, Massachusetts, who spoke with a Boston social worker in 1905. Since childhood, Sarah had borne primary responsibility for caring for her home and four other siblings. She began full-time work in Fall River's textile mill at age twelve. Sarah's mother, herself a mill worker from the age of nine, died after two years of paralysis and, lacking medical insurance, being cared for at home. Sarah's younger sister, her alcoholic father, and at times a brother with his wife and child also lived in the family home, contributing to household income only erratically. Sarah had lived under her parents' roof all her life, and had long served as the family's main breadwinner. Millwork had impaired her eyesight and hearing and compromised her health. Illiterate, inarticulate, and worn, she had come to Boston hoping to find more "decent" work, but was ill prepared to do so.[21] Sarah's story highlights the chasm between the dependent-homemaker gender script and the economic realities of women's paid and unpaid labor for the majority of non-elite families.

The family wage norm cast women, regardless of class or wage-earning status, as primary guardians of the domestic sphere. In this capacity, wives, mothers, and daughters contributed great quantities of unpaid labor within and around the home. Housewives' diaries detailed, and at times lamented, their domestic labor's toil and endlessness, yet seeming insignificance.[22] Because it involved no monetary exchange, socially reproductive labor within the household was—and is to this day—excluded from official measures of US national economic productivity. Household spending did register on the radar of the formal economy—as consumption. Meanwhile, copious amounts of domestic work performed largely by women, including emotional labor and labor necessary for consumption, such as grocery and clothing shopping, remained invisible on the official economic map.[23] "Do you work?"—the guileless question posed to adult women through most of the twentieth century—perfectly and frustratingly reflects the persistence of this ethos.

US Catholic Thought on Gender and Livelihood

John Ryan and other US Catholics accepted the distinction of public wage earning and private, dependent household economies assumed by the culture at large, and their church's teaching lent religious approval to the gendering of this distinction. As did Popes Leo XIII and Pius XI, Ryan regarded the family living wage as a right due every adult working male by virtue of his patriarchal destiny in the social and familial order. Since, Ryan reasoned, a man's legitimate flourishing normally includes marrying, supporting, and raising a family, every workingman has the right to a family-supporting wage.[24]

Like most of his contemporaries, Ryan assumed that women had a special vocation for domesticity springing from qualities inhering in feminine nature, especially qualities related to motherhood. "Woman," he held, "is less individual and more domestic because both her functions and her limitations make her so."[25] Grace Sherwood, in a 1932 pamphlet issued by the US Bishops' Social Action Department that Ryan directed, sums up the then prevalent view. Sherwood extols the gifts and the genuine "feminism" of great Catholic women from Catherine of Siena, to Hildegaard of Bingen, to Joan of Arc. But, she reminds her readers, "woman's greatest privilege, after all, her supreme and abiding privilege[,] is that of motherhood." This privilege has its price, and it comes with specific role obligations:

> Above the road to . . . [motherhood] is set the sign of sacrifice. Everywhere upon it is to be found suffering, toil, self-forgetfulness. Motherhood is the result of marriage, and marriage, to be successful, means the subordination of the wife's interests to that of her husband. . . . There *is* an order in marriage, as in everything else in life. And in that order the husband's interests come first. To make a home for him, to encourage him and comfort him, to have children, God willing, these

are the first duties of a married woman. After they are done, properly, then can come outside things, the cultivation of what talents she may possess. But when outside things interfere with home life, THEY must be curtailed, not home duties.[26]

Ryan agreed, decrying equal rights feminists of his day for "false notions of freedom and the emancipation of woman as a personality." In the economic arena, he judged, "women should in general, not compete with men but cooperate with them, and be their complement, thus developing their own capacities instead of becoming a bad imitation of men." And those women who "do compete with men in the tasks that are more suitable to men's nature, . . . will inevitably suffer because they will have to abide by the rules of the game, and men will make the rules." Deeming economic independence for married women "incompatible with proper care of a family," Ryan brushed aside suggestions that working mothers "might nurse their babies during the rest periods in store or factory" or that they "might hire women to care for the children and the house." The dangers and disadvantages of housewives' economic dependence upon a male breadwinner—major first-wave feminist concerns—were, for Ryan, nonissues: "The dependence of a wife upon her husband for a living is no more degrading than his dependence upon her for his meals, his household comforts, and his children."[27]

Ryan was well aware, as we have noted, that multitudes of women did work outside the home, mostly out of economic necessity.[28] But he was firmly convinced that wives' main sphere of activity must be the home and that a good social order ought to make this possible. Middle-class feminists who insisted otherwise were "social reactionaries" who ignored the commonweal and spurned the moral law.[29] Ryan's experiences with working-class women confirmed his view that "the great majority of working women would prefer to be married, and at home only."[30] Working-class women exhibited a more realistic grasp of equality as proportional to differences in talents and abilities between different classes of persons.[31] In their orientation toward domesticity, Ryan also saw ordinary working women as more attuned than middle-class feminists to what Pope John Paul II would later call the "special genius of woman."[32]

Behind Ryan's arguments lay a deeply romanticized Catholic ideal of womanhood, captured in a quotation with which he liked to conclude addresses to women's groups:

Into her arms we are born, on her breast our helpless cries are hushed, and her hands close our eyes when the light is gone. Watching her lips, our own become vocal; in her eyes we read the mystery of faith, hope and love; led by her hand we learn to look up and walk in the way of obedience to law. We owe to her, as mother, as sister, as wife, as friend, the tenderest emotions of life, the purest aspirations of the soul, the noblest elements of character, and the completest sympathy in all our joy and sorrow. She weaves flowers of Heaven into the vesture of earthly life. In poetry, painting, sculpture, and religion, she gives us ideals of the fair and beautiful. Innocence is a woman, chastity is a woman, charity is a woman.[33]

Popes from Ryan's day to the present would continue to envisage women as bringing different qualities, strengths, and vulnerabilities into home and workforce, and to regard mothers, especially, as having a primary and indispensable role in the familial household.[34]

A FLEETING MIDCENTURY ZENITH FOR THE ASPIRATIONAL IDEAL

For white American workers, and US Catholics in particular ways, the years between 1945 and 1970 were a kind of golden moment for the American dream of livelihood. Postwar cultural stability and economic expansion made this a particularly auspicious moment to be an American worker. More working- and lower-middle-class workers than ever before enjoyed the sufficiency, security, and status of a family-supporting job; and more families than ever before were able make a good living on the wages of one full-time breadwinner partnered with a full-time housewife. For Catholic families, some persisting cultural anti-Catholicism notwithstanding, social and economic circumstances improved steadily, and second- and third-generation Euro-American Catholics felt more assimilated into US culture and accepted as American citizens than ever before.

A number of factors accounted for this felicitous moment for the Catholic family wage ideal. These included historical confluences of Catholic economic teaching and programs put in place by the New Deal; housing and educational benefits to (primarily white) working-class families conferred by government supports offered to returning soldiers; a strong economy; an influential labor union movement; and wide availability of family-supporting jobs for white working-class men. That their church's teaching on gender, work, and family seemed to track closely with US middle-class cultural norms further enhanced Euro-American Catholics' sense that full inclusion in the American dream was within their reach.

But like most golden eras, this one was more ambiguous than its public and media images allowed, and more short-lived than its beneficiaries expected. First, even at its ideological peak, in practice, the family-supporting male breadwinner/fulltime female homemaker arrangement remained out of reach for over half of white working- and middle-class families, and it all but eluded families of color.[35] Second, beginning in the 1960s, dramatically shifting economic and cultural conditions exposed flaws in the family living wage agenda and its dual-spheres gender ideology.[36] Alongside the social upheavals of the 1960s, US Catholics experienced seismic changes in their church sparked by the Second Vatican Council. Calls for a new status for women began to echo in both US society and the Catholic Church.[37] Meanwhile, Catholic teaching on work and economy held steady, but an increasingly neoliberal economic outlook coupled with constricting economic conditions for working-class families began to take their toll.

LATER-CENTURY WORKING FAMILIES, GENDER, AND LIVELIHOOD

Over the course of the twentieth century the US labor market underwent significant change as "industries dominated by primary production occupations, such as farmers and foresters[, were replaced by] those dominated by professional, technical, and service workers." In 1900, 38 percent of the labor force worked on farms; by 1999, less than 3 percent did so. Workers in "goods-producing industries, such as mining, manufacturing, and construction, decreased from 31 to 19 percent of the workforce." Meanwhile, "service industries" jumped "from 31 percent of all workers in 1900 to 78 percent in 1999."[38]

This same period saw a steep rise in working-age women's labor force participation, from 19 percent in 1900 to 60 percent in 1999.[39] In the 1870 census, 70 percent of women listed their primary occupation as homemaker; by 2000, 70.5 percent were working for pay, concentrated in the service and professional care industries.[40] Working-class mothers had always been more likely to work outside the home, but by 2012, 71 percent of all women with children under eighteen years of age, including 61 percent of women with children three and younger (compared to under 35 percent in 1970), were in the paid labor force.[41]

Increasingly, too, labor trends among US workers were enmeshed in the larger dynamics of a globalizing economy. Internationally, women's engagement in paid work trended upward in both developed and developing countries. By 2008, there were 1.2 billion women wage earners—40 percent of wage earners—worldwide, and they were especially heavily represented in the service sector (46.3 percent of total workforce) and processing industries.[42] Recent scholarship investigates both ground-level particularities and larger patterns characterizing the "feminization of employment" in globalizing labor markets, focusing on the wide participation of poorer women in international supply chains.[43] Across the globe, poorer women work in suboptimum conditions in garment, electronics, and other light industries of so-called global assembly lines. Poorer women also help compose global care work supply chains, emigrating to richer countries to take domestic caregiving jobs in order to support their own children, whom they must mother long-distance.[44]

Internationally, advocates for gender equality have, with reason, emphasized the benefits of bringing women into the waged workplace. Paid work offers indisputable monetary benefits to women and their families. Earning their own paychecks also affords women greater freedom, power, and voice in both their households and their communities.[45] But valorizing wage earning can obscure other problems related to women's household and civic participation. In her study of women garment workers in Bangladesh, economist Naomi Hossain makes this point: "Paid work may enable some women to negotiate the "structures of constraint" that shape their lives and relationships, but what of the structures of constraint themselves? What has mass, highly visible employment in the economically central RMG [ready-made garment] sector meant for recognition of women's rights and roles within the care [household] economy and as citizens and political actors within the public sphere?"[46]

Moreover, the benefits of paid work depend heavily on the quality of the jobs women procure, and as Ingeborg Wick documents, an enormous and growing percentage of women's work is "being performed in the vulnerable areas of the formal as well as informal sectors."[47] In 2008 the *informal* economy comprised an estimated 60 percent, or 1.8 billion, of the 3 billion wage earners throughout the world. Informal workers often live in poverty, and "the vast majority of vulnerable workers in the informal economy are women."[48] In addition, the rise in women's waged employment has not correspondingly reduced their unpaid labor at home.[49] Both in the United States and globally, the painful conflicts between the demands of waged and household economies run directly through the lives of wage-earning women. Among economically vulnerable women caring for families, these conflicts cut the most deeply and exact the highest costs.[50]

Several broad social dynamics have helped entrench and exacerbate these conflicts and costs. First, rising female workforce participation across the twentieth century corresponded with the consolidating influence on policy of neoclassical economics and a corresponding orthodoxy that treats markets as socially disembedded arenas, coordinated by the impersonal workings of the price system, where rational individuals compete for profit and control over scarce resources by freely exchanging goods and services. Though in practice modern markets involve a great deal of cooperation and reciprocity, they deliver the highest returns to those most adept at competitive, self-interest-maximizing behavior, and to employees whose performances best approximate the geographically and relationally unencumbered, single-minded, and unrelenting focus on the job demanded of the masculinized, "ideal worker."[51]

Second, like men moving into wage labor a century prior, women entering the workforce reallocated time and physical presence to gainful employment, and away from family and household. Also like men before them, women's growing labor force participation was motivated by family needs, by material and self-actualizing aspirations, and by the status and social benefits that having a job entailed. But there was one major difference from nineteenth-century men's experience: twentieth-century female labor force entrants lacked a crucial "backstage support"—another adult present in the home, whose primary job was to ensure that its necessary work was performed.[52]

Third, despite gains in civil rights and public opportunities, cultural assumptions about women's primary responsibility for the work of the household and care economy persisted.[53] Recognizing this work's necessity and significance, most wage-earning women could or would not relinquish their long-held positions as CEOs of the household economy.[54] As increasing numbers of married women and mothers entered the paid workforce, their continued, unpaid domestic labor in what sociologist Arlie Hochschild dubbed the "second shift" frequently undercut their ability to meet workplace standards of undivided attention and dedication to the job.[55] The fact that most wage-earning women are "working caregivers" and thus cannot be "ideal workers" diminishes their opportunities for professional advancement. For poorer working women, it can create crushing double binds when, for example, they must jeopardize the health and safety of their children in order to work for income their families desperately need.[56]

Women's caregiving responsibilities coupled with unpaid work's social and economic devaluation have also contributed to labor force segmentation, labor market dualism, and inequality. Post-1980 US labor markets show a trend toward market dualism, with jobs increasingly clustering at very high or very low ends of the wage scale.[57] Compounding this is labor market segmentation, which relegates disproportionately certain groups (e.g., women, non-whites, new immigrants—and recently, workers in informal and nonstandard

working arrangements) to secondary, lower-paying and lower-status job categories, many of which involve female-identified care work.[58] Driven in part
by these factors, wealth and income disparities both in the United States and
globally have increased steeply over this period, with women overrepresented
in the lowest deciles.[59]

Finally, twentieth-century women's workforce participation crested in the
context of a mass-consumerist culture that calculates sufficiency, success, and
standards of living against ever-receding horizons of growth, improvement,
and novelty. Frequently the primary household spending decision-makers,
women have been frontline participants in these consumerist dynamics. As
wage earners, women are subject to consumerist pressures to assure their
families' continued access to the changing standards and accoutrements of
a respectable and successful lifestyle.[60] When, after 1973, stagnating wages
and the disappearance of family-supporting jobs required households to
put in more hours of paid work just to keep from losing economic ground,
the resulting time squeeze and consumer frustration hit lower-middle- and
working-class families with special force.[61]

Assessing the US situation in 1999, economists Julia Heath and colleagues
argued that household members' increased efforts in paid labor under current
market conditions impedes families' ability to perform unpaid but crucial
"socially reproductive" functions. Moreover, most families operate "in an environment devoid of institutional support for these non-market functions."[62] In
a culture that touts freedom of choice, families' options concerning paid and
unpaid work are constrained by a range of "family, market and social-political
forces." Abetted by slow-to-adapt patriarchal family structures, "the market
system has been slow to provide mechanisms by which family members can
be effective agents in both the labor market and at home."[63] Current market
culture exacerbates families' difficulties by maintaining "an environment in
which family members must labor longer in both spheres" and, even more
seriously, through trends that are "transforming the labor market from a complex institution to a spot market where labor is treated as any other commodity."[64] Finally, social policy, business, and government have failed to create or
foster "institutions that inhibit the commodification of modern labor or that
would further the transformation of gender roles in families."[65]

This state of affairs does not simply place additional stress on individual
families. "Society is stressed as well," for these dynamics "diminish the family's ability to perform the unpaid work that forms the basis of community:
the production [and replenishment] of social capital, and the performance of
caring labor."[66] "Social capital" here refers to families' contributions to "the
institutions, relations, and norms that shape the quantity and quality of a

society's social interactions."[67] Regarded by policy experts as critical to the societal cohesion required for economic prosperity and sustainable development, social capital is "not just the sum of the institutions which underpin a society—it is the glue that holds them together."[68] Underlying these strains on families' socially reproductive and social-capital-building activities are ideological and power dynamics in which gender plays a significant part. Over the past century, efforts to understand these gendered dynamics fueled new forms of social-critical and economic analysis and sparked movements of political protest and social reform.

MODERN FEMINIST MOVEMENTS AND SCHOLARSHIP

Like the ever-practical Monsignor Ryan, twenty-first-century inclusive livelihood advocates will have little use for abstract, theoretical gobbledygook. Here I engage critical social analysis and examine historical developments as resources for building effective strategies for actually advancing work justice. To this end, feminist scholarship can help us address two related questions about the economic status quo: What roles do norms concerning gendered difference play, to whose advantage? And how does gender influence the ways waged and household economies are organized, related, and valued?

The rise of the modern industrialized economy was accompanied by a "modern bourgeois culture," which, as we have seen, "assumed masculinity and femininity to be mutually exclusive and yet complementary opposites."[69] The nineteenth- and early twentieth-century US women's movements variously resisted and embraced this gendered cultural imaginary. This resulted in a dual-track feminist rhetoric on equality and difference, that in subsequent decades continued to shape practices and discourse concerning sexual and gender identities and roles.

Many first-wave feminists framed their arguments for women's political and economic rights in terms of women's presumed familial and feminine competencies. Women's hands-on experiences of housekeeping, childbearing and child-rearing, and family life, it was believed, gave them unique and valuable perspectives on cultural, political, and economic life.[70] These "difference feminists" were convinced that heightening the influence of feminine sensibilities and values in public arenas would foster a world that was more peaceful, well-ordered, and safe for all families.[71] By contrast, other influential movement leaders argued that men's and women's common humanity, not distinctive feminine gifts, warranted women's equal rights, opportunities,

and responsibilities. In campaigns for female economic and political enfranchisement, these two lines of argument intertwined; early twentieth-century
appeals for women's suffrage, for instance, employed both equal rights and
women's difference arguments.[72] And across a range of positions on women's
identity and roles, suffragists agreed that gaining access to the vote would not
only increase women's civic power but enhance their economic well-being.[73]

In the 1960s and 1970s the United States experienced a second wave of
feminism, initially dominated by white, middle-class women whose political
agendas were primarily liberal-progressive- and equal-rights-focused. Other,
more heterogeneous voices, some advocating for women's distinctive perspectives and contributions, soon came to the fore.[74] And by the turn of the
twenty-first century, contestation and dialogue over group identity and differences, enriched and fruitfully complicated by women who do not identify
as white, or middle class, or heterosexual, was fueling a diverse, intersectional,
third wave of feminism. Problematizing racial, class, and sexual dualisms and
binaries, these feminists strove to reflect and be better accountable to the
variety and complexity of women's racial cultural, class, and sexual experiences and histories.[75]

Today, scholars and activists continue to grapple with ways that sex- and
gender-attributed differences help construct and maintain social patterns that
advantage some—primarily white, nonpoor, heterosexual men—and disadvantage women; in particular, women who are not white, affluent, or heterosexual.[76] The social interpretation of sexual difference, they find, "organizes
the world in concrete ways" at once enormously "variable and contingent"
and highly structured or "patterned."[77] A focal concern is to understand, in
particular social and cultural circumstances, the roles such interpreted differences play in the distributions of power, status, voice, and resource access.
And because gender roles and relations remain deeply implicated in modern
labor and economy, undertaking this analysis is important for identifying
obstacles and avenues to inclusive and equitable livelihood.

Women, Gender, and Systemic Injustice

Feminist critical analysis asks how beliefs and practices surrounding sex and
gender operate to encode unjust and oppressive economic and social relations, especially for women and girls. Historically and today, women and
girls are distinctly vulnerable to every one of the fivefold forms of oppression
that Iris Marion Young has identified: economic exploitation, marginalization, cultural imperialism, powerlessness, and violence.[78] Women routinely
suffer exploitation by way of "the systematic and unreciprocated transfer of

material, emotional and sexual energies to men," especially through their labor in the unpaid care economy. Women's overassignment to the unpaid household economy, in turn, systematically deepens their political and economic marginalization. Workplaces and other public spaces where success requires conforming to masculine-keyed cultural codes or work schedules that demand freedom from household responsibilities inscribe regimes of patriarchal, cultural imperialism that force women (and other nonconformers), as Ryan saw, to decipher and play by a set of "men's rules" to which they are systemically impeded from measuring up.[79] In modern labor markets, gender segmentation and inequities in access and opportunity accord most working women and most female-associated jobs relatively less power compared to similarly situated men and "men's jobs." And in both workplaces and households, women are disproportionately vulnerable to violence that ranges from harassment and intimidation to sexual or physical assault. These facets of oppression are at times stark and obvious but equally often subtly woven into attitudes, routines, and structures of daily living. In the mundane activities of everyday life, susceptibilities to oppression simply come with the territory of being female in a male-dominated culture, economy, or society.[80]

Joan Williams, Jean Baker Miller, Nancy Fraser

Three twentieth-century US feminist scholars—law professor Joan Williams, psychologist Jean Baker Miller, and political theorist Nancy Fraser—offer useful perspectives on how gender has implicated women and men in economic arrangements that may serve certain valuable social purposes but do so by marginalizing and exploiting spheres of work, activities, and human qualities coded as feminine or associated with women.

Williams analyzes the late twentieth-century US iteration of the gendered relationship between household and waged economies. This "domesticity system" has two defining characteristics. First, it organizes market work around assumptions about an "ideal worker" who is employed full-time, even overtime, and takes little or no time off for childbearing or childrearing. The ideal worker performs as if he or she has no responsibilities or needs beyond the workplace, a trompe l'oeil made possible by dependence on the background labor of—typically female, unpaid or poorly paid—care workers. This has important economic consequences for the caregivers, who simply cannot fulfill the demands made of ideal workers. Because of this, the system has a second defining characteristic: it "provid[es] for caregiving by [economically and socially] marginalizing the caregivers."[81]

Domesticity ideology, Williams contends, decisively shaped how twentieth-century Americans saw, felt about, and enacted their work and family lives.[82] Its normative force took a particular toll on working-class and poor families whose aspirations for both economic security and gender-role success were routinely thwarted. Nuancing Ryan's perceptions of working-class women's domestic sensibilities, Williams notes that both the negative familial impacts of trading time in unpaid family labor for waged work and the impossibility of simultaneously living up to the standards of both ideal worker and full-time caregiver roles are often experienced more directly and viscerally by non-elite, low-wage-earning women than by affluent working women.[83]

In her study of power and gender ideology, psychologist Jean Baker Miller describes dominant Western cultures' repression or splitting-off of certain human traits, such as vulnerability or dependency, along with the costs this inflicts, both on those who deny those traits and those who become the symbolic carriers of those traits. When such denied or repressed qualities get projected on subordinated social groups, their members are believed to be especially endowed with them and thus to be uniquely capable of and uniquely obligated to do the socially necessary work associated with them. Writing in the 1980s, Miller contended that in the modern West, "the large element of human activity that involves doing for others has been separated off and assigned to women." This false splitting, she claims, feeds beliefs and practices that harm both women and men. Men as a group end up being "seriously deprived of knowing what it is like to fully integrate living for oneself and for others." Service out of love "threatens" men "with being like a woman." And insofar as women and what they do are invisible and under-valued, to take on caring or nurturing traits or labor threatens both women and men with diminishment, even erasure: for "to be like a woman, is almost to be nothing."[84]

These scholars illumine gender's powerful impact on the milieux in which US families pursue their livelihoods. Over the past century and into the present, domesticity's gender scripts have pulled or steered men and women into different roles with distinct emotional and character requirements. Much like the "pink" and "blue" aisles in twentieth-century children's megastores, gender differences and expectations were, and to a large extent are still, communicated as existing in reality, normative, and largely dichotomous. Today, compared to a century or even fifty years ago, these gendered roles are arguably more porous and flexible; in countries like the United States, dramatic shifts in public awareness and wider acceptance of nonheteronormative persons and families have contributed to this. Yet Williams rightly observes that, to different degrees, older gender scripts continue to act like an unseen force field, exerting subtle but steady pulls on women and men, policing attitudes and behaviors, and perhaps most importantly legitimating (while diverting attention from) the consequential differences in perception, value, and power that genderings of work and economy have generated and sustained.

A third feminist thinker, political theorist Nancy Fraser, limns ways that work-family ideologies have reflected and served shifting phases in modern capitalist economies. Scholars, she notes, commonly narrate the history of modern capitalism as "a succession of different regimes of accumulation." Successive eras—nineteenth-century liberal capitalism, twentieth-century state-managed (or social-democratic) capitalism, and late-twentieth- to twenty-first-century neoliberal financialized capitalism—are described and distinguished by their state-economy relationships. Yet in modern political economies, "the relation between production and reproduction . . . is equally consequential. That relation is a defining feature of capitalist society and belongs at the center of our analysis of it."[85] Taking this tack, Fraser traces a path through modern capitalism: "In a nutshell: liberal capitalism *privatized* social reproduction; state-managed capitalism partially *socialized* it; financialized capitalism is increasingly *commodifying* it. In each case, a specific organization of social reproduction went with a distinctive set of gender and family ideals: from the liberal-capitalist vision of 'separate spheres' to the social-democratic model of the 'family wage' to the neoliberal financialized norm of the 'two-earner family.'"[86] During the first phase, "states largely looked on from the sidelines as industrialists dragooned newly proletarianized people, including women and children, into the factories and mines," leaving working people and their families economically disempowered and vulnerable. The resulting "crisis of social reproduction" elicited "public outcry and campaigns for 'protective legislation.'"[87] Over time there arose "a new, state-managed variant of capitalist society" based on "mass production and mass consumption." In this period, social reproduction—what I have been calling the work of the domestic economy—was "partially socialized, through state and corporate provision of 'social welfare.'" During this era, the gendered and aspirational norm of the family living wage predominated.[88]

Later twentieth-century feminists vocally opposed the family wage model's patriarchal constraints. During the 1960s and 1970s "liberal feminists pushed for the removal of barriers to participation in the workforce, embracing the idea of waged employment."[89] The resulting "feminization of the workforce" provided increases in material and personal freedom for many women. Yet, Fraser notes, "this drive was easily co-opted into efforts to make the workplace more insecure and to push pay down." Madeleine

Schwartz summarizes Fraser's claim: "Women's entrance into the work force coincided with the international deregulation of markets and crumbling job protections. Women's labor was used to ramp up this assault on the working class."[90]

This happened on several fronts. For one thing, "women's entrance into the labor force was key to expanding low-wage work. It provided most of the workers in the fastest-growing areas of poorly paid employment." Simultaneously, seeking to increase women's freedom to both work for wages and care for their families (pursuing what Fraser calls a "breadwinner-caregiver parity" ideal), feminists advocated for workplace flexibility and greater availability of job sharing, part-time, and contract-based arrangements. However, "this vision of autonomy, which might have fulfilled a utopian ideal for control over work, did not anticipate that shifts toward flexibility would become a boon to the employer, not the employee, as the decades unfolded." Today, she argues, forms of popular feminism typified in Facebook CEO Sheryl Sandberg's widely read book *Lean In* "encourage women in the boardroom and in low-level jobs to see their work as a facet of their independence."[91]

Two concomitant forces—"the fall in real wages, which makes it impossible to support a family on a single salary (unless one belongs to the 1 percent)" and second-wave feminism's success in making wage earning a hallmark of women's liberation—constituted the "one-two punch" that opened the way for a new cultural norm: the two-earner family.[92] The benefits of the two-earner family ideal disproportionately accrued to middle- and upper-middle-class women with spouses or partners who could afford to outsource household work. But for nearly everyone else, the two-earner model has contributed to "depressed wage levels, decreased job security, declining living standards, a steep rise in the number of hours worked for wages per household, and exacerbation of the double shift."[93] In short, "the fight against the family wage has inadvertently lent moral credence to changes in the work force that weaken working people" and run "directly counter to feminist visions of a just society."[94]

Why is this so? Because, like the family wage ideal that preceded it, the two-earner family norm "is an obfuscation." "It mystifies the steep rise in the number of hours of paid work now required to support a household," which structurally disadvantages families, especially single-parent families or families with vulnerable members needing care at home.[95] Making matters worse, contemporary US households find themselves under the two-earner (or two-plus-earner) regime during a time of cutbacks in social and state welfare provisions. The thinning of social provision has had especially deleterious effects on families' capacities to perform the necessary work of the care economy.

"Between the need for increased working hours and the cutback in public services, the financialized capitalist regime is systematically depleting our capacities for sustaining social bonds." Fraser sees the genesis of this "crisis of care" as less intentional than structural: the latest expression of "a tendency to social-reproductive crisis that is inherent in capitalist society."[96]

To build a framework for a better way forward, Fraser draws on the work of economic historian Karl Polanyi, whose 1944 *The Great Transformation* depicted the disembedding of markets from traditional, locally rooted communities as a central dynamic of modern capitalism. Accompanying this great disembedding, Polanyi argued, were two major, conflicting social projects. The first created strong trends to marketization, increasingly commodifying and reducing to market terms sectors of society such as households and human labor. Against marketization, a movement for "'social protection' attempted to uphold the fabric of society," but often proved no match against massive market pressure.[97]

In Fraser's critical feminist view, Polanyi failed to recognize the social protection project's crucial underside: the "preserv[ation of] inequity and entrenched hierarchies." To remedy this Fraser proposes adding to Polanyi's double movement a third: "emancipation, the force of non-domination." A triple-movement model enables "a more nuanced social analysis in which emancipation serves as a corrective to both marketization and social protection."[98] It also enables Fraser to expose some of the economically consequential blind spots that beset second-wave feminism. By valorizing freedom through waged work, and seeking women's emancipation from patriarchal protections, liberal feminists "did not realize that by rejecting social protection, they might be allying themselves with marketization."[99]

For integrating waged and household work within an inclusive vision of personal and communal life today, Fraser proposes a "universal caregiver" model. Against state-managed capitalism's breadwinner-homemaker model that divides sectors by gender and subordinates the so-called women's sphere, or the financialized universal wage earner model that marketizes or short-changes the household economy, the universal caregiver model foregrounds and prioritizes the work of care as falling to all citizens, men and women alike, and arranges waged work to support that, including by shortening work hours and leaving time not only for caregiving but civic participation and leisure. Without providing detailed programs or strategies, Fraser's work contributes to a twenty-first-century livelihood agenda by posing, then pointing out directions toward answering, this question: "How do we stop giving priority to work over the fullness of social life, individual success over collective justice, and men over women?" Significantly, the universal caregiver scheme suggests that work justice has a great deal to do with regaining control not so much over labor as over time.[100]

Feminist Economics and the Care Economy

To effectively advance economic justice for women, children, and men, Fraser argues that the "dangerous liaisons" between feminism and neoliberalism must be exposed, understood, and addressed. To do this, without abandoning important cultural recognition and identity concerns, twenty-first-century feminists must maintain an unrelenting focus on political economy. Advancing inclusive justice will require connecting "projects of cultural 'recognition' with . . . economic restructuring and parity."[101] Fraser's exhortations point us to another resource for an inclusive livelihood agenda: the contemporary field of feminist economics, whose practitioners typically locate themselves within heterodox or social economics and in the broader tradition of political economy.

Deliberately in contrast to neoclassical or neoliberal economics, feminist social economists take a normative, social-provisioning approach to their field.[102] Deborah Figart, following fellow economist Marilyn Power, identifies five methodological premises that characterize feminist economics: (1) "Ethical judgments are endemic to economic analysis," and (2) in order to make sound economic judgments, "we must have a vision of the purpose of economic life and activity." (3) Adequate economic analysis places not only economic outcomes but "human agency and economic processes" under descriptive and normative scrutiny. (4) Nonmarket processes, in particular, care labor and household labor, are "central, not peripheral, to economic life" and must be incorporated into economic analysis. (5) Finally, for understanding economic realities, examining the diversity of human experiences and situations, especially as shaped by historically specific categories such as gender, class, and race/ethnicity, is more effective than focusing on ostensibly universal laws.[103]

One of feminist economists' most important contributions has been to foreground the significance of unpaid, reproductive, or caring labor, and the vast economic contributions of the so-called care sector to both household and monetized economies. Their work, in tandem with feminist philosophical and social-scientific scholarship, is in the forefront of increasingly influential efforts to reorient economic and policy analysis accordingly.

Relatedly, feminist scholars in a variety of fields have sought to reconnect Western ideals of freedom and personhood to their inescapable roots in humans' embodied vulnerability, our dependence, and our undulating needs for (and responsibilities to provide) care.[104] Challenging Western cultural tendencies to see dependence as a flaw to be shunned, minimized, or dealt with in private, feminist "care ethicists" argue boldly that attention to dependence "must suffuse any successful attempt to address the local and global economic, political and ecological crises in which our century is enmeshed." Economic theory and labor policies need to be reoriented to acknowledge embodied dependence as a central feature of human life and human relationships, and interdependency rather than independence as a central goal in human development.[105]

Catholic feminist ethicist Sandra Sullivan-Dunbar offers a helpful sketch of dependency as integral to our humanity, and thus a fundamental consideration for approaching our institutional life:

> Dependency is a central aspect of human existence. We begin life ensconced within and dependent upon the body of another human person. . . . When we emerge into the world as a separate body, we remain utterly dependent upon other human beings. . . . We are bodily dependent again when we are sick, or when we are disabled, and if we live to old age, we are often dependent on others in the frailty of our final years.[106]

Indeed, even "at those points in our lives when we seem most autonomous, we nevertheless remain deeply dependent on others in countless ways that we often fail to acknowledge."

Yet we moderns, especially in the United States, strongly identify our humanity and our dignity with "human autonomy, not human dependency." Dependency is regarded as repugnant, something to be minimized, or at least hidden from public view. It is not surprising, then, that "much dependent care is sequestered in the sharply privatized family, now seen as separate and qualitatively different from the economic and political sectors of human life." Nor is it surprising that "care is provided with little political and economic support, and assigned to persons with less social power."[107]

This state of affairs is ironic, since the exigencies of embodied human vulnerability and neediness are arguably the economy's originating raison d'être. Work, and the householding—*oikonomia*—that work makes possible, are motivated most basically by our dependencies on food, shelter, clothing, warmth, relationships, and nurture. Against social contract paradigms' tendency to imagine society as roving, autonomous adults who then decide to relate to each another, scholars like Sullivan-Dunbar and Eva Kittay underscore the indispensable, mutually conditioning connections between human dependence and social institutions. Kittay writes:

People do not spring up from the soil like mushrooms. People produce people. People need to be cared for and nurtured throughout their lives by other people, at some times more urgently and more completely than at other times. Who is available to do the labor of care and who gets the care they require is contingent on political and social organization. Similarly, norms surrounding both the giving and receiving of care, while dictated in part by the nature of human need, are also conditioned by cultural and ethical understandings and by economic and political circumstances.[108]

People's universal and incorrigible need for care points to a further fact: the essential roles that care work and the care economy play in making civic, political, and economic life possible at all. Kittay notes that "the very possibility of the independence and individualism prized in justice-based moral theories depends on care labor and on some having the values that enable care to take place."[109] Because they enable, improve, and sustain "productive human capabilities," economist Nancy Folbre affirms, "care services have an important public good component," as "the benefits of providing good care 'spill over' to improve the well-being of the community as a whole."[110]

Yet current US economic culture and market arrangements underacknowledge workers' dependencies and needs and foster standards for successful workplace behavior that ignore exigencies of workers' human embodiment (including our embodied relationships in families and communities). As the story of fictional corporate downsizer Ryan Bingman, told in the 2009 film *Up in the Air*, poignantly illustrates, in the ideal-worker regime, the most desirable and successful employee is the one best able to perform *as if* he or she has no material, temporal, or relational commitments, responsibilities, or needs, or at least none that will interfere with total dedication to the job.[111]

For care providers, anyone with family responsibilities, and ultimately, anyone with a body, this setup is indeed a setup: it supports an economy that distributes financial rewards and penalties in unequal and disingenuous ways. To meet ideal-worker standards means depending heavily on backstage caregivers, whose indispensable work is most often concealed and underrewarded. Wage earners who lack, or who themselves perform, such supportive caregiving labor are subject to the same marginalization. If this analysis is correct, it points to a deep systemic flaw in our presently accepted economic and work practices.

Feminist economists' insistence that caring labor must be registered and rewarded equitably in both paid and unpaid economies coheres with Catholic social thought on family and work; both pose sharp challenges to standard economic theory and much business practice. For both social Catholics and feminists, redesigning work cultures and policies to respect and adequately support the care economy is a nonnegotiable task for building a livelihood regime that serves the well-being of everyone who provides and depends upon caring labor.

Resistance, Persistence, and Gendered Livelihood on the Ground

In later twentieth-century United States, the loudest criticisms of the gendered family living wage, breadwinner/homemaker setup came from second-wave feminists, whose iconic leaders—Betty Friedan, Gloria Steinem, and others—were predominantly white and middle class. These feminists assailed the gender-dichotomized household and public economies for depriving women of equal opportunities to employ their talents, to pursue economic independence, and to contribute to society through satisfying jobs or careers. Especially for married, middle-class women, this feminist era—abetted by economic dynamics and further spurred by the consumerist demands of an ever-rising American standard of living—contributed to women's increased paid workforce participation, accompanied by pushes for legislative, business, and education reforms aimed at overcoming gender disparities and discrimination.[112] For large numbers of US women, the post-1960s years brought new economic opportunities, and women's attachment to the waged workforce became stronger across all demographics.

At the same time, economic changes linked to globalization began to affect the US labor landscape in ways that hit non-elite workers and families with special force. Falling real wages after 1973 combined with deindustrialization and the outsourcing of high-paying factory jobs made it increasingly difficult to maintain middle- or working-class living standards with the wages of only one household member. These changes added to the factors pushing wives and mothers into the paid workforce.

During the 1980s the challenges of working mothers, dual-earner families, and—in part due to dramatic increases in middle-class divorce rates—the struggles of single-parent heads of households, became news. Time use studies showed that as most households devoted more hours per week to wage earning, lost time for unpaid care work was offset partially by substituting commodified care. But wage-earning women, particularly working-class women, continued to devote many extra hours to the second shift.[113]

The tenacity of the gendered family work ideology contributed to three enormously significant social effects. First, the collective transfer of women's (especially mothers') time and energies from domicile to workplace during these decades was not accompanied by a similar transfer of men's time and energy into the household, leaving women in the full-time workforce to be measured by the ideal-worker standard but without the wealth of backstage support that married men have typically received from their wives. Second, women now in the waged workforce continued to perform a disproportionate share of the crucial work of the home. Fewer hours of adult time devoted to family work created a "care gap" that afflicted all families; for nonaffluent families, this care gap was further complicated by scarcities of money and time.[114]

Third, the systemic contradiction involved in moving domestic caregivers into an ideal-worker job market without either reformulating the relations between household and public economy or establishing other avenues for reinvesting energy and attention into the household (such as paid parental or caregiver leave policies, or shorter work hours) went largely unrecognized. Employers and corporations had little incentive to question the ideal-worker setup.[115] Further impeding structural critique was the privatized lens through which resulting burdens on families were viewed: "Work-family" conflicts were problems to be solved by individual families, and most often, individual women. Thus, writes Hochschild, "a giant public issue appears to us as millions of individual problems, each to be solved privately at home." And in trying to work things out, most workers find that "companies have far more power over families than families have over companies. So time demands at work come to seem implacable while those at home feel malleable."[116]

All this gives the lie to the view commonly voiced by century's end—including by many younger women—that, at least in developed Western societies and economies, the fight for gender equity was history, a "done deal." Genuine gains for many women notwithstanding, "domesticity did not die: it simply mutated."[117] Its influence lingers, especially in "a gendered structure of market work," "a gendered sense of how much child [and other family] care can be delegated," and "gendered pressures on men to structure their identities around work."[118] Between 1900 and 2000 the major shift was, rather, from a system "where (middle-class and some working-class) men were breadwinners and (middle-class and some working-class) women were housewives, to one where men are ideal workers and their wives (or ex-wives) are workers marginalized by caregiving."[119] Facing greater obstacles with fewer resources, circumstances were even more complicated and precarious for working-poor families and single-parent households.[120]

Obstacles to full gender equity in contemporary US workplaces and homes were subtler in 2000 than in 1900. Still, in different variations, "the old roles and stereotypes have proven remarkably resilient." Explicitly and implicitly gendered assumptions and practices act as gravitational forces that reinforce the status quo even for those who believe the environment is neutral. Women and men whose lives are full enough already find resisting or reshaping gender's multifactored cultural force field difficult, and often, just impractical. Daily living is already challenging enough, and "gender carries such a load of meanings that individuals change only what irks them most immediately."[121]

The continued pulls toward gendered divisions of waged and household labor also bespeak the crucial social functions they were installed to serve. Faced with the immediate and often urgent needs arising from embodied dependency, people in caregiving roles see and feel acutely the nonoptional significance of these responsibilities and relationships. Perceiving the importance of sustaining care as the wheat amid the weeds of an inequitable system, marginalized caregivers continue cooperating with domesticity, despite its flaws. And because the work caregivers do must continually be done, families or communities can't simply throw out the old system without a better one to take its place. It's as if, Williams says, "we are in a boat trying to rebuild it. But we have to preserve all we can because we are in the middle of the sea."[122] And no one sees more clearly how precious and fragile is the cargo that this leaky boat carries than those assigned to care about care.

AVENUES TOWARD
GENDER-EQUITABLE LIVELIHOOD

Substantive political and economic equality for women, and by extension for all working adults and families, will require reshaping attitudes, culture, policies, and institutions to support a society and economy that give practical priority to embodying equality, to emancipating difference, and to valuing and supporting the care economy.

Embodying Equality, Acknowledging Dependency

Sullivan-Dunbar points out that humans' dependency and needs for care complicate both Christian and standard liberal notions of equality. "Equality is a crucial value" for Christians, who ground it in our shared God-given dignity, and for modern Western political thought, which links it to autonomy and freedom. "Notions of equality have been responsible for many social developments that we hold dear," including advances in freedom and civil rights for women and other marginalized groups. But if dependency is an inextricable part of the human condition, pursuing the norm of equality becomes more complicated. "These two realities, dependency and equality, stand in a paradoxical tension, because when we are dependent on another, there are important ways in which we are not equal to that other." Alongside this is the fact that historically, "many groups of persons have had their dependency exaggerated and enforced precisely in order to exclude them from equality and autonomy."[123]

To address these complexities, Sullivan-Dunbar argues that in order to respect human dignity and cultivate freedom and agency in interpersonal or social relations, dependency must be neither imposed, exaggerated, nor abused. At the same time, "in creating more egalitarian social structures, we must continue to account for that dependency which is intrinsic to human life, or else we will undercut the very equality we seek." An economic ethics and society that supports inclusive access to livelihood, therefore, "must integrate human equality with human dependency."[124]

For an inclusive livelihood agenda, the task of recalibrating household and wage-earning economies to more equitably incorporate the realities of dependency and caregiving is not simply a matter of gender justice. Doing so is essential to ensuring access to sufficiency, security, and status/dignity for all those who give care, and all those who depend upon it. That includes in special ways children, the sick, the frail elderly, and those with special physical or mental needs. For Christians, caring labor is also an exercise of solidarity with and for the vulnerable—a group every one of us belongs to at different stages of our lives. And politically, arranging market and household economies to equitably address dependencies and care needs is prerequisite to enabling citizens to actualize their capabilities for agency, freedom, and productive participation in and for the commonweal.[125]

As previously noted, in most political economies dependency-related care work continues to be undervalued, and to be delegated disproportionately to women and girls. Efforts to promote greater equity for women, and finding more equitable ways to ensure and support care, are therefore closely intertwined endeavors. On this front, one promising development has been recent advocacy by the United Nations and related nongovernmental organizations for policies that advance "substantive equality" for women. Whereas formal equality "refers to the adoption of laws and policies that treat women and men equally, substantive equality is concerned with the results and outcomes of these: 'ensuring that they do not maintain, but rather alleviate, the inherent disadvantage that particular groups experience.'"[126]

Prioritizing substantive equality leads international human rights orga-nizations "to assess laws and policies for their actual effect on women and girls on the ground," and to focus on tackling "structural causes of inequal-ity" and "the obligations of States to address them." Taking this perspective, a 2016 UN report on the progress of women concludes that achieving substan-tive equality for women and girls will require "coordinated public action on three interrelated fronts: redressing women's socio-economic disadvantage; addressing stereotyping, stigma and violence; and strengthening women's agency, voice, and participation."[127] The goal is to create "a virtuous cycle through the generation of decent work and gender-responsive social protec-tion and social services, alongside enabling macroeconomic policies that pri-oritize investment in human beings and the fulfillment of social objectives."[128] A substantive-equality approach will succeed to the extent that it incorpo-rates, as well, attention to the ways that dependency needs are addressed through care work, and to institutionalizing equitable ways to support those who do that work.

Significantly, the report suggests that making labor economies fair for workers and families will require shared and coordinated action that reflects a solidary perspective in culture, in legislation, and in business: "Human rights emphasize the dignity and freedom of the individual, but their realization depends heavily on solidarity and collective action." Putting in place policies that foster substantive gender equality "requires collective financing," and in this regard, historical experience recommends prioritizing policies that make common protections and benefits available to all, not only the poor.[129] Also needed are reforms aimed at depenalizing gender-ascribed and other differ-ences and at fairly valuing and supporting care work in both the waged and household economies.

Emancipating Difference

Given a historical record marked by sex and gender oppression, many contem-porary feminists cast a critical eye on all gender-based divisions of waged and household labor. Still, for many people in many—perhaps most—cultures, gender-differentiated practices and social roles are neither merely oppressive nor undertaken solely under duress. Across many communities and families, a range of gender-differentiated customs, roles, and expressions are valued, enjoyed, and passed down over generations. Perceptions, convictions, tastes, and norms concerning gender are complicated and shaped by cultural, racial/ethnic, religious, aesthetic, and other factors. They are also influenced by people's differing social positions and experiences. To give one, previously

mentioned example, twentieth-century US women's approaches to domestic work and the homemaker role often differed among women of varying
classes, cultures, and racial/ethnic communities.[130] In attempting to overcome the constraints of traditional work and family gender scripts, equality
advocates have at times promoted gender-precluding or gender-dismantling
solutions. But rather than finding such solutions liberating, many women,
particularly those outside the circles of cultural, class, and racial elites, find
such solutions constraining, incredible, or even belittling. In the face of wide
value differences, work-family policy proposals that assume or depend on
strong descriptive or normative consensus about gender and gender roles
have tended to founder or fail.[131]

Today, further questions about gender and gender roles are being raised
by increases in (and heightened public awareness of) the numbers and types
of partnership, household, and family configurations that differ from the
male-female dyad that the dual-spheres gender system has assumed. These
include single-parent families, same-sex couples with or without children,
blended and adoptive families, and intergenerational households. Even as
the heterosexual-couple-headed nuclear family retains a strong normative,
legal, and practical hold in the United States, an increasingly pluralist range of
household and family arrangements seems here to stay.[132]

The upshot is that for the foreseeable future, efforts to erase gender-based
economic discrimination in households and workplaces by insisting that
people either agree on one particular form of gendering or abandon gendering altogether are not likely to succeed. To make headway, just-livelihood
initiatives need to garner broad-based support among groups who may hold
differing views on the salience of gender for family and social life. Is it even
possible to devise social, economic, and political strategies that accommodate the values and sensibilities of both "gender maximizers and gender
minimizers" while also respecting and including persons and families across
the whole nondualist spectrum of sexual and gender diversity we are seeing
emerge today?[133] It seems a very tall order.

To tackle it, legal scholar Christine Littleton suggests that rather than
seeking to eliminate or dictate gender roles or gendered differences, we
work to create laws and policies that equalize the costs associated with
them.[134] Littleton, Joan Williams, and others propose putting aside debates
about how exactly women and men differ to focus on addressing "the ways
in which differences are permitted to justify inequality." Littleton contends
that "eliminating the unequal consequences of differences is more important
than debating whether such differences are 'real,' or even trying to eliminate
them altogether." In the spirit of substantive equality's attention to outcomes,

she focuses attention on the consequences rather than the causes of gender-encoded differences, arguing that "equality can be *applied across* difference." This strategy does not require leveling every possible difference. Rather, it calls for "equalization across only those differences that the culture has encoded as gendered complements." Gender-coded roles or work may differ in content, but they should not be systematically more economically or socially rewarding or costly for those who perform them.[135]

So, in the labor force, jobs requiring culturally feminine-coded skills such as nurturing or emotional attentiveness would be expected to command salaries on a par with jobs requiring culturally masculine-coded skills like assertiveness or initiative. Within households and families, reproductive labor's economic value and rights to support would be accorded on a par with similarly skilled and socially necessary paid work. Benefits and protections for doing socially needed and valuable work would accrue both to those who embrace culturally gendered work scripts and to those who prefer to improvise. This bridging approach to achieving economic equity across contested gender differences—and across differences over gender differences—can be applied flexibly in pluralist or changing cultural contexts, and it offers one promising avenue toward more justly valuing care and household work. To this end, Williams emphasizes, cultivating cross-class and cross-cultural respect and humility, especially for elites, will be indispensable for creating political coalitions powerful enough to advance the cultural and policy changes that a truly gender-equitable economy demands.[136]

In reshaping work-family policies for substantive equality, it will be important to resist assuming that gender differences or gendered roles as they appear under historical or present conditions are fixed or universally normative. Policies and practices that provide access to social benefits, roles, or status exclusively on the basis of sex or gender should, as a rule, be disallowed. Exceptional cases where differential treatment is warranted (for example, affirmative action hiring to redress historical exclusions, or in matters explicitly tied to male or female anatomy such as delivery of medical care) demand careful scrutiny and regular evaluation that gives special attention to the underlying assumptions about difference and to the asymmetries of power such laws or policies may underwrite or perpetuate.

Valuing and Economically Supporting Care

Along with freeing work roles and job valuations from rigid gender scripts, creating a livelihood framework that ensures substantive equality for women and men requires reorienting currently dominant social thought, culture, and policy to more realistically acknowledge and justly support the work of care in both household and public economies. This is the backdrop for the questions posed by Danny Dorling, questions that have become even more resonant and pressing in a post-COVID-19-pandemic economic context:

> Think about how you might end up if you are lucky enough to die old.... In what sort of a society, with what kind of care, do you want to end up? Do you want your relatives to have time to visit you, or would you rather they were working all available hours to perform better economically? Do you want the people who are caring for you ... to be worrying more about how they will pay their own bills on their low income or worrying more about you? Will you end up feeling like a burden to everyone around you? Being cared for in old age in a care home that is being run at the lowest possible cost, being looked after by people who can find no other work—people who leave their jobs as fast as they can get a better one—what kind of an old age will that be?[137]

A 2009 study conducted for the International Labor Organization by economist Rania Antonopoulos reaches five conclusions that summarize current research findings concerning relationships between unpaid and paid work in today's market economy.[138] First, for those responsible for doing it, "unpaid care work shapes the ability, duration and types of paid work that can be undertaken."[139] Second, because unpaid household work does not offer monetary remuneration, it reduces practitioners' exercise of "voice" over household decision-making and harms their ability to accumulate savings and assets.[140]

Third, insofar as it is regarded as woman's "natural" work—performed in the "private" sphere of the family—unpaid care work's economic dimensions and contributions are concealed and undervalued.[141] This point, made already, lifts the curtain on a central fiction legitimating the economic status quo. Masculinized *Homo economicus*, the unencumbered ideal worker, is a mythic creature; his performance on the public economic stage depends continually on the nonmythic material toil and care work of a cadre of supporters in the familial household and beyond. But in most measures of economic productivity, the actual work that makes up this care infrastructure and those who perform it remain invisible, excluded, or underrepresented.[142]

Fourth, waged work involving social reproduction and care tends to be low-prestige and poorly paid, providing slender options for promotion and scant social protection.[143] Partly because society constructs it as something other than "real" work, partly due to its feminized—and therefore, its "less-than"-but-"must-be-done"—valuation, and partly because "a large proportion of care is unpaid care, which in turn depresses the wages for paid care," even professionalized domestic and care-related jobs continue to be relatively cheaply priced by the market.[144] Performed predominantly by women (and often involving dealing with bodies' messiness or dirt) such care-related jobs include childcare, cleaning, housekeeping, food service and cleanup, early and young child education, and hands-on care for the frail, ill, and elderly.

Antonopoulos underscores her fifth conclusion: "Unpaid care work entails a *systemic transfer of hidden subsidies to the rest of the economy* that go unrecognized, imposing a systematic time-tax on women throughout their life cycle." These hidden subsidies connect the so-called private worlds of households and families with the public spheres of marketplace and state in systemically exploitative ways.[145] The time and energy (physical, emotional, and intellectual) expended by those doing household and care work create a hidden transfer from these workers' pockets, clocks, and lives into the pockets, clocks, and lives of those who benefit from their cheap or free labor. The "tax" that such work extracts constitutes a form of structural exploitation occurring across developed and developing economies. It is paid daily by everyone engaged in unpaid or paid care work. "It is important to shed light on these interconnections," she concludes, for only then can we "draw attention to a pervasive [and self-perpetuating] form of inequality" that riddles business-as-usual under modern economic regimes.[146]

Women and men who invest in the work of care perform what domestic labor organizer Ai-jen Poo calls "the work that makes all other work possible."[147] Yet "when care work is paid it is performed by a disregarded workforce—nearly all women, and disproportionately women of color—employed in some of the fastest-growing and lowest-paying jobs in the economy. Their 'priceless' work, of such critical importance to families, rarely offers more than miserable wages and poor benefits."[148]

Whether care work is paid or unpaid, the harshest impacts of the inequities and conflicts created by the current system fall on those least able to absorb them: the poorest and most vulnerable women, children, men, and families. In efforts to press for policies and laws that can change this, some economists are seeking ways to better account for the contributions of women's unpaid and informal work in national measures of productivity.[149] At the same time, a persistent bias toward market participation as the primary avenue to women's empowerment continues to lead many policymakers to stress the value of getting women into paid work but to underplay the importance of an all-in commitment to redesigning economic and workplace cultures and practices to effectively support the interdependent, provisioning functions of both markets and households. In sum, despite its utter necessity,

> Public investment in care in the US is generally indirect, complex, and entirely inadequate in scale. Most of the work is done by family members "for free," and yet the US family policy is uniquely weak among developed nations, with no national paid family and medical leave program to support families with new additions or other intense care demands, meager public nursing support for newborns, very little publicly provided child care, inadequate health care for part-time employees, and only partial support for the elderly and people with disabilities.[150]

Taking a cross-cultural, global view, Sakiko Fukuda-Parr identifies the structural tension involved here: "The current ways in which societies reproduce themselves—an essential aspect of sustainability—perpetuate inequalities that compromise capabilities and human development."[151]

In one important example of this vicious cycle, women factory workers in poorer countries whose labor contributes to complex global supply chains for products sold in the United States suffer grievously from the disregard for care work responsibilities embedded in ideal-worker job arrangements and policies. As epidemiologist Jody Heymann's studies document, work-family tensions that pose challenges for working- and middle-class caregivers in the United States regularly become insurmountable, desperate, and dangerous for vulnerable workers and families in developing countries.[152] In another instance, in many poorer countries, "care drains" are being created as poor women leave their families to work as migrant caregivers in richer countries. In a cascading effect, as migrant caregivers grieve the loss of proximity to care for their own children and families, and "host countries enjoy the benefits of the relatively inexpensive care that migrants provide," the availability of this cheap care labor in turn "reduces the pressure [on host country policymakers] to provide greater public funding for dependent care."[153]

Later-Century Catholic Teaching, Contributions and Limits

Post-1960s papal social teaching has affirmed the importance of and need for women's participation and contributions in all realms of public life.[154] At the same time, Pope John Paul II and his successors emphasized a "feminine genius" that equips women uniquely for motherhood and family. "Womanhood and manhood," John Paul writes, "are complementary not only from the physical and psychological points of view, but also from the ontological. It is only through the duality of the 'masculine' and the 'feminine' that the 'human' finds full realization."[155] On this strong "papal complementarian" view, femininity denotes distinctive capacities, attunements, and sensibilities that have theological, moral, and social import.[156] The "feminine genius" is portrayed as a particular attunement and sensitivity to receiving and welcoming "the other." As women engage in domestic and waged work, particularly in jobs that involve the sustenance and nurturing of vulnerable life, John Paul writes, they "exhibit a kind of *affective, cultural and spiritual motherhood* which has inestimable value for the development of individuals and the future of society."[157]

Fathers' presence in families is important, but the pope maintains that "the woman's physical motherhood constitutes a special 'part' in this shared parenthood, and the most demanding part."[158] Besides the bearing and feeding of the infant, a woman's centrality in the work of home springs from her special capabilities for care: "It is commonly thought that *women* are more capable than men of paying attention *to another person*, and that motherhood develops this predisposition even more." Therefore, even though "the child's upbringing, taken as a whole, should include the contribution of both parents . . . the mother's contribution is decisive in laying the foundation for a new human."[159]

Pope John Paul regularly invoked *Gaudium et spes*'s affirmation that "humanity only finds itself through the sincere gift of self." Notably, papal praise for the "genius of women" refers to women's special ability to enact this universal human and Christian vocation of self-giving in service of the other. "Woman," and hence, every flesh-and-blood woman, is an embodied symbol of the vocation to receive and give love that all humans share.[160] This feminine genius, John Paul insists, is also urgently needed in the work world and the culture at large.[161]

As women in the United States and worldwide streamed into the waged workforce later in the century, official Catholic rhetoric expanded to champion women's full and equitable participation in all social sectors, while continuing to insist that economic participation ought not require that women give up their duties and unique role in the care economy of the household, especially as mothers of young children.[162] Left unaddressed, however, were structural tensions between the de facto interdependence of the waged and household economies and a system that locates economic value and power in the first economy while both relying upon and undervaluing the contributions of the other. To use and depend upon the labor of others while systematically undervaluing and underrewarding that labor constitutes a textbook case of exploitation, morally inimical to both feminist and Catholic justice traditions. In every country today, moreover, women's heavier responsibilities for unpaid household labor limit their abilities to be ideal-worker wage earners, with corresponding economic and social penalties. These tensions are reflected but not confronted in the mix of "equal rights and participation talk" and "gender complementarity talk" one finds in recent Catholic teaching concerning women, family, and work.[163]

Recent popes have continued to describe women simultaneously as men's social equals and as having distinctive "feminine" contributions to make to the world, especially within home and family. The official magisterium, as Sullivan-Dunbar points out, has yet to engage more heterogeneously focused social science literature concerning care work and the care economy.[164] Especially given official Catholicism's tendency to sidestep critical power analysis, popes' emphasis on women's distinctive (and fixed) nature diminishes this tradition's ability to effectively challenge (or even to clearly see) the harm done by problematically gendered ways of organizing and relating public and domestic economies.[165] Gregory Baum's critique of Pope John Paul II's treatment of gender can be applied to recent papal teaching overall: it insufficiently acknowledges "the institutionalized injustices to which women are exposed in society, culture, and church"; it lacks "an analysis of how this inferiorization affects women at the workplace and at home"; and it fails to inquire "what agents in society derive benefits from these oppressive conditions."[166]

Granting these lacunae, Catholic teaching on livelihood also harbors resources for imagining more just and wholesome ways to relate the household and waged economies today. As we have seen, Catholic thought has envisioned economic support for families as normally requiring the work of two adults, and it is illuminating to consider this two-person paradigm apart from its gendered features. One is an adult wage earner whose reasonable amounts of honest labor returns pay and benefits sufficient to support self and family "in frugal comfort," providing "a decent livelihood" for all members. A second adult prioritizes the unpaid labor of caring for home and family, particularly for children and frail or elderly members. Debates over the patriarchy or gendering of this arrangement ought not distract us from key facts: to champion the right to a "family living wage" was, first, to acknowledge that creating a good livelihood for families ordinarily involves the full-time labor of two adults; but, second—and against the "dual earner family norm" that Fraser critiqued—to posit that in a just economy, forty to fifty hours per week of waged work, combined with a similar amount of unpaid household labor, should yield enough to modestly support a household (if necessary, as in the case of single-parent families, with assistance from neighbors, relative, employers, or the state).[167] Taken seriously, this normative paradigm throws into serious question many taken-for-granted features of contemporary US work culture.

By highlighting the subjective or human dimension of work, insisting on the priority of the person who labors over the importance of work processes or products, and, significantly, including household and family work—the care work sector—within the category of societally necessary labor that deserves economic support and recompense, modern papal social teaching offers resources and support for constructing a livelihood agenda that equitably accounts for paid and unpaid labor.[168]

Further, and despite the assumptions of many past popes and believers, the moral purposes of work and economy affirmed by Catholic social teaching—to satisfy people's material and dependency needs, to develop and utilize their talents and potentialities, and to further the common good of family and community—are neither inherently patriarchal nor necessarily gendered. They can be, and historically have been, fulfilled by a range of different economic arrangements and divisions of labor. And, like Ryan's, papal complementarian treatments of men's and women's economic roles have retained a certain elasticity in light of needs to adapt them, in changing circumstances, for the good of families and for the common good.

In the end, a primary historical impetus for both Catholic and secular family wage agendas has been to honor and preserve, not a masculine or feminine genius, but the "genius" of the familial, household, and care economies, and the multifaceted aspects of a good living that these help generate and sustain. In a newly modernizing market economy the gendered breadwinner/ homemaker division of labor was a way to secure both wage-based economic sufficiency and adult presence and labor in the household. But it was not, and has never been, the only possible way.

CONCLUSION

In its varied renderings, the modern family living wage agenda has been suffused with gendered perceptions of economy and men's and women's roles within it. Later twentieth-century economic and cultural developments challenged both this agenda's goal of universal economic livelihood and its gendered strategy for attaining it. Second-wave feminists decried the family wage's masculine bias and pressed for women's full inclusion in economic and public life on equal terms with men. But continued social disregard for the care economy and persisting ideal-worker norms undermined progress toward substantive equality for wage earners who also shouldered domestic caregiving responsibilities. In addition, by century's end, larger economic forces were squeezing non-elite workers' capacities to attain economic sufficiency, security, and status either on the job or for their households.

Throughout this period, Catholic teaching never wavered in its insistence on economy's obligation to deliver livelihood for all members, on the economic primacy of households and families, and on the need for cultures and institutions that ensured supportive relationships between household and waged economies. As we have seen, gender received a more complicated treatment.[169] In the early twenty-first century, feminists, including many Catholic feminists, moved to more self-consciously pluralist and more socially radical analyses and proposals concerning livelihood and household/waged economy relations, focusing more sharply on the obstacles to livelihood facing women and families in nondominant cultural, class, or racial/ethnic contexts. Meanwhile, for both US Catholics and society at large, issues surrounding gender, in relation to livelihood and elsewise, remained contested and far from resolved.

NOTES

1. World Health Organization, "What Do We Mean by 'Sex' and 'Gender'?" (archived), accessed August 18, 2015, https://web.archive.org/web/20150818074425/http://apps .who.int/gender/whatisgender/en/index.html.

2. Some material in this chapter draws from these previously published works: Firer Hinze, "U.S. Catholic Social Thought, Gender, and Economic Livelihood"; Firer Hinze, "Women, Families, and the Legacy of *Laborem Exercens*"; Firer Hinze, *Glass Ceilings, Dirt Floors*.

3. Thomas Tusser's *Five Hundred Pointes of Good Husbandrie*, originally published in 1570, enumerates an extensive list of the housewife's jobs (sections 72–94).

4. But not everyone assumed these roles to be innately fixed, including Adam Smith. See Dimand, Forget, and Nyland, "Gender in Classical Economics," 231–32.

5. See Glickman, *Living Wage*; Kessler-Harris, *Woman's Wage*.

6. Muller, "Capitalism and Inequality," 33.

7. Glenn, *Forced to Care*, 184.

8. Two reasons commonly adduced are: (1) social perceptions of homemaking and socially reproductive labor as "unskilled," and (2) the supply of free labor in the unpaid household economy, which keeps its price on the wage market depressed.

9. Glenn, *Forced to Care*, 35.

10. Folbre, "Unproductive Housewife"; Glenn, *Forced to Care*, 29, 35.

11. Glenn, *Forced to Care*, 36. Moreover, "kin care labor is not considered real work, and the lack of monetary compensation for it means that kin care does not fulfill one's citizenship duty to earn and support oneself" (Glenn, 184). Note the conflation of exercising citizenship with earning money and economic independence.

12. Glenn, 36. Cf. Palmer, *Domesticity and Dirt*; Glenn, "From Servitude to Service Work"; Firer Hinze, "Dirt and Economic Inequality."

13. Glenn, *Forced to Care*, 37–38.

14. See, e.g., Glickman, *Living Wage*; Kessler-Harris, *Woman's Wage*.

15. See, e,g., Institute for Women's Policy Research, "Pay Equity and Discrimination," https:// iwpr.org/issue/employment-education-economic-change/pay-equity-discrimination/. See also, with thanks to Vanessa Williams, Claire Cain Miller, "As Women Take Over a Male-Dominated Field, the Pay Drops," *New York Times*, March 30, 2016, https://www .nytimes.com/2016/03/20/upshot/as-women-take-over-a-male-dominated-field-the -pay-drops.html; Levanon, England, and Allison, "Occupational Feminization and Pay."

16. See, e.g., O'Neill, *Feminism in America*; Andolsen, *"Daughters of Jefferson, Daughters of Bootblacks"*; Cobble, *Other Women's Movement*.

17. Glickman, *Living Wage*, 1–35, 61–77. Cf. Roediger, *Wages of Whiteness*, 43–92. The racial overtones of "free labor" versus "wage slavery" rhetoric were not coincidental.

18. Glickman, *Living Wage*.

19. See, e.g., Sylvia Hewlett, *Lesser Life*, chs. 10, 11; Coontz, *Way We Never Were*.

20. Kessler-Harris, *Woman's Wage*, 10. Cf. Couture, *Blessed Are the Poor?*, introduction.

21. Barnum, "Story of a Fall River Mill Girl," 242.

22. E.g., Hoy, *Chasing Dirt*, ch. 1.

23. See Schor, *Overworked American*; Glazer, *Women's Paid and Unpaid Labor*.

24. Ryan, *Living Wage*, 188–89; Ryan, *Church and Socialism*, 59–60; Ryan, *Distributive Justice*, 282–84; Kessler-Harris, *Woman's Wage*, 9–11.

25. John A. Ryan, "Address to Educated Catholic Women," John A. Ryan Archives, Mullen Library, Catholic University of America, Washington, DC.

26. Grace H. Sherwood, "The Church and the Dignity of Woman," *Christian Marriage and the Family*, Washington, DC: National Catholic Welfare Council, Family Life Section, Social Action Department, 1932, John A. Ryan Archives, Mullen Library, Catholic University of America. Washington, DC. See also Ryan, baccalaureate sermon, Trinity College, June 3, 1923, p. 8, box 37, file: "Commencement Addresses," John A. Ryan Archives, Mullen Library, Catholic University of America, Washington, DC.

27. John A. Ryan, "Fallacies of the Feminist Movement," John A. Ryan Archives, Mullen Library, Catholic University of America. Washington, DC; John A. Ryan, *Declining Liberty*, 101–14. A contrasting, contemporaneous analysis is Rathbone, *Disinherited Family*.

28. Most wage-earning women contributed to other family members' support; "black women were eight times as likely to earn wages as white women." Kessler-Harris, *Woman's Wage*, 10–11. See also Penn, "Survival Strategies among African-American Women Workers."

29. Ryan regarded much of first-wave, liberal feminism as motivated by "selfishness," "the desire for self-indulgence," and (in the extreme) a socially destructive "anarchic individualism like that of the thief, the adulterer, and the wife deserter." Since the welfare of society requires "that woman's chief functions shall be in the home . . . this is the way of her own true development also." Ryan, "Fallacies of the Feminist Movement," 4; cf. Ryan, *Declining Liberty*, 113–14.

30. Ryan, "Fallacies of the Feminist Movement," penned-in addition. Also, Ryan, *Church and Socialism*, 236–45; Tentler, *Wage-Earning Women*.

31. Middle-class feminists, Ryan believed, ignored the fact that "women may be equals of men as persons and yet inferior to them in economic power and in physical capacity." Thus, "instead of demanding identical laws for unequal economic groups, [Leo XIII]

declared that the working classes and the poor stood in need of special laws for their weaker economic condition. The same principle applies in the economic and social relations of women." *Declining Liberty*, 113.

32. John Paul II, *Laborem exercens*, §19; John Paul II, *Evangelium vitae*, §99. Cf. Caldecott, "Sincere Gift."

33. Ryan, quoting Archbishop John Spalding (1840–1916) in a baccalaureate sermon, June 3, 1923, 2–3; see also Ryan, "Fallacies of the Feminist Movement," 4.

34. Leo XIII, *Rerum novarum*, §33; Pius XI, *Quadragesimo anno*, §71.

35. See Coontz, *Way We Never Were*; Ta-Nehisi Coates, "The Case for Reparations," *Atlantic*, June 2014, https://www.theatlantic.com/magazine/archive/2014/06/the-case-for -reparations/361631/.

36. Feminists were key critics. Mainard, "Politics of Housework," e.g., recounts difficult negotiations with her otherwise egalitarian husband over redistributing work at home in 1969.

37. John XXIII, *Pacem in terris*, §§41, 19; *Gaudium et spes*, 1965, §§9, 52, 60, 67; Paul VI, *Octogesima adveniens*, §13.

38. Donald M. Fisk, "American Labor in the 20th Century," US Bureau of Labor Statistics, January 2003. https://www.bls.gov/opub/mlr/cwc/american-labor-in-the-20th -century.pdf.

39. Fisk. "In 1900, only 1 percent of the lawyers and 6 percent of the nation's physicians were women. In 1999, the figures were 29 percent for lawyers and 24 percent for physicians."

40. Folbre and Nelson, "For Love or Money," 126–27. Cf. Hernandez, "Changes in the Demographics of Families," 23–26.

41. US Department of Labor Women's Bureau, "Facts over Time: Women in the Labor Force," 2016, https://www.dol.gov/wb/stats/NEWSTATS/facts/women_lf.htm. Cf. Goldin, "Quiet Revolution."

42. Wick, *Women Working in the Shadows*, 14, citing United Nations Development Fund for Women, *Who Answers to Women*, 54.

43. Wick, *Women Working in the Shadows*, 14.

44. See Kittay, "Global Heart Transplant"; Parreñas, *Servants of Globalization*; Osborne, "Migrant Domestic Careworkers."

45. Cf. Harkness, "Women's Employment and Household Income Inequality," 207.

46. Hossain, "Exports, Equity, and Empowerment,"

47. Wick, *Women Working in the Shadows*, 14, 11.

48. Wick, 15.

49. Wick, 14, 11. Cf. Philipps, "Silent Partners."

50. Heymann and Barrera, *Addressing Poverty in a Globalized Economy*. See the tragic story of Irene Echeverria Perez. Heymann and Barrera, 5.

51. Williams, *Unbending Gender*, 1–4, inter alia.

52. Hochschild, *Second Shift*, 250–68.

53. Feminist scholars employ "care economy" to speak of the wide sector of human activity wherein "care work," or the work of "social reproduction" (terms used in variously overlapping ways) is performed. See, e.g., Alexander and Baden, *Glossary on Macroeconomics from a Gender Perspective*; Dresser, King, and Reddy, *Oregon's Care Economy*; International Labour Office, *ABC of Women Workers' Rights and Gender Equality*.

54. Glenn, *Forced to Care*, 10, 11. Cf. Damaske, *For the Family*; and Williams, *Unbending Gender*, 37–39, on gender as "force field."

55. Cf. Hochschild, *Second Shift*; Williams, *Unbending Gender*.

56. For instance, the story of Honduran single mother Gabriela Saavedra, recounted in Heymann, *Forgotten Families*, 3–6.

57. Autor, Katz, and Kearney, " Polarization of the U.S. Labor Market;" Goldin and Katz, "Long-Run Changes in the Wage Structure."

58. Reid and Rubin, "Integrating Economic Dualism and Labor Market Segmentation." Kenneth Hudson argues that the temporary or gig economy is creating a new form of labor market segmentation; see Hudson, "New Labor Market Segmentation."

59. See Ortiz and Cummins, "Global Inequality"; Folbre, Gornick, Connolly, and Munzi, "Women's Unemployment, Unpaid Work, and Economic Inequality."

60. See Schor, *Overspent American*, 1–21; Cloutier, *Vice of Luxury*: chs. 6, 7.

61. See, e.g., Daphne Spain and Suzanne M. Bianchi, "Women in the Labor Market," *Focus: Newsletter of the University of Wisconsin–Madison Institute for Research on Poverty* 20, no. 1 (1998–99): 1–46, https://www.irp.wisc.edu/publications/focus/pdfs/foc201.

62. Heath, Ciscel, and Sharp, "Work of Families," 502.

63. Heath, Ciscel, and Sharp, 502.

64. Heath, Ciscel, and Sharp, 504, italics added. Cf. 518.

65. Heath, Ciscel, and Sharp, 503.

66. Heath, Ciscel, and Sharp, 503.

67. Mark Smith, "Social Capital," *The Encyclopedia of Pedagogy and Informal Education*, last updated March 28, 2013, https://infed.org/mobi/social-capital/.

68. Heath, Ciscel, and Sharp, "Work of Families," 503. Cf. Nelson, *Economics for Humans*, 77.

69. Young, *Justice and the Politics of Difference*, 139, 136.

70. An exemplar is Frances Willard, the Wisconsin Evangelical Lutheran who founded and led the Women's Christian Temperance Union. Couture, *Blessed Are the Poor*, ch. 6.

71. Nineteenth-century women's movement leaders like Elizabeth Cady Stanton, Susan B. Anthony, and Frances Willard held sometimes conflicting views on gender differences and roles. See Couture, *Blessed Are the Poor*, 141–45.

72. In "Why Women Should Vote," published in 1905, Alice Stone Blackwell cites both equal rights and women's different (and more noble) moral sensibilities and concerns in support of women's suffrage.

73. Blackwell, "Why Women Should Vote," also offers economically related reasons for women's suffrage, e.g., *"Because disenfranchisement helps to keep wages down.... Because it would help those women who need help the most ... working women especially ... In the States where women vote, there is far better enforcement of the laws which protect working girls."*

74. For one overview, see Krøløkke and Sørensen, *Gender Communication Theories and Analyses*, ch. 1, "Three Waves of Feminism."

75. Here Young emphasizes "the importance of difference within and between subjects," distinguishing between the "oppressive meaning of group difference ... as absolute otherness, mutual exclusion, categorical opposition" and difference's positive meaning as "specificity, variation, heterogeneity"—which difference and liberationist (Latina, etc.) feminists have sought to forward in distinct ways. Young, "Ideal of Community," 305; Young, *Justice and the Politics of Difference*, 169–71.

76. Freeden, *Ideologies and Political Theory*, 491.

77. Bair, "On Difference and Capital," 203, 205. Especially since 1990, a burgeoning field of LGBTQ analysis, discourse, and activism has further expanded this work.

78. Still, women's indispensable role in preserving the human species prevents any society, however misogynistic, from completely excluding them. Under patriarchy, women are simultaneously necessary and intimate insiders and perennially marginalized outsiders, in relation to dominant races, classes, and male-dominated institutions.

79. Young, *Justice and the Politics of Difference*, 64; Ryan, "Fallacies of the Feminist Movement."

80. See also Lebacqz, "Love Your Enemy." In 2017 and 2018, #MeToo, a movement exposing and seeking to redress sexual harassment endemic in a range of workplace cultures, shed light on one of these oppressive patterns.

81. Williams, *Unbending Gender*, 1, 241.

82. E.g., Albrecht, *Hitting Home*, 71, 93. Cf. Tom W. Smith's data-rich "Emerging 21st Century Family."

83. See, e.g., Ryan, *Declining Liberty*, 113–14; cf. Clark-Lewis, *Living In, Living Out*; Hochschild, *Second Shift*, ch. 5; Couture, *Blessed Are the Poor*, ch. 1.

84. Miller, *Toward A New Psychology of Women*, 70–77.

85. Nancy Fraser, "Capitalism's Crisis of Care," interview by Sarah Leonard, *Dissent*, Fall 2016, https://www.dissentmagazine.org/article/nancy-fraser-interview-capitalism-crisis-of-care.

86. Fraser, "Capitalism's Crisis of Care."

87. Fraser, "Capitalism's Crisis of Care."

88. Fraser enumerates the limits and biases of the family living wage norm mentioned above in "Capitalism's Crisis of Care."

89. Madeleine Schwartz, "Kicking Back, Not Leaning In," review of *Fortunes of Feminism*, by Nancy Fraser, *Dissent*, Summer 2013, 3.

90. Schwartz, 3.

91. Schwartz, 4. Cf. Fraser, *Fortunes of Feminism*, ch. 4.

92. Fraser, "Capitalism's Crisis of Care."

93. Schwartz, "Kicking Back," 4.

94. Schwartz, 4.

95. Fraser, "Capitalism's Crisis of Care."

96. Fraser.

97. Fraser, 6. Cf. Fraser, *Fortunes of Feminism*, ch. 10.

98. Schwartz, "Kicking Back," 6; Fraser, *Fortunes of Feminism*, ch. 10.

99. Schwartz, "Kicking Back," 7.

100. Schwartz, 7. Cf. Nancy Folbre's earlier articulation of this goal in Folbre, *Who Pays for the Kids*, 103.

101. Schwartz, "Kicking Back," 2.

102. Figart, "Social Responsibility for Living Standards," 394–95. Social provisioning and political economy paradigms also predominate in Catholic social and economic thought. See, e.g., Michael Sean Winters, "Francis's Critique of Libertarianism Echoes the Gospel," *Distinctly Catholic* (blog), *National Catholic Reporter*, May 3, 2017, https://www.ncronline.org/blogs/distinctly-catholic/francis-critique-libertarianism-echoes-gospels.

103. Figart, "Social Responsibility for Living Standards," 394–95; citing Power, "Social Provisioning," 6; cf. 3–4. Figart notes that for many feminist economists, Amartya Sen's focus on "human well-being—defined as the capacity to pursue functionings that one has reason to value—provides such a vision."

104. Prominent scholars include Alison Jaggar, Virginia Held, Sara Ruddick, and Eva Feder Kittay.

105. Kittay, Jennings, and Wasunna, "Dependency, Difference and the Global Ethic of Long-term Care," 454n22.

106. Sullivan-Dunbar, *Human Dependency and Christian Ethics*, 1–2.

107. Sullivan-Dunbar, 2.

108. Kittay, Jennings, and Wasunna, "Dependency, Difference and the Global Ethic of Longterm Care," 443.

109. Kittay, Jennings, and Wasunna, 453, citing Kittay and Feder, *Subject of Care*; Cf. MacIntyre, *Dependent Rational Animals*.

110. Folbre, "Measuring Care," 189.

111. Williams, *Unbending Gender*, 1, 241.

112. Betty Friedan's *The Feminist Mystique*, published in 1963, was a catalyst for second-wave, "liberal" feminism. Yet, contra the "well-educated, trapped, middle-class suburban housewife" persona presented in her famous book, Friedan brought to her writing a long history of progressive and radical political involvement. See Boucher, "Betty Friedan and the Radical Past of Liberal Feminism."

113. Hochschild, *Second Shift*, introduction.

114. Hewlett, *When the Bough Breaks*, describes a "time famine" afflicting middle-class families, compounded for working-class and poor families by a "resource famine." Cf. Burggraf, *Feminine Economy and Economic Man*, 19.

115. See, e.g., Wallace, *Selling Ourselves Short*, 170.

116. Hochschild, *Time Bind*, 191–92, quoted in Wallace, *Selling Ourselves Short*, 167. Cf. Williams, *Unbending Gender*, ch.1; Stone, *Opting Out*; Goldin, "Quiet Revolution."

117. Williams, *Unbending Gender*, 124. Cf. Siegel, "Home as Work," 1073.

118. Williams, *Unbending Gender*, 124.

119. Williams, 124.

120. See, e.g., Albrecht, *Hitting Home*; Rubin, *Families on the Fault Line*; Newman, *No Shame in My Game*.

121. Williams, *Unbending Gender*, 254.

122. Williams, 254.

123. Sullivan-Dunbar, *Human Dependency*, 2.

124. Sullivan-Dunbar, 2, also chs. 7, 8.

125. On participation as essential to social and economic justice, see, e.g., World Synod of Bishops, *Justicia in mundo*, §18. See also Paul VI, *Octogesima adveniens*, §§22, 24, 41; US Catholic Bishops, *Economic Justice for All*, §§77, 297; Pontifical Commission for Justice and Peace, *Compendium*, 189–91.

126. United Nations, *Progress of the World's Women, 2015–2016*, 4, citing United Nations Committee on Economic, Social, and Cultural Rights, Article 3, Comment.

127. *Progress of the World's Women, 2015–2016*, 4.

128. *Progress of the World's Women, 2015–2016*, 4.

129. The report also considers means-tested versus universal-provisioning policies for addressing care needs, noting that "universal systems can actually expand financing options by increasing the willingness of middle and higher income groups to pay taxes for well-functioning education, health, or pension systems that they also use." *Progress of the World's Women, 2015–2016*, 7n16.

130. See, e.g., Clark-Lewis, *Living In, Living Out*.

131. Williams makes this case in *Unbending Gender*, esp. chs. 5, 7, 8.

132. Williams, 186–98; also Schneebaum, "Economics of Same-Sex Couples;" Weisshaar, "Earnings Equality"; Kurdek, "Allocation of Household Labor"; Maldonado, "Doing Better for Single-Parent Families."

133. For "maximizers" and "minimizers," see Callahan, "Homosexuality, Moral Theology, and Scientific Evidence," 210.

134. Littleton, "Reconstructing Sexual Equality."

135. Littleton, 32. "There must be choices beyond those of ignoring difference or accepting inequality."

136. See Williams, *Unbending Gender*; also, Williams, *Reshaping the Work-Family Debate*; Williams, *White Working Class*.

137. Dorling, *Better Politics*, 27, 37.

138. Antonopoulos, "Unpaid Care Work–Paid Work Connection."

139. Antonopoulos, iii, 1, 11–19. See also Antonopoulos, Masterson, and Zacharias, *Interlocking of Time and Income Deficits*.

140. Antonopoulos, "Unpaid Care Work–Paid Work Connection," 1.

141. Antonopoulos, "Unpaid Care Work–Paid Work Connection," 1–2, 35, 54.

142. E.g., Folbre, "Measuring Care," 183–98.

143. Antonopoulos, "Unpaid Care Work–Paid Work Connection," 1, 11–19.

144. Sullivan-Dunbar, "Care Economy as Alternative Economy."

145. Antonopoulos, "Unpaid Care Work–Paid Work Connection," 2, 6–10.

146. Antonopoulos, 2.

147. Leigh Dodson, "The Work That Makes All Other Work Possible': A Dialogue with Ai-jen Poo and Premilla Nadasen," University of California Humanities Research Institute, May 13, 2013, https://uchri.org/news/leigh-dodson-the-work-that-makes-all-other-work-possible/.

148. Dresser, King, and Reddy, *Oregon's Care Economy*, 7.

149. Folbre, "Measuring Care," 187, provides a detailed grid for "distinguishing among forms of care work according to their relationship to the market, characteristics of the labor process, and types of beneficiaries."

150. Dresser, King, and Reddy, *Oregon's Care Economy*, 7.

151. Fukuda-Parr, Heintz, and Seguino, "Critical Perspectives on Financial and Economic Crises," 25.

152. See, e.g., Heymann, *Forgotten Families*.

153. Folbre, "Measuring Care," 190. Cf. Kittay, "Global Heart Transplant"; Parreñas, *Servants of Globalization*. Such examples underscore the importance of recent work by Daniel K. Finn and others on the ethics and obligations arising from affluent consumers' participation in global supply chains whose "links" often involve mistreatment or exploitation of vulnerable workers. See Finn, *Consumer Ethics in a Global Economy*.

154. On women's social equality: John XXIII, *Pacem in terris*, §41; Vatican II, *Gaudium et spes*, §60; John Paul II, *Letter to Women*, §§2–6, 8. On women's distinctive traits and family role: Paul VI, *Octogesima adveniens*, §13; John Paul II, *Laborem exercens*, §19; John Paul II, *Mulieris dignitatem*, §§18, 29, 31; Joseph Ratzinger, "Letter to the Bishops of the Catholic Church on the Collaboration of Men and Women in Church and World," July 31, 2004.

155. John Paul II, *Letter to Women*, §7.

156. John Paul II, §11, see also §12.

157. John Paul II, §9. See also John Paul II, *Mulieris dignitatem*, §29.

158. "Parenthood—even though it belongs to both—is realized much more fully in the woman, especially in the prenatal period." John Paul II, *Letter to Women*, §18.

159. John Paul II, *Mulieris dignitatem*, §§18, 19, emphasis in original. Cf. Ratzinger, "Letter to the Bishops," §13.

160. *Gaudium et spes*, §24. Cf. John Paul II, *Letter to Women*, §9; *Mulieris dignitatem*, §§ 10, 11.

161. See John Paul II, *Letter to Women*, §2; John Paul II, *Evangelium vitae*, §99.

162. See Pontifical Commission for Justice and Peace, *Compendium*, §295; John Paul II, *Laborem exercens*, §19. On the global rise in female paid labor, 1960–2000, see, e.g., Heymann, Fischer, and Engleman, "Labor Conditions," 75–78. See also "Labor Force, Female (% of Total Labor Force), 1990–2016," World Bank, https://data.worldbank.org /indicator/SL.TLF.TOTL.FE.ZS.

163. Recent popes' persistent focus on male/female differences as binary and fixed problematically limits dialogue with important contemporary discourses questioning these categories from philosophical, scientific, and experiential perspectives. See, e.g., Firer Hinze and Hornbeck, *More than a Monologue*; Jung and Coray, *Sexual Diversity and Catholicism*.

164. Recent Catholic teaching and leadership have been anemic in their support for economic policies that practically account for and justly remunerate work done by women, in particular, care work, paid or unpaid. Sullivan-Dunbar, *Human Dependency*, ch. 1, correctly attributes this to the persistent gendering of this work. Underattention to ideology and to power analysis are also contributing factors.

165. More problematically, binary and fixed understandings of sexuality and gender risk occluding Catholicism's longstanding commitment to attending to and learning from "the signs of the times" by carefully examining the data of philosophy, the sciences, and the experiences of the faithful and others of good will. Cf. Firer Hinze and Hornbeck, *More than a Monologue*; also Pope, "Scientific and Natural Law Assessments of Homosexuality"; and Pope, "Magisterium's Arguments against 'Same Sex Marriage.'"

166. Baum, *Priority of Labor*, 78, 79.

167. A recent official (and notably gender-neutral) formulation of the living wage norm is Pontifical Commission for Justice and Peace, *Compendium*, §250. Cf. John Paul II, *Laborem exercens*, §19; Pontifical Council on the Family, "Charter of the Rights of the Family," Vatican City, 1983, §10, http://www.vatican.va/roman_curia/pontifical_councils/family /documents/rc_pc_family_doc_19831022_family-rights_en.html.

168. Schiltz, "Motherhood and the Mission," 426–27, referring to *Laborem exercens*, §19. Dorr, *Option for the Poor and for the Earth*, 319–22.

169. Left aside in my analysis is much-needed further treatment of the significant connections between Catholic social thought concerning gender and the ways that gender has been interpreted to position women in both Catholic sexual teaching and Catholic ecclesiology.

CHAPTER 4

Livelihood Racialized

Across US history, race and ethnicity, like gender, have profoundly shaped the ways work and economy have been understood, organized, conducted, and rewarded. Today, racialized dynamics and divisions, intertwined in complicated ways with gender and class, thread through the fabric of US politics, economy, and work. Attending to race illuminates the importance of the cultural and institutional contexts in which Americans' quest for a decent living takes place. In addition to their own industriousness, US workers and families have always also required specific social and institutional supports in order to succeed: a government that ensures civic and property rights, laws that provide advantageous economic policies and equal protection, and a culture that accords individuals and groups respect and fair opportunities for education, employment, wages, and advancement. Across US history, however, every one of those supports has been riddled with racialized inequities and exclusions, barring portions of the population, regardless of their efforts, from full access to a good living.

At the root of this troubling fact lie modern Western notions of race and racial hierarchy. Over its history, this nation's population has comprised peoples of many ethnic and cultural identities. Groups have celebrated and taken pride in their particular shared histories, cultures, and traditions while simultaneously identifying as patriotic Americans. From the late nineteenth century through the twentieth, ethnic pride, and an immigrant narrative about a people going from being struggling outsiders to being fully enfranchised American citizens, frequently went hand-in-hand.

Polish American immigrant Joseph Podles's story offers a typical example of this combination. Interviewed in 1979, Podles, whose family arrived in the "new country" by freight ship in 1906, described his hardscrabble life as one of fourteen children in a family where all members worked for low wages at arduous seasonal jobs. He recalled summers, at ages six and seven, laboring alongside his parents and siblings harvesting strawberries, peas, and corn; steaming and peeling tomatoes and "snipping beans" in Baltimore canneries; and in winters, traveling to Mississippi where the family steamed and shucked oysters. Podles took pride in the many members of his generation who grew up to attain comfortable livings. He also underlined their patriotism: "I think some of the best American citizens you have today are Polish-Americans. . . . There's no more patriotic people in this whole country than the Poles are."[1] Podles' Polish American pride was genuine, justified, and positively cast. But for Poles, like many European American groups who began as outsiders, the journey to being fully American also included "progress" toward classification as, collectively, "white"—a racial identity that barely existed prior to the European colonization of the Americas but has profoundly shaped global history, including economic history, since the sixteenth century.

In the United States, freedom- and rights-based political discourse has long coexisted with discrimination and stratification calibrated according to differences attached to race. Beginning in colonial times, racialized group distinctions were deployed to map and maintain social divisions and differential access to power over labor, land, resources, and money. Bolstered in the nineteenth and early twentieth centuries by pseudoscientific "race studies," beliefs about purportedly innate racial differences helped to legitimate the power and privilege of some and to justify the subordination, exploitation, and exclusion of others.[2] Native American and African peoples were portrayed as "wild," "savage," "pagan" races over which members of a civilized, disciplined, and virtuous Anglo-Saxon race were destined by nature and providence to rule.

Over time, a potent social psychology that closely identified full US citizenship with being "white" became culturally and institutionally entrenched, securely marginalizing the black, brown, yellow, and red peoples in the "North American box of colors."[3] These racialized dynamics have permeated every phase of American history and influenced every sector of American society, including the spheres of work and economy. Today as in the past, group othering and its divisive and oppressive outcomes pose enormous obstacles to the economic solidarity on which a radically inclusive livelihood agenda depends. To advance this agenda in our US context, therefore, we must take the time to examine the quintessential modern form of oppressive othering that is white racism and how it has shaped the lives and livelihoods of everyone in the United States, but especially peoples deemed to be on the other side of the "color" divide.

DEFINING RACE AND RACISM

Native American legal scholar Bethany Berger defines *race* as "the complex body of social meanings that attach to group differences of ancestry and appearance."[4] Though often linked to biology and bodily characteristics, in fact race is not naturally occurring but socially constructed and continually evolving amid shifting social, political, legal, and economic conditions.[5] The history of US census classifications indicates how racial categorization of different ethnic groups has changed over time, and suggests, too, the degree to which racial identity involves subjective factors like self-identification or the opinions of neighbors, rather than objective measures. Nineteenth- and early twentieth-century US legal history also demonstrates that whether a person or group was "white" was not a given but frequently subject to courtroom wrangling and litigation.

This mention of legal history brings us to another highly salient fact about race: it may not exist, scientifically speaking, but as a social fact it has real, profound, effects. In the United States, assignations of race have for hundreds of years shaped life outcomes and people's everyday experiences, including how they are treated by the government (including police and the courts), where they live and go to school, and the economic opportunities and outcomes they are able to attain. But if "race" is so hard to pin down, how did it develop as such a powerful factor in the United States, and why does it remain so today? A full answer is well beyond what can be discussed here, but many recent historians argue that the modern hierarchical system of racial classification developed largely to benefit Europeans in an age of colonization.[6] Because this racial hierarchy continues to benefit "white" descendants, it has been strongly resistant to change. On this view, the notion of "race" itself is an invention of racists, in the service of racism.

The term *racism* is used to describe both subjective feelings of prejudice about those lower on the hierarchy and the objective effects of an economic and social system built around that hierarchy. On the social-psychological side, Anthony Giddens's parsing of everyday consciousness and agency is helpful for distinguishing among (1) consciously racist attitudes and actions (expressions of "discursive consciousness"); (2) habituated, subtle, racist reactions and behaviors that operate at the edges of actors' direct awareness (operating as "practical consciousness"); and (3) only liminally conscious, affectively driven dynamics of "ontological security/safety vs. insecurity/ fear" that fuel racism's workings at the visceral psychic level of what Giddens calls the "basic security system."[7] This last suggests that racism capitalizes and feeds on our human propensities to fear difference and otherness and to draw self-protecting lines between "us" and "them" that can easily become abusive of outsiders.[8] Focusing on the connections between social psychology, othering, and domination, philosopher Albert Memmi defines racism broadly, as the "generalized, and final assigning of values to real or imaginary differences, to the accuser's benefit and at his victim's expense, in order to justify the former's own privileges or aggression."[9] In racist ideology, the valued or disvalued difference is regarded as applicable to every member of the racialized group, and unchangeable. For Memmi, racist ideology functions primarily to legitimate racialized hierarchies, and the privileged race's power over, hostility toward, or mistreatment of subjugated groups.[10]

Encounters with difference do not inevitably elicit racism but can become the occasion for it. Memmi traces racism's roots to a species-adaptive tendency to react with ambivalence to anyone and anything perceived as unfamiliar or foreign.[11] When encountering novelty or difference, we human animals react with curiosity and attraction; at the same time, we hesitate and are wary.[12] Memmi sees in this latter reaction the seed of "heterophobia"— habituated fear of the other or of the different. And racists, he observes, are always people who are afraid.[13] Whether motivated by self-protection or self-aggrandizement, racism channels our natural ambivalence in the face of difference in aggressive ways, for dominative ends.[14] Memmi's analysis highlights "the organic connection between racism and oppression," including, importantly, economic oppression.[15]

Writing contemporaneously with John A. Ryan in 1919, English author Rudyard Kipling poetically comments on the unconscious and ubiquitous nature of humans' othering practices. His words also point to the fact that race and racism in their modern, colonizing forms did not arise merely as an unfortunate side effect of our evolutionary tendency to identify others as similar to or different from ourselves.

> "Father, Mother, and Me
> Sister and Auntie say
> All the people like us are We
> And everyone else is They.
> And They live over the sea,
> While We live over the way.
> But would you believe it?—They look upon We
> As only a sort of They! . . .
> All good people agree,
> And all good people say,

All nice people, like Us, are We
And everyone else is They:
But if you cross over the sea,
Instead of over the way,
You may end by (think of it!) looking on We
As only a sort of They!

The poem slyly evokes the universal tendency to assume the normalcy and superiority of our own "we" in the face of unfamiliar and foreign "theys." Kipling also sticks a pin in his British readers' presumed monopoly on the civilized, valuable, and beautiful. Yet by implying equivalence and reciprocity between the "we's" the poem invokes, Kipling also elides the influence of—and sidesteps accountability for—the vast disparities of power between colonizer and colonized, inequalities that rendered the poetic narrator's disingenuous attitudes anything but benign for those subjected to them. Within the imperial matrix, widely deployed racist beliefs and practices othered and subordinated British "subjects" and worked to occlude, expropriate, or destroy the traditions and cultures of colonized peoples while advancing colonizers' political and economic power.[16]

Millions of people over several centuries have wielded whiteness to shore up their groups' social and economic power, and to disempower and exploit outgroups. From slavery through colonialism to the present day, identifying other peoples as inferiorly raced has been one way to justify why their members should, for example, lose their ancestral lands, receive low or no wages for work, take on low-status or "dirty" jobs, and be aggressively policed when they object to this treatment. Racist cultures and institutions arise, then, through the actions of people and groups over time and become embedded in "reflexively monitored action, the aggregate effects of that action, and the unintended consequences of action."[17] Once entrenched, as Kipling's poem also signals, racist ideology makes patterns of raced advantage and disadvantage, honor and denigration appear natural, legitimate, and unchangeable. And as we saw with gender, racist ideology works to conceal the patterns it justifies, perhaps especially from its beneficiaries.[18]

In the United States and elsewhere, despite gradations in the racial hierarchy, the group at the top is always composed of those labeled "white"—hence the label *white supremacy* for a racist ideology that contends simultaneously and contradictorily that this hierarchical order is not invented but natural and that it must be maintained through aggressive and if necessary violent action. White supremacy here does not refer simply or solely to extremist hate groups or their views. It denotes something more subtle and pervasive:

"a political, economic, and cultural system in which whites overwhelmingly control power and material resources, conscious and unconscious ideas of white superiority and entitlement are widespread, and relations of white dominance and nonwhite subordination are daily reenacted across a board array of institutions and social settings."[19] So understood, racist ideology's primary function is legitimation: to justify perpetrators' privileges and their hostility toward or mistreatment of racialized others.

Terms like *white supremacy* and *white privilege* often evoke resistance or protest, particularly from white Americans.[20] But the historical record confirms that white-benefiting ideas about race and forms of racism have decisively shaped the maps of cultural and institutional power in the United States, including the institutions of property, labor, and economy. As we will see, these racial dynamics also shaped the story of a range of European Catholic immigrants who came to call themselves "white" in the United States.

RACE AND ECONOMY IN THE SIXTEENTH THROUGH NINETEENTH CENTURIES

To get a proper handle on how race and racism have influenced twentieth- and twenty-first-century US families' quest for economic livelihood, we must begin by looking, even if briefly, at their formative role in the country's longer history. Taking this look is difficult but imperative, because, as writer James Baldwin explains incisively:

> History is not merely something to be read. And it does not refer merely, or even principally, to the past.... We carry it within us, are unconsciously controlled by it in many ways, and history is literally present in all that we do. It could scarcely be otherwise, since it is to history that we owe our frames of reference, our identities, and our aspirations. And it is with great pain and terror that one begins to realize this.[21]

Baldwin's last observation signals the difficulty of this chapter's subject matter, especially perhaps for those of us upon whom US history has bequeathed the mantle of whiteness. But as his words also make clear, each of us, our communities, and our institutions are deeply shaped by and continue to embody our country's raced history. This being so, a twenty-first-century agenda for inclusive livelihood cannot sidestep the work of grappling with that history and its legacy.

Colonial Economics and the Invention of Whiteness

Berger traces the origins of modern racism to a constellation of historical developments in which, from the beginning, economics played a central role. In early modern Europe, nascent nationalism fed colonial competition "to achieve national economic superiority by dominating newly discovered continents and their resources."[22] Abetting this colonial quest, intellectual developments such as "new systems of biological classification . . . of racial 'types'" gave Europeans and American colonizers purportedly scientific warrants to "depart from the biblically derived belief in a common human origin" and "to posit innately inferior races." Berger contends that racism's hallmark, the lesser value placed on some human lives, also "emerged naturally" from Europeans' sense of religious superiority, which fueled conquerors' and missionaries' convictions about their God-given civilizing and evangelizing missions.[23] A matrix of belief and practice developed a system in which race and economics would continue to be deeply and persistently intertwined.

In 1782 Congress selected the motto "E Pluribus Unum"—"out of many, one"—for the official seal of the United States.[24] From their many cultures of origin, the motto suggested, US citizens would now forge a national identity centered on shared civic ideals and republican virtue. This new identity would be the glue binding an otherwise diverse people within an American culture, polity, and commerce. Two and a half centuries later, the survival and success of the United States witnesses to remarkable achievements in this regard.

But from the beginning this achievement had a shadow side. The originally proposed design for the Great Seal incorporated symbols of the "six nationalities" populating the original thirteen colonies: England, Scotland, Ireland, France, Holland, and Germany. Notably absent were the nations of Spain and Portugal, along with Native Americans and people of African descent. The ideal of a unified American "we" was already wedded with racialized thinking that opposed a "fully American," Anglo-Saxon citizenry—imagined as "original" or even "native"—to peoples whose nonwhiteness diluted or disqualified their claims to belonging. Far from being inconsistent with the fledgling nation's republican ideals, "inclusions and exclusions based on whiteness did not contradict, but rather constituted" those ideals. Across subsequent US history, often unrecognized by those whom it benefited, the ideology and practice of white supremacy have pervaded Americans' self-understandings, practices, and institutions.[25]

The original design for the Great Seal also reflected the founders' understanding of the new nation as providentially chosen. Emerging very early in the national story, this exceptionalist self-understanding drew on an "Anglo-Saxon myth" that focused initially on Europeans' supposed legacy of superior political institutions. But as Kelly Brown Douglas details, proponents soon became convinced that "the secret of Saxon success lay not in the institutions but in the blood"—blood that did not course through the veins of Spanish, Native/indigenous, or African peoples.[26] Powerful quasi-religious and quasi-natural-law claims about American exceptionalism coalesced around the nation's purportedly superior Anglo-Saxon identity and "stock," and America's calling to embody Anglo-Saxon superiority in the country's social and political institutions. The ties between chosenness and race became tightly bound.[27]

Whiteness as Property

Intricate intersections between racism and economic power mark US history. From the start a tool for dehumanizing, dividing, and dominating othered peoples, whiteness became a prerequisite for accessing civic freedoms and economic opportunities. Legal scholar Cheryl Harris notes that a central feature of capitalist property ownership is "the absolute right to exclude," and she observes that "the right to exclude was the central principle, too, of whiteness as identity, for mainly whiteness has been characterized, not by an inherent unifying characteristic, but by the exclusion of others deemed to be 'not white.'"[28] This right to exclude, backed up by a legal system that privileges white interests, "inexorably gives way to other fundamental rights—the right to claim land and the right to stake out space."[29]

In the American colonial context, white racial entitlement and superiority served to justify both usurping native lands and owning Black bodies and their labor.[30] "On the eve of the American Revolution," Berger notes, "Indians were the group whose disintegration and absorption would facilitate and justify the march of white American colonization, and Africans were those who would do the work when they got there."[31] Gaining, possessing, and keeping economic power over land (space), resources, and labor were primarily white prerogatives, around which the places and destinies of nonwhites would be fixed. By the late 1700s, thanks to a concatenation of law, force, and custom, "the transformation of Africans into a permanently inferior labor force and Indians into a permanently inferior nation" was largely complete.[32] African Americans were racially fixed in the role of slave or menial laborers, and American Indians "fixed in their role of absorption and disappearance."[33] This linkage of ascribed racial inferiority with constricted access to civic participation and economic opportunity has been deeply etched into the subsequent fortunes of these two communities and has served as the template for the treatment of other "nonwhite" groups over the course of US history.[34]

Impacts on Economy and Livelihood

Average families' chances to make a decent living and establish financial security have always depended on the existence of cultural, legal, and institutional supports. But from colonial times forward, these necessary supports were systematically denied or rigged to the disadvantage of workers and families excluded from whiteness. What have been called America's two original sins—the expropriation of Native American lands and the institution of African chattel slavery—deployed racism in violent and oppressive ways to advance and secure white economic interests. Their harmful effects have infected US culture, economy, and politics in every generation since, with families of color and their children bearing the brunt of racism's compounding impacts.[35]

Colonial Americans' racialized understanding and legislating of property and ownership contributed to "a fusion of what [came] to be known as race with capitalism."[36] Two important elements in this fusion were, first, the merging of "settler" and "white" identities, and second, the distinguishing of relevant from expendable populations based on who was superior and civilized (or at least, civilizable) versus who was inferior, savage, and wild.[37] On this logic, African Americans, Native Americans, and—with slightly greater elasticity—immigrant groups deemed nonwhite were stigmatized as other, culturally demeaned, relegated to menial or degraded work, cordoned off from political enfranchisement or economic opportunity, and treated as threats to white possession, purity, safety, and security.[38] The gendered and raced framing of republican citizenship as the purview of "free white men" went hand-in-hand with a system of usurping land and labor, and partitioning and apportioning economic power.

Harris details the historical establishment of whiteness as prerequisite to the right to hold property, and, in turn, whiteness itself as cherished property, something to be fought for, guarded, and protected:

> Slavery linked the privilege of whites to the subordination of Blacks through a legal regime that attempted the conversion of Blacks into objects of property. Similarly, the settlement and seizure of Native American land supported white privilege through a system of property rights in land in which the "race" of the Native Americans rendered their first possession rights invisible and justified conquest. This

racist formulation embedded the fact of white privilege into the very definition of property. . . . *Possession—the act necessary to lay the basis for rights in property—was defined to include only the cultural [and legal] practices of whites.*[39]

"This definition," Harris continues, "laid the foundation for the idea that whiteness [itself] is valuable . . . property."[40] If possession denoted spaces and prerogatives exclusive to whites, nonwhites entered those spaces or claimed those prerogatives at their peril.[41]

White Americans were never wholly unaware of the contradiction between their treatment of African and Native Americans and the ideals of freedom, equality, and inalienable natural rights upon which their national discourse rested (and to which, for most, their Christian faith pointed). Over the ensuing years, neither cultural amnesia or benign retellings of American history were able to fully erase the stubborn facts: robbing, disenfranchising, cheating, and killing indigenous American peoples, and dispossessing, dehumanizing, and exploiting the bodies, labor, and lives of African peoples had been constitutive to creating, building, and expanding "the land of the free and home of the brave."

The long shadow cast by these realities helps explain the striking degree to which white fear and anxiety mark the history of race relations in the United States. In his famous study of 1830s America, Alexis de Tocqueville speaks of witnessing "white people's fear of free blacks" in both North and South. The French ethnographer attributes whites' fear in part to status threat: "As the separations between whites and Negroes are lessened legally there is a sense of 'danger' that overcomes whites." What a white person dreads most, he hypothesizes, is "resembling the Negro, his former slave, and descending below his white neighbor." Tocqueville found strong aversions to "blacks 'intermingling' into the free space of white people. To do such a thing suggested an equality that was intolerable."[42] Pervasive white fear helped fuel a culture of avoidance, and more often oppression, of nonwhite others.[43]

Strong threads link this past to present-day US cultural, civic, and economic life. For many among a white community haunted by this dimly realized history, people of color are seen as "more than just inferior to white people. They are perceived as a threat. They are viewed as a chronic danger to cherished white property."[44] What a distorting white gaze perceives as Black people's—especially Black men's—implacable dangerousness has legitimated a historical litany of mistreatment and violence, from slavery to Jim Crow, lynching, mass incarceration, shootings of unarmed Black youth (like teenager Trayvon Martin in 2012) who were "in the wrong place at the wrong time," and the subtle, everyday harms inflicted by racism's hold on whites' practical consciousness and existential security systems. Recent scholars trace a clear trajectory from chattel slavery to post–Civil War constructions of free Black persons as threatening and dangerous, to the twentieth-century constructions of "the guilty Black body," Black economic dependency, and Black criminality, to the persistence, in the twenty-first century, of implicit or overt presumptions of guilt applied to law-abiding Black citizens perceived to be in white space (e.g., driving, shopping, walking).[45]

This history held profound implications for ordinary people and families pursuing livelihood over the past century. For African Americans, Native Americans, and other peoples of color, the story is written statistically—in disparities in wages, wealth, and well-being—and personally—in narratives of discrimination, dispossession, and loss, but also of courage, dignity, resistance, and forward movement, often at great cost, against seemingly insurmountable forces. In 2014, by recounting the story of Clyde Ross, whose life experiences spanned a childhood marked by economic exploitation and loss in Jim Crow Mississippi, migration north to Chicago, and decades of struggle to acquire and keep a house under the city's regime of redlining and price-gouging real estate practices, Ta-Nehisi Coates lifted up but one among a host of powerful witnesses in his widely read and much-discussed *Atlantic* piece titled "The Case for Reparations."[46]

Catholic Immigrants and Whiteness

Race and racism also had important consequences for white working people. In the nineteenth and early twentieth centuries, whiteness afforded non-elite working families greater access to the economic sufficiency, security, and status of a good living. As waves of Catholic immigrants began arriving during the nineteenth century, first from Ireland and Germany, then in growing numbers from Italy and Eastern Europe, they were quick to recognize the United States' racial hierarchy, and the desirability of rising to its top. Their ability to do so, however, was frequently called into question.[47]

Matthew Frye Jacobson identifies three shifts in the political-economic and cultural shape of whiteness in the United States between 1790 and 1924. In 1790 Congress declared that only "free white" immigrants could become citizens. During the nineteenth century, influxes of "peasants and laborers from unanticipated regions of Europe" raised new questions about the "equation of whiteness with fitness for self-government." In response, "a second regime of racial understanding emerged . . . cataloguing the newcomers as racial types, pronouncing on their innate biological distance from the nation's [Anglo-Saxon] 'original stock' and speculating as to their fitness for citizenship."[48] This regime fed a nativist movement that had as its apogee the passage in 1924 of the Johnson-Reed Act, a racially based and highly restrictive immigration law. Johnson-Reed sharply curtailed "the influx of immigrants from south and eastern Europe that had begun around 1900," groups nativists regarded as inferior to the original "Aryan" or "Anglo-Saxon" racial stock of northern and western Europe.[49] Among the non-Aryan undesirables who sparked the nativist—and racist—backlash behind Johnson-Reed were large numbers of Catholics.

Nineteenth-century nativist cartoons depicting Irish immigrants as apes reveal a tendency to classify them either with or near to African Americans—that is, as less than human, and at the bottom of the hierarchy. By 1900, newly arriving Italians, Slavs, and Poles were also widely treated as, if not fully racialized minorities, "in-between peoples" whose ethnicities and religion kept them from full civic and racial belonging.[50] In 1909, Stanford professor of education Ellwood Cubberly described these largely working-class immigrants in terms that jibe with rhetoric historically applied to American Indians and African Americans. Immigrants arriving after 1882, Cubberly contended, were "a very different type from the north European who preceded them. Illiterate, docile, lacking in self-reliance and initiative and not possessing Anglo-Teutonic conceptions of law, order, and government, their coming has served to dilute tremendously our national stock, and to corrupt our civic life." Still, many policymakers held out hope that with proper education and cultural assimilation, these European "racial groups" could, over time, become fully American. For racialized Asian, Native, and African Americans, no such hope was held; federal officials in the 1920s declared that among new immigrants, "race disappears after the third generation" with the exception of "Orientals, Negroes, and American Indians."[51]

The flexibly racialized status of newer European immigrants, Catholics included, meant that, over time, what Jacobson calls an "alchemy of race" could transform them into "white ethnics."[52] But this transformation came at a price. Strong cultural pressures to assimilate, felt especially by immigrant children, threatened cherished traditions and often caused rifts within families and between generations. Italian American educator Leonard Covello recalls that public schools during these decades aggressively promoted Americanization of speech, customs, and even food. As first-generation children were pressed to shed their home languages and cultures, their schooling frequently created painful fissures. "We were becoming American," Covello laments, "by learning how to be ashamed of our parents."[53]

Immigrants Americanized, too, by assimilating American racial categories. Italian and Eastern European workingmen quickly caught on to the benefits that being "white" could offer on a job site or when seeking a home. Immigrant women, too, working in their own and others' households, learned that part of their job was to conform with, and to train their children to practice, the customs of antiblack racism.[54] Immigrant Slovak, Polish, and Italian Catholic women whose families lived in poor, substandard neighborhoods and housing encountered strong incentives to embrace attitudes and practices that would align them and their families with whiteness. The painfully intimate locality of racism's manifestation and transmission is evident in 1920s social workers' reports, which show how ideology and emotions surrounding race, class, purity, and Americanization all "came together dramatically over the question of whether new immigrant children should play with African American children."[55]

Social workers repeatedly reported on immigrant parents' worries about such play and their efforts to stop it. In Chicago by 1925, Italian residents' "resistance to having black neighbors focused on teaching that 'no decent Italian family' would let their children play interracially, and on the more general stricture: 'Don't visit the n—rs in their houses.'" In Connecticut a Slovak woman recounted: "I always tell my children not to play with the n—r people's children, but they always play with them just the same. I tell them that n—r children are dirty and that they will get sick if they play.... If we had some place for the children to play here I'm sure that the white children they would not play with the n—r children.... All people are alike— that's what God says—but just the same it's no good to make our children play with the n—r children, because they are too dirty."[56] These quotations reveal fears and anxieties among—most likely Catholic—immigrant families about their children's racial status, as well as the mechanisms, both physical (racially segregating children by prohibiting play or friendly contact) and social-psychological (discourses of separation-purity versus contamination-dirtiness that supersede religious affirmations of human equality), they deployed to secure their whiteness.[57]

RACE AND LIVELIHOOD IN THE EARLY 1900S

Against this longer historical backdrop, we now revisit the story of early-twentieth century working families' quest for a dignified livelihood, paying particular attention to the ways in which economic opportunities, experiences, and outcomes diverged for differently racialized groups.

Native Americans and African Americans

The year 1900 found non-elite and working-class families in the economically vulnerable conditions that prompted the activism of Ryan and other Progressive Era reformers. We can see why European Catholic immigrants sought so strenuously to acquire whiteness, and why they so forcefully defended their claim to it, when we look at the situations of those who were not able to acquire this possession—including former Mexican residents in the American Southwest, Asian immigrants on the West Coast, and Native and African Americans.

Echoes of their distinctive histories of oppression sounded in the differently racialized experiences of Native and African American communities during this period. In the late nineteenth and early twentieth centuries, Berger explains, "the basic racist move at work in Indian law and policy" was "to racialize the *tribe*, defining tribes as racial groups in order to deny tribes the rights of governments."[58] Scholars and government leaders theorized tribal societies "as fatally and racially inferior" while at the same time urging Indian individuals to leave their communities and join the ranks of non-Indians.[59] Between 1887 and 1928, the most decisive blow toward breaking down tribal societies was struck by the Dawes Allotment Act, which mandated the breakup of tribal lands among individual households, giving over whatever remained for white purchase or settlement.[60]

Accompanying "direct intrusion on tribal economies" were a series of policies and educative measures whose aim was the "absorption of the Indian race into the body politic of the nation." These included establishing boarding schools, many run by Catholic religious orders, which separated Indian children from their families for the express purpose of "killing all the Indian there is in the race."[61] Native Americans at the turn of the twentieth century, Berger writes, were caught in a double bind. Their tribal nations were stripped of their sovereign status and now treated as "racial groupings fixed at an earlier moment of social evolution." But individual assimilation as "Americans" came at the price of abandoning one's historical identity and conceding white superiority.[62]

Persons of African descent continued to be barred by law and sanction-backed custom from equal participation in civic and economic life. Soon after the Civil War, the federal government rescinded earlier promises to economically enfranchise freed slave families through grants—"forty acres and a mule"—that would have made their independent pursuit of livelihood viable.[63] Though by 1900 African Americans had gained legal citizenship and male voting rights, in practice the majority remained socially, politically, and economically oppressed. In the South, the Jim Crow regime of legislated seg-regation and economic subjugation, backed by vigilante groups such as the Ku Klux Klan and punctuated by thousands of gruesome lynchings, had taken firm hold. Lynchings, not limited to the Deep South, commonly involved mobs dragging accused Black people from jail cells to mete out extralegal punishment in well-attended public spectacles of torture, castration, burn-ing, shooting, hanging, and dismemberment.[64] As a handful of courageous journalists like Ida B. Wells amply documented, lynchings were acts of terror, designed to keep Black Americans in their political, social, and—importantly—economic places by making horrifying examples of those per-ceived to have stepped out of line.[65]

In northern cities, Black migrant families who had fled blatant racial oppression in the South encountered social and economic discrimination, including geographical confinement to underresourced ghettos. In every region, a racially segmented job market ensured that jobs offering better pay, prestige, or advancement were denied to workers of color.[66] Assumptions about Black people's inferiority, dirtiness, and abjection made African Amer-icans' segregation from whites, and confinement to the least-dignified and lowest-paying forms of labor seem both natural and right.

It was W. E. B. Du Bois's up-close encounter with the brutal lynching of farmworker Sam Hose in April 1899, witnessed by thousands of spectators in Atlanta's courthouse square, that prompted the renowned African American scholar and social critic's decisive turn to activism and public advocacy.[67] In his famous 1903 work, *The Souls of Black Folk*, Du Bois poignantly describes African Americans' enforced "peculiar double-consciousness" and the mar-ginal citizenship, marginal livelihood, and marginal humanity that being Black in white America entailed.[68] Keenly aware of both the economic and social planks in the "doors of Opportunity," Du Bois was an astute analyst of the interactions of race and class. For the white US working class—who at the time included great numbers of Catholics—low wages and poor work-ing conditions were offset in part, Du Bois saw, by "the wages of whiteness." In both South and North white workers gained substantive advantages from "a public and psychological wage": "They were given public deference ... because they were white. They were admitted, freely, with all classes of white people, to public functions [and] public parks.... The police were drawn from their ranks and the courts, dependent on their votes, treated them with leniency ... and while this had small effect upon the economic situation, it had great effect upon their personal treatment."[69]

Du Bois's description of whiteness as a wage bespeaks what Harris under-lines as the property value of racial superiority for even the poorest white person: "White workers could, and did, define and accept their class positions by fashioning identities as 'not slaves' and as 'not Blacks.'"[70] A racially segmented labor market also afforded white workers higher wages and status than nonwhites. Simultaneously, however, the dynamics of antiblack racism tamped down and dissipated working-class unity, and accordingly, power. Racial divisions among working-class people advantaged employers and capitalists by helping to keep cheap labor cheap, and its providers docile.[71]

African Americans and the "Great Migration"

Amid the violence of the Jim Crow South and surging Eastern and Southern European working-class immigration in the north, millions of African-American men, women, and children joined a "great migration" from the rural south to the urban north in search of better lives and jobs. Between 1910 and 1940, a first wave of 3.5 million migrants "doubled the percentage of Blacks living in the North and West." In the 1940s, a second wave further increased Black populations in northern cities—in Chicago, for example, by over 70 percent.[72] Jacqueline Jones's history of African American women and work provides a window into Black families' quest for better livelihood through northern migration, as well as the obstacles they encountered.[73]

As Jones points out, both European immigrant and Black migrant families grappled with the shift from the meager self-sufficiency of rural farm life to a fully cash-dependent consumer economy of large northern cities.[74] Both faced inferior housing and exploitative work conditions and sought to preserve their cultural traditions, relying on family and kin to ease the transition between rural and city life. But their different patterns of adjustment reflected their divergent experiences in the work force. African Americans—despite being native-born, English-speaking, (mostly) Protestant Christians, often with superior levels of educational attainment—remained heavily concentrated in menial labor and domestic service, "and the anticipated rewards of northern life—decent jobs and good housing—eluded them and many of their children and grandchildren as well."[75]

As Polish immigrant Joe Podles's story attested, life was also difficult for poor European immigrants during these years, but Black migrant workers confronted additional challenges. In the cities of the North, "industrial employers preferred white foreign-born workers (most from southern and Eastern Europe)" over US-born Black workers who were included only when the supply of immigrant labor diminished. "This initial preference on the part of northern employers shaped the respective fates of blacks and the 'New Immigrants' for years to come."[76] Here Jones hints at the stark divergences in intergenerational economic mobility and asset accumulation that would divide the grandchildren of European immigrants and the grandchildren of Black migrants.[77] In all cases, women of color, especially among the poor, found themselves in the most vulnerable and marginalized cultural, economic, and social spaces.

Black women arriving in northern cities eagerly sought factory jobs, which they saw as paths out of poverty and servility. Factory work was arduous and wages, especially for women of color, were low, but compared to sharecropping or domestic work they delivered higher status and pay for fewer working hours. As a twenty-two-year-old Black woman working in a box factory put it in 1920, "I'll never work in nobody's kitchen but my own anymore. No indeed!"[78] Sadly, Jones observes, the realities of the racialized labor market made it likely that this woman might soon have had to return to washing dishes and clothes for white families. Black migrant women's qualifications frequently matched or exceeded those of European immigrants, yet "immigrant women continued to find expanded job opportunities in manufacturing" during this period, while "black women formed an ever larger proportion of laborers in the shrinking fields of hand laundry work and personal service."[79]

As we have seen, business practice, labor law, and public policy at this time reflected powerful cultural assumptions about wives' and mothers' primary mission in the home.[80] But economic necessity meant that few African American wives and mothers could conform to full-time homemaker gender norms.[81] The fact that low-paying domestic service was the only job option for large numbers of married Black women only underscored their exclusion from the domestic opportunities and recognition available to middle-class white women.[82] In many ways, writes Jones, "the white mistress-black maid relationship preserved the inequalities of the slave system," and in every field of work, "a black female wage earner encountered a depth and form of discrimination never experienced by a Polish [Catholic, immigrant] woman, no matter how poor, illiterate, or lacking in 'factory sense' she was."[83]

African American men encountered equally demoralizing obstacles to fulfilling masculine breadwinner roles. Mary Church Terrell, the prominent Black educator and civil rights activist, reflected poignantly in a 1906 lecture on the painful disillusionment that beset Black youth as they became aware of the obstacles to dignified economic livelihood that faced even the most highly skilled and educated among them.

> The colored laborer's path to a decent livelihood is by no means smooth. . . . I am personally acquainted with skilled workmen who . . .

are not admitted into the unions because they are colored. Even when they are allowed to join . . . they frequently derive little benefit owing to certain tricks of the trade. . . . Early in life many a colored youth is so appalled by the helplessness and hopelessness of his situation in this country that in a sort of stoical despair he resigns himself to his fate. 'What is the good of our trying to acquire an education? . . . [T]here is almost nothing for colored people to do but engage in the most menial occupations, and we do not need an education for that.' More than once such remarks, uttered by young men and women in our public schools who possess brilliant intellects, have wrung my heart.[84]

Recent work by scholars like Michelle Alexander, James Logan, and Kahlil Muhammad demonstrate another powerful cementer of racist ideology and practice during these decades: the criminalization of Black people and Black bodies, specifically Black men, in white American cultural imagination and institutional practice.[85] In both South and North, narratives of Black male criminality were bolstered by myths of the hypersexual, predatory Black man surrounding lynching culture, a myth widely disseminated in popular culture and media.[86] As Margaret Denike details, this narrative has fed a racist social imaginary that, to this day, tags dark bodies as menacing and antisocial.[87] Early twenty-first-century crises surrounding mass incarceration and police mistreatment of unarmed Black citizens testify to the cumulative impacts of this criminalizing apparatus on the lives and livelihoods of generations of families of color.

The Depression, the New Deal, and Race

The Great Depression and New Deal eras created unprecedented openings for a public discussion of democracy as entailing not only political but economic rights. Gloria Albrecht recalls that New York senator Robert F. Wagner, author of the groundbreaking 1935 National Labor Relations Act, argued that safeguarding democracy demanded that political, civic, and economic rights be recognized as interdependent.[88] "What does it profit a man to have so-called 'political freedom,'" Wagner contended, "if he is an economic slave?"[89] Yet given the many categories of workers (including agricultural, domestic, small business, and contract workers) not covered by New Deal labor reforms, Albrecht observes, "the New Deal was no deal for millions of white women and majorities of women and men of color."[90]

Concurring, labor historian Joe Trotter writes that as the "'Last Hired and the First Fired,' African Americans entered the Depression era earlier and deeper than other racial and ethnic groups."[91] When unemployment soared, Black workers found themselves pushed out by whites from even the menial jobs, like domestic and railroad service, to which Black people had routinely been relegated.[92] Northward migration continued, and unemployment and poverty for African Americans in the cities worsened: "By 1932, black urban unemployment had reached well over 50 percent, more than twice the ratio for whites."[93]

Adding to the financial burdens for already strapped families of color were the discriminatory features of many of Franklin D. Roosevelt's signature economic-recovery policies. These included the aforementioned exemptions of agricultural and domestic workers (occupations with high percentages of African Americans and Latinos) from coverage under the Social Security Act and from the wage and work protections of the Fair Labor Standards Act. Many municipalities, especially in the South, impeded or denied nonwhite families' access even to government relief programs for which they were legally eligible. In addition, the strengthening of white-dominated labor unions under the New Deal frequently worked to the detriment of nonwhite workers.[94]

Racial discrimination by labor unions was widespread. Speaking at historically Black Howard University in March 1943, Monsignor Ryan addressed this discouragingly persistent problem: "Sometimes the Negro is excluded from certain occupations by the rules and practices of labor unions. This is even more reprehensible than exclusion by employers; for the wage earners have themselves been victims of oppression by stronger classes." Ryan declared racial discrimination and exclusion "a blot on the history of American labor unionism." Yet labor was "not a unique offender" in this regard. "Other social groups, and even whole nations, that have felt the miseries of subjugation have in turn oppressed their less fortunate fellows after reaching a position of domination. That is human nature in one of its un-lovely manifestations." His Howard University audience likely felt the limitations of Ryan's dispassionate natural-law discourse as he intoned: "The sooner the unions discard this practice, the sooner will they bring about a rational and ethical resolution of this very real difficulty. My conclusion, then, is that these discriminations by the unions are nearly always against charity and frequently against justice."[95]

Racially discriminatory New Deal homeownership policies channeled nonwhites into inferior housing and laid the groundwork for white resistance to so-called open housing and neighborhood integration during the postwar years. Housing policies, especially around loan eligibility, framed homeownership as "a white entitlement to a home in a racially homogenous neighborhood."[96] Rather than challenging whites' image of the person of color as antineighbor, writes historian David Roediger, "the New Deal blessed, rationalized, and bankrolled that notion. In doing so it imparted powerful lessons and expectations to new immigrants and their descendants regarding the extent to which social reformers tolerated and forwarded white privilege." Bluntly, many New Deal policies "encouraged—and in some ways required—[people] to literally invest in whiteness. Insofar as housing policy also discriminated against urban neighborhoods of mixed nationalities, it encouraged the descendants of new immigrants to borrow in order to suburbanize and whiten."[97]

By "linking the pursuit of happiness to the homogeneous neighborhood," and "freedom of choice" to the right to associate with whom one chooses, urban white homeowners and buyers could deny racist motives even as they benefited from racially rigged policies and systems. Labor and housing policies "empowered and advantaged new immigrants, but as white, not as new immigrants. . . . [thus] raising the stakes for the claiming of white identity" and assimilation.[98] In so doing, "the New Deal took in, and coerced, members of new immigrant communities"—many of them Catholic communities—"via appeals to *both* race *and* class."[99]

Communities of color were by no means passive during these decades. Recent historians record persistent efforts by Black citizen groups and leaders who, often at great, even mortal cost, resisted, protested, and fought to improve economic conditions and opportunities for their constituencies. Thomas Sugrue recounts the active parts played by Black (and some white) community organizations in struggles over Federal Housing Administration funding for low-income public housing and private homes in northern cities. Thanks to the work of these activists and organizations, by the late 1930s what African Americans had originally dubbed FDR's "Raw Deal" policies were being implemented in ways somewhat more beneficial to Black communities. Black workers' and citizens' experiences of organizing and solidarity during these years, Trotter notes, laid down foundations on which the civil rights movement of the 1950s and 1960s would rise.[100]

Gender, Race, and Livelihood

Evelyn Nakano Glenn's finely grained research on productive (waged) and reproductive (unpaid, caring) labor by non-elite women in three racialized groups reveals race and gender's compounding impacts on the quest for a dignified livelihood among nonwhite US women and their families. Tracking the different experiences of working-class Chinese American, Mexican American, and African American women, Glenn also identifies commonalities. She attributes these to women's "similar positions in the colonial labor system and the similar difficulties the system created for their families." In each racial group, men were often barred from earning a family wage, so that "women had to engage in subsistence and income-producing activities both in and out of the household. In addition they had to work hard to keep their families together in the face of outside forces that threatened their integrity."[101]

Race entered deeply into the gendered ideology we examined in chapter 3, as "the dominant culture calculated the relative value of productive versus reproductive labor differently for different groups. Motherhood and domesticity were elevated as virtues for white women. White men were seen as requiring and deserving a wife's services, and white children were viewed as future citizens to be nurtured and protected." But the domestic work that nonwhite, working-class women performed for their own families "was not deemed as worthy of protecting." These attitudes were reflected in welfare policies that judged "poor black and Latina mothers . . . to be 'employable,' and not requiring or deserving of charity." In many cases, "women of color who were not employed were even deemed 'vagrants' and put to work forcibly."[102]

Society's devaluing of nonwhite women's family labor complicated the impact of the family living wage ideology on women and families of color. Recall that one motivator for the breadwinner/homemaker ideal was social resistance against the commodification of family labor. "In opposing a purely economic or market calculation" for all work, advocates for a family living wage "were asserting that not all human labor should be commodified, but rather that some—particularly women's—labor ought to be retained for the benefit of family members." Society's disregard for their right to perform care work in their own homes gave working-class families of color an additional impetus for embracing the homemaker ideal: For these families, aspiring to remove "women's reproductive labor [from the capitalist market] was a form of double resistance to the incorporation of the whole family into capitalist regimes of labor *and* to white control of family life."[103]

US Catholics, Race, and Livelihood

As we have seen, the new immigrants pouring into the United States at the turn of the twentieth century included great numbers of Roman Catholics. Seeking political inclusion and economic opportunity, these largely southern and Eastern European newcomers, like their Irish and German predecessors, quickly recognized the value of whiteness. Being part of a religious community still working toward full acceptance in Protestant America may have been an additional impetus for these Catholics to seek and secure dominant racial status. In any event, with few exceptions, interracial solidarity was neither emphasized nor practiced among early twentieth-century US Catholics, or by their church.

Recall that for early twentieth-century urban Catholics in the Northeast and Midwest, life was centered on local, frequently ethnically specific parishes and neighborhoods. In both large and smaller cities, immigrant Catholics routinely sorted themselves into "national parishes" in different neighborhoods. The small southeastern Wisconsin town of Cudahy, for instance, covered less than five square miles. Between 1900 and 1910, as Cudahy saw its population increase nearly tenfold (from 1,366 to 10,631), three different Catholic parishes with schools were established: a north-side parish in 1896, Saint Frederick's, attended by primarily German Catholics; a south-side parish, Holy Family, for Polish speakers, in 1900; and in 1909, a Slavic, mid-town parish, Saint Joseph's.[104] Urban ethnic communities guarded their neighborhood and parish boundaries, engaged in mutual prejudices ("ethnic" jokes mocking purported characteristics of different groups were freely traded), and "mixed" cross-ethnic marriages were discouraged. In late 1940s Detroit, for instance, an Irish and Italian American couple's Catholic marriage evoked such deep dismay that most family members in the groom's first-generation Italian family refused to attend the wedding. Before a 1950 Chicago wedding between an Irish American and a German Slavic Catholic, the bride's Irish mother worried aloud that the couple's children would be taunted as "Polish."[105]

But between the 1920s and 1940s, as the migration of southern Black workers into northern cities reached a crescendo, and cross-ethnic marriages continued take place among postimmigrant generations, Euro-American Catholics increasingly closed ranks around a more homogeneous, white identity. Through the post–World War II years, as John McGreevy recounts, bitter battles over racial integration raged in many Catholic urban neighborhoods, with whiteness regularly trumping Catholic residents' religious bonds with nonwhite Catholic newcomers.[106] Those deemed nonwhite, especially African Americans, were treated as antineighbors whose mere presence contaminated neighborhoods and downgraded property values.[107]

The northward movement of southern Black people coincided with the decades in which Ryan and the Catholic bishops championed wage justice, in theory, for all.[108] But white working-class Catholics, fearing competition from black migrants for similar jobs and opportunities, rarely questioned and at times benefited from the cultural and economic disadvantages to which racism subjected their neighbors of color. Some racial mixing did occur in urban workplaces, but in housing, social interactions, and parish life, white Catholic working-class families with few exceptions chose hunkering down among other whites over cross-racial neighborliness or cooperation.[109]

At workplaces, scuffles, strikes, and at times riots occurred as whites rebelled alongside Black workers. Interracial toilet facilities and social mixing sparked white fears of "racial contamination" and were especially incendiary topics.[110] In 1940s northern cities, the particularly strong animus of "newly white" Italian, Polish, and Slavic Catholic workers toward mixing with persons considered "colored" has been well documented. And as we have seen, Ryan's beloved New Deal often reinforced patterns that systematically lessened nonwhites' access to employment, housing, and wealth-building opportunities.[111]

In northern cities, residential patterns shifted from older mosaics of ethnic enclaves to neighborhoods divided by race. In the Midwest, the evolution of heavily Catholic, industrial Detroit was typical:

Immigrants in late nineteenth-century Detroit chose ethnic neighborhoods over all other factors in locating housing. The logic of ethnicity overrode employment location and class considerations when people decided where to live. . . . By 1920 this had begun to change, however, with employment-related "mill villages" emerging, multi-ethnic and defined predominantly by occupation. One enormous exception occurred for the growing number of black Detroiters, who were segregated into racially distinct ghettoes. In other words, as most ethnic neighborhoods lost their linguistic and cultural distinctiveness, black neighborhoods gained theirs. Race and class, more than ethnicity, began to define city neighborhoods after 1920.[112]

Subordination and marginalization of nonwhite workers were enforced vigorously, yet most whites evinced little awareness that their privileged position was anything other than natural. White majorities ascribed racialized identities and cultures to nonwhites, but rarely to themselves.[113] Only toward the end of the century would the invisibility (to dominant whites, primarily) of whiteness and white privilege begin to be analyzed and challenged by scholars in the social sciences, followed, considerably more slowly, by Catholic thinkers and leaders.[114]

Catholic leaders' general lack of empathy toward Black workers and families during this period is evident in Monsignor Ryan's previously mentioned 1943 lecture on race and work justice, one of his only recorded speeches on the subject. Ryan counseled his Howard University audience to patience, reminding them that "history teaches at least five lessons that should never be ignored by oppressed minorities":

First, they must themselves be vigilant, active and constant in struggling to remove by all legitimate means the disabilities under which they labor; second, in countries possessing representative and constitutional government, they must avoid methods of violence; third, the greater disabilities and the longer the tradition of inferiority, the slower will be the rate of progress; fourth, one of the most useful virtues to be practiced by the oppressed group is that of patience; fifth, the struggling minority must not disregard or discourage the assistance that can be obtained from men of good will in the dominant group.

Ryan continues:

If Christ's Gospel of love were adequately put into practice by all classes, neither the Negroes [n]or any other minority group could honestly complain of unfair treatment. But brotherly love does not, or should not, travel a one-way street. While the white man ought to love the Negro, as Christ loved all men, the Negro is . . . equally bound to love the white man. And he should especially love white friends [of the Negro] . . . even when they advocate patience and a realistic approach to interracial conditions and practices.[115]

Coming from the country's most distinguished Catholic advocate for labor justice, Ryan's paternalist—and racially self-serving—words and tone are shamefully disappointing. Even more upsetting—and telling—is the contrast between his long record of vigorous advocacy for workers' dignity and rights and the rights of organized labor, and his consistently tepid response to the rampant mistreatment of African Americans on every one of these fronts. In the end, it seems clear, "the workingman" Ryan so ardently defended had not only a normative gender but a racial identity: he was white. In this failure Ryan exemplifies a wider failure of antiracist awareness or commitment that continued in subsequent decades to shape and mar US Catholic leaders' attempts to promote "economic justice for all."[116]

RACE AND LIVELIHOOD, LATE TWENTIETH TO EARLY TWENTY-FIRST CENTURIES

In the late twentieth and early twenty-first centuries, the longstanding economic and social disparities afflicting racialized groups in the United States morphed, in some cases lessened, but did not disappear. By many measures, the economic lots of nonwhite groups improved in comparison to their early twentieth-century forebears. Yet the overall economic advantages of white people over people of color persisted, and in some cases increased. Well into the twenty-first century, race-based wage, employment, and especially wealth gaps remained wide, and even in times of economic boom they improved only at close-to-glacial paces.

Native, African American, and Other Racialized Workers

This was patently true for Native Americans.[117] Economic and work opportunities in Native American communities continued to be poor, and clashes between indigenous and white people over property or natural resource rights were regularly racialized. Berger describes "ugly, racist protests by white sports fishermen and businesses with interests in fishing stocks" in Wisconsin treaty disputes during the 1980s and 1990s, which eventually were settled in favor of the Lac Du Flambeau Chippewa tribes.[118] In the 2000s, white antipathy toward Indians and tribal-run gambling casinos displayed the "racially fixed image of the tribe" and illustrated the slippery ways that racialization functions in service of white economic interests. The romanticized white image of "the accepted and honored tribe," Berger observes, "is poor, traditional, and close to the earth. By engaging in profitable commercial enterprises, tribes act as modern governments and violate this accepted Indian image." Berger cites whites' reactions to successful gaming operations run by the Pequot tribe in her home state of Connecticut, where many critics—asking "But are they really Indians?"—"challenged the right to game on the grounds that tribal members [operating casinos] are not racially Indian enough."[119] Berger underlines the racialized catch-22 here: "The rights of Indian tribes are thus fixed by their race, but efforts to assert those privileges in ways that interfere with white expectations result in challenges to racial authenticity."[120]

Circumstances for later-century African American citizens had improved in some significant respects over the previous era of legalized, overtly dominative and violent racism.[121] The striking down of legal segregation by the highest courts, the passage of the Civil Rights Act of 1964 and the Voting Rights Act of 1965, and other hard-won gains by the civil rights movement disrupted historic patterns of discrimination and yielded positive economic benefits for many families of color. In 1960, for example, "only about 10 percent of African American households were in the middle class. In 1990, 30 percent of African American households had middle-class incomes and their number in high-paying professional and technical occupations had increased by over 100 percent." Yet in the early twenty-first century, "with the exception of some Asian Americans, white families [still] enjoyed advantages over all other groups in the areas of housing, household income, net worth, employment, education, and job status."[122]

In 2007, 8.2 percent of whites fell below the poverty threshold, "by sheer headcount dominating the face of poverty." But while constituting only 12.4 and 14.8 percent of the overall population, respectively, 24.3 percent of African Americans and 20.6 percent of Hispanics fell below the federal poverty line. These communities were also overrepresented among the working poor: compared to 12 percent of whites, 31.8 percent of Blacks and 30.2 percent of Hispanics had incomes low enough (below 130 percent of the poverty line) to qualify for the federal food stamp program. Some economists peg the upper limit of "working poverty" at 200 percent of the federal poverty line, and in the economically prosperous, prefinancial crisis year of 2007, "22.9 percent of whites, and a startling 48 percent of blacks and 50.9 percent of Hispanics" fell below this level.[123] Native Americans' economic situation was similar: in 2012, their median annual household income hovered at around $36,000, with an overall poverty rate of nearly 29 percent.[124]

Shifting immigration and migration patterns also affected the post-1960s labor landscape. Numerically, culturally, and economically, the greatest impact came from large influxes of immigrants from various Spanish-speaking countries in Central, Latin, and South America, along with internal migration streams of Puerto Ricans moving to the mainland and Latinx workers from the rural Southwest to large cities in the Southeast and Northeast. Like European immigrants a century earlier, these migrants came from diverse communities, were largely working class, and were treated as racialized or "in-between peoples" whose fitness for citizenship was in doubt and whose labor was simultaneously essential and exploited.[125] With their African American neighbors, working-class Hispanics, particularly Mexican Americans and Puerto Ricans, suffered disproportionately over the decades of economic restructuring and intermittent crises that began in the 1970s. Rust Belt and Sunbelt manufacturing job losses hit racial minorities with particular force.[126]

Racial gaps in unemployment rates also persisted. In the nonrecession year of 2005, for instance, overall unemployment rates hovered between 5.1 and 5.5 percent. Yet, David Jensen writes, "during this same year, African-American unemployment rates were double the national average, with younger African Americans looking for work (ages sixteen to nineteen) at 35%."[127] Unemployment among Native Americans was equally inflated.[128] Both during and outside of official economic recessions, Seth Wessler concludes, "disparate unemployment rates for whites and people of color" are a persistent feature of the US economy. In fact, unemployment among peoples of color is consistently higher than recession-level unemployment levels for whites, leading Algernon Austin and others to speak of a "permanent recession" for members of nonwhite communities in the United States.[129]

Wages and labor force outcomes for nonwhite working-class immigrants also showed evidence of racialized inequity. While in 2007 immigrant workers as a whole earned "about 10 percent less than native-born U.S. workers," writes Melissa Snarr, "foreign-born workers from Mexico and Central America earned 27 percent less than their U.S.-born counterparts," with undocumented immigrants especially concentrated in low-wage jobs.[130] Joan Moore emphasizes that each subpopulation of Hispanic immigrants and in-migrants "is very diverse racially," with varying percentages identifying as white. As a whole, however, along with darker-skinned new immigrants from northern Africa, the Middle East, and Asia, "darker-hued Hispanics suffer housing and employment discrimination similar to that of blacks."[131] And while African Americans and US-born Latinxs saw some gains in median wages between 1982 and 2007, the wage gap between whites and nonwhites remained nearly unchanged. At every level of educational attainment, white workers' mean earnings exceeded those of Black, Latinx, or Asian workers.[132]

Statistics also reveal the enduring links between whiteness and "valued property." In residential housing, racial penalties were attached to housing values for native-born nonwhites in both cities and suburbs. "Suburban residence is considered symbolic of the American dream;" but when suburban communities become "contaminated" by US-born families of color, white residents tend to move out, and housing values tend to drop. Echoing racialized disparities of a century earlier, Samantha Friedman and Emily Rosenbaum's study of suburban minority and immigrant populations found that in diversifying suburbs, "many foreign-born households reside in significantly *better* neighborhoods than their native-born counterparts." Even when nonwhite families make the move "up" to suburban communities, researchers found, "the effect of race/ethnicity is generally a more consistent predictor than nativity status of households' neighborhood conditions," with American-born Black and Hispanic families continuing to experience disadvantages.[133]

Perhaps the most telling evidence of the intergenerational effects of racial economic disparity is the household wealth gap between white families and families of color. Always significant, in the late twentieth century this gap increased dramatically, from a mean of $84,000 in 1990 to $142,000 in 2007. Mean white household wealth had increased from $101,000 to $170,000, while among families of color wealth grew from a paltry $17,000 to $28,000.[134] Not unrelatedly, concentrated neighborhood poverty, abetted by continuing racial segregation and antiblack prejudice, encourages "the physical association between black people and poverty"; as "black and His-panic bodies, especially younger, male bodies, are marked in the public imagi-nation as more likely to be poor, more likely to be criminal, and dangerous." Research also shows that "this implicit bias feeds into patterns of discrimina-tion in housing and job opportunities."[135]

The surge in Latinx and other populations of color during these decades complicated the historically dominant Black/white racial narrative. Yet the most foundational American binary, white versus nonwhite, continued in force, its lingua franca etched in skin, both in the United States and in what Howard Winant calls the twenty-first-century "re-racialization of the world" within new, globalized social and economic hierarchies.[136] These hierarchies dictate, writes theologian M. Shawn Copeland, a cruel calculus: "The darker your skin is, the less you earn; the shorter your life span, the poorer your health and nutrition, the less education you can get."[137]

And as this book went to press, racialized disparities in the health and eco-nomic consequences of the COVID-19 pandemic for white versus nonwhite US families were already reflecting these same, inequitable patterns.[138]

Racism Reconfigured

Why do these problems persist? By the late twentieth century, a portfolio of antiracist policies were the law of the land, and many white Americans dis-avowed dominative racism.[139] With the support of legislation and public pol-icies, racial inclusion had increased in many sectors, and overtly racialized practices and discourse, accepted a century earlier, had given way to a more widespread ethos of racial civility.[140] "Oafish racism" was ruled out of court, its errant perpetrators the frequent butts of elite liberal disdain. But studies and surveys revealed racism's persistence beneath layers of public civility, often in practical consciousness and through gut reactions at the level Gid-dens calls basic security system.[141] This less crass, "elegant racism," as Coates dubbed it, persisted in racialized attitudes and power relations, continuing to reproduce systemic inequities and to subject nonwhites to racism's chronic, wearing harms.[142] Meanwhile, people—most often people of color—who "disturbed the routines" by publicly pointing out "mundane signs of sys-tematic oppression" were frequently met with gaslighting-type "denial and powerful gestures of silencing," or dismissed as "picky, overreacting, making something out of nothing, or of completely misperceiving the situation."[143]

Surveying these dynamics, sociologist Eduardo Bonilla-Silva perceived a contemporary ideology he called "color blind racism." Through interpretive frames that deny, minimize, or distract from racism's reality or perniciousness, color blind racism functions to construct "an impregnable yet elastic wall that barricades whites from the United States' racial reality." This ideology bolsters white group identity and cohesion; simultaneously it "blurs, shapes, and provides the terrain and terms of the discourse for blacks, Latinos, and east Asian, south Asian, and middle eastern diasporic communities."[144] Often adopting political liberalism's dominant vocabulary of individualism, equality, and freedom, this breed of racism operates ideologically, delegitimating and confounding efforts to expose white supremacy's infection of the economic and social status quo. In a public arena marked by such structured blindness, honest communication is thwarted, divisions harden, and racialized inequities remain entrenched.

Post-1970s economic circumstances also disadvantaged non-elite whites, but racialized divisions impeded the formation of working-class coalitions to advance cross-racial economic interests.[145] And as economic inequality steadily increased, so did class- and race-based social and geographic isolation. Geographic and symbolic distances between affluent white enclaves and Black and Brown urban ghettos fostered elite indifference to concentrated economic distress in central cities. Social scientists found mounting evidence that inequality, socioeconomic isolation, and racial divisions were "tightly intertwined."[146]

By the 2000s researchers were beginning to chart, across states and regions, correlations between high or growing economic inequality and "a status-based us-and-them mentality that heightens race bias," especially, they found, among non-elite whites.[147] When one's own economic sufficiency, security, and status feel threatened, data suggests, people's attention to and compassion for the plights of neighbors outside their immediate circles lessen.[148] In addition, white US citizens' well-documented tendencies to closely connect race, poverty, and undeservingness fed skepticism toward public efforts to alleviate poverty or lessen economic inequality.[149] As a result, research shows, "many [white] people simply don't feel very motivated to support fighting poverty when they imagine that minorities will be the beneficiaries."[150] Other studies have found that simply living in areas of greater economic inequality correlates with higher overt and implicit racial bias.[151]

Increasingly divergent political views among white and nonwhite American citizens is one final feature marking this period. Barack Obama's election in 2008 as the nation's first African American president led many—white people in particular—to hope or believe that the country was finally laying to rest its racist past. But the ensuing years quickly confirmed that this was not to be the case, and among some demographics, including economically beleaguered white working-class communities, discourses of racial resentment and hostility made at-times dramatic comebacks to the public stage.[152]

As we will discuss further in the next chapter, large numbers of white working-class Americans experienced the later twentieth century as a time of economic decline and cultural displacement.[153] Beginning in the 1970s white working- and lower-middle-class families in many parts of the country watched job opportunities diminish, wages stagnate, and benefits and job security erode. At the same time, their communities' once-mainstream American values and cultures seemed increasingly marginalized and undermined.[154] Fears and anxieties about families' short- and longer-term economic prospects mingled with confusion and grief over what many saw as the dissolution of the religious values and cultural bonds that had long identified and grounded working-class people and their communities. There was also growing anger.[155] And by the early twenty-first century, working-class distress was manifesting in declining health, rising levels of addiction and related disease, and higher suicide and overall death rates, especially among middle-aged white men without a college degree.[156]

Keith Payne's research traces the health crisis among white working-class men to, among other factors, racialized disappointment: the once-reliable wages of whiteness now seemed, for them, to have been rescinded. The declining physical and mental health among white working-class communities is striking, he contends, "because it speaks to the power of subjective social comparisons. *This demographic group is dying of violated expectations.* Although high school educated whites make more money on average than similarly educated blacks, the whites expect more because of their history of privilege."[157]

Surveys of non-elite white voters during the 2016 presidential election cycle appeared to validate Payne's claims about ties between economic insecurities and racialized social comparisons.[158] Pre-2016 election polls conducted by the Pew Foundation and by political scientist Michael Tesler found large numbers of white voters—and an overwhelming majority of Republicans— agreeing that "the average American does not get their fair share in this country." This is not surprising, as the sluggish economic recovery following the 2007–09 recession left Americans in all but the highest income brackets economically less well off. Despite the persistence of significant interracial economic and social disparities, however, these same white respondents did not agree that "African Americans do not get their fair share in this country." A majority of these white voters further agreed that, "today, too much attention is paid to racial issues."[159] On all these points, majorities of non-white voters thought otherwise.

A reader's comment on a May 2017 *Wall Street Journal* article bespeaks the deep antipathy that Tesler's polling data implied. Responding to a previous commenter, C. Cook declares:

Your "minority" narrative is no longer valid. We have had a black President (OK, half black, but the media insisted he was Black), Women,
Blacks, Hispanics, CEOs, Senators, Governors, Congressmen, and
representatives in all aspects of American society. But, the guilty
White left STILL needs the '60s narrative, because dealing with a new
reality would shatter their philosophical base. The world HAS changed.
Dealing with our social problems with a racial bias does not fix anything. It just funds leeches on society and distorts help and treatment
for those who are truly needy.[160]

Many among the working-class whites who formed a core sector of Donald
Trump's voting base found elites' antiracist analysis and rhetoric to be abstract
and unconvincing.[161] As the next chapter discusses in more detail, these non-
elite voters tended to aim their resentment at two targets: nonwhite or poorer
groups they regarded as unfairly advantaged by the government, and out-of-
touch cultural and political elites whom they saw as demeaning their religious
and cultural values and exacerbating, then ignoring their economic struggles.[162]

During the 2016 presidential campaign, non-elite whites' sense of disenfranchisement and anger came sharply into public view. Journalist Hsu
Hua's conversations with voters in rural and working-class communities suggested that "in working-class America, an élite-resenting identity politics has
emerged in which whiteness," instead of providing its former cultural and
economic wage, "spells dispossession."[163] Between communities separated
by geographical region, race, class, and/or culture, sociologist Arlie Hochschild observed clashes between what she calls "deep stories"—the shared,
viscerally felt communal narratives through which members makes sense of
their social and political identities and situations. Absent avenues for con-
structively addressing them, reinforced by competing media echo chambers,
deep-story clashes feed cycles of misunderstanding and alienation that isolate
factions, erode civility, and cement cultural and political impasse.[164] None of
this is good for democracy, commentators from across the political spectrum
agreed. Nor is it conducive to building the pluralist, solidary ethos that an
inclusive livelihood agenda requires.

US CATHOLICS, LIVELIHOOD,
AND RACIAL SOLIDARITY IN
THE TWENTY-FIRST CENTURY

What does recent Catholic teaching offer that might help us understand and
address these dilemmas—and in what ways have the blindness of US Catholic

leadership and social teaching helped to maintain them? When it appeared in 1979, *Brothers and Sisters to Us (BSTU)* was the most astute, forceful anti-racist statement that the US Catholic bishops had ever issued. Several key elements of *BSTU*'s analysis of racism give it enduring salience.[165] First, the letter framed racism in strongly theological and spiritual terms as a profound evil, a sinful affront to the image of God in all persons: "Racism is not merely one sin among many; it is a radical evil that divides the human family and denies the new creation of a redeemed world." Because the evil of racism is deep-seated, "to struggle against it means an equally radical transformation, in our own minds and hearts as well as in the structure of our society."[166]

Second, the bishops describe racism in complex personal, cultural, and institutional terms. Overtly expressed in prejudiced attitudes and speech, consciously biased behavior or violent acts, racism also permeates culture and society in ways that are "systemic, subtle, and covert."[167] Despite genuine progress in US race relations, the bishops point to "an unresolved racism that permeates our society's structures and resides in the hearts of many among the majority." Because it is less blatant, this "subtle form of racism is in some respects even more dangerous—harder to combat and easier to ignore." Covert racism "manifests in the tendency to stereotype and marginalize whole segments of the population whose presence is perceived as a threat. It is manifest also in the indifference that replaces open hatred."[168]

Finally, the bishops explicitly connected racial and economic injustice, declaring, "Racism and economic oppression are distinct but interrelated forces which dehumanize our society. Movement toward authentic justice demands a simultaneous attack on both evils." Presciently, the bishops observed that "our economic structures are undergoing fundamental changes which threaten to intensify social inequalities in our nation." And in an era of economic instability and anxiety, the poor and racial minorities are especially vulnerable to harm. Tightening economic pressures "exacerbate racism, particularly where poor white people are competing with minorities for limited job opportunities." This being the case, "We must fight for the dual goals of racial and economic justice with determination and creativity."[169]

This document's analysis of racism's dimensions and sinfulness superseded by miles Ryan's tepid treatment four decades earlier. Yet while it inspired action by some white Catholics and clergy, overall, *Brothers and Sisters to Us* was a flop. Its primary intended audience—white Catholics—scarcely noticed its appearance, and its impact was correspondingly scant. Reviewing *BSTU*'s lackluster reception and anemic outcomes in 2010, Black Catholic ethicist Bryan Massingale drew the undeniable conclusion: the US Catholic community's responses to even their leaders' most eloquent calls to confront racism have been, much like Ryan's responses years earlier, singularly devoid of passion.[170]

But why? Massingale finds one clue embedded in the title of the 1979 document: the implied "us" in "Brothers and Sisters to Us"—both leaders and members—is "we white Catholics."[171] In their thoughtless elision of "Catholic" and "white," the bishops ignored and marginalized millions of faithful nonwhite Catholics, while performing one of the hallmarks of white privilege: blithe ignorance that one is participating in it.[172] Massingale also points to three major deficiencies in the bishops' approach: it is not informed by sustained social analysis of the phenomenon of racism; its theological and ethical arguments against racism are weak; and "third and perhaps most importantly, 'the bishops developed no formal plan for implementing the teachings and exhortations of the document.'"[173] Building on advances made by some individual bishops in subsequent pastoral letters on race, the national bishops' conference in 2018 published a new document, *Open Wide Our Hearts*, that attempts, with a degree of success, to do better on all three of these fronts.[174] But in the eyes of many Catholic theologians and laity, the new document still fell badly short.[175]

By 2019, US Catholics' racial demographics were undeniably trending less white: Whereas "in 1987 U.S. Catholics were 85% white, 10% Hispanic, and 5% black or other," by 2014, "white U.S. Catholics numbered 58%, Latinos 34%, and black/other 8%." But in its leadership and power structures the US Catholic Church remained what it had been throughout its history: a predominantly white institution.[176] White Catholics' blindness to this fact concealed their church's—and their own—possessive investment in whiteness. Jeff Lustig's earlier observation holds true for white Catholics during this period: while most may not be conscious racists, "in the absence of a larger vision or shared purpose whites oppose any effort to devalue these investments."[177]

Over their history in the United States, Euro-American Catholics and their church have regularly traded the larger vision and demands of the Gospel for a share in the privileges bestowed by an American identity that has required being white. During the period we are studying, a Euro-American majority habitually allowed its attachment to whiteness to trump core tenets of the Catholic social justice tradition. Human dignity, the common good, solidarity—even solidarity with the most vulnerable—were conceived in racialized terms that made whites central, and that drained these principles of their power either to call white Catholics' racism to account or to provide a mandate and direction for dismantling white supremacy in its ecclesial, social, and economic aspects.

As noted, for working- and lower-middle-class whites, the post-1973 years were a time of growing animus against arrogant, amoral, and irreligious "liberal elites"; and against what they perceived as undeserving minorities and foreigners, with whom "limousine liberals" indulged in shows of faux solidarity while hard-working, law-abiding (white, Christian) families were ignored, derided, and further disadvantaged.[178] Overall, white Catholics followed these same attitudinal trends. Beginning in 1980 as "Reagan Democrats," non-elite white Catholics' political allegiances shifted steadily toward the Republican party.[179] In the 2000s, surveys recorded increasingly negative views on racial issues among white Republicans, including Catholics. Although Obama won the *overall* Catholic vote in 2008 and 2012, strong majorities of *white* Catholics twice voted for his Republican opponent.[180] And in 2016, white Catholics cast their votes for Trump by a 23-percent margin.[181]

Why, as Christians called to neighborly love and as descendants of groups who themselves historically experienced racialized social and economic marginalization and discrimination, have white US Catholics been so lacking in solidarity with communities of color struggling for respect and inclusion in US civic and economic life?[182] One reason is surely the lure of the wages of whiteness, combined with the "amnesic power" whiteness confers.[183] In the United States, citizenship, economic livelihood, and the components of a good living—for instance, access to homeownership in a "good" neighborhood—all were painted in hues of white. And after 1973, white working-class Catholics' economic and social anxieties made them susceptible to new forms of identity politics laced with nativist and antiglobalist sentiments.

CONCLUSION

The complex history sketched in this chapter—and the vast literature that surrounds it—makes it clear that cultivating racially reconciling economic solidarity requires learning to navigate difficult terrain. Political theorist Jodi Dean proposes that to advance this tricky agenda, our practices of solidarity must be "reflective."[184] Reflective solidarity obliges political interlocutors, as they think and talk through their own conflicts and differences, to habitually ask: what specific groups does the dialogue or negotiation at hand risk ignoring or excluding? Copeland, meanwhile, calls for an incarnational solidarity, emphasizing actual, embodied encounters with excluded or oppressed others, and engaging in concrete, collaborative action for the common good.[185] In politics shaped by these forms of solidary practice, people with differing identities and conflicting economic interests will disagree and contest, but will strive to do so with respect, humility, mutual accountability, and an attentive ear to voices on the periphery.

While acknowledging the "security, belonging, and self-respect" that particular group identities can provide, practicing reflective, racially reconciling solidarity also demands reaching across group boundaries to forge larger narratives that can connect interdependent people and groups, while respecting their ineluctable differences. "Rather than basing the strength of our association on our common experiences of pain and oppression, or tradition and affection," Dean writes, this deeper solidarity "anchors it in our ability to recognize each other as mysterious, inviolate, and worthy of respect." By providing a trustworthy foundation of mutual regard, such bonds "allow us to assert and contest the claims each raises as we attempt to come to understanding," in different times and circumstances, about what being authentically American (and authentically human) means and requires.[186]

As chapter 7 will further discuss, there are places where this bridge building is happening today, including in parishes, schools, neighborhoods, and community coalitions where cross-racial relationships are being formed, racism's legacy confronted, and equitable, neighborly bonds nurtured. In addition, beginning in 2014 two specific trajectories have emerged addressing the social and especially the *economic* legacy of slaveholding and its long aftermath. First, attention began to be paid by some Catholic institutions to Catholics' historical complicity in the sins of slaveocracy, including the buying, owning, and selling of enslaved human beings. In one notable example, Georgetown University's Slavery Project has exposed the ways nineteenth-century Jesuit colleges were financed in part through funds raised from the sale of enslaved men, women, and children owned by priests of the Society of Jesus. An 1838 contract of sale between Georgetown Jesuit father Thomas Mulledy and the Louisiana buyers reads in part:

> Thomas F. Mulledy sells to Jesse Beatty and Henry Johnson two hundred and seventy two negroes, to wit:—Isaac, a man sixty five years of age, Charles, his eldest son, forty years of age, Nelly his daughter, thirty eight years of age, Henny, a girl thirteen years of age, Cecilia, a girl eight years of age, Ruthy, a girl six years of age, Patrick a man thirty five years of age, Letty, his wife, thirty years of age, Cornelius, thirteen years of age, Francis, a boy twelve years of age, Susan, a girl of ten. . . . [The buyers] agree on their part to pay to Thomas F. Mulledy for the said negroes, the sum of one hundred & fifteen thousand dollars . . . on delivery . . . It is further stipulated, that [if] the said negroes herein named shall be of different ages from that affixed to their names, and

their value thereby impaired, or shall be unhealthy, or in any manner unsound, a fair deduction shall be made for such difference in age, or for such defects as shall lessen their value; and if the parties shall not agree as to the amount to be deducted, the question shall be submitted for decision to two arbitrators.[187]

Today, the chilling and shameful historical realities to which these legal documents attest cry out to white Catholics and Americans for acknowledgement, repentance, and repair. Georgetown leaders and students have taken initial steps in this direction: publicly acknowledging the university's slaveholding history; stripping Jesuit slaveholders' names from campus buildings; researching, making contact with, and offering public apologies to the descendants of the enslaved people sold by the Jesuits; and in conversation with descendants, creating reparative programs such as offering college tuition.

In a second instance, Coates's 2014 *Atlantic* essay, mentioned earlier, helped sparked the most serious public conversation since the Civil War on the matter of reparations for the wider, compounding economic harms—what Coates calls "theft" and "plunder"—inflicted on generations of African Americans up to the twentieth century. As Coates reflects in a 2019 interview, progress on this front has barely begun, but the fact that publicly raising the subject of reparations no longer evokes only laughter and jokes, he avers, signifies a step forward.[188]

The journey through the United States' racially fraught history and toward reconciling forms of civic and economic solidarity is complicated, arduous, slow, and uneven. It requires believers and citizens willing to make long-haul commitments to racial literacy and to the work of respectful bridge building across entrenched and painful racial divides, and civic and religious communities who educate for and strive to practice reconciling solidarity amid differences. Difficult and messy though it is, this work is both necessary and a *bonum honestum*, an authentic human good. And it is work that those who pursue a twenty-first-century livelihood agenda in the key of radical sufficiency must intentionally and steadfastly undertake.

NOTES

1. Joe Podles, interview by Michael Tiranoff, August 9, 1979, archives, Mullen Library, Catholic University of America, Washington, DC, https://cuomeka.wrlc.org/exhibits /show/howmuch/documents/hm-doc1. Cf. Lewis Hine's photographs of children and families performing these jobs in the 1900s: "Teaching with Documents: Photographs of

Lewis Hine: Documentation of Child Labor," National Archives, https://www.archives
.gov/education/lessons/hine-photos#documents.

2. On the politicized nature of "racial identifications," demonstrated via studies of US census categories between 1850 and 1930, see Hochschild and Powell, "Racial Reorganization and the United States Census, 1850–1930," 59–96.

3. Berger, "Red," 593.

4. Berger, 656.

5. This evolution in relation to workplace law, e.g., is discussed in Carbado and Gulati, "Law and Economics of Critical Race Theory."

6. See Allen, *Invention of the White Race*, and Fields and Fields, *Racecraft*.

7. Cited in Young, *Justice and the Politics of Difference*, 131.

8. Susan J. Stabile, "Othering and the Law," 382. "Othering" is a process by which the determination that certain people are "not us" creates "a devalued and dehumanized Other" from whom one can affectively and morally distance. Stabile cites Todres, "Law, Otherness, and Human Trafficking," 605.

9. Memmi, *Racism*, 180. Clarkson, "Tribal Bondage," 75, 78, employs Memmi's definition of racism and postcolonial theorist Homi Bhabha's notion of "colonial discourse" as an apparatus of power whose object is "to justify conquest and to establish systems of administration and instruction." Homi K. Bhabha, "Other Question," 101.

10. For racism as a social process to operate, (1) a difference—real or invented—must be singled out and emphasized; (2) a negative valuation on the difference must be made by one group against the "different" other; and (3) the valuation must be systematically deployed, through discourse and practice, to the power and privilege advantage of one group over and against another. Memmi, *Racism*, 184.

11. Memmi, 23.

12. Hannah Arendt articulates something similar concerning the modern origins of "race-thinking." Denike, "Scapegoat Racism," 124, citing Arendt, *Origins of Totalitarianism*, 158, 160–61.

13. Memmi, *Racism*, 23, 119–21.

14. Memmi, 55.

15. Memmi, 92–93. Group differences of any sort can be used in the hostile othering that "racism" describes; Memmi describes isomorphisms between racism and other forms of oppression such as sexism, ableism, classism, and homophobia.

16. Barbara J. Fields and Karen E. Fields, "How Race is Conjured," interview by Jason Farbman, *Jacobin*, June 29, 2015, https://www.jacobinmag.com/2015/06/karen-barbara-fields-racecraft-dolezal-racism/.

17. Young, *Justice and the Politics of Difference*, 131, citing Giddens, *Constitution of Society*, 79.

18. These attitudes were bolstered by natural law theories intended to legitimate chattel slavery and white supremacy. These theories expose "a menacing vulnerability of natural law, at least when it is applied in a racially bigoted context. . . . Natural law theory in the hands of subjugating power can become a dangerous tool. For it serves to justify unjust structures, and thus it sanctifies an oppressive status quo." Douglas, *Stand Your Ground*, 56.

19. Harris, "Whiteness as Property," citing Ansley, "Stirring the Ashes," 1024n129.

20. A June 2016 Pew Research report documents sharp differences between white and Black Americans' views on progress (or lack thereof) toward racial equity. Pew Research Center, "On Views of Race and Inequality, Blacks and Whites are Worlds Apart," June 27,

2016, https://www.pewsocialtrends.org/2016/06/27/on-views-of-race-and-inequality
-blacks-and-whites-are-worlds-apart/. Cf. political scientist Tesler, *Post-Racial or Most-Racial*, esp. chs. 7–9.

21. Baldwin, "White Man's Guilt," 410.

22. Berger, "Red," 602.

23. Berger, 605. Hill Fletcher, *Sin of White Supremacy*, examines historical connections between Christianity and white supremacy in North America.

24. The 1776 committee's (Thomas Jefferson, John Adams, and Benjamin Franklin) original proposal for the Great Seal's design is telling: "First Great Seal Committee – July 1776," GreatSeal.com, http://www.greatseal.com/committees/firstcomm/.

25. Jacobson, *Whiteness of a Different Color*, 26ff. Allen, *Invention*, vol. 1, labels this inadvertence in most accounts of US history "the Great White Blind Spot."

26. Douglas, *Stand Your Ground*, locs. 1544–46. Cf. Douglas, locs. 425–28, citing Horsman, *Race and Manifest Destiny*. This myth did not go entirely unquestioned; see, e.g., Detweiler, "Anglo-Saxon Myth in the United States," 183–89.

27. Douglas, *Stand Your Ground*, locs. 396–97.

28. Harris, "Whiteness as Property," 1737: "At the individual level, recognizing oneself as 'white' necessarily assumes premises based on white supremacy . . . privileging 'white' as unadulterated, exclusive, and rare. Black 'blood'—including the infamous 'one drop'—consigned a person to being 'Black' and evoked the metaphor of purity and contamination."

29. Douglas, *Stand Your Ground*, loc. 812. Harris, "Whiteness as Property," 1716.

30. Denike refers to Charles Mills's use of "racial contract" in "Scapegoat Racism," 121–22, citing Mills, *Racial Contract*, 14.

31. Berger, "Red," 617.

32. Berger, 603.

33. Berger, 600.

34. Berger, 655–56.

35. Berger, 591. See also Wallis, *America's Original Sin*.

36. Fletcher, "How Race Enters Class," 37, referring to the work of Manning Marable.

37. The term "white race" and its assumptive superiority arises in context of sixteenth- and seventeenth-century colonialism. Irene Silverblatt traces its emergence in Latin America, illustrating with the 1648 work by Rev. Francisco de Avila, *Tratado de los evangelios*, in Silverblatt, *Modern Inquisitions*, 99–116.

38. Cheryl Gilkes underscores Robert Blauner's distinction between immigrant and colonized minorities in "Storm and the Light," 195.

39. Harris, "Whiteness as Property," 1720, emphasis added.

40. Harris, 1720.

41. Douglas, *Stand Your Ground*, locs. 777–80.

42. Douglas, locs. 2378–90. See Wilkinson and Pickett, *Spirit Level*, 51–52, citing Tocqueville, *Democracy in America*, 371, 650, 400.

43. Tocqueville, ch. 18, "The Future of the Three Races in the United States."

44. Douglas, *Stand Your Ground*, locs. 1416–17; cf. locs. 1349–51.

45. Douglas, locs. 1349–51. On the guilty Black body, see also Muhammad, *Condemnation of Blackness*.

46. Ta-Nehisi Coates, "The Case for Reparations," *Atlantic*, June 2014, http://www.the atlantic.com/magazine/archive/2014/06/the-case-for-reparations/361631/.

47. On the history of racism and the US Catholic Church, see Stevens, "Challenging the Catholic Church," esp. ch. 2.

48. Jacobson, *Whiteness of a Different Color*, 8, 23–24. The exclusion of not only Native and African Americans but Americans of Spanish lineage from this "original stock" ideology is telling.

49. Jacobson, 8–13. In the first decade of the twentieth century, for instance, an average of two hundred thousand Italians entered the United States each year. The 1924 Act reset the annual quota for Italians to less than four thousand. Asians, including Indians, had been completely excluded decades earlier by the Chinese Exclusion Acts in the late 1880s—laws that remained in force till the 1960s. "Who Was Shut Out? Immigration Quotas, 1925–1927," History Matters, http://historymatters.gmu.edu/d/5078/, citing *Statistical Abstract of the United States*, 100.

50. Roediger, *Working toward Whiteness*, 18.

51. Roediger, 12. In a 1923 Supreme Court decision concerning the immigration appeal of a "high-caste Hindu" from India, *United States v. Bhagat Singh Thind*, Chief Justice Sutherland denied the appeal because "free white persons," in common understanding, connoted peoples whose physical distinctiveness could over time be assimilated into "whiteness," which did not apply to Indians.

52. Jacobson, *Whiteness of a Different Color*, 8.

53. Orsi, *Madonna of 115th Street*, 161.

54. Roediger, *Working toward Whiteness*, 184–93.

55. Roediger, 191.

56. Roediger, 190, 193.

57. On links among purity codes, racism, and inequality, see Firer Hinze, "Dirt and Economic Inequality," 45–62.

58. Berger, "Red," 529, 628, emphasis added.

59. Berger, 593–94, cites historian (later president) Theodore Roosevelt in 1899: "The rude, fierce settler who drives the savage from the land lays all civilized mankind under a debt to him. . . . [I]t is of incalculable importance that America, Australia, and Siberia should pass out of the hands of their red, black, and yellow aboriginal owners, and become the heritage of the dominant world races."

60. Berger, 629. The policy was meant to open reservation land to white settlement, but US officials regarded it as "inspired by the highest motives" and "as a panacea which would make restitution to the Indian for all that the white man had done to him in the past." In truth, Berger contends, the law was "a mighty pulverizing engine for breaking up the tribal mass" and "separating the individual from the tribe."

61. Berger, "Red," 630. Cf. studies like Adams, *Education for Extinction*.

62. Berger, 639.

63. Foner and Brown, *Forever Free*, 64–65, 77–78.

64. Oklahoma District Judge Caruthers's 1911 jury instructions in a lynching investigation demonstrate racist assumptions' sway among even justice-minded officials: "The people of the state have recently said, by adopted constitutional provision, that the race to which the unfortunate victims belonged should in large measure be divorced from participation in our political contests, because of their known racial inferiority and their dependent credulity. . . . All the more, then, does the duty devolve upon us of a superior race and of greater intelligence to protect this weaker race from unjustifiable and lawless attacks." James Allen and John Littlefield, *Without Sanctuary: Photographs and Postcards*

of Lynching in America. https://withoutsanctuary.org/. See too the 1919 Jackson, Mississippi, newspaper announcing the preplanned lynching and burning of John Hartfield. "A Lynching Survivor Returns," Equal Justice Initiative, September 18, 2015, https://eji.org /news/lynching-survivor-mamie-lang-kirkland-returns-to-mississippi.

65. Close friends of Wells were lynched after their Atlanta grocery store began to take Black business away from local white merchants. Henry Louis Gates Jr., *Life upon These Shores,* 175–76. See also Megan Ming Francis, "Ida B. Wells and the Economics of Racial Violence," *Items: Insights from the Social Sciences* (blog), Social Science Research Council, January 24, 2017, https://items.ssrc.org/reading-racial-conflict/ida-b-wells-and-the -economics-of-racial-violence/. Cf. Francis, *Civil Rights,* ch. 2.

66. Cf. Glenn, *Unequal Freedom,* "From Servitude to Service Work."

67. See Gates, *Life upon These Shores,* 189, 198–202, 230–35.

68. "One ever feels his twoness—an American, a Negro; two souls, two thoughts, two unreconciled strivings." Du Bois, *Souls of Black Folk,* 3. In 2019 Ibram Kendi argued that "what Du Bois termed double consciousness may be more precisely termed *dueling* consciousness." Kendi, *How to be an Antiracist,* 29.

69. Roediger, *Wages of Whiteness,* 11–13, citing Du Bois, *Black Reconstruction,* 700–701.

70. Roediger, *Wages of Whiteness,* 13.

71. "White men often defined their identity as citizens in terms of being not black and not women." Forbath, "Caste, Class, and Equal Citizenship," cited in Glenn, *Unequal Freedom,* 29.

72. Harris, "Whiteness as Property," 1993n4, citing Myrdal, *American Dilemma,* 183. Lemann, *Promised Land,* 70.

73. Jones, *Labor of Love.* Cf. Banks, "Uplifting the Race through Domesticity."

74. Jones, *Labor of Love,* 187, 188.

75. Harris, "Whiteness as Property," 1710–12, recounts the story of her Mississippi grandmother's migration to Chicago in the 1930s. A divorced mother, she held a family-supporting department store job—but only because she was sufficiently light-skinned to be able to "pass" as white. "Accepting the risk of self-annihilation was the only way to survive."

76. Jones, *Labor of Love,* 153.

77. Janelle Jones, "The Racial Wealth Gap: How African-Americans have been Shortchanged out of the Materials to Build Wealth," *Working Economics Blog* (blog), Economic Policy Institute, February 13, 2017, https://www.epi.org/blog/the-racial-wealth-gap-how -african-americans-have-been-shortchanged-out-of-the-materials-to-build-wealth/. Cf. Algernon Austin, "Three Lessons about Black Poverty," Economic Policy Institute, September 18, 2009, https://www.epi.org/publication/the_lessons_of_black_poverty/.

78. Jones, *Labor of Love,* 154.

79. Jones, 133.

80. For instance, Glenn, *Unequal Freedom,* 44–45, cites an 1871 Supreme Court case *Bradwell v. Illinois,* which upheld the denial of a law license to Myra Bradwell.

81. Jones, *Labor of Love,* 187. Cf. Clark-Lewis, *Living In, Living Out.*

82. See Palmer, *Domesticity and Dirt,* x–xiii; ch. 7; Firer Hinze, "Dirt and Economic Inequality."

83. Jones, *Labor of Love,* 182.

84. Mary Church Terrell, "What it Means to be Colored in the Capital of the United States," lecture, 1906, *New York Independent,* January 24, 1907, https://loa-shared.s3.amazonaws .com/static/pdf/Terrell_What_It_Means.pdf.

85. See Muhammad, *Condemnation of Blackness*, chs. 1, 2; Alexander, *New Jim Crow*; also Logan, *Good Punishment*.

86. Cf. Francis, "Ida B. Wells and the Economics of Racial Violence"; see also Gates, *Life upon These Shores*, 175–76, 257–58.

87. Denike, "Scapegoat Racism," 120. Cf. Urbina and Alvarez, eds., *Ethnicity and Criminal Justice*; O'Connell, *If These Walls Could Talk*, chs. 9–11.

88. Albrecht, "Forget Your Right to Work," 125, citing Dorrien, *Reconstructing the Common Good*, 45–47.

89. Albrecht, "Forget Your Right to Work," 125, citing Robert Wagner quoted in Dubofsky, *State and Labor in Modern America*, 119.

90. Albrecht, "Forget Your Right to Work," 125.

91. Trotter, "Perspectives on Black Working-Class History," 2. Adapted from Trotter, *From a Raw Deal to a New Deal*.

92. Trotter, "Perspectives on Black Working-Class History," 3–5, 6.

93. Trotter, 3.

94. Trotter, 7–10.

95. John A. Ryan, "The Place of the Negro in American Society," lecture, Howard University, March 2, 1943, archives, Catholic University of America, https://cuomeka.wrlc.org /files/original/778bc0967ca0d94c09b6c5716ee990a3.pdf. In an edgy interview with Ryan published by the *Baltimore Afro-American* (featuring a photograph of Ryan in full ecclesial regalia, delivering his Howard lecture three weeks prior), reporter Michael Carter exposes Ryan's unreflective racial biases, to cringeworthy effect. See Michael Carter, "Colored Girls May Not Live in Catholic University Dorms," *Baltimore Afro-American*, March 1943, Catholic University Archives, https://cuomeka.wrlc.org/files/original /e0106799f3edfc8707e841b6d61a71f4.pdf.

96. Roediger, *Working toward Whiteness*, 230. Cf. Sugrue, *Origins of the Urban Crisis*, esp. ch. 9.

97. Roediger, *Working toward Whiteness*, 224–25. Coates also discusses this history.

98. Roediger, *Working toward Whiteness*, 230–31. "Thus while helping the descendants of new immigrants get more favorable credit and cheaper homes, the FHA and VA also directed them away from the mixed urban areas containing immigrant neighborhoods and ethnic institutions." Suburbanizing Catholic families were part of these trends.

99. Roediger, *Working toward Whiteness*, 243.

100. Sugrue, *Origins of the Urban Crisis*, 11–19.

101. Glenn, "Racial Ethnic Women's Labor," 92. See also Glenn, "From Servitude to Service Work."

102. Glenn, *Unequal Freedom*, 75, citing Gwendolyn Mink, *Wages of Motherhood*, 49–52; Kerber, *No Constitutional Right to be Ladies*, 47–80. In the Jim Crow South, vagrancy laws were also routinely used to incarcerate, and then extract forced unpaid labor from, poor Black men.

103. Glenn, *Unequal Freedom*, 76, citing Martha May and others. Wolcott, *Remaking Respectability*, 8; and Attfield, "Rejecting Respectability," 48, identify "respectability" as a trope in African American rhetoric around these issues.

104. US Census Bureau, "Real Median Income by Race and Hispanic Origin: 1967 to 2016," https://www.census.gov/content/dam/Census/library/visualizations/2017/demo /p60- 259/figure1.pdf; personal anecdotes related to the author.

105. These personal anecdotes are stories related to me by my own family and neighbors in Detroit when I was growing up.

106. See McGreevy, *Parish Boundaries*; Massingale, *Racial Justice*. On the history and contributions of African American Catholics since their 1565 arrival in Saint Augustine, Florida, see Davis, *History of Black Catholics*.

107. In 1957, "Daisy and Bill Myers, the first black family to move into Levittown, Pennsylvania, were greeted with protests and a burning cross. A neighbor who opposed the family said that Bill Myers was 'probably a nice guy, but every time I look at him I see $2,000 drop off the value of my house.' The neighbor had good reason to be afraid, [as] housing policy almost guaranteed that [the Myers'] neighbors' property values would decline." Coates, "Case for Reparations."

108. Black Catholics among the working-class families who moved to northern cities were most often relegated to separate parishes serving Black congregants. Black Catholics' numbers increased through migration and conversion but remained dwarfed by large European ethnic Catholic communities in the urban North. See McGreevy, *Parish Boundaries*, ch. 2; Cressler, *Authentically Black and Truly Catholic*, chs. 1–3.

109. Putnam "E Pluribus Unum," describes the phenomenon of "hunkering down" in identity groups as a typical initial response to diversifying communities; in racially changing communities, this strategy can prove more permanent than transitional.

110. Roediger, *Working toward Whiteness*, 223.

111. Roediger, 224–34.

112. Monkkonen, *America Becomes Urban*, 205, citing the ethnography of Oliver Zunz, *Changing Faces of Inequality*.

113. See Roediger, *Colored White*, 180. Later twentieth-century Euro-Americans began to rediscover and celebrate in their own ethnic histories and roots. Jacobson, *Roots Too*.

114. In the early twenty-first century, some white US Catholic theologians and ethicists undertook sustained research and self-reflection on racial privilege. See, e.g., Cassidy and Mikulich, eds., *Interrupting White Privilege*; Hill Fletcher, *Sin of White Supremacy*.

115. Ryan, "Place of the Negro," 8. McGreevy, *Parish Boundaries*, ch. 7, describes pushback from some Howard faculty in response to Ryan's address. Cf. Michael Carter's *Baltimore Afro-American* article referenced above, note 95.

116. Massingale, *Racial Justice*, ch. 2, details this history of episcopal inattention to racism, including in the US Bishops' major 1986 pastoral on the economy, *Economic Justice for All*.

117. Gavin Clarkson analyzes racism's role in native tribal struggles to attain economic livelihood within the US regime in "Tribal Bondage."

118. Berger, "Red," 650–51, citing Lac du Flambeau Band of Lake Superior Chippewa Indians v. Stop Treaty Abuse Wis., 843 F. Supp. 1284, 1289 (W.D. Wis. 1994), at 1294.

119. Berger, "Red," 650–51.

120. Berger, 652.

121. E.g., Equal Justice Initiative, "Lynching in America: Confronting the Legacy of Racial Terror," https://lynchinginamerica.eji.org/. Public Religion Research Institute polling in 2016 found that roughly six in ten Black (62 percent) and Hispanic (57 percent) Americans said American society has changed for the better since the 1950s; strikingly, a majority of white Americans said the opposite. See Cooper, Cox, Lienesch, and Jones, *Divide over America's Future*.

122. William Thompson, Joseph Hickey et al., *Focus*, 256. Cf. extensive data on racial economic disparities in 2014 in Pew Research Center, "Demographic Trends and Economic Well-Being," June 27, 2016, https://www.pewsocialtrends.org/2016/06/27/1-demographic-trends-and-economic-well-being/.

123. Snarr, "Religion, Race, and Bridge Building," 75–76. Hispanic, African American, and Native American families also show greater levels of "multidimensional poverty" (low incomes, unemployment, poor educational opportunities, and other factors). See Reeves, Kneebone, and Rodrigue, *Five Evils*.

124. In 2011, poverty rates for American Indians and Alaska Natives were 26.4 percent, compared to 11 percent of whites. Austin, "Native Americans and Jobs." See also Valerie Wilson, "2013 ACS Shows Depth of Native American Poverty and Different Degrees of Economic Well-Being for Asian Ethnic Groups," *Working Economics Blog*, Economic Policy Institute, September 18, 2014, https://www.epi.org/blog/2013-acs-shows-depth-native-american-poverty/.

125. Described in Glenn, *Unequal Freedom*, inter alia. See also Moore, "Social Fabric of the Hispanic Community," 6. Between 1960 and 1990, the Hispanic population grew to 22 million, increasing by 53%—7.6 million—between 1980 and 1990.

126. Moore, "Social Fabric of the Hispanic Community," 6–7, 15.

127. Jensen, *Responsive Labor*, 5–7, cf. 130n11.

128. Between 2009 and 2011, the American Indian employment rate among twenty-five-to-fifty-four-year-olds (i.e., the share of that population with a job) was 64.7 percent—13.4 percentage points lower than the white rate, with unemployment rates for prime workforce-age men ranging from a high of 73.4 percent (Nebraska) to a low of 54.8 percent (South Dakota). The overall unemployment rate for prime-working-age Native Americans during this period was over double that for whites (14.6 vs. 7.7 percent). Austin, "Native Americans and Jobs."

129. Seth Wessler, "Race and Recession: Report 2009," Race Forward, May 18, 2009, https://www.raceforward.org/research/reports/race-and-recession-report. Wessler cites Austin, "Three Lessons about Black Poverty."

130. Snarr, "Religion, Race, and Bridge Building," 75. "Foreign-Born Workers Made 83.1 Percent of the Earnings of Their Native-Born Counterparts in 2016," *TED: The Economics Daily* (blog), Bureau of Labor Statistics, May 24, 2017, https://www.bls.gov/opub/ted/2017/foreign-born-workers-made-83-point-1-percent-of-the-earnings-of-their-native-born-counterparts-in-2016.htm.

131. Moore, "Social Fabric of the Hispanic Community," 7.

132. Wessler, "Race and Recession," 19, citing Bureau of Labor Statistics, "2009 Current Population Survey," 2009, https://www.bls.gov/cps/cps_aa2009.htm.

133. Friedman and Rosenbaum, "Does Suburban Residence." See also Benjamin, *Searching for Whitopia*. On the self-fulfilling consequences of white homeowners' belief that once a critical mass of Black or Latinx residents moves into a neighborhood, housing values will fall, see, e.g., Wilson and Taub, *There Goes the Neighborhood*.

134. Federal Reserve Survey of Consumer Finance, 2007, cited in Wessler, "Race and Recession." Cf. Wheary and Shapiro, *Downslide before the Downturn*. For recent data see Asante-Muhammed, Collins, Hoxie, and Nieves, *Road to Zero Wealth*.

135. Lani Guinier, "Race and Reality in a Front-Porch Encounter," *Chronicle of Higher Education*, July 30, 2009, https://www.chronicle.com/article/RaceReality-in-a/47509/. Michael D. Tanner makes similar points from a libertarian perspective in *Inclusive Economy*, ch. 2.

136. Copeland, *Enfleshing Freedom*, 66, citing Winant, *New Politics of Race*, 131.

137. Copeland, *Enfleshing Freedom*, 67.

138. Ibram X. Kendi, "What the Racial Data Show," *Atlantic*, April 6, 2020, https://www.theatlantic.com/ideas/archive/2020/04/coronavirus-exposing-our-racial-divides

/609526/. Max Fisher and Emma Bubola, "As Coronavirus Deepens Inequality, Inequality Worsens Its Spread," *New York Times*, updated March 16, 2020, https://www.nytimes.com/2020/03/15/world/europe/coronavirus-inequality.html.

139. See, e.g., McConahay, Hardee, and Batts, "Has Racism Declined."

140. A brief review of this progress is Dusty Sklar, "Is Racism Really in Decline?" *Jewish Currents*, January 30, 2017, https://jewishcurrents.org/is-racism-actually-in-decline/.

141. Denike, "Scapegoat Racism," 12.

142. Ta-Nehisi Coates, "This Town Needs a Better Class of Racist," *Atlantic*, May 14, 2014, cited in M. Shawn Copeland, "Black Theology and a Legacy of Oppression," *America*, June 24, 2014, https://www.americamagazine.org/faith/2014/06/24/black-theology-and-legacy-oppression.

143. Young, *Justice and the Politics of Difference*, 134.

144. Copeland, *Enfleshing Freedom*, 68–69, 73, citing Bonilla-Silva, *Racism without Racists*, 25–31, 48, 265.

145. See, e.g., Fletcher and Gapasin, *Solidarity Divided*, ch. 7.

146. Jensen, *Responsive Labor*, 7, referring to studies by William Julius Wilson and others.

147. Payne, *Broken Ladder*, 168.

148. So, "as one competes for jobs in a scarce economy, solidarity with the unemployed gradually slips away." Work, Dorothy Soelle writes, "'becomes a commodity some persons possess and others do not.'" Jensen, *Responsive Labor*, 5, citing Soelle, *To Work and to Love*, 69.

149. See, e.g., Gilens, *Why Americans Hate Welfare*; Neubeck and Cazenave, *Welfare Racism*; Quadagno, *One Nation, Uninsured*.

150. Payne, *Broken Ladder*, 174.

151. Payne, 174–75.

152. Wise, *Between Barack and a Hard Place*, 24.

153. See, e.g., Raines and Day-Lower, *Modern Work and Human Meaning*; Williams, *White Working Class*.

154. Victor Tan Chen describes the post-1970s deterioration and loss of an entire, working-class "moral economy," which comprised social supports, faith, marriage, and workers' union-supported security and voice on the job. Chen, "All Hollowed Out: The Lonely Poverty of America's White Working Class," *Atlantic*, January 2016, https://www.theatlantic.com/business/archive/2016/01/white-working-class-poverty/424341/.

155. See Gest, *New Minority*, esp. chs. 1, 2, 7; historian Anderson, *White Rage*; and Tom Ciccotta's *Breitbart* review of Anderson (along with over three thousand revealing reader comments), "Black Professor Blames African-American Struggle on White Rage," *Breitbart*, June 22, 2016, https://www.breitbart.com/tech/2016/06/22/black-professor-blames-african-american-struggle-on-white-rage.

156. Payne, *Broken Ladder*, 120. Payne, who himself grew up in a poor rural Tennessee community, observes that "the wounds in this group seem to be largely self-inflicted. They are not dying from higher rates of heart disease or cancer. They are dying of cirrhosis of the liver, suicide, and a cycle of chronic pain and overdoses of opiates and painkillers."

157. Payne, 120–21, emphasis added.

158. E.g., Christopher Ingraham, "Two New Studies Find Racial Anxiety is the Biggest Driver of Support for Trump," *Washington Post*, June 6, 2016, https://www.washingtonpost.com/news/wonk/wp/2016/06/06/racial-anxiety-is-a-huge-driver-of-support-for-donald-trump-two-new-studies-find/.

159. Tesler, "Trump Voters Think African Americans are Much Less Deserving than 'Average Americans,'" *Huffington Post*, December 19, 2016, http://www.huffingtonpost.com /michael-tesler/trump-voters-think-africa_b_13732500.html.

160. Reader comment on Janet Adamy and Paul Overberg, "Rural America is the New 'Inner City,'" *Wall Street Journal*, May 26, 2017, https://www.wsj.com/articles/rural-america-is -the-new-inner-city-1495817008. Not unrelated are practices of "racial transposition" by the political right, discussed in Hosang and Lowndes, *Producers, Parasites, Patriots*.

161. Jacobson notes that "attention to *structures* of inequality remains one of the most potent distinctions separating the contemporary right and left" *Roots Too*, 180.

162. See, e.g., Gest, *New Minority*, 15–16, 98–101.

163. Hsu, "White Plight."

164. See Hochschild, *Strangers in Their Own Land*, chs. 1, 9. For a theological-ethical perspective on racial and class impasses, see O'Connell, *If These Walls Could Talk*.

165. US Catholic Bishops, *Brothers and Sisters to Us*.

166. US Catholic Bishops.

167. Beyer, "Continuing Relevance."

168. US Catholic Bishops, *Brothers and Sisters to Us*. For context and analysis, see Massingale, *Racial Justice*, ch. 2; Mich, *Catholic Social Teaching and Movements*, ch. 5.

169. US Catholic Bishops, *Brothers and Sisters to Us*.

170. Massingale, *Racial Justice*, 77; ch. 4. This pattern has continued, despite some bishops' efforts; e.g., Bishop Edward Braxton, "The Racial Divide in the United States: A Reflection for the World Day of Peace 2015," *Messenger*, January 1, 2015, http://bellevillemessenger .org/2014/12/bishop-braxton-writes-a-letter-on-racial-divide-in-the-united-states/; and Braxton, "Catholic Church and the Black Lives Matter Movement."

171. Massingale, *Racial Justice*, 61–70. African American church historian Cyprian Davis, OSB, provided suggestions to the *BSTU* drafters (he later recalled convincing the bishops to underscore the point that racism is a systemic, structural problem as his greatest contribution), but Davis, too, regarded *BSTU* as written by white authors (US bishops) for a white audience. Rice, *Healing the Racial Divide*, 7–9.

172. Massingale, "James Cone and Recent Catholic Episcopal Teaching on Racism." O'Connell, *If These Walls Could Talk*, 104–5, analyzes "white ways of 'not knowing'" in this regard. See Michael Pasquier, "White Catholics Have to Talk about Race and to Admit their Racism," *America: The Jesuit Review*, July 27, 2016, https://www.americamagazine .org/politics-society/2016/07/27/white-catholics-have-talk-about-race-and-admit -their-racism.

173. Massingale, *Racial Justice*, 74–77, discussed in Daniel Horan, "The Bishops' Letter Fails to Recognize that Racism is a White Problem," *National Catholic Reporter*, February 20, 2019, https://www.ncronline.org/news/opinion/faith-seeking-understanding/bishops -letter-fails-recognize-racism-white-problem.

174. US Catholic Bishops, *Open Wide our Hearts*. On individual bishops' post-1979 pastorals on racism, see Massingale, *Racial Justice*, ch. 2; also, Braxton, "Racial Divide."

175. See Horan, "Bishops' Letter"; also essays in Matthew Shadle, ed., "Symposium on *Open Wide Our Hearts*," Political Theology Network, February 15, 2019, https://political theology.com/symposium/open-wide-our-hearts/.

176. In Michael Lipka, "A Closer Look at Catholic America," *Fact Tank: News in the Numbers* (blog), Pew Research Center, September 14, 2015, https://www.pewresearch.org/fact -tank/2015/09/14/a-closer-look-at-catholic-america/. Church leadership remained

predominantly white. In 2010, "just 250 of America's 40,000 priests and only 16 of the 434 bishops in the United States" were Black; 273 (13 percent) of priests and 29 (9 percent) of active US bishops were Hispanic. Jim Graves, "Black and Catholic," *National Catholic Register*, January 6, 2012, https://www.ncregister.com/daily-news/black-and -catholic/blank.htm; US Catholic Bishops, "Hispanic Ministry at a Glance," http:// www.usccb.org/issues-and-action/cultural-diversity/hispanic-latino/demographics/ hispanic-ministry-at-a-glance.cfm.

177. Lustig, "Tangled Knot," 50; emphasis added. Lustig cites Lipsitz, *Possessive Investment in Whiteness*, vii–viii, ch. 3.

178. Fraser, *Limousine Liberal*; Jacobson, *Roots Too.*

179. As evidenced, for example, in presidential voting patterns. See Center for Applied Research on the Apostolate (CARA), "Presidential Vote of Catholics," https://cara .georgetown.edu/presidential%20vote%20only.pdf.

180. Gregory A. Smith and Jessica Martínez, "How the Faithful Voted: A Preliminary 2016 Analysis," *Fact Tank: News in the Numbers* (blog), Pew Research Center, November 9, 2016, https://www.pewresearch.org/fact-tank/2016/11/09/how-the-faithful-voted-a -preliminary-2016-analysis/.

181. E.g., Sean McElwee, "White America's Obama-era Freakout: What Research Can Tell Us about Racial Animus since 2008," *Salon*, April 17, 2016, https://www.salon.com/2016 /04/17/white_americas_obama_era_freakout_what_research_can_tell_us_about _racial_animus_since_2008/; Jon Henley, "White and Wealthy Voters Gave Victory to Donald Trump, Exit Polls Show," *Guardian*, November 9, 2016, https://www.theguardian .com/us-news/2016/nov/09/white-voters-victory-donald-trump-exit-polls.

182. The story of pre-nineteenth-century Catholics and slavery raises a different set of questions and reveals a different set of trajectories. See, e.g., Farrelly, "American Slavery, American Freedom, American Catholicism"; Dolan, *American Catholic Experience*, ch. 4.

183. Hooker, *Race and the Politics of Solidarity*, 114.

184. Dean, *Solidarity of Strangers*, 4–10.

185. Copeland, *Enfleshing Freedom.*

186. Dean, *Solidarity of Strangers*, 178.

187. Articles of agreement between Thomas F. Mulledy of Georgetown, District of Columbia, and Jesse Beatty and Henry Johnson, of the State of Louisiana, 19th June 1838, *Georgetown Slavery Archives*, Maryland Province Archives, https://slaveryarchive.georgetown .edu/exhibits/show/gallery/item/1. See also Rothman, "Reckoning with Slavery at Georgetown."

188. Coates, "Case for Reparations"; also "Ta-Nehisi Coates Revisits the Case for Reparations," interview with David Remnick, *New Yorker*, June 1, 2019, https://www .newyorker.com/news/the-new-yorker-interview/ta-nehisi-coates-revisits-the-case -for-reparations. Summer 2020 saw further developments whose outcomes remain to be seen: a nationwide crescendo of public anger, grief, and protest over police killings of unarmed Black citizens, and a dramatic rise in publicly voiced support for systemic efforts to combat cultural and institutional racism.

CHAPTER 5

Class, Inequality, and Livelihood

Does every worker and every family deserve access to a decent living? In principle, most would likely say yes. Yet in our fractious times, what realistic chance does a universal livelihood agenda have to be seriously considered, much less put into practice? What enables and impedes the bonds of economic solidarity and the political will that this would demand? Previous chapters examined how socially interpreted differences such as gender and race/ethnicity have sorted, divided, and influenced access to social and economic opportunities and power among US families. Research and experience show that relative socioeconomic position has done the same. To understand what is required to make dignified livelihood in the United States a truly inclusive matter, therefore, we also need to talk about class.

CLASS IN THE UNITED STATES

Class both emerges from and reproduces distinctions of wealth and power among groups. Most scholars agree that class is fundamentally determined by one's position in the system that produces, distributes, owns, and controls economic wealth. Lifestyle, educational attainment, or even one's job may reflect one's class position but does not constitute it. In modern capitalist economies, access to and control over social and economic capital and the influence and the power accompanying these most decisively determine class.

Ownership creates "social power over workers' lives, the nation's priorities, and the society's paths of development."[1] This makes class about more than disparities in wealth and status. "Class," writes labor economist Michael Zweig, "is about the power some people have over the lives of others and the powerlessness most people experience as a result." Further, "the heart of class is not about lifestyle. It is about economics."[2] Classes arise in "relationships of economically based social power, visible, and invisible"; and this economic power regularly translates into political and cultural influence.[3] Asymmetrical economic power places higher classes in advantageous, frequently conflictual, and often exploitative relationships with classes below them.

Catholic social teaching joins social theorists like Max Weber, Talcott Parsons, and C. Wright Mills in affirming class stratification and its significant economic foundations.[4] Also with such thinkers, modern social Catholicism disputes Marxian analyses that "see the relation between classes as inherently conflictual."[5] But whether oppositional or merely stratified, inherently or only situationally conflictual, class-based power differences make relations of inequality and oppression—in the multifaceted forms described by Iris Young—a persistent possibility and a frequent reality.[6]

Capitalist systems engender conflict between but also within classes. Here, as in many of capitalism's fundamental dynamics, writes scholar-activist Bill Fletcher, "intent is irrelevant." The capacity to divide and conquer the working class, often by exploiting racial/ethnic difference, is, Fletcher avers, "not something that has to be introduced from outside the system. It exists within the system, much like a virus."[7]

Distinguishing Classes

Class boundaries are inevitably fuzzy around the edges, and one's class position can shift. Some people are class migrants; others are class straddlers.[8] Nor is class predictive of one's every action or viewpoint. Nevertheless, our class standings locate us in our economies and societies, immerse us in distinctive cultures, school us in particular values, priorities, attitudes, and ways of behaving, and enable or constrain countless aspects of our work, family, and community lives.

Two factors—income and wealth—are most frequently used to delineate classes in the United States. In a tripartite division of lower, middle, and upper classes, tiers may be variously defined or emphasized. Theda Skocpol and Joan Williams, for instance, highlight "the missing middle," defined as the 53 percent of US households with incomes between the lowest 30 percent and the upper 20 percent (in 2019, those making between $42,000 and $131,000 per year).[9] However configured, these breakdowns are always inexact and risk eliding important economic and cultural commonalities and differences, especially between families earning at the upper and lower ends of each category. The life-worlds and concerns of "middling" families making $42,000 per year who struggle on the brink of poverty, for instance, are quite different from those of families making $131,000. By the same token, the experiences of a family making $42,000 per year may have much in common with their lower-class neighbors earning somewhat less.

With these caveats, our focus on non-elite and working-class US families argues for making more finely grained distinctions on the class spectrum. Looking additionally at educational attainment, occupational status, and control over work process, working-class scholars like Betsy Leondar-Wright distinguish four broad class categories: (1) poor/low income; (2) working class (ranging from struggling to "settled"); (3) middle (from lower-middle to professional/managerial); and (4) upper (upper-professionals to owning) classes. Writing in 2005, Leondar-Wright reports: "About two-thirds of Americans are working-class, low-income, or lower-middle-class. Fewer than one in ten Americans remains in the poverty class for a generation or more, although many working-class people spend part of their lives in poverty. About three percent of Americans belong to the owning class. Almost a third of Americans are in professional middle-class families."[10]

On an upper-middle-lower class spectrum, a vast majority of Americans locate themselves as middle class, while only small percentages self-identify as "rich/upper class" or "poor/low income." But when surveys offer the choice, US citizens since 1973 have self-identified as "working class" and "middle class" in nearly equal numbers of around 44 to 46 percent each.[11] Today, by many objective measures, a majority of US workers are experiencing conditions traditionally attributed to the working class: minimal wealth; restricted rights, respect, and autonomy in the workplace; and low job security. Add to this financial fragility—being one or two paychecks or one serious emergency away from being unable to pay one's bills—and the declaration by scholars like Zweig that the United States is now home to a "working-class majority" becomes persuasive.[12]

This broad, middling-to-working-class majority is by no means a unified community, and significant cultural and political differences obtain within its ranks. Still, class position enmeshes members in a particular set of shared structural relationships, divisions, and conflicts. Echoing Marxian themes, Zweig describes "a basic conflict in class interests that divides workers from capitalists," arising from "the way a capitalist economy organizes production, generates profit and distributes goods and services to the people."[13] By contrast, social stratification theorists distinguish between economically defined classes and social "status groups," averring that social hierarchies are importantly, but not solely, economic.[14] Most scholars do agree that, "classes are formed in the dynamics of power and wealth creation," that class categories "are by their nature a bit messy," and that "classes are more complicated, more interesting, and more real than the arbitrary income levels used to define class in the conventional wisdom."[15]

Allergy to Class Discourse

A national ethos that celebrates equality, individualism, and socioeconomic opportunity has helped to render class consciousness and discourse much less prominent in the United States than in most European countries. Historically, Americans have spurned both rigid class differences, and socialist notions of a classless society. Dominant nineteenth-century narratives portrayed the United States as a land where, unlike Europe, class was not a primary determinant of life circumstances or opportunities. Horatio Alger's popular "rags to riches"—or more accurately, poverty-to-middle-class-respectability—tales revolved around class mobility attained by a poor, young, male protagonist through a combination of "luck, pluck, and virtue" (often with assistance from a rich benefactor). In the American imaginary that Alger's stories celebrated, class boundaries were porous, and any individual could rise above humble circumstances.[16]

Over the twentieth century, public discourse around class flowed and ebbed. The Progressive and New Deal eras were marked by attention to working-class issues and the ascendance of the labor movement. Then, during the decades after World War II, a period of general prosperity conspired with Cold War anticommunism to move talk about class, often associated with Marxism, to the edges of the public stage. Amid later-century advances in civil rights and freedoms for women and racial minorities, and even during the long post-1973 period of economic stagnation for most workers, public, class-focused discourse remained sparse. In contrast to Ryan's era a century earlier, political leaders, when they mentioned class at all, spoke of a broad middle class in which the vast majority of their constituents, it seemed, were presumptively included, at least aspirationally.

"Almost everyone's middle class"

Scholar and activist Jack Metzgar examines the uses and abuses of people's predilection for "envisioning American society as made up of a sprawling middle class that includes almost everyone, all those who are neither rich nor poor."[17] While statistically inaccurate, as "an everyday way of fitting oneself into a bigger picture," this we're-mostly-middle-class vernacular is a powerful frame that, for Metzgar, expresses something "deep and abiding" in American culture that deserves a nuanced interpretation. On one hand, this vernacular honors "everybody who is not particularly distinguished, but who works hard, looks out for others (particularly their families), pulls their own weight, and does not hold themselves out to be any better than anybody else."[18] "When it refers to 'just ordinary people living ordinary lives,' just 'regular,' 'normal' folks doing the best they can," the middle-class label appeals to many Americans across social strata. Historically, "the egalitarian ethos inherent in this notion of middleness has been seen as both peculiarly American, and essential to democracy, by political sociologists from Alexis de Tocqueville to Alan Wolfe."[19] Imagining ourselves as a vast and inclusive middle class can help create an "us" across our economic differences.

On the other hand, Metzgar cautions that this unifying embrace of middleness is worth preserving only if two problems are addressed.[20] First, as Nancy Isenberg and others document, the "mostly middle-class" identification conceals the different realities of the rich and working classes, while ignoring or stigmatizing the poor.[21] Second, the "illusion of equal power and life prospects" that imbues "middleness" discourse demands critique. To call most everyone middle class "first hides the working class (by including it within the ubiquitous middle), and then forgets [the working class] is there by assuming that almost everybody is college-educated, professional, and has a reasonably comfortable standard of living—mistaking the part for the whole, substituting the small, affluent 'middle class' for the big, inclusive one."[22] In so doing, this "middle-class two-step" misidentifies and disserves large swaths of the working public. To make non-elite working families visible, we need the distinctive category "working class." But to preserve the middle-class vernacular's egalitarian intentions, Metzgar advocates "emphatically avoiding hierarchical uses that remove the 'working class' from the vernacular's moral and status inclusiveness." Citing prescient research in 2000 identifying the white working class as the "forgotten majority" in party politics, Metzgar elaborates: "The working class to which we refer is different from, not less than, the professional middle class. It refers to people ... 'whose economic interests and experience diverge fundamentally—in terms of culture, class, and history—from those of soccer moms and 'wired workers.' ... It is a complicated class with lots of differences within itself, but it is there in the middle with the rest of us, neither rich nor poor, but above all 'working.'"[23]

Our class analysis must also attend to the fact that "social classes are not all about power in the workplace. They are also about the distribution of status (shame and honor), of freedom, of opportunities, of living standards and working conditions." All of these, Metzgar adds, "have to do with the distribution of money." In terms of how money and power get dispersed across classes, he observes, "the capitalists are getting much more than they deserve or need. But so, in general, are we, the professional middle class—and as a class, we have a cultural power that even the capitalists envy." Meanwhile, "the working class generally gets much less of everything as compared to what its work contributes."[24]

Class and the American Dream

Also complicating awareness of class in this country is the American dream of upward mobility through individual effort; or as the phrase's popularizer, James Truslow Adams, described it in 1931, "That American dream of a better, richer, and happier life for all our citizens of every rank . . . with opportunity for each according to his ability or achievement."[25] We noted earlier President Bill Clinton's concise rendering in 1993 of the dream's "simple but powerful" essence: "if you work hard and play by the rules you should be given a chance to go as far as your God-given ability will take you."[26]

Recall the tenets that Jennifer Hochschild identified in this American dream credo: First, the dream is open to everyone. Second, though no one is guaranteed it, anyone who pursues it can reasonably anticipate success. Third, one achieves the dream by dint of hard work and virtue—attitudes and actions that are under one's control. Finally, success in attaining the American dream is associated in various ways with virtue.[27] In light of historical divisions of race and class, Hochschild finds this fourth tenet—a theme reaching back to Benjamin Franklin and the colonial era—especially fraught.[28]

As one of the nation's defining ideological motifs, the American dream has proven an energizing source of positivity, action, and hope for countless people. Across generations, it has bolstered a sense of agency and possibility, encouraging self-reliance, discipline, and a strong work ethic. At critical historical junctures, leaders have harnessed American dream discourse to galvanize support for agendas for justice and public progress. Its influence has persisted even in times of economic crisis, and even among Americans whose circumstances and experiences have seemed to belie it.

But as Hochschild in 1996, David Kusnet, Lawrence Mishel, and Ruy Teixeira in 2006, and Robert Putnam in 2015 have detailed across three successive decades, American dream ideology can also function negatively. For one thing, it feeds a cultural tendency to take individual credit for economic achievements and to blame only oneself for one's economic failures (and others for theirs). The dream's emphasis on individual effort and achievement conceals or denies impediments to success—often, as we have seen, linked to race, gender, or class—that are baked into economic and social structures. Further, although there have been moments when the American dream has been effectively reframed as a shared, communal project, its dominant ethos gravitates toward "each of us is on our own" far more than it does to "we are all in this together."[29] And given American proclivities to admire "big winners" who attain fabulous success while scorning economic "losers," American dream ideology can easily devolve into adulating the financially successful while blaming or demeaning people thwarted by structural barriers to livelihood. By diluting class consciousness and discouraging cross-class solidarity in these and other ways, the American dream that binds us together also keeps us apart.

Class Cultures

Class discourse in the United States has frequently been muted, but as writers from Tocqueville to Thorstein Veblen to Richard Sennett attest, awareness of class cultures and differences has not. For building the inclusive bonds of solidarity that a radical sufficiency agenda requires, therefore, learning to recognize, respect, and communicate across class-cultural differences are important tasks.

Every culture shares normative beliefs, values, and practices.[30] Recent cultural studies by social psychologist Jonathan Haidt and his colleagues point to a palette of six normative foundations, each springing from communally shared moral intuitions: care; fairness (emphasizing concepts like reciprocal altruism and proportionality—people getting what they deserve); authority; loyalty; purity/sanctity; and liberty (emphasizing freedom, and hatred for oppression). Haidt's research team found that US rural and working-class communities tended to cherish and draw on all six of these moral foundations. In contrast, upper-middle-class cultures foregrounded care and fairness and tended to sideline authority, loyalty, and sanctity; they prized autonomy and freedom from oppression, yet were willing to limit or override liberty for the sake of advancing fairness or assuring care.[31] Haidt's central claim has salience for our project: Americans in different social locations differ not only over political but *moral* values and priorities. These morally freighted differences help explain the passion of people's in-group convictions, and their incredulity or animus toward groups who fail to equally prize or respect them.[32]

Haidt's analysis jibes with reflections by scholars with family roots in working-class communities.[33] Also emphasizing culture's normative features, psychologist and class migrant Barbara Jensen, for example, avers: "Working- and middle-class people live in different cultures." One reason for this, she proposes, is that "communication processes taught in early childhood . . . select different skills and meanings for children of different social classes, which lead to different world views." While cautioning against reductive stereotypes, Jensen contends that, broadly speaking, middle- and working-class communities differently access and express some important aspects of being human resulting in different, characteristic strengths and blind spots.[34] This being so, if working- and middle-class people can learn to respectfully listen, dialogue, and collaborate with, rather than deride or spurn one another, everyone benefits.

Like her fellow class migrant Zweig, Jensen recognizes that classes are never "entirely discrete cultures." Yet, she argues, even everyday experience suggests that class-cultural differences are real. "One knows in a moment which is the teacher and which the construction worker."[35] Daily, people of varied classes meet, interact, and affect one another, "but this does not alter the fact that each has come from a different world, each with its own integrity." Writing in the late 1990s, Jensen observed that because professional middle-class culture dominates centers of social power, US institutions like the media, education, and politics tend to reflect middle-class values; meanwhile, "the insights and values that working class people hold" often get ignored or misrepresented.[36] Differences between working-class and middle-class cultures shape distinctive, at times conflicting perspectives, values, and customs. Absent adequate cross-class understanding and respect, such differences can foment division, mutual disdain, or worse.[37]

Professional middle-class culture, for instance, "values and recreates individuality and competition," educating its members to strive and to achieve. To this end, "middle class families socialize their children into a consciousness that is communicative and future-oriented" and "driven by language and its linearity."[38] In emotional matters, the favored style is diplomatic and indirect, and overt conflict is avoided. Financially and educationally advantaged, professional middle-class people also tend be more geographically mobile, more cosmopolitan, and more generally "unrooted" compared to their working-class peers. Leondar-Wright suggests reasons for this: "Prior generations may have left behind distinct ethnic cultures. Then they unroot themselves further by leaving their families to go to college, often never returning to their hometowns. Professional middle-class work schedules are more mobile, less rooted in schedules set by others. They have more options and can more easily move on to a new job or home. Professional middle-class people also unroot their minds by filling them with book knowledge that exceeds and supersedes their own lived experience."[39]

The result is people who have weaker loyalties to particular persons, places, groups, or institutions but stronger skills at networking and greater openness to learning from people who are different or distant. These competencies may make professional middle-class people adept at building and maintaining what Putnam calls "bridging social capital."[40] Professional middle-class people also value social sophistication, which, combined with orientations to competition and achievement, can foster status anxieties and continual comparisons with peers. "Self-worth among college-educated middle-class people often rests on feeling smarter than others," or "more than" in other ways. This means subjective status security is chronically at risk, which in turn can be a "major obstacle to cross-class alliance building."[41]

In working-class culture, by contrast, people prize belonging and loyalty to "personal and particular" relationships with family, place, and community. Flowing from this are other values working-class people esteem: stability, sharing and cooperation, honesty, responsibility, and hard work. Drawing in part on her own experiences, Jensen describes a working-class family culture "based on intimacy, on meaningful silences, on a sense of belonging" that manifests in a more subtle communicative style. "Children are taught to tune into many things other than words." And words are fewer, more like "buoys that float on a sea of shared assumptions."[42] Concrete and narrative-focused, working-class culture is less driven by the linear, verbally elaborate thinking that is the hallmark of professional middle-class culture.[43]

At the heart of working-class culture Jensen perceives a commendable dedication to nurturing and preserving "deep, loyal, we-are-part-of-one-another bonding"—put differently, a genius for creating and nurturing what Putnam calls bonding social capital. Professional middle-class children are groomed to individuate, to achieve, to prove themselves, and to stand out. Working-class children develop their sense of self amid "a culture which does not encourage them to grow out of that mutuality, to develop and defend their 'individual' identity."[44] And versus the hierarchies and powermongering they encounter at work and in society, working-class people "value a kind of 'peerness,' an egalitarian attitude that recognizes that no one as better than anyone else." People prize familiar relationships among peers, where "there is a relative freedom from having power and 'role negotiation' interwoven with communication." Closely linked to this is appreciation for honest, plain, and direct speech. This helps explain why the indirectness and diplomacy favored by middle-class professionals tend to sound inauthentic and phony to working-class ears.[45]

Research by Michele Lamont with working-class men, by Lillian Rubin with working-class families, and by Arlie Hochschild and Joan Williams with working-class white communities augments these descriptions, especially with respect to working-class viewpoints concerning "those above them and those below them" in the socioeconomic scheme of things.[46] Against popular media stereotypes of working-class people as uneducated, unambitious, and bigoted (Williams cites TV characters like Archie Bunker and Homer Simpson), these studies highlight positive values and convictions that shape working-class people's identities and from which they derive dignity and pride.[47] "Settled" working-class people (as opposed to their "hard living" neighbors who flout or fail to live out these values), Lamont found, cherish dedication to family and local community; responsibility, self-reliance, and hard work; maintaining the discipline needed to persevere in toilsome or stressful jobs and working conditions in order to support oneself and one's family; personal integrity and directness; traditional morality; interpersonal sharing, and altruism.[48] Black working-class men in Lamont's study emphasized two additional values: social solidarity and generosity.[49]

Their values and convictions lead settled working-class people to find fault with both those above them—the professional middle and upper classes—and those below them—the "hard-living" working class and the poor. Lamont found that working-class men "construct the upper half as having socioeconomic status to aspire to but values to be rejected."[50] Critical of what they experience as the snobbish insularity and subtle scorn of professional elites, working-class people take pride in "being part of the group that actually does the work." They look askance at what they see as professional elites' status consciousness, egocentrism, competitiveness, and pushiness. They are skeptical of upper-middle-class individualism, and childrearing practices that coddle children but also push kids upward and away from family roots. They resent professional middle-class liberals' apparent lack of patriotism and disrespect for "traditional family values" and elite-run popular media's seeming readiness to dismiss or ridicule values that working-class communities hold dear.

Tending to see themselves as "on their own in the struggles to make ends meet and to get ahead," working-class people take pride in surviving economic and social adversity through self-reliance and perseverance.[51] By the same token, they find social narratives of victimhood or helplessness repugnant, whether applied to themselves or to others.[52] Government programs that appear to discourage self-reliance and hard work are impugned. Policies providing the poor with unearned benefits for which working-class people do not qualify, and for which their hard-earned tax dollars must pay, are especially resented.[53]

Social psychologist Keith Payne lifts up one more important, frequently class-linked, difference in Americans' approaches to social and economic analysis. Research finds that political conservatives, including many in the working and lower-middle classes, tend to think and judge in ways that foreground individual actions and responsibilities. Political liberals, including professional middle-class elites, more often highlight systemic and structural social interpretations.

> Conservatives focus on the individuals within the system. This young man is responsible for getting a job. That young woman should make choices that enable her to avoid being a single mother. If they don't, then they suffer the consequences. Liberals look at the system and perceive that places where poverty is the norm just keep reproducing generations of poverty. Even when kids work hard, few can escape. If you want to predict who gets a job or who becomes a single mother, start by assessing their parents' incomes and the quality of their schools.[54]

When considering social and economic questions, Payne observes, "You can focus on the individual or the system, but it's hard to see both at once." Moreover, evidence shows that "both perspectives are oversimplifications," insofar as choices *and* structures are always at play and influence one another. Such groups may share many values but foreground them differently. "Conservatives and liberals generally agree that individual responsibility, talent, and hard work are important factors in achieving success, and they agree that context matters as well. One group's main emphasis, however, is the other's background. When the system is in the spotlight, hierarchy and inequality come sharply into focus. When the individual is in the spotlight, hierarchy and inequality fall where they may."[55] As inclusive-livelihood advocates engaged in the difficult work of coalition-building, Payne's nonbinary framing can be useful for opening doors for dialogue across differences in political and class-cultural perspectives.

Early twenty-first-century surveys found that true to their self-reliant cultural bent, most working-class people tended to think that "what they have going for themselves in this 'new economy' is their own wits" and willingness to hustle, work, and persevere.[56] If they were gaining or even holding ground amid generally hostile economic conditions, it was "because of their own efforts, and the sacrifices that they and their family members [were] making." Embracing a key tenet of the American dream, working-class citizens held "themselves and others responsible for their circumstances, and their success or failure."[57] They saw "a very limited role for the government, particularly in their own lives, and regard[ed] having to accept assistance as a violation of their own moral standards."[58] Yet working-class people did see government as having important responsibilities to fulfill on behalf of ordinary "people like themselves" who work hard and play by the rules. Thus, programs that reward work and protect workers and their families (Medicare, Social Security, disability, earned income credit, Federal Housing Administration mortgage subsidies) have consistently drawn strong working-class support.[59]

For building the economic solidarity that a radical sufficiency political economy requires, such studies can be significant resources. Besides illuminating value differences that often fuel class-based misunderstandings and conflicts, they challenge each class's kneejerk assumptions about their own cultural superiority. What is needed, scholars like Jensen and Leondar-Wright argue, is an approach that respects different class cultures' attunement to distinctive aspects of human experience and that strives, in particular, "to increase awareness of *the value of working-class cultures to a truly inclusive American society.*"[60]

Class and Status Competition

Etched into the US story of social class and economic livelihood is a profoundly important fact about our human species: we seem hardwired to crave status.[61] Like sufficiency and security, status is not only an element of economic livelihood but something more fundamental to human well-being, in this case our need to be acknowledged, respected, and capable of expressing our dignity and agency. So important is this hunger to feel and to be regarded as worthy, competent, and respectable (both in our own eyes and in the eyes of others) that psychologist Abraham Maslow included status, along with sufficiency and security, in his well-known hierarchy of basic human needs. Without sufficient esteem and status, Maslow believed, humans are incapable of self-actualization or flourishing.[62]

Status is deeply relational. One way we derive status is through group belonging: by being part of an "us" that accepts and regards "me" as someone of value, with a respected position or role(s). Status is also exquisitely relative. We see and measure status comparatively and, often, competitively. Like our primate kin, we notice, react to, and vie to improve—or at least maintain—our places within various social pecking orders. Here the context for status is one of ongoing struggle for superiority or dominance, in which we are constantly comparing ourselves, and others, with those above and below us. Today, traditional communities with fixed and stable roles and status hierarchies have been replaced by a dominant modern social and economic culture marked by fluidity, possibility, and insecurity. This fluidity fosters a heightened sense of individual responsibility for our own fortunes and failures, even as the goal posts for attaining the American dream and its attendant prestige are continually moving. The upshot is a highly, and anxiously, comparison- and status-conscious socioeconomic culture.[63] While most of us in the United States today will read-ily recognize this culture as our own, Jennifer Hochschild notes,

> This state of affairs is not altogether unique to our day. In the early nineteenth century Alexis de Tocqueville was already observing: "Every American is eaten up with longing to rise. In America I have seen the freest and best educated of men in circumstances the happi-est in the world; yet it seemed to me that a cloud habitually hung on their brow, and they seemed serious and almost sad even in their plea-sures. The chief reason for this is that . . . [they] never stop thinking of the good things they have not got. . . . They clutch everything but hold nothing fast, and so lose grip as they hurry after some new delight."[64]

Notwithstanding an ideology of egalitarianism and class fluidity, Amer-icans then and now have found themselves enmeshed in complicated dynamics of social comparison and sorting, status seeking and insecurity, honor and shame. Always linked to economics and power, class relations and divisions additionally involve different histories, values, and cultural practices. Because class structures consist of power gradations between asymmetrically resourced "we's" and "theys," and because status and power are tightly linked, class helps mark our relative positions both within and between our groups. Internally, classes create spaces where members construct, then compete according to common, if shifting, meanings for what social and economic "sufficiency, security, and status" entail. Externally, different class belongings locate groups "above and below" one another on a socioeconomic ladder against which degrees of separation and otherness, aspirations for advance-ment, and fears of falling are continually being recalibrated.

Class and Injustice

Conflicting interests born of differential access to socioeconomic power and life possibilities put classes into structured relations wherein, historically, members of less-powerful classes are vulnerable to oppression by the more powerful. For many non-elite workers, Young writes, "a hierarchical division of labor that separates task-defining from task-executing work enacts domina-tion, and produces or reinforces at least three forms of oppression."[65] For these Americans, she explains, structured economic disadvantage—exploitation—translates into the further injustices of lack of voice and influence—social powerlessness—and elites' devaluation or occlusion of working-class culture and values—cultural imperialism.

Lower-working-class, working poor, and poor families feel class-related denigration and invisibility especially keenly. As Isenberg documents, the labeling, deriding, and shaming of groups of "throwaway persons" is a venerable US tradition extending back to the early colonial era. Alongside the exploitation and dehumanization of Native, African, and other peoples deemed "not white," Isenberg traces poor white people's class-based marginalization and vilification as "waste people," "rubbish," and "white trash." Complicating the legacy of racism and white supremacy (from which poor and working-class whites have also sought to benefit), the history Isenberg recounts persists today, in twenty-first-century stereotypes of poor- and working-poor whites as hillbillies, ignorant rednecks, or trailer trash.[66]

Against this background, in 2016 Isenberg called out presidential aspirant Senator Bernie Sanders for reflecting a widely shared, American "blindness to class-race realities when he stated in one debate: 'When you're white . . . you don't know what it's like to be poor.'" "Today," she pointed out, "19.7 million people below the poverty line (42.1 percent) are white." Meanwhile, eking out livings close to the poverty line, the working poor and precarious working classes of all races and ethnicities struggle to stay afloat and maintain their dignity in conditions that threaten at any time to plunge them financially underwater and into (or back into) the ranks of the scorned poor.[67]

This, along with "the frequent powerlessness and physical exhaustion of working-class work," contributes to the injustices behind what Sennett famously called "the hidden injuries of class": "a psychology of shame and self-doubt . . . as one struggles to reduce the cognitive dissonance of colliding value systems."[68] From higher rungs of the class ladder, the upper-middle class's influence extends beyond workplaces and bank accounts. They also set the standards for "respectability," what is considered cultured, socially acceptable, and esteemed.[69] Performances of respectability (cleanliness, manners, dress) may gain poor and working-class people at least limited recognition by higher classes. But respectability regimes never fully deliver respect or inclusion to racial or class outsiders.[70] The resulting cultural inequalities, write Kate Pickett and Richard Wilkinson, "affect people almost as profoundly as inequalities in income." Experiences of low social status, research shows, negatively affect both physical and mental health. These negative impacts are most severe for people at the lowest rungs of the social ladder but are not limited only to them.[71]

Class, Race, and Gender

Class cannot be reduced to race or gender. But in the story of Americans' quest for livelihood these three have operated, from the country's beginnings, in interweaving and mutually formative ways. "It is not that the U.S. lacks a working class," Fletcher notes. But "this class has multiple, often-contradictory interests that are affected by race, ethnicity, gender, and empire."[72] We have seen Fletcher describe the "fusion of what comes to be known as race with capitalism" from the early settler period forward.[73] As the previous chapter also discussed, "whiteness" provided those so deemed with both economic benefits and a social/status "wage." The resulting racial divisions undermined working-class unity and effective action for change, as the conferral of whiteness "served to blunt white workers' efforts to plumb the real sources of their degradation on the job and before the law."[74] Progressive Era and New Deal policies that inscribed differential treatment for white and non-white families continued and contributed to working-class racial segmentation.[75] In the end, though, racialized pseudosolidarity between white workers and white elites notwithstanding, "class distinctions among whites were not ended, but secured by whiteness."[76]

Gender has also entered US class identity and relations in significant and evolving ways. Through the mid-twentieth century, a masculinized image of the average worker and the framework of the family living wage charted a path to manly dignity and the American dream for breadwinning (male, white), working-class, household heads. To white men, this gendered arrangement offered modest economic status and power that women and non-whites could not easily access. At the same time, it reinforced wage dependence and workplace discipline among men who needed their jobs in order to successfully fulfill their roles as family heads, providers, and self-supporting citizens.

White male workers' relative independence and status were often defined through racialized and gendered comparisons: over and against economic "dependents" such as their wives and children, the less-than-self-sufficient poor, or socially marginalized racial and immigrant groups. However, this ideology of masculine independence obscured the fact that only a minority of working-class male breadwinners actually received a family-supporting living wage. It also concealed the extent to which such workers remained dependent on volatile market forces and the shifting interests of employers for the jobs and wages that made their "independence" operative.

As labor unions arose to protect and advance the interests of workers against powerful owners, they too invested in a gendered notion of work, workers, and the manly liberty that unions existed to champion. Besides legitimating the exclusion or marginalization of women members, this ideology discouraged union leaders from supporting pro-worker legislation or government regulations that appeared to threaten male members' independent self-image.[77] By employing the language of manly liberty to reinforce workers' suspicions of government intervention and preferences for benefits negotiated between unions and employers, trade union leaders helped steer US policy away from more robust European-style social programs.[78]

As we have seen, class and race also influenced women's economic situations and relationships in myriad ways. Working-class wives who had to earn wages to make household ends meet were disqualified from attaining the feminine success that full-time homemaking ideally conferred. This was doubly true for working-class women of color, who up through the later twentieth century were disproportionately relegated to low-status jobs such as domestic service in white households, with their underpaid labor often allowing middle- and upper-class white women to fulfill homemaker-role expectations in ways these working women of color could not. Besides facing and engaging with different challenges surrounding gender than did white women, women of color also encountered and negotiated class strictures and demands in distinctive ways. Research by Virginia Wolcott on Black women's savvy strategies for employing the rules of bourgeois respectability to the advantage of their own communities limns some of the astute and creative ways women of color helped their families resist and persist in a culture and economy that stacked the odds against them.[79]

Later in the twentieth century these racialized and gendered frames for livelihood morphed and evolved, but never disappeared. Notably, job segregation and market segmentation rarely served working-class economic interests. Combined with the economic devaluation of women's work whether waged or in households, segmentation of the labor force by gender and race increased profits for business owners and employers by providing them with a vast, secure reserve of cheap (or, in the case of women's household labor, free) labor.[80]

CLASS AND LIVELIHOOD, LATE NINETEENTH TO MID-TWENTIETH CENTURY

Scholars of varied ideological stripes regard worker precarity as an inevitable byproduct of modern capitalism. "From its very beginnings," writes economic historian Jerry Muller, "the creativity and innovation of industrial capitalism were shadowed by insecurity for members of the work force."[81] In the late nineteenth- and early twentieth-century United States, a large working class—with high percentages of Catholics—suffered in manifold ways: pay was insufficient; job, health, and retirement security were rare to nonexistent;

and workers' power and status on the job, and in civil society, were far less than their dignity, rights, and contributions merited. Insufficient pay, insecurity, and low status defined and diminished the lives of millions of workers and their families.

If worker insecurity was endemic to industrial capitalism, countervailing institutions and policies were needed to reduce or buffer it. Late nineteenth and early twentieth-century reformers fought for and established a range of legal, governmental, and economic measures to constrain or offset the negative impacts on workers of largely unfettered capitalist markets. By the mid-twentieth century, all Western democracies had embraced some type of welfare state, whose provisions included "old-age and unemployment insurance and various measures to support families."[82] Within civil society, labor movement and labor unions, by harnessing workers' collective power to advance their interests, played an especially important role in countering industrial capitalism's power.

Trade Unionism, the Common Man, and the "National Bargain"

The communitarian—also called solidarist or corporatist—ethos and mindset that animated organized labor directly challenged the individualist focus of the economics that dominated the United States and Europe during this period.[83] The union movement rallied workers to solidarity, to join together to wrest a decent livelihood from owners and managers. Class language was used liberally by both union leaders and labor-supportive politicians. In the United States, no more than one-third of the workforce ever became unionized; but workers' associations, industrial and craft unions, and union federations became highly significant players in struggles to improve workers' wages, benefits, and working conditions. Union membership and legislative gains for workers grew dramatically during the New Deal years, but pro-labor policies bore their greatest fruit during the economic boom that followed the close of World War II.[84]

Labor union strength was among the forces that made the period between 1933 and 1970 a kind of golden era in the United States for the "common man." Pictured as honest, hard-working, family-oriented, patriotic, and white, the everyday working-class American was celebrated in Norman Rockwell's popular paintings, including the famous 1943 "Four Freedoms"; in the Hollywood films of Frank Capra and stars like Jimmy Stewart; in Vice President Henry Wallace's 1942 speech declaring that America was entering a "century of the common man," and in Aaron Copland's iconic 1943 musical composition

"Fanfare for the Common Man." Progressive religious leaders and political elites also played key roles in helping promote and establish worker-favorable policies and legislation during this period. On the political side, no one was more emblematic of this than the upper-class New York scion Franklin D. Roosevelt and his spouse and partner, Eleanor. Assuming the presidency amid dark times of depression and, later, war, Roosevelt masterfully connected with voters by projecting an inclusive, flexible populism focused on advancing the well-being of "ordinary, hardworking people" against the forces of elite control.[85]

By the 1950s "industrial workers had become the largest single group in every developed country," and in the United States and abroad, most "unionized industrial workers in mass production industry (which was then dominant everywhere) had attained upper-middle-class [or at least, comfortably middle-class] income levels."[86] In the 1950s and 1960s, a union factory worker in an industrial city like Detroit or Chicago could afford to own and maintain a well-equipped single-family home with one or more automobiles; enjoyed generous employer-provided health, vacation, and retirement benefits; and often participated in decision-making and stock- and profit-sharing options on the job. Indispensable to this achievement were the governmental supports to working families (including free college education for veterans via the GI Bill, and low-interest loans for purchasing homes through the Federal Housing Administration) provided by the further expansion of the welfare state in the decades after World War II.

Because this expansion "took place at a time when the capitalist economies of the West were growing rapidly," states were able to procure ample funds for social welfare programs through taxation.[87] What resulted was a period of "temporary equilibrium during which the advanced capitalist countries experienced strong economic growth, high employment, and relative socioeconomic equality."[88] During these acutely anticommunist Cold War years, many argued that Marxist ideas had failed to gain traction in the United States because workers, finding that capitalism was delivering for them, had no interest in class struggle or class warfare. A flourishing economy, coupled with working-class favorable business and welfare policies, reinforced the popular sense that with very few exceptions, upward mobility, or at minimum, solid middle-class status, were within the reach of every American family.

The postwar period was also an auspicious moment of cross-class reciprocity between workers and political and business elites. The ascendancy of the blue-collar worker at this time, writes Peter Drucker, "was the result of, and formed the basis . . . for a 'national bargain': Big Business, Big Labor, and the public at large would subsidize high-volume production in order to gain greater efficiencies of scale, which in turn would employ a growing middle class of Americans capable of buying the expanded output."[89] There arose, concurs economist Joseph Stiglitz, "a deal between the top and the rest of our society that went something like this: we will provide you jobs and prosperity, and you will let us walk away with the bonuses. You all get a share, even if we get a bigger share."[90]

Worker-employer antagonism by no means disappeared, but by fulfilling their sides of the national bargain, all parties had the opportunity to be good citizens and enjoy a good living. Through their employment policies, corporations "did tend to promote the general welfare, thus lending credence to the optimistic view that within the democratic capitalism promoted in the United States, one could usually 'do well while doing good.'"[91]

Unions' Wider Benefits

Beyond demonstrable improvements for union members, labor strength yielded benefits for the public at large. Union successes had echo or halo effects, producing gains for nonunion workers as well.[92] Civically activated union members contributed to an engaged and empowered democratic citizenry.[93] On their own, many working-class people lack the resources and social capital that make voting and other forms of civic participation likely.[94] Labor unions' effectiveness in rectifying this made union membership one of the "'principal paths by which members of the working classes were accepted into the fabric of societies as political and economic citizens.'"[95] Functioning as what Sara Evans and Harry Boyte call civic "free spaces," wherein members can meet and talk with one another, learn from one another, and receive practice and training in political participation and leadership, "the labor movement helped channel and organize the political energies of the working class." In so doing, organized labor helped "'counter the inequalities . . . that Americans otherwise experience' and 'equalize participation across class lines.'"[96]

Bruce Western and Jake Rosenfeld underscore one final, key public benefit: the union movement helped anchor a *social moral economy* that legitimated economic rights and helped buffer the negative effects of the competitive marketplace. "U.S. unions often supported norms of equity that extended beyond their own membership. Contributing to a sort of moral economy, unions help[ed] materialize labor market norms of equity"—culturally, through public speech about economic inequality and "social solidarity"; politically, by influencing social policy; and institutionally, by promoting and participating in rules governing the labor markets that help ensure fairness to workers.[97] Doing all this enabled unions to function as "a normative presence that helps sustain the labor market as a social institution [not just a factor of production], in which norms of equity shape the allocation of wages outside the union sector."[98]

EARLY-TWENTIETH CENTURY CATHOLIC TEACHING, US CATHOLICS, AND CLASS

In the later nineteenth century, concerns surrounding class, inequality, and worker justice in the industrial capitalist order sparked a new era of Catholic social engagement and teaching. In 1891 Pope Leo XIII trained his attention on challenges to social and class harmony, and to the economic well-being of the vast, vulnerable working classes that the new industrial economy had engendered. The usual English rendering of *Rerum novarum's* title, "On the Condition of Labor/the Working Classes," reflects Leo's intended focus.

Rerum novarum's treatment of class remained tied to a traditional understanding of society as a hierarchically structured organism in which different groups had specific and stable roles. In an era under pressure from capitalist industrialization and urbanization, rapid political democratization, and socialist movements, Leo, with a traditionalist's appreciation for order and stability, took class distinctions for granted. He enjoined mutually charitable and just relations between classes, underscored their mutual bonds, and emphasized the obligations of the richer and "owning" classes toward the working and unpropertied classes. Subsequent popes, until the 1960s, also assumed that a socially unequal, class-stratified society was inevitable and, at least to some degree, the result of natural, indelible differences among persons.[99] Class was understood as economically grounded but also culturally embodied in practices and customs.

In upholding ordered and harmonious class relations as natural and just, *Rerum novarum* took issue with economic liberals and socialists alike, rejecting laissez faire markets and unrestricted competition, as well as endemic class struggle and complete social equality.[100] But Leo—and even more sharply, Pius XI in 1931—harshly criticized extreme economic inequality, calling out greed and wealth concentration among what we today call the 1 percent. The popes pressed business, government, and civic leaders to ensure that workers were not mistreated or underpaid, to prevent egregious social and economic inequalities, and to check concentrations of wealth, property, and power in the hands of the advantaged few.[101]

US Catholics and Class

Monsignor John A. Ryan was highly educated and traveled in elite political circles. But he never forgot his working-class roots. Passionately concerned for ordinary workers and families, he decried the evils and injustices confronting vulnerable wage earners and was strategic about how these might be addressed. Focused on "social reform through legislation," his US interpretation of a Catholic livelihood agenda, largely adopted by the national bishops, aimed to ensure for all families access to dignified work and modest material comfort. Class distinctions were not expected to disappear. But universal livelihood, by ensuring decent work and a dignified standard of living to poor and working-class families, would honor their social rights and enable them to more fully participate in and contribute to the commonweal. To achieve this goal would, Ryan judged, require significantly redistributing wealth and ameliorating the extreme economic disparities that allowed an upper-class minority to live in extreme extravagance while a working-class majority struggled in near deprivation.

In rallying US Catholics on behalf of working-class justice, Ryan and the bishops spoke of social reform and reconstruction, not revolution. This reflected in part Catholicism's traditional attachment to social order, and in part US Catholics' desire to be regarded as patriotic citizens rather than rabble-rousers, thus their desire to distance themselves from radical socialism and communism. Yet this Catholic program for worker justice was in many ways structurally transformative and class subversive, particularly in its insistence on government's duty to assure all working families a modest standard of material well-being and in its vision of an industrial democracy whose workers would become active social citizens through workplace participation that afforded them a share in management and profits. These elements—inclusive access to livelihood, social citizenship, and economic democracy—augured changes to capitalist business as usual that, if enacted, would change the face of the US political economy. Particularly during the New Deal years, Ryan both contributed to and epitomized a rich moment of interface between Catholics' social ideology and the economic striving of the US working class.

Catholic engagement on behalf of workers' rights in this period had critics both inside and outside the church. Intellectuals who regarded Catholics as traditionalist authoritarians were suspicious of the motives behind the church's public advocacy.[102] And not all US Catholic leaders and clergy approved of their church's shift to the papal-teaching-inflected ideology that Ryan at times framed as "true economic liberalism."[103] Outspoken Catholic critics of Roosevelt's New Deal, including New York's John Cardinal O'Connor, accused the president of fomenting illegitimate government interference. But as the Roosevelt administration's programs began to benefit the working-class, primarily white, Americans who dominated the rank and file of urban Catholic parishes, "Catholics became key New Deal supporters." Especially in large metropolitan areas, white Catholic voters strongly supported the Democratic party in 1936 and 1940, remaining a reliable Democratic voting bloc for decades thereafter.[104]

Labor Unions

Their high concentration in the industrial working classes placed US Catholics in the thick of early twentieth-century workers' struggles, and therefore in the thick of the labor movement.[105] In large, tight-knit, and paternalistically run urban Catholic parish communities, clergy leaders known as "labor priests" played crucial roles in encouraging and supporting parishioners' political and labor union activism. One of these labor priest was Charles Owen Rice, who, inspired by papal teaching and Dorothy Day's Catholic Worker movement, became an influential leader in Pittsburgh's Catholic Radical Alliance. Rice worked tirelessly with laity and local unions on behalf of labor justice. Speaking to textile workers in Utica, New York, in 1938, Owen stressed the solidarist sensibilities and economic justice goals that animated much Catholic labor activism: "Unionization is a perfectly normal, Christian thing. . . . Why should not the worker organize? Why should he be compelled to go through his working life like a grain of sand and not like the social organism he is? Why does anyone want to keep the workers apart, disorganized? Why other than through the desire to keep them weak and easy to exploit?"[106] What was needed, Rice urged, was not less but more "CIO"—Congress of Industrial Organizations, the national union for unskilled laborers—"and progressive legislation." Seamlessly melding labor's agenda with Pope Pius XI's call for social reconstruction, Rice urged his listeners to fortitude, for "labor is on the march. On the march to a goal that will bring justice and happiness to all classes of people. Labor's fight is everyone's fight. It is a fight for decency, justice, and a Christian social order."[107]

In other working-class parishes, Catholics were similarly exhorted. During the dreary Depression year of 1936, Detroit pastor Erwin Lefebvre deployed an ingenious strategy for bringing the Church's message on labor to his heavily working-class congregation. Weekly, he began devoting the later-morning Sunday mass sermon to reading and commenting on *Rerum novarum*. Attendance soared. Lefebvre's Labor Mass experiment "quickly became developed and integrated into the official devotional calendar of the Detroit Arch-diocese," as part of the liturgical cycle and "Catholics' routine living of their faith."[108]

Three years later, in 1939, parishes across the Detroit archdiocese hosted recruiters for local chapters of the lay-led Association of Catholic Trade Unionists (ACTU). "Local bulletins announced: 'CATHOLIC WORKERS! God needs you in your labor union! Labor's fight for justice is in vain unless labor follows the principles of Jesus Christ.'" Citing Archbishop Edward Mooney's plea that Catholics not be intimidated by false corporate press reports dis-paraging unions, ACTU newsletters urged, "'Catholics! Get in the labor parade. Don't just stand on the sidelines and find fault.'" A small but influen-tial movement dedicated to infusing Catholic social principles into the labor unions, the ACTU's inroads in Detroit were mirrored in other cities across the country.[109]

Matthew Pehl comments on the religiously grounded sense of empower-ment among working Catholics these stories reflect. "One senses a libera-tion and excitement appropriate for people newly confident in their agency and newly self-aware of the forces shaping their lives and identities." Now, "workers were no longer background players in the Catholic vision of history; they were, in fact, the main sites."[110] Because they were steeped in an ethnic-religious solidarity that prepared them to understand and engage in worker solidarity, Pehl argues that these Catholics developed not simply a "working class consciousness" but a unique synthesis of piety, faith, and action better described as "working-class religion."[111] During this same period, a similar synthesis fueled the rise of a remarkably successful series of "labor schools." In these labor schools, some hosted by universities, many others located in urban Catholic parishes, workers were trained in "public speaking and par-liamentary procedure, labor ethics and law, in economics and trade union methods." In over one hundred Catholic labor schools, such as the Xavier Labor School in New York City led for decades by Jesuit "labor priest" Father Edward Carey, workers of all faiths (or no faith) also learned about Catholic social teaching on work and economy. [112]

As the previous chapter explored, however, working-class solidarity during these years was marred by exclusions based on race. And in their willing-ness to trade faith- or civically based principles of equal human dignity for the advantages that racism's coin of "other/better/over" could buy, most US Catholics proved indistinguishable from their neighbors. In Northeast and Midwest cities, perceived economic and social threats posed by the influx of African Americans from southern states accelerated shifts in Euro-American Catholics' racial/ethnic self-identifications and loyalties from Polish, Irish,

Italian, and so forth to "white." Most white Catholic workers and families resisted racially integrating labor unions, and many more resisted the integration of working-class neighborhoods and schools.[113]

CLASS AND LIVELIHOOD, LATE TWENTIETH TO EARLY TWENTY-FIRST CENTURY

During the post–World War II period, capitalism seemed, overall, to be a friend to working families. In the United States, a climate of anticommunist patriotism and unprecedented working-class prosperity served to tamp down class consciousness and class-related discourse. "By the end of the 1950s," many Catholics had embraced "the 'New Capitalism'—the 'People's Capitalism'—that many believed had evolved in the United States, and they resisted calls to change it."[114] But some Catholics challenged the Ryanesque economic positions of the US bishops, including their support for labor unions. In his 1953 book, *Christianity and American Capitalism*, for instance, Monsignor Edwin Keller mounted a typical conservative critique of the state of the US labor movement. Keller denied that the social encyclicals called for "a partnership-contract whereby workers would share with owners the right to manage business."[115] Citing Catholic teaching on subsidiarity, in fact, he warned, "the greatest threats to the freedom of the American people came from 'Big Government' and 'Big Labor.'" For Keller, government overreach was the primary threat to liberty, with a close second being union leaders, who had come to wield "economic power greater than that of big business." The victims were no longer the vulnerable workers but, rather, "business owners and managers . . . bullied by unions that controlled their fate with unreasonable demands."[116] Though Keller's was a minority view in 1953, critiques like his presaged rising popular disaffection with US labor unions that the next few decades would bring.

Fading class consciousness and conservative critiques notwithstanding, clear differences in power, autonomy, and economic vulnerability remained in place between working-class wage earners whose union contracts afforded them modest financial security, their managerial supervisors and bosses, and wealthy corporate owners. But the sense of urgency and commitment to labor struggles of previous decades had waned, while persistent racial divisions further diminished prospects for broad working-class solidarity.

Perhaps the most important driver of what one scholar calls the "les trente glorieuses" years of postwar class harmony was a widely shared sense of abundant opportunities for economic sufficiency and security, enhanced by shrinking gaps between rich and poor. For large swaths of the white working classes in particular, a modest but real version of the American dream felt within reach; and in this climate, the socially peaceable aura of what Danny Dorling calls "the equality effect" enjoyed a season of influence.[117]

Beginning in the later 1960s, however, the postwar prosperity and security that had bouyed so many workers and families began to erode. After 1973, a long season of decline set in as working-class families across the country faced stagnant or falling real wages, the decoupling of rising productivity from raises in income, the loss and replacement of high-paying industrial jobs with lower-wage and often benefit-free service-sector jobs, declines in labor union participation and strength, and rising inequality.[118] Economic and social vulnerabilities that had been lessened or obscured reemerged.[119] And as non-elite families were buffeted by new threats to their sufficiency, security, and status, millions in middle-class managerial, professional, and corporate positions also began to find their jobs, wages, and benefits increasingly insecure.

A sobering hallmark of this post-1970s period was the dismantling of what had been a widely shared US ethos concerning the meaning of a "job contract": that in return for their competent, dedicated, and loyal performance, workers could expect from employers secure employment, decent pay, and good benefits over the course of a career. By the end of the twentieth century this worker-friendly job contract was in danger of disappearing. In its place, a range of so-called "new job contracts" and an ascendant temp or gig economy offered workers only short-term or rescindable deals, contingency, and lower or no benefits.[120]

In the new era, upholding workers' dignity and their right to a decent and secure livelihood receded as public priorities. Earlier decades' focus on labor solidarity and "the common man" were now overshadowed by the profile of "Me, Inc."—everyone their own individual contractor, peddling their labor on an open market. For a small cosmopolitan-class elite, highly educated and mobile, this new work climate proved energizing and highly profitable. But for great majorities in both the middle and working classes, these changes put families' access to livelihood under chronic, often severe, threat.[121]

For non-elite Americans these post-1970 shifts signaled the coming apart of the aforementioned, cross-class national bargain that had provided economic security during the previous twenty-five years. Always fragile, the tacit agreement between the rich and the rest now unraveled; the rich continued to get richer, but "the majority of Americans simply [were] not . . . benefiting from the country's growth." By the new millennium, these trends had weakened the position and bargaining power of workers in all but the most select fields.[122] Approximately 62 percent of Americans held a widely diverse set of working-class-level jobs; 36 percent held the professional, managerial, or entrepreneurial jobs that qualified them as middle class; while 2 percent of the workforce inhabited the most powerful, upper echelons of the corporate or capitalist class.[123] Automation, offshoring of manufacturing jobs, and the dominance of neoliberal economic policies left labor increasingly vulnerable to the vagaries of supranational market forces. In sector after sector, and now within a globalizing market, older supports for "fair wages" were put aside; "competitive" or "market" wages once more ruled the day.[124]

Meanwhile, several historical dynamics combined to move the social and economic well-being of white working-class communities, previously at the center of much Catholic and US political concern, out of the cultural and policy spotlight. Postwar economic stability and reasonable educational costs enabled many children of working-class families to migrate into the middle and professional classes Beginning in the 1960s many liberal elites and government leaders directed new, and needed, attention to racial and gender injustice, creating policies and programs to remediate historical inequities suffered by women and people of color. Simultaneously, post-1960s cultural shifts put previously mainstream working-class sexual, family, and religious values under increasing pressure. By the early twenty-first century, large swaths of the white working class had begun to feel, and act, more like a marginalized minority.[125]

Women were distinctly affected by later-century trends. In the 1960s and 1970s second-wave feminism valorized and advanced the rights of middle-class women to self-and career development through workforce participation. But after 1970, working- and middle-class women's engagement in paid labor—particularly among female heads of households and mothers of young children—was motivated even more by the need to maintain slipping standards of living and to combat families' economic vulnerability. This was particularly true for working-class women and acutely true for women among the working poor.[126] Meanwhile, labor force segmentation channeled these women disproportionately into jobs where their wages lagged behind those of men. For working-class women of color, wages and employment opportunities remained even more depressed.[127]

Labor union decline proved another bellwether of changing working-class fortunes.[128] Union vitality requires a congenial civic environment in which government and law, cultural values, and public opinion all play parts. Amid postwar economic expansion, the removal of one or another piece of this Jenga-like support structure seemed less consequential. But by the early 1970s the effects of a slow postwar deterioration of labor union supports were becoming increasingly evident.[129] The 1949 Taft-Hartley Act had been the first of a series of legislative restrictions on labor and union activities, as the more communitarian New Deal ethos gave way to policies that prioritized individuals and a competitive market economy.[130] These legal and policy shifts, Michael Wachter argues, were key drivers of the "unrelenting decline in union membership" after 1960, alongside other factors including unions' overbureaucratization, corruption, and narrowly self-interested strategies.[131] Weakening unions tracked with the erosion of the US public's perception of labor markets as valuable social institutions, whose function was to serve the common good by enabling a decent livelihood for all workers. This cycle appears to be self-reinforcing: "as organized labor's political power dissipates, economic interests in the labor market are dispersed and policymakers have fewer incentives to strengthen unions."[132] In an individualist, competitive economic culture, inherently collectivist unions are anomalous and marginalized.

What were the consequences of labor unions' dwindling power? Major studies correlated declines in union membership with lower wages and benefits for union members, declines in wages for nonunion workers, and rising income inequality. In the United States these effects track especially strongly with private sector union decline, and collateral wage losses for nonunion members are especially great among private sector male workers without a college degree.[133] While correlation is not necessarily causation, evidence strongly suggests that "the near disappearance of private-sector unions from the economic landscape removes an important institutional buffer" against working-class vulnerability and economic inequality in the United States.[134]

Union decline also eroded an important pathway to political empowerment among working-class citizens. Unions have long been an avenue by which non-elite citizens have become participants in the political arena. In their union locals, workers get grassroots education and formation for civic activism and leadership; more union members, particularly in private sector unions, vote than do nonmembers in similar industries. Civically engaged and politically empowered working-class citizens are another casualty of ebbing labor union strength.[135] Beyond this, union decline and the unraveling of labor movement solidarity signaled the undoing of one pillar of a twentieth-century "moral social economy." Strong unions contributed to and benefited from a shared ethos that framed the labor market not just as a manipulable factor of production but as a "political institution in which norms of equity shape the allocation of wages" both inside and outside the union sector.[136]

Overall declines in civic solidarity and community engagement signaled a larger, troubling development for the health of the US polity. Sociological studies—emblematically, Putnam's 2000 book *Bowling Alone*—documented the attrition of civic bonds, community engagement, and social trust in the United States, across classes. These trends, Putnam warned, drained crucial reserves of social capital, those networks of connection among citizens that make for peace, neighborliness, and positive quality of life.[137] While affecting all classes, these trends (plus others such as lower marriage rates, rises in prime-age male unemployment, and more children born out of wedlock) had especially damaging impacts on more economically vulnerable working-class communities in both urban and rural America.[138]

Race, Racism, and Class

Class and race remained salient, and intertwined, into the twenty-first century.[139] But, "because the lens through which [class] is looked at ... has tended to be racial," class remains difficult to see, especially for white workers. Racialized capitalism's obfuscation of class places "objective limitations" on labor organizations' power.[140] Organizations that do become multiracial or multiethnic find their unity and efficacy threatened whenever what Fletcher calls "the racial tripwire"—working-class fragmentation along lines of racialized conflict—"is breached." Unless this racial tripwire can be disarmed, "the closest we may ever come to working-class consciousness is tactical unity on economic issues among all workers, and right-wing populism among a significant sector of white workers." Writing in the early 2000s, Fletcher predicted the subsequent resurgence of right-wing populist leaders who would weaponize traditional racist tropes in service of "the basic notion that under the white working class there should be a cushion," formed by the lesser advantage of those below—most often, workers of color.[141] Racism today, Lustig laments, "by providing a lightning rod for ultimately class-based fears and worries, "masks the major causes of social inequality."[142] Class-focused questions that might lead to united action "cannot be raised because the groups that might raise them remain divided between racializers and racialized, fighting in a box without questioning the box itself." The upshot: "The color of power [remains] white."[143]

By 2016 several intersecting developments in this race-class nexus were coming to a head. Racialized wealth and income disparities persisted. In many white working-class communities, feelings of economic marginalization and cultural alienation had become palpable, and a new form of white identity politics was taking hold. As we have seen, white and Black public opinion concerning racism's social power and economic effects diverged sharply, as polling revealed that increasing numbers of working-class whites believed that historic disadvantages had been supplanted by unfair advantages for Black people in workplaces and society. Simultaneously, the racial complexion of the working class as a whole was darkening, with the Bureau of Labor Statistics predicting a shift to a "majority-minority" working class by as early as 2032.[144] Economist Valerie Wilson emphasizes that "wage stagnation and economic inequality can't be solved without policies aimed at raising living standards for the working class." But to secure their economic betterment, this diverse working class will need to forge a "sustainable" solidarity "that supersedes the racial and ethnic tensions present among all groups of people, not just between whites and people of color."[145]

Probing a related development was political scientist Justin Gest's 2016 study of the white working classes in the United States and the United Kingdom. In what he calls "post-traumatic cities"—"exurbs and urban communities that lost signature industries in the mid- to late-twentieth century"—Gest found working-class white people grappling with a series of disempowering conditions. In fact, Gest argues, a combination of "systemic, psychological and rhetorical, and political forces" have put white working-class people in marginalized social circumstances that qualify them as a new "minority group." If this is true, he concludes provocatively, this group's downwardly mobile social status "demands the attention of minority politics scholars and alters the way we conceptualize minorities."[146] I will return to this proposition below.

Moving toward working-class solidarity under these circumstances, Wilson concludes, will require "honesty and a collective reckoning about race, white privilege, and institutional racism." And if Gest is correct, this reckoning must include finding ways to bridge divides and to build bonds of respect between working-class people of color and what many white working-class families now believe is their own beleaguered minority. To the extent that white working-class discontent also remains rooted in a history of clinging to and exploiting their whiteness, building cross-racial solidarity in a majority-minority working class will be extremely tricky and challenging business. But no path to a future of inclusive economic justice will be able to circumvent the difficult, long-haul work of unraveling the tangled knot of class and race.

Growing Economic Inequality and its Effects

Accelerating economic inequality after 1970 has been convincingly correlated with heightened class segregation and social fragmentation. Scholars and social justice leaders further argue that unless moderated or checked, growing socioeconomic inequality undermines the conditions for participative democracy and breeds the exclusion or exploitation of lower-downs by higher-ups.[147] The period from 1979 to 2014 saw a striking increase in higher-end middle-class households earning more than $100,000 per year; and the size of the upper middle class (the majority white, married, and college educated) grew from 13 percent to over 29 percent of the US population.[148] Meanwhile, the percentages of middle- and working-class families decreased.[149]

In many ways this was good news for the American dream: more families seemed to be achieving it. But concomitant distributional shifts created a deepening economic (and inevitably, social) gap between a burgeoning professional-managerial elite and the rest of the population. "In 1979," economist Stephen Rose reports, "the bottom three income groups controlled 70 percent of all incomes, and the upper middle class and rich controlled 30 percent. By 2014, this distribution shifted to 37 percent for the bottom three groups and 63 percent for the upper middle class and rich groups. The middle class alone saw its share of income decline from 46 percent in 1979 to 26 percent in 2014." Non-elite family incomes increased, but at much slower rates. In 2016, as political efforts to limit gender and racial segregation continued, Rose continues, "segregation by income (which is growing) was [increasingly] accepted as a fact of life." And because "most metropolitan areas differ greatly by the size and price of the homes in their neighborhoods and communities," compounding income differences were also widening geographic and cultural separations between classes.[150]

Family wealth also grew at significantly different rates for different segments of the US population. In 2013, after adjusting for changes in prices, the wealth of families at the ninetieth percentile had grown 54 percent since 1989. The wealth of those at the median was 4 percent greater, while the wealth of families at the twenty-fifth percentile had declined by 6 percent from 1989 levels. Not surprisingly, wealth distribution was also more unequal in 2013 than it had been in 1989. The net difference (in 2013 dollars) between wealth held by families at the ninetieth percentile and by those in the middle widened from $532,000 to $861,000 over this period. Even more striking, the share of wealth held by families in the top 10 percent of the wealth distribution increased from 67 to 76 percent, while the share of wealth held by families in the entire bottom half of the distribution declined from 3 to 1 percent.[151]

Statistics on inequality also reflect continued intergenerational impacts of racism on economic opportunities and outcomes. Black and Hispanic households continued to lag behind white households in mean annual income.[152] Between 1986 and 2013, racial and ethnic wealth disparities, both median and average, grew.[153] Even as families of color were on track to become the majority of the US population, most continued to fall far behind white families in accumulating wealth.[154] The racial wealth gap also increased sharply with age, as differences in earnings over a lifetime accumulated. African Americans and Hispanics in particular lost ground on major wealth-building measures like homeownership and retirement savings. "In 2013, white families had over $100,000 more (or 7 to 11 times more) in average liquid retirement savings than African American and Hispanic families," a difference that had quadrupled over the previous quarter century.[155]

Contributing to these discouraging trends, federal programs intended to promote asset building continued disproportionately to serve families already enjoying higher incomes. "The federal government spent $384 billion to support asset development in 2013 but ... [a]bout two-thirds of homeownership tax subsidies and retirement subsidies go to the top 20 percent of taxpayers, as measured by income. The bottom 20 percent, meanwhile, receive less than 1 percent of these subsidies."[156] Due to lower average incomes, African American and Hispanic families received far fewer of these asset-building benefits, reinforcing the historical cycle of racialized wealth inequalities.

Researchers and activists emphasize the significant differences between providing lower-income Americans with "safety nets," and contributing to their capacities—through well-paying work, tax credits, and savings incentives—to acquire and keep economic assets: "Low-income families benefit from safety net programs ... *but most of these programs focus on income— keeping families afloat today—and do not encourage wealth-building and economic mobility in the long run.* What's more, many programs discourage saving: for instance, when families won't qualify for benefits if they have a few thousand dollars in assets or when they have to give up rent subsidies to own a home."[157]

An extensive 2013 study of developing countries conducted under the auspices of the United Nations Development Programme detected similarly rising inequalities internationally.[158] Both less- and more-advantaged countries showed high and growing levels of inequality.[159] Among developed countries in 2014–15, the United States and Turkey competed for the third-highest level of inequality, behind Chile and Mexico.[160] Within the United States, inequality lessened slightly in 2009 and 2010, largely due to Great Recession wealth losses among the rich. But between 2010 and 2014, growth at the very top again surged, while wages and wealth for those in the bottom 50 percent remained largely stagnant.[161]

Many economists regard inequality and its negative side effects as endemic to modern capitalist markets.[162] But does growing inequality necessarily harm non-elites' economic well-being? An earlier generation of analysts argued that such inequalities were not problematic when also accompanied

by growth, the predominating assumption reflected in the old saw "a rising tide lifts all boats." But more recent research yields strong evidence that
"beyond a certain threshold, inequality harms growth and poverty reduction,
the quality of relations in the public and political spheres of life and individuals' sense of fulfilment and self-worth." Further, "greater income inequality between households is systematically associated with greater inequality in
non-income outcomes."[163]

Dorling synthesizes the research to make a compelling case for the benefits that accrue when countries install policies designed not to eliminate economic inequality but to keep it within moderate bounds.[164] Dorling calls these
compounding positive outcomes "the equality effect." "Greater economic
equality benefits all people in all societies," Dorling writes, "whether you
are rich, poor, or in-between. Countries that have chosen to be more equal
have enjoyed greater economic prosperity while also managing to develop in
a more environmentally sustainable fashion." Evidence shows that "in more
equal countries, human beings are generally happier and healthier; there is
less crime, more creativity, more productivity, more concern over what is
actually being produced, and—overall—higher educational attainment."
Putting it colloquially, he concludes, "Greater economic equality makes us all
less stupid, *more* tolerant, *less* fearful and *more* satisfied with life."[165]

CLASS IN LATER TWENTIETH-CENTURY CATHOLIC TEACHING AND PRACTICE

Pope John XXIII's treatment of economic issues in the social encyclical *Pacem
in terris* (Peace on Earth), released just before his death in June 1963, reflects
its historical moment: a time of great change and insecurity mixed with great
hope. Pointing out "three things that characterize our modern age," Pope John
first cites "progressive improvement in the economic and social condition of
working men" attained, he emphasizes, by workers' *own* action, their "loud
demands," and their determined efforts to claim their just rights and benefits.
"Working men all over the world . . . insist on being treated as human beings,
with a share in every sector of human society: in the socio-economic sphere,
in government, and in the realm of learning and culture."[166] Two years later
the Vatican II bishops reconfirmed their modern social tradition's insistence
on the primacy of workers and their labor over any economic factor or system: "Human labor which is expended in the production and exchange of
goods or in the performance of economic services is superior to the other
elements of economic life, for the latter have only the nature of tools."[167]

Support for workers' associations, including labor unions "structured...
to safeguard the workers' legitimate professional interest," remained a steady
theme in later twentieth-century Catholic social teaching.[168] Popes from John
to Francis reaffirmed Leo's defense of workers' rights to enter freely into associations to advance their own well-being and to "contribute to the organizing of economics in the right way."[169] In 1981 John Paul framed economic
justice in terms of "the priority of labor over capital," and described workers
and unions as principal agents of the struggle for labor justice. Yet Catholic leaders situate workers' pursuit of self-interest within a larger context of
service to the public good: "Union demands cannot be turned into a kind
of group or class 'egoism,' although they can and should also aim at correcting—with a view to the common good of the whole of society—everything
defective in the system of ownership of the means of production or in the way
these are managed."[170]

As post–Vatican II teaching continued a tradition of support for workers
and for worker associations, its treatments of class and inequality developed
and sharpened, aided by new and significant emphases on solidarity and the
preferential love for the poor.

Inequality

In 1963 Pope John, departing from Leo's assumptions about classes within a
fixed, hierarchical social order, set the tone for a new approach to inequality
and social stratification. "Today," John wrote, "the conviction is widespread
that all men are equal in natural dignity," animating movements against racism, colonialism, and gender discrimination. Limning social inequality's evil
effects on dominators and dominated alike, John further states (in hindsight,
overly sanguinely) that "all over the world . . . the longstanding inferiority
complex of certain classes because of their economic and social status, sex,
or position in the State, and the corresponding superiority complex of other
classes, is rapidly becoming a thing of the past."[171]

Vatican II struck a tone of prophetic critique in the face of yawning and
persistent inequalities: "At the very time when the development of economic
life could mitigate social inequalities . . . it is often made to embitter them; or,
in some places, it even results in a decline of the social status of the underpriv-
ileged and in contempt for the poor." The existence of great wealth alongside
great poverty is deemed especially scandalous. "Extravagance and wretch-
edness exist side by side. While a few enjoy very great power of choice, the
majority are deprived of almost all possibility of acting on their own initiative and responsibility, and often subsist in living and working conditions

unworthy of the human person." The situation is urgent: "the demands of justice and equity" require that "strenuous efforts" be made to remove "immense economic inequalities which now exist and in many cases are growing."[172]

Pope Paul VI, who was pope from 1963 to 1978, continued to emphasize the need to curb inequality, foregrounding as Christian and human values "the aspiration to equality and the aspiration to participation, two forms of man's dignity and freedom."[173] Pope Paul also "insisted on the need to balance the value of equality with the value of solidarity" so that concern with individuals' agency and participation is blended with concern for the common good.[174] Pope John Paul II (1979–2005) continued to flag modern conditions marked simultaneously by rapidly growing interdependence and rapidly increasing inequalities. "Stoked by various forms of exploitation, oppression, and corruption," gaping inequalities create injustice, division, and conflict.[175] Dismantling sinful social structures and building a more just and equitable social and economic order, John Paul contends, requires cultivating and practicing solidarity and a preferential option for the poor.[176]

Their differing theological sensibilities notwithstanding, Pope Benedict XVI (2005–13) and Pope Francis (2013–) share their predecessors' alarm at "the systemic increase of social inequality" within and between nations. In his 2009 encyclical *Caritas in veritate*, Benedict enumerates inequality's negative effects, including harm to social cohesion, danger to democracy, and damage to the economy due to "the progressive erosion of 'social capital': the network of relationships of trust, dependability, and respect for rules, all of which are indispensable for any form of civil coexistence."[177] Francis, echoing *Gaudium et spes* fifty years prior, frequently decries a culture of indifference to the injustice and suffering caused by "enormous inequalities" that persist in our midst, indifference that further entrenches ways of proceeding "whereby we continue to tolerate some considering themselves more worthy than others." Blinded by our indifference, "we fail to see that some are mired in desperate and degrading poverty, with no way out, while others have not the faintest idea of what to do with their possessions, vainly showing off their supposed superiority and leaving behind them so much waste which, if it were the case everywhere, would destroy the planet. In practice, we continue to tolerate that some consider themselves more human than others, as if they had been born with greater rights."[178]

Class Struggle and Preferential Solidarity

While evincing little tolerance for extreme inequality, Catholic Church teaching since Vatican II has also revisited class struggle, more fully acknowledging the need to take sides in societal conflicts between the poorer and the more powerful. Pope John Paul II significantly reframed official social teaching concerning the working class, class conflict, and solidarity within and between classes. In his 1981 *Laborem exercens*, the first social encyclical devoted completely to the subject of work, John Paul, recognizing that issues surrounding class and inequality have been transposed into the larger context of an interdependent global economy, put a new emphasis on examining and transforming unjust structures on "a more universal scale."[179]

Doing this, John Paul frankly acknowledges, will entail struggle. So, labor unions can be "*a mouthpiece for the struggle for social justice*, for the just rights of working people." This struggle, which "in controversial questions [may take] a character of oppositions to others," is neither an anomaly nor an unfortunate breakdown of class harmony. Rather, struggle is part of "a normal endeavor *for* the just good" of working people in their various jobs and professions. Still, battling for workers' rights "is not a *struggle 'against' others*" but rather is conducted "*for* the good of social justice, not for the sake of struggle or in order to eliminate the opponent."[180] Invoking the longer tradition, John Paul emphasizes that the "fundamental structure of all work" is that "it first and foremost unites people," with labor and capital both indispensable components of production. However inevitable or fierce, interclass struggle and conflict are legitimate only insofar as they seek and serve peace and right relations between classes.

In a pithy 1984 essay, Canadian political theologian Gregory Baum contended that *Laborem exercens* represented a key development in Catholic social thought on class conflict, one he perceived to be trickling up from grassroots movements and regional bishops' conferences into official papal teaching, beginning in the late 1960s. At that time, "a new note" in church thinking about class struggle began to sound, beginning in Latin America. At their 1968 regional synod in Medellín, Colombia, the Latin American bishops undertook a theological analysis of the situation of the poor in their region that led them to consensus on four major points: a more conflictual understanding of society; the urgent need for both structural change and personal conversion; social struggle for justice as a form of Christian discipleship; and the oppressed as agents of social transformation.[181] All four points, Baum argued, were affirmed in subsequent papal teaching.[182]

For Baum, these developments signaled a new embrace by the official church of a solidarity that gives preference to the poor and most vulnerable— Baum calls this "preferential or partial solidarity"—as indispensable for advancing social justice.[183] While earlier Catholic teaching looked to the powerful in society as the drivers of social change, preferential solidarity affirms that "the key agents of social reconstruction [are] the victims of society, united in a joint struggle for justice, supported by all citizens committed to justice."[184]

Baum describes this solidarity, and distinguishes it from Marxian class struggle, in four points. First, Catholic preferential solidarity "does not aim at the victory of one class over another." This enables solidary justice seekers to welcome likeminded people from other social strata to join the poor and oppressed in their struggle for justice. In cross-class coalitions each group "must modify its aim somewhat" and make the ethical choice to "sacrifice certain elements of its immediate self-interest in order to build and protect solidarity" in working toward an inclusive, common good.[185] Second, Catholic preferential solidarity is nourished by positive yearning for justice and liberation. As the histories of labor and civil rights struggles attest, this solidarity is characterized by a holy impatience for justice for the poor and oppressed who have been denied it. But the rich and powerful are not demonized as enemies of the poor: "the enemy, rather, are the institutions that oppress and damage the people. Solidarity desires the transformation of these institutions."[186] Third and fourth, Catholic preferential solidarity movements eschew violent means to structural change, as well as deterministic understandings of history and expectations of a this-worldly utopia. On this side of God's final kingdom any historical achievement of justice remains incomplete and liable to setbacks or reversals.[187] Every movement, and every institution, "remains in need of ongoing guidance" by ethical reflection and by its preferential commitment to justice for the vulnerable.[188]

US Catholic Economic Teaching

In the United States, the most dramatic and detailed later twentieth-century attempt in official teaching to express the Catholic church's solidarity with economically struggling workers and families was undoubtedly the May 1986 promulgation—after nationwide listening sessions, input and feedback gathering, then repeated drafting and revisions—of the US bishops' major pastoral letter *Economic Justice for All.*[189]

This lengthy text marshals church tradition, social science data, and results from widespread consultation with experts and everyday people to address the economy at all levels, focusing particularly on the widespread struggles and insecurities that families in all but the most affluent classes seemed to be confronting: "Many working people and middle-class Americans live dangerously close to poverty. . . . Many in the lower middle class are barely getting by and fear becoming victims of economic forces over which they have no control."[190] That said, the bishops take seriously the emerging emphasis on preferential solidarity with the poor, stressing that *"the obligation to provide justice for all means that the poor have the single most urgent economic claim on the conscience of the nation."* In this regard, *"the fulfillment of the basic needs of the poor is of the highest priority."*[191] With modern popes, the bishops regard work, decently conditioned and remunerated, as a key to both meeting non-elite families' basic needs and to relieving their economic insecurity. The document details workers' rights to employment, living wages, "adequate health care, security for old age or disability, unemployment compensation, healthful working conditions, weekly rest, periodic holidays for recreation and leisure, and reasonable security against arbitrary dismissal," as well as the rights to unionize, bargain, and, when necessary, to strike.[192]

Moving to the institutional and systemic levels, the bishops echo Ryan's earlier call for industrial democracy, urging that economic justice in the United States be taken to a new level.[193] "The time has come," they declare, "for a 'New American Experiment'—to implement economic rights, to broaden the sharing of economic power, and to make economic decisions more accountable to the common good."[194] Like the experiment in political democracy that has animated the nation's identity and history, the bishops call for *"a similar experiment in securing economic rights: the creation of an order that guarantees the minimum conditions of human dignity in the economic sphere for every person . . .* a new venture to secure economic justice for all."[195] The bishops aver that "a new experiment in bringing democratic ideals to economic life calls for serious exploration of ways to develop new patterns of partnership among those working in individual firms and industries." On this front, worker associations and labor unions are urged to partner with management to experiment with "innovative methods for increasing worker participation within firms," and for developing other forms of employee-employer partnerships.[196] Here, unlike much antecedent teaching, power is addressed explicitly. Underscoring that "partnerships between labor and management are possible only when both groups possess real freedom and power to influence decisions," the letter emphasizes that power-based injustices and tensions cannot be papered over for the sake of avoiding conflict. "Workers," the bishops note, "rightly reject calls for less adversarial relations when they are a smoke screen for demands that labor make all the concessions. For partnership to be genuine it must be a two-way street, with creative initiative and a willingness to cooperate on all sides."[197]

In 2009 Pope Benedict XVI returned to the issue of workers' rights in a globally interconnected economy. He challenged contemporary labor unions to be "open to the new perspectives that are emerging in the world of work," urging them to look beyond simply their own particular trades or professions in order to address larger questions related to work and economy, such as consumerism. Work's global context further demands that national labor unions no longer limit themselves to defending registered members' interests but rather "turn their attention to those outside their membership, and in particular to workers in developing countries where social rights are often violated."[198] Benedict summarizes eloquently social Catholicism's inclusive vision of work and livelihood:

> [Just work] means work that expresses the essential dignity of every man and woman in the context of their particular society: work that is freely chosen, effectively associating workers, both men and women, with the development of their community; work that enables the worker to be respected and free from any form of discrimination; work that makes it possible for families to meet their needs and provide schooling for their children, without the children themselves being forced into labor; work that permits the workers to organize themselves freely, and to make their voices heard; work that leaves enough room for rediscovering one's roots at a personal, familial, and spiritual level; work that guarantees those who have retired a decent standard of living.[199]

US Catholics' Shifting Class Alignments

The 1950s and 1960s were decades of economic mobility for many Catholic families, but multitudes of working-class white Catholics continued to be subject to class-based prejudices and constraints that class-blind popular discourse only thinly disguised.[200] After midcentury, the longstanding identification of US Catholics with the working class began to give way during what would be a decades-long trend toward upward social mobility for many of the (particularly, white) Catholic families who now made up over 22 percent of the country's population.[201] Unlike their union-identified parents and grandparents, for upwardly mobile US Catholics after 1950, Craig Prentiss reports, "being 'working class' was less likely to be seen as a badge of honor . . . but was instead seen as a burden. When Catholics finally had the opportunity to gain their piece of the proverbial pie, many lost interest in those things that had marked their status as industrial laborers."[202] Euro-American Catholics, benefiting from a Catholic-school-inculcated culture of industriousness and increasing access to higher education, realized steady gains in economic status on both income and wealth measures during the second half of the century.[203] By the late 1960s Chicago priest-sociologist Andrew Greeley was detecting "twin revolutions" apace in US Catholic communities: the first a religious shift from a counterreformation to an ecumenical, Vatican II church; and the second, a shift in socioeconomic class location, from blue-collar ethnic immigrants to white-collar professionals.[204]

By the dawn of the new millennium, large numbers of white Catholics had traversed into professional and managerial circles and higher class status. Numerous children or grandchildren of poor and working-class immigrants became class migrants, straddling the class identities of their families of origin with the new positions and cultures into which their education, occupations, and incomes had propelled them. As class migrants married and raised their own children, a settled Catholic middle- and professional-managerial class was being forged. Accompanying these changes came geographic shifts as successful white Catholics exited urban parish enclaves for the greater privacy and homogeneity—class and racial—of suburban living.

In the march of economic progress, however, American Catholics often left behind some key social values that had been baked into their urban, working-class cultures. Among the casualties of Catholic upward mobility were the strong local community bonds, connections to neighborhood and place, more constrained consumerism, and more critical perspective on capitalist economy that their working-class forebears had taken for granted. As the "working-class religion" of the 1930s, 1940s, and 1950s receded in prominence, few were reflecting on the consonances or tensions between Catholic social teaching and "middle-class religion" or "professional-elite-class religion." Also unclear was what class- or cross-class solidarity might mean for the prosperous US minority, including many US Catholics, inhabiting what Matthew Stewart dubbed in 2018 the "new aristocracy" of the 9.9 percent.[205]

Working-Class Catholics' Changing Faces and Fortunes

Meanwhile, the percentage of US Catholics who were white shrank steadily. By 2014, compared to the US population at large, the Catholic community had "fewer non-Hispanic whites (59 percent vs. 66 percent) and blacks (3 percent vs. 12 percent)," and larger percentages of Hispanics (34 percent vs. 15 percent). Catholic communities in 2014 also included a higher percentage of first- and second-generation immigrants (42 percent) than their non-Catholic neighbors (35 percent). Regionally, white Catholics continued to predominate in the Northeast and Midwest. In the South, 50 percent of Catholics were Hispanic. The Southwest boasted the most diverse Catholic population—the most Hispanic, and the least white (31 percent white, 57 percent Hispanic, 8 percent, Black, Asian, other).[206] Though still majority white, US Catholics had become the least white and most racially diverse among the major US Christian denominations, and these trends were expected to continue.[207]

Income disparities among Catholics reflected those in the population at large. In 2014 white Catholic households were doing the best, with 61 percent earning more than $50,000 per year. Latino Catholic households were faring worst: 60 percent were in poverty, and only 21 percent earned more than $50,000 per year, with Black Catholics faring only slightly better.[208] The 2010 US census showed that 29 percent of Hispanic Catholic millennials had less than a high school education, and less than 10 percent had college degrees. By contrast, over one-third (35 percent) of non-Hispanic Catholic millennials had college degrees. Educational differences were reflected in incomes. "More than half of Hispanic millennials (52 percent) made less than $25,000 a year," while 55 percent of non-Hispanic millennials were making between $25,000 and $99,999. More than other Catholic demographics, "many Catholic Hispanic millennials and their friends and relatives are poor. They know those who struggle to work with undocumented status. Poverty is not an abstract concept—it is a fact of their lives."[209]

As a burgeoning sector of the US population who in 2018 encompassed many lower- and working-class people, Latinos were poised to play a leading role in advancing a twenty-first-century livelihood agenda. But racial/ethnic and class divisions, including among US Catholics, posed major challenges. Timothy Matovina observed in 2011 that "the concerns of Hispanics reveal . . . a prominent divergence in U.S. Catholicism along class and cultural lines." Interactions between white and Hispanic Catholics still tended to be "between predominantly working-class Hispanics, a number of them immigrant newcomers, and their more established coreligionists." With many Euro-American Catholics now in the middle classes, in many ways Hispanics' economic, work, and ecclesial experiences had become "more akin to those of European immigrants of yesteryear than to present-day Euro-Americans."[210] By the early twenty-first century, a culturally diverse, majority non-elite, Latinx Catholic community was rapidly changing the face of a church whose leaders, membership, and dominant culture had long been largely white, and more recently, largely middle class.

White working-class Catholics also remained numerous, but were often overshadowed as other racial and cultural demographics drew the public's attention. Not coincidentally, Charles Murray's (2013) and Robert Putnam's (2016) studies of white working-class marginalization and discontent spotlighted heavily Catholic communities.

CONCLUSION

In the United States, the seismic demographic shifts transforming a majority-white to a majority-minority, majority-working-class population also sent tremors through Catholic communities. These transformations, fraught with class, cultural, and racial tensions, portend critical decision points for Catholics and citizens committed to a future of inclusive and sustainable economic livelihood. Faced with the class-related dynamics and shifts discussed in this chapter, US Catholics may ignore or attempt to insulate themselves from the challenges and opportunities these changes pose. But advancing inclusive livelihood will require taking steps to confront and engage them, drawing on the full complement of riches—teachings, piety, embodied practices, and more—that the tradition provides. Undertaking a "Catholic examination of class-consciousness" within local and diocesan faith communities may be one valuable first step. Absent intentional efforts to chart a different course, however, our currently racialized, consumerist, and economically and culturally fragmented US working and middle classes, Catholic or not, are likely to remain distracted from their shared interests, divided, and deprived of their transformative power.

US Catholicism's strongly working-class and immigrant past *and* present, combined with its class and racial/ethnic diversity, make contemporary Catholic communities sites where people who are joined by bonds of faith might forge strategies for more fruitfully addressing our complicated class, racial, and cultural belongings and differences. With demographics that reflect the socioeconomic inequalities and divisions marking the country as a whole, Catholics in the 2020s were especially well positioned for this work. Later twentieth-century economic mobility created a significant Catholic professional-managerial, upper middle class. Catholics are also strongly represented among the large, "missing middle" of less affluent, middle- and working-class citizens. As significantly Catholic Latinx families surged into the majority in the West and Southwest, large numbers of Catholics populated white middle- and working-class communities in urban and rural communities in the Northeast and Midwest. US Catholics also counted among their ranks large numbers of class migrants and class straddlers, with embodied appreciations for the virtues, strengths, inconsistencies, and failures of their multiple class cultures.

Their robust social tradition and history of practical advocacy for the poor and working classes also positioned twenty-first-century US Catholics to play integral roles in public efforts to advance inclusive economic justice. Their faith community harbors important resources for cultivating bridges of dialogue, respect, and common cause across class, racial/ethnic, and political divides. And with societal energies coalescing around political movements to ensure people dignified livelihoods within ecologically sustainable economies, the time seemed ripe for Catholics to more fully unleash the power of their religious faith to impel solidary action in service of these goals.

But by largely mirroring, rather than resisting, contemporary socioeconomic, race/ethnic, and political dividing lines, US Catholics have too often been part of the problem rather than agents of transformation toward a solidary, inclusive-livelihood political economy. As the next chapter details, mass consumerist culture and a looming ecological crisis compound the challenges facing the radical sufficiency economic agenda we need. They also make even more clear this agenda's importance, and its urgency.

NOTES

1. Lustig, "Tangled Knot," 49.
2. Zweig, *What's Class to Do with It*, 11.
3. Zweig, 12.
4. On harmonies and differences between Max Weber and Karl Marx on class and social stratification see, e.g., Coser, *Masters of Sociological Thought*, 228–30.
5. Lustig, "Tangled Knot," 48. Cf. Talcott Parsons's functionalist theorizing of conflict as not inevitable but "a matter of empirical investigation." Parsons, "Sociology and Economics of Class Conflict," 17.
6. Recall Young's "five faces of oppression": economic exploitation, cultural imperialism, marginalization, powerlessness, and violence. *Justice and the Politics of Difference*, ch. 2.
7. Fletcher, "How Race Enters Class," 36. Cf. Nick Coles, "A Class on Class," *Working Class Perspectives* (blog), July 30, 2012, https://workingclassstudies.wordpress.com/2012/07/30/a-class-on-class/.
8. Leondar-Wright, *Missing Class*, 39 (class straddlers); Williams, *White Working Class* (class migrants).
9. Williams and Boushey, *Three Faces of Work-Family Conflict*. Dollar equivalents for 2018 calculated using CPI Inflation Calculator, http://www.in2013dollars.com/us/inflation/2008.
10. Leondar-Wright, *Class Matters*, 2.
11. Over the last forty-two years, 45.9 percent have self-identified as "working class" and 45.7 percent as "middle class." National Opinion Research Center at the University of Chicago, *Trends in Public Evaluations of Economic Well-Being, 1972–2014*.
12. Zweig, *Working Class Majority*.
13. Zweig, *What's Class Got to Do with It*, 17. On this point, G. William Domhoff cautions against confusing freedom with social power. Workers may have the liberty to "say and do what they want within very broad limits," and their children are free to study hard in school so that they can perhaps "join the well-off professional class." But as for social power, "most Americans have very little of it if they are not a part of the power elite."

Domhoff, "Wealth, Income, and Power," *Who Rules America*, https://whorulesamerica .ucsc.edu/power/wealth.html.

14. On Weber, see Coser, *Masters of Sociological Thought*.
15. Zweig, *Working Class Majority*, 39.
16. See, e.g., Weiss, *American Myth of Success*.
17. Metzgar, "Politics and the American Class Vernacular," 72.
18. Metzgar, 63.
19. Metzgar, 64.
20. Metzgar, 65.
21. Isenberg, *White Trash*.
22. Metzgar, "Politics and the American Class Vernacular," 65.
23. Metzgar, 64, citing Joel Rogers and Ruy Teixeria, "The Forgotten Majority," *Atlantic*, June 2000, https://www.theatlantic.com/magazine/archive/2000/06/americas-forgotten -majority/378242/. Cf. Teixeira and Rogers, *America's Forgotten Majority*.
24. Metzgar, "Politics and the American Class Vernacular," 65.
25. See David Kamp, "Rethinking the American Dream," *Vanity Fair*, April 2009, https:// www.vanityfair.com/culture/2009/04/american-dream200904; Adams, *Epic of America*.
26. Hochschild, *Facing Up to the American Dream*, 18.
27. Kamp, "Rethinking the American Dream"; Hochschild, *Facing Up to the American Dream*, 23. Cf. Streib, Ayala, and Wixted, "Benign Inequality."
28. Success in attaining the American dream may be measured absolutely, relatively, or com- petitively. In situations of perceived scarcity, the competitive meaning becomes more salient. Hochschild, *Facing Up to the American Dream*, 24–28.
29. Kusnet, Mishel, and Teixeira, *Talking Past Each Other*.
30. Graham et al., "Moral Foundations Theory," 59.
31. See Haidt, *Righteous Mind*; Graham et al., *Moral Foundations Theory*.
32. Hochschild, *Strangers in Their Own Land*, illumines cultural and moral dimensions of Tea Party members' political convictions.
33. Authors Lillian Rubin, bell hooks, Michael Zweig, Barbara Jensen, Keith Payne, Jack Metzgar, and Betsy Leonard-Wright are all class migrants or class straddlers. Others, like Arlie Hochschild, Joan Williams, and Barbara Ehrenreich, are middle-class professionals who engage in immersive- and participant-observation of working-class cultures.
34. Jensen, "Becoming versus Belonging," 1, 6.
35. Jensen, 1, 6; Zweig, *Majority*, 9.
36. Jensen, "Becoming versus Belonging," 6.
37. Jensen, 2.
38. Jensen, 3, citing Shands and Meltzer, *Language and Psychiatry*.
39. Betsy Leonard-Wright, "Are There Class Cultures?" Class Matters, July 2007, http:// www.classmatters.org/2005_07/class-cultures.php.
40. Putnam, *Bowling Alone*, 1, 22, 24; Putnam, "E Pluribus Unum."
41. Leonard-Wright, "Are There Class Cultures?"
42. Jensen, "Becoming versus Belonging," 3.
43. Jensen, 4.
44. Yet "any clinical psychologist knows how many suffering middle class people spend their lives yearning and searching for a sense of connection to others." Jensen, 4.
45. Consider the often derisive use of the phrase "political correctness."

46. See Rubin, *Worlds of Pain*; Hochschild, *Strangers in Their Own Land*; Williams, *White Working Class*.

47. Joan C. Williams, "Class Creeps into Our Times," *Huffington Post*, July 20, 2010, updated May 25, 2011, http://www.huffingtonpost.com/joan-williams/class-creeps-into-our-tim_b_652127.html.

48. Lamont, *Dignity of Working Men*, 17–55; 21.

49. Lamont, 46–51.

50. Lamont, 97–147, 100.

51. Kusnet, Mishel, and Teixeira, *Talking Past Each Other*, 4.

52. Kusnet, Mishel, and Teixeira, 45–47.

53. Kusnet, Mishel, and Teixeira, 47.

54. Payne, *Broken Ladder*, 88.

55. Payne, 88.

56. Kusnet, Mishel, and Teixeira, *Talking Past Each Other*, 17.

57. Kusnet, Mishel, and Teixeira, 18, quoting Stanley Greenberg, *Middle Class Dreams*.

58. Kusnet, Mishel, and Teixeira, *Talking Past Each Other*, 47.

59. Kusnet, Mishel, and Teixeira, 48–49.

60. Cover copy, Jensen, *Reading Classes*.

61. Payne, *Broken Ladder*, 21, 45.

62. Danny Dorling discusses Maslow's hierarchy in relation to basic needs for esteem in *Better Politics*, ch. 2.

63. See, e.g., Payne, *Broken Ladder*.

64. Hochschild, *Facing Up to the American Dream*, 28–29, quoting Tocqueville, *Democracy in America*, vol. II, section 2, ch. 13.

65. Young, *Justice and the Politics of Difference*, 12.

66. Isenberg shows that consistently, the white poor have been identified with trash or idleness; associated with inferior kinds of lands, localities, and living places; labeled vagrants who failed to contribute to the economy; and dehumanized using comparisons with inferior breeds of animals. Nancy Isenberg, "Class in America and Donald Trump," interview by Karin Kamp, *Moyers*, August 1, 2016, https://billmoyers.com/story/class-america-donald-trump/.

67. Isenberg.

68. Jensen, "Becoming versus Belonging," 5. Cf. Payne, *Broken Ladder*, ch. 8.

69. See Wuthnow, *American Misfits*, introduction, on "respectability" as a sought-after requisite for inclusion in the American dream.

70. Attfield, "Rejecting Respectability," 47–48, citing Wolcott, *Remaking Respectability*. Cf. hooks, *Where We Stand*, 17, 112.

71. Wilkinson and Pickett, *Spirit Level*, loc. 1113.

72. Fletcher, "How Race Enters Class," 39.

73. Fletcher, 37.

74. Lustig, "Tangled Knot," 51.

75. Lustig, citing Lipset and Bendix, *Social Mobility in Industrial Societies*, 106.

76. Lustig, "Tangled Knot," 51–52.

77. Despite its biases in favor of working men, many women during this period engaged actively in the labor movement and union organizing. See, e.g., Cobble, *Other Women's Movement*; Milkman, ed., *Women, Work, and Protest*; Kessler-Harris, *Out to Work*.

78. Men's unions did support protective legislation for women, such as shorter hours for working women or aid to widows and children. See Kessler Harris, *Out to Work*, ch. 7.

79. Wolcott, *Remaking Respectability*. Another important example was the Black Women's Club Movement.

80. See, e.g., Glenn, *Unequal Freedom*, 56–92.

81. Muller, "Capitalism and Inequality." Cf. Stiglitz, *Price of Inequality*, xliii.

82. Muller, "Capitalism and Inequality," 36.

83. On European corporatism and Catholicism, see Mark G. Nixon, "Economic Foundations of Modern Catholic Social Teaching," ch. 3; and the more skeptical Chappel, *Catholic Modern*.

84. See, e.g., Wachter, "Labor Unions"; Crain and Matheny, "Beyond Unions."

85. See Franklin Roosevelt, "A Rendezvous with Destiny," acceptance speech at the Democratic National Convention, June 27, 1936, https://teachingamericanhistory.org/library /document/acceptance-speech-at-the-democratic-national-convention-1936/.

86. McCann, "Catholic Social Teaching," 56, citing Peter F. Drucker, "The Age of Social Transformation," *Atlantic*, September 2004, 53–80.

87. See Philip Scranton, "Tax Rates Mid-Twentieth Century," *Teachinghistory.org*, https:// teachinghistory.org/history-content/ask-a-historian/24489. The fifteen-year period of 1945–1960 saw historically high progressive tax rates; by 2011, "Americans remained among the least-taxed citizens of advanced industrial nations."

88. Muller, "Capitalism and Inequality," 37.

89. McCann, "Catholic Social Teaching," 58, citing Reich, *Work of Nations*, 6–7.

90. Stiglitz, *Price of Inequality*, loc. 199ff.

91. McCann, "Catholic Social Teaching," 58.

92. See Crain and Matheny, "Beyond Unions"; Western and Rosenfeld, "Unions, Norms, and the Rise in US Wage Inequality."

93. Rosenfeld, "Economic Determinants," 379–80.

94. Rosenfeld, 379, citing Verba, Schlozman, and Brady, *Voice and Equality*, 520.

95. Rosenfeld, "Economic Determinants," citing Lipset, "Radicalism or Reformism," 6.

96. Rosenfeld, "Economic Determinants," 379–80, citing Skocpol, "Civic Transformation and Inequality," 739. Cf. Evans and Boyte, *Free Spaces*.

97. Western and Rosenfeld, "Unions, Norms, and the Rise in US Wage Inequality," 518–19.

98. Western and Rosenfeld, 519.

99. Leo XIII, *Rerum novarum*, §17. Leo argues that "it is impossible to reduce civil society to one dead level," and "striving against nature is in vain." Moreover, the "manifold differences" among people actually serve the common good.

100. Leo XIII, *Quod apostolici muneris*, §5. See also *Rerum novarum* §19. The great mistake . . . is . . . the notion that class is naturally hostile to class. . . . Each needs the other: capital cannot do without labor, nor labor without capital."

101. E.g., Leo XIII, *Rerum novarum* §§14–16, 26; Pius XI, *Quadragesimo anno*, §§104–9, 58.

102. Many liberals "failed to understand that a significant wing of the American Catholic Church was simultaneously anti-Communist, antifascist, and anti-laissez-faire capitalist." Heineman, "Catholic New Deal," 366.

103. Calo, "True Economic Liberalism."

104. Heineman, "Catholic New Deal," 365.

105. Mazzenga, "One Hundred Years," discusses the ACTU's nineteenth-century antecedents (Orestes Brownson, Knights of Labor), plus contemporaneous figures (Dorothy Day, Peter Maurin) whose radical Catholicism contrasted with its approach.

106. Heineman, "Catholic New Deal," 382.

107. Heineman, 382.

108. Pehl, *Making of Working-Class Religion*, locs. 1555–72.
109. Pehl, locs. 1806–9. "When the ACTU chapter of Chrysler UAW Local 7 met for the first time in July of 1939" the call-to-meeting notice blared: "'WE, AS CATHOLICS, HAVE A SPE-CIAL RESPONSIBILITY TO SEE THAT OUR UNIONS ARE EFFECTIVE, MILITANT, AND RUN PROPERLY! . . . The welfare of Local 7 is PART OF OUR RELIGION!'" Pehl, locs. 1813–22.
110. Pehl, loc. 1821.
111. Pehl, locs. 1555–87.
112. "School for Organizers," *Time*, November 19, 1951. University of Wisconsin, a labor school center during the movement's midcentury heyday, in 2020 continued to operate a "School for Workers." University of Wisconsin–Madison School for Workers, https://schoolforworkers.wisc.edu/.
113. Pehl, *Making of Working-Class Religion*, locs. 382–83, 389–90. Cf. McGreevy, *Parish Boundaries*; Roediger, *Working toward Whiteness*.
114. Prentiss, *God's Economy*, 173, ch. 4.
115. Prentiss, 169, 227.
116. Prentiss, 169, 170.
117. Dorling, *Equality Effect*.
118. See Bivens, Gould, Mishel, and Shierholz, "Raising America's Pay." See also Mishel, Gould, and Bivens, *Wage Stagnation in Nine Charts*.
119. Zweig, *Working Class Majority*, 44. Cf. Albrecht, "Forget Your Right to Work."
120. Andolsen, *New Job Contract*; Hatton, *Temp Economy*; Kochan, "Building a New Social Contract at Work."
121. See Draut, Wheary, and Shapiro, *By a Thread*; Temin, *Vanishing Middle Class*.
122. Zweig, *Working Class Majority*, esp. chs. 1–3.
123. Zweig, 35.
124. Clawson and Clawson, "What Happened to the U.S. Labor Movement." "In order to suc-ceed, unions *must* raise the price of labor above what would exist if conditions were left entirely to capital and the market," 101.
125. Poignantly documented in Hochschild, *Strangers in Their Own Land*. Cf. Williams, *White Working Class*.
126. US Bureau of Labor Statistics, "Working Poor, 2016." See also Katherine S. Newman's award-winning *No Shame in My Game*.
127. See, e.g., Albrecht, *Hitting Home*, chs. 1, 2, 5; Ehrenreich, *Nickel and Dimed*.
128. The most-unionized sectors of the economy saw the greatest post-1950s declines: con-struction, mining, manufacturing, and transportation. Troy, "Is the U.S. Unique." See also Angela B. Cornell, "Sharing Prosperity: Why We Still Need Organized Labor," *Com-monweal*, June 7, 2016, https://www.commonwealmagazine.org/sharing-prosperity; US Bureau of Labor Statistics, "Union Members in 1999," January 19, 2000, https://www.bls.gov/news.release/history/union2_01272000.txt.
129. McCartin, *Collision Course*; McCartin, "Fire the Hell Out of Them."
130. Wachter, "Labor Unions," 583. See also Blanchflower and Freeman, "Going Different Ways," 6, 42; Troy, "Rise and Fall of American Trade Unions."
131. Wachter, "Labor Unions," 583. See also Fletcher and Gapasin, *Solidarity Divided*, chs. 3, 4, 5; Fitch, *Solidarity for Sale*.
132. Western and Rosenfeld, "Unions, Norms, and the Rise in US Wage Inequality," 533.
133. Rosenfeld, Denice, and Laird, *Union Decline Lowers Wages of Nonunion Workers*.
134. Rosenfeld, Denice, and Laird. Cornell, "Sharing Prosperity," concurs. Cf. Holland, "Cri-sis of Family and Unions."

135. Rosenfeld, "Economic Determinants," 394.

136. Western and Rosenfeld, "Unions, Norms, and the Rise in US Wage Inequality," 519.

137. See Putnam, "E Pluribus Unum" and *Bowling Alone*; also Putnam, *Our Kids*; Murray, *Coming Apart*, 244–51.

138. Murray traces the changing fortunes between 1960 and 1999 of a heavily Catholic working-class community near Philadelphia. On civic engagement and trust, see Putnam, *Bowling Alone*, chs. 8, 9. See also Victor Tan Chen, "All Hollowed Out: The Lonely Poverty of America's White Working Class," *Atlantic*, January 2016, https://www.theatlantic.com/business/archive/2016/01/white-working-class-poverty/424341/.

139. Lustig, "Tangled Knot," 49. "It would be a mistake to reduce race *to* class. But it would also be a mistake . . . to try to understand it *without* class," and vice versa. Lustig, 53.

140. Fletcher, "How Race Enters Class," 40.

141. Fletcher, 44.

142. Lustig, "Tangled Knot," 53.

143. Lustig, 56, cf. Zweig, introduction to *What's Class Got to Do with It*, 4–8.

144. Wilson, *People of Color*.

145. Wilson. Cf. Sean McElwee and Jason McDaniel, "Fear of Diversity Made Voters More Likely to Vote Trump," *Nation*, March 14, 2017, https://www.thenation.com/article/fear-of-diversity-made-people-more-likely-to-vote-trump/.

146. Gest, "White Working-Class Minority"; Gest, *New Minority*.

147. Valuable essays include Cloutier, "Exclusion, Fragmentation, and Theft"; Himes, "Catholic Social Teaching"; Ward and Himes, "'Growing Apart.'"

148. Rose, "Growing Upper Middle Class," 14.

149. Rose, 1, 6.

150. Rose, 14.

151. Congressional Budget Office, *Trends in Family Wealth*.

152. US Census Bureau, "Real Median Income by Race and Hispanic Origin: 1967 to 2016," https://www.census.gov/content/dam/Census/library/visualizations/2017/demo/p60-259/figure1.pdf.

153. Urban Institute, "Nine Charts about Economic Inequality in America," October 5, 2017, http://apps.urban.org/features/wealth-inequality-charts/.

154. In 1963, white families' average wealth was $117,000 higher than nonwhite families. By 2013, the average wealth of white families was over $500,000 higher than the average wealth of African American families ($95,000) and of Hispanic families ($112,000). Urban Institute, "Nine Charts," 4.

155. Urban Institute, 9.

156. Urban Institute, 11.

157. Urban Institute, 11. Cf. Bailey, *Rethinking Poverty*.

158. The United Nations Development Programme reports that average income inequality increased by 11 percent in developing countries between 1990 and 2010.

159. Organisation for Economic Co-operation and Development (OECD), "Inequality," http://www.oecd.org/social/inequality.htm.

160. OECD, *Income Inequality Remains High*.

161. Heather Long, "U.S. Inequality Keeps Getting Uglier," *CNN Business*, December 22, 2016, https://money.cnn.com/2016/12/22/news/economy/us-inequality-worse/index.html. In 2014, "after-tax income shows that the bottom half averaged just $25,000 per person in 2014," just $4,000 adjusted dollars more than in 1980; while the top 1 percent's average incomes rose from $344,000 to $1,000,000.

162. E.g., the much debated Piketty, *Capital in the Twenty-First Century*; cf. Muller, "Capitalism and Inequality," 31.

163. United Nations Development Programme, *Humanity Divided*, 3. See also Moyn, *Not Enough*.

164. See Ferrer-i-Carbonell and Ramos, "Inequality and Happiness" (2012), 13; and Ferrer-i-Carbonell and Ramos, "Inequality and Happiness" (2014).

165. Dorling, *Equality Effect*, 9–11.

166. John XXIII, *Pacem in terris*, §40.

167. *Gaudium et spes*, §67. John Paul II, *Laborem exercens*, §6, adds, "What gives work its dignity and value is the person doing it."

168. John XXIII, *Mater et magistra*, §22.

169. *Gaudium et spes*, §68.

170. John Paul II, *Laborem exercens*, §20.

171. John XIII, *Pacem in terris*, §43. A thoughtful, Catholic reconsideration of economic inequality is Hirschfeld, "Rethinking Economic Inequality."

172. *Gaudium et spes*, §66.

173. Paul VI, *Octogesima adveniens*, §22.

174. Dorr, *Option for the Poor and for the Earth*, 193.

175. Pontifical Commission for Justice and Peace, *Compendium*, §192. Cf. John Paul II, *Sollicitudo rei socialis*, §14.

176. Pontifical Commission for Justice and Peace, *Compendium*, §§36–42.

177. Benedict XVI, *Caritas in veritate*, §32; cf. Dorr, *Option for the Poor and for the Earth*, 379.

178. Francis, *Laudato si'*, §90.

179. John Paul II, *Laborem exercens*, §2.

180. John Paul II, §20.

181. Baum, "Class Struggle and the Magisterium," 692.

182. Baum, 696, citing *Laborem exercens*, §8. Cf. Twomey, "John Paul II and the 'Preferential Option for the Poor.'"

183. Baum, "Class Struggle and the Magisterium," 695, 696.

184. Baum, 696.

185. Baum, 698.

186. Baum, 698–99.

187. Baum, 700–701.

188. Post-1981, John Paul II speaks of "structures of sin" and "love of preference for the poor," (*Sollicitudo rei socialis*, §§36–42, 47), nuances his treatment of "class struggle" (*Centesimus annus*, §14), and emphasizes solidarity as a commitment to the common good (*Sollicitudo rei socialis*, §§ 36–40). Benedict XVI highlighted none of these themes; Francis returned to them. See, e.g., Francis, *Evangelii gaudium*, §§186–90; Francis, *Laudato si'*, §§86, 158.

189. US Catholic Bishops, *Economic Justice for All* (*EJA*). *EJA* drew widespread interest and debate within and beyond Catholic circles. Pro-capitalist critics castigated the bishops' "warmed-over New Deal policy proposals," for overreliance on government activism that endangered market freedom and productivity, and for focusing on redistribution at the expense of economic creativity, entrepreneurial initiative, and productivity, all also crucial to economic and worker well-being. Progressives and liberationists criticized *EJA*'s lack of radicality. See Curran, "Reception of Catholic Social and Economic Teaching"; Allman, introduction to *Almighty Dollar*, 11–18.

190. US Catholic Bishops, *Economic Justice for All*, §85.

191. US Catholic Bishops, §§86, 87–89, 90.

192. US Catholic Bishops, §§103, 104.

193. On Ryan and "industrial democracy," see, e.g., Firer Hinze, "John A. Ryan," 181–84.

194. US Catholic Bishops, *Economic Justice for All*, §21.

195. US Catholic Bishops, §95.

196. US Catholic Bishops, §§298, 301. Invoking Ryan's legacy, §300 states, "In our 1919 Program of Social Reconstruction we observed 'the full possibilities of increased production will not be realized so long as the majority of workers remain mere wage earners. The majority must somehow become owners, at least in part, of the instruments of production.' We believe this judgment remains generally valid today."

197. US Catholic Bishops, §302. A rejoinder to *EJA*'s first draft by a group of conservative Catholic intellectuals led by Michael Novak, published in 1985, became known as "the Lay Commission's letter on the economy." Novak, Joyce, and the Lay Commission on Catholic Social Teaching, *Toward the Future*. Cf. Jeffrey Tucker, "Papal Economics 101: The Catholic Ethic and the Spirit of Catholicism," *Crisis Magazine*, June 1, 1991, https:// www.crisismagazine.com/1991/papal-economics-101-the-catholic-ethic-and-the-spirit -of-capitalism; Deslippe, "For Faith and Free Markets."

198. Benedict XVI, *Caritas in veritate*, §64.

199. Benedict XVI, §63. Cf. Matheny, "Disappearance of Labor Unions," 33–34.

200. Jonathan Cobb and Richard Sennett's 1972 study, *Hidden Injuries of Class*, drew its stories of people negotiating working-class life primarily from interviews with white ethnic, largely Catholic, Bostonians.

201. David Briggs, "Counting U.S. Catholics: Signs of Growth and Decline on the Road to 100 Million," *Huffington Post*, December 27, 2012, https://www.huffpost.com/entry /counting-us-catholics-signs-of-growth-and-decline-on-the-road-to-100-million_b _2315142.

202. Prentiss, *Debating God's Economy*, 138.

203. By 2011, "53 percent of Catholics had at least some post-secondary education, and 27 percent had college or graduate degrees." Compared to 20 percent in 1987, by 2011, "60 percent of Catholics reported family incomes of $40,000 or more, with 22 percent of that number reporting incomes of $100,000 or more." 51 percent of Catholic families reported incomes of $55,000 or higher, roughly matching the population at large. William D'Antonio, "New Survey Offers Portrait of U.S. Catholics," *National Catholic Reporter*, October 24, 2011, https://www.ncronline.org/news/new-survey-offers-portrait-us-catholics.

204. See Greeley, *Catholic Myth*, 20, 73; ch. 4. See also Keister, "Upward Wealth Mobility," 23, citing Oats, "Catholic Laywomen."

205. Matthew Stewart, "The 9.9 Percent Is the New American Aristocracy," *Atlantic*, June 2018, https://www.theatlantic.com/magazine/archive/2018/06/the-birth-of-a-new -american-aristocracy/559130/.

206. Michael Lipka, "A Closer Look at Catholic America," *Fact Tank: News in the Numbers* (blog), Pew Research Center, September 14, 2015, https://www.pewresearch.org/fact -tank/2015/09/14/a-closer-look-at-catholic-america/.

207. Lipka. Smith et al., "America's Changing Religious Landscape." See also Emma Green, "There Are More Black Catholics in the U.S. Than Members of the A.M.E. Church," *Atlantic*, November 2017, https://www.theatlantic.com/politics/archive/2017/11 /black-catholics/544754/.

208. Pew Research Center, "Income Distribution among Catholics by Race/Ethnicity," 2014, https://www.pewforum.org/religious-landscape-study/compare/income-distribution /by/racial-and-ethnic-composition/among/religious-tradition/catholic/.
209. "Survey Highlights Struggles of Young Hispanic Catholics," *National Catholic Reporter*, October 24, 2011, https://www.ncronline.org/news/survey-highlights-struggles-young -hispanic-catholics.
210. Matovina, *Latino Catholicism*, 346.

CHAPTER 6

Livelihood Consumed

This book advocates an inclusive livelihood agenda, animated by an ethic of radical sufficiency. The past several chapters have engaged the "radical" part of this ethic by critically analyzing ideological and structural dynamics around gender, race/ethnicity, and class differences, asking how these factors have influenced work and livelihood for non-elite families over the past century. This chapter delves more explicitly into the "sufficiency" side of the ethic by examining one further, crucial twentieth-century plotline: the story of mass consumerism and its profound economic and ecological impacts. Arguably, two of the most significant forces impeding progress toward sustainable, inclusive livelihood are the consumerist system and ethos that dominate contemporary US life. In a world where underconsumption still wracks the lives of millions, consumerism's powerful economic and cultural apparatus normalizes patterns of excess and, like an anti-Goldilocks fairy tale, disarms our capacities to judge rightly what is too little, too much, or "just right," whether for ourselves, for vulnerable neighbors, or for the well-being of our environment and planet.

The problem, to be clear, is not consumption per se—acquiring, ingesting, or using what enables us to survive and flourish. Consuming in this sense is necessary, and a genuine human good.[1] Nor is this chapter a takedown of economies that successfully produce and amply provide their members with consumer goods and services. Rather, I critique the mass consumerist culture, practices, and institutions currently ascendant in the United States. In this system, commodifying and consumerist ways of thinking, valuing, and behaving transgress market boundaries, constituting a cultural *habitus* that invades and shapes both noneconomic spheres of life, and our own psyches.[2] Observing these developments in the 1950s, Hannah Arendt lamented: "In our need for more and more rapid replacement of the worldly things around us, we can no longer afford to use them, to respect and preserve their inherent durability; we must consume, devour, as it were, our houses and furniture and cars as though they were the 'good things' of nature which spoil uselessly if they are not drawn swiftly into the never-ending cycle of man's metabolism with nature."[3]

Fifty years later, Jennifer Lambert tells a childhood story that poignantly illustrates consumerism's power to colonize and shape perceptions and desires, even among the very young.

> I learned at an early age that what you have in your toy chest is a reflection of what your worth in society amounts to. At five years old I knew that having "real" Barbie dolls, along with their "authentic" accessories, was the ticket to being cool. This ticket of material coolness is a ticket to power and to most, power equals acceptance. When you are a five-year-old latchkey kid, and you live in low-income housing, you will do or attempt to do whatever it takes to be liked and accepted by your peers.
>
> [As each Christmas holiday approached,] most of my days were spent asking Santa for the "real" Barbie Dream House. I believed that it had the power of making me fit in and making others accept me, despite my family's circumstances. I am sure I wanted it more because Lisa, the girl who lived about a block and a half down the street . . . had not one, but two Barbie Dream Houses and every accessory imaginable.
>
> In the end I never got my five-year-old hands on one, but I did find the Barbie RV under the tree in 1980. I cannot even put into words the feeling of power that RV gave me. I believe I was the only kid on the block to have one, so all of the other "Barbies" wanted to go on Barbie vacations at my house (much to the chagrin of Lisa).
>
> [Meanwhile, my mother worked overtime, and each Christmas and birthday my grandmother went into further debt, all to provide me with the consumer happiness and positional power I craved.] This "trickle up effect" (my needs and desires making those who care about me succumb to the effects), is a great example of the effects of consumerism.
>
> I am nearing my thirty-second birthday and I can say, without hesitation or doubt, that after falling victim to the clutches of consumerism and the ways in which we mass produce and waste, I have not yet been able to crawl out from under the spell. Capitalism is alive and well in my brain and I am aware of it; but I am paralyzed by it.[4]

As Jennifer's story attests, the key problem here is not the activity of consuming, nor the production and exchange of consumer goods. It is that she, her family, and our society are entangled in a *consumerist regime* that permeates and deeply informs our contemporary North American economy and culture.

It hasn't always been this way. As capitalist productivity ramped up in the late nineteenth century, business leaders sought to ensure political and cultural conditions conducive to business's optimal—in their definition, most profitable—functioning. Their solution wedded a "mass production, high growth" economy to a "long work hours, high consumption" middle-class lifestyle. Over the ensuing century, this mass-consumerist culture reframed both the shape and substance of the good livelihood workers and families sought. Consumerism changed how American families understood and experienced sufficiency, security, and status, in particular by removing stable criteria for determining when sufficiency has been reached, or what constitutes excess. And its dynamics and consequences implicated the mass-consumerist economy in what, by century's end, would be called the environmental or ecological crisis. All this makes examining and contending with consumerism imperative tasks for advocates of an inclusive-livelihood political economy.

THE ASCENDANCE OF MASS CONSUMERISM, EARLY TWENTIETH CENTURY

The rise of modern capitalism, writes economic historian Jerry Muller, brought "new forms of commerce and manufacturing" that, along with the commodification of goods and the division of labor, enabled an explosion of production and distribution unprecedented in the history of the world. The positive benefits of these developments were many. Besides making goods like food and medicine widely available at low cost, Muller underlines "the extent to which modern capitalism's creation and increasingly cheap distribution of new cultural commodities" provided more people than ever before with resources of "self-cultivation." Access to books and newspapers paired with astonishing developments in communications technologies facilitated connections and information sharing across great physical and social distances. The cross-class dispersion of "cultural commodities" like art, music, and theater has enabled "an expansion of not only our awareness but also our imagination, our ability to empathize with others and imagine living in new ways ourselves." In multiple ways, Muller contends, capitalism and commodification have facilitated not only material prosperity but also "humanitarianism and new forms of self-invention."[5]

Historian Jan de Vries points out another effect of these modern developments: "an awakening of the appetites of the mind—an expansion of subjective wants and a new subjective perception of needs," all critical in the birthing of what we are here calling mass consumerism. Accompanying the industrial revolution, de Vries argues, was an "industriousness revolution," as households were induced to invest their time and labor into wage earning in order to access the streams of commodities (goods and services) that made up an ever-rising "standard of living."[6] Motives for wage earning changed: people were no longer spurred to labor solely or primarily to alleviate the material scarcities of poverty. Long after meeting basic material and social needs, workers in a consumerist economy—eager to acquire new, improved, luxury, or positional goods—would continue to work.[7]

The early twentieth century, as Sharon Beder details, witnessed the consolidation and entrenchment of a particular form of mass-production, high-growth market economy. In the United States, "production between 1860 and 1920 increased by 12 to 14 times," while the population only tripled. With more goods being produced than populations with "set habits and means" could consume, two schools of thought emerged on the proper way to respond.[8] One camp, dominated by "intellectuals, labor leaders, reformers, educators, and religious leaders" like John A. Ryan, held that "work hours should be decreased and the economy stabilized so that production met current needs and the work was shared around." If, as was widely believed, "consumer desires had limits that could be reached," then "production beyond those limits would result in increased leisure time for all."

An opposing camp advocated addressing market saturation by increasing consumption, in particular among economic non-elites. This solution had two primary attractions. First, continually expanding production would enable manufacturers to reap continually growing profits. The alternative, a stabilized economy that delivered moderate livelihoods for all and shorter hours of work, might stagnate growth, harm business competitiveness, and jeopardize some firms' survival. Second, a high-consumption, high-work economy was seen as conducive to social order: many feared that increased leisure time for non-elites would erode their work ethic, breed dissoluteness and disorder, and create conditions ripe for political "radicalism." Because "increasing production and consumption guaranteed the ongoing centrality of [waged] work," taking this route "would help to ensure a peaceful and well-behaved working class."[9]

Leading businessmen and economists therefore advocated "expanding the consuming class beyond the middle and upper classes to include the working classes," and "extolled the virtues and pleasures of work." In 1929,

National Association of Manufacturers President John E. Edgerton summarized this viewpoint: "I am for everything that will make work happier but against everything that will further subordinate its importance.... [T]he emphasis should be put on work—more work and better work, instead of upon leisure." For, he warned, "nothing breeds radicalism more quickly than unhappiness unless it is leisure. As long as the people are kept profitably and happily employed there is little danger from radicalism." For business leaders, keeping non-elite families too busy to become radicalized was among the many benefits that mass consumerism promised.[10]

At this critical juncture, the "inclusive employment, moderate consumption, less hours" economic model became the road not taken.[11] Corporations, communities, and workers opted instead into a high-growth, high-consumption, high-hours culture and economy. Meanwhile, economists and policymakers projected a picture of the market economy as a high-productivity, low-unemployment machine that would churn out jobs, profits, and a plethora of consumer choices for all.[12]

But the attitudes and practices that this high-consumption model required had to be taught and learned: "'People had to move away from habits of strict thrift toward habits of ready spending.'"[13] Corporations thus set out to reform and reeducate people's habits according to "the new economic gospel of consumption," employing mass advertising as a key pedagogical tool.[14] Business leaders like Boston merchant Edward Filene "spoke frankly about the need for social planning in order to create a consumer culture where industry could 'sell to the masses all that it employs the masses to create' and about the need for education to train the masses to be consumers in a world of mass production." Filene further contended that "consumer culture could unify the nation and, through education," social change could be limited to pursuing the changing commodities that industry produced.[15]

The historical record thus reveals that consumerism—"the mass participation in the values of the mass-induced market"—was less "a natural historical development" than "an aggressive device of corporate survival." Business leaders knew that "discontent in the workplace could lead to a challenge to corporate authority" and demands for governmental redress. But discontent in the consumer sphere, by focusing workers' attention on scratching the itch of consumer desire, "provided an incentive to work harder and reflected an acceptance of the values of the capitalist enterprise." By "shifting the locus of discontent from people's work to arenas that advertisers could promise would be satisfied by consumption," writes Stuart Ewen, "workers' frustrations and unhappiness could then be redirected towards buying rather than political protest against working conditions or other elements of industrial society."[16]

Capitalists' efforts to stoke consumerism did not meet much resistance; accounts of early twentieth-century working-class life attest to the popular pursuit and enjoyment of consumerist goods and pleasures. For many working people and their families, the escape provided by the latest cheaply available consumer products or leisure activities helped sweeten what could "otherwise be a dreary and downtrodden existence." As one 1920s journalist noted, "To those who cannot change their whole lives or occupations, even a new line in a dress is often a relief."[17]

United States consumption rates increased, and by the mid-1920s, "the idea that there were limits on consumer wants began to be eclipsed by the idea that such wants could be endlessly created." In its 1929 report President Hoover's Committee on Recent Economic Changes stated matter-of-factly that consumer wants "are almost insatiable; ... one want satisfied makes way for another." Approvingly, the Committee noted that "by advertising and other promotional devices, by scientific fact finding, and by carefully predeveloped consumption, a measurable pull on production ... has been created."[18]

This same period completed the transformation of households' economic function to their new, commodity-dependent identity as "units of consumption."[19] Women formerly absorbed with home-based productive labor took on the new mantle of "consumers-in-chief," serving as the family's principal shoppers, and as consumerism's primary mediators, inculcators, and at times selective resisters. Simultaneously, a booming advertising industry was teaching the public to equate upward mobility and the American dream with access to bountiful, continually upgraded commodities, its running curriculum captured in commercial slogans such as "Some Day Your Boy will Own a Buick."[20] Labor unions also gradually shifted their focus from solidarity in class struggle to bargaining with employers for the annually increasing wages and benefits that members needed to maintain their consumption-focused, ever-rising "American standard of living."[21]

The burgeoning consumerist regime had an air of democracy about it: "Every American, regardless of income, class, ethnicity, or race was considered a potential consumer."[22] And buoying consumerism's popular acceptance and socially stabilizing effects was a powerful distributive narrative that Roland Marchand calls "the parable of the democracy of goods." According to this parable, "although there was a social hierarchy with wealth concentrated at the top," thanks to our capitalist economy "ordinary people could enjoy the same products and goods" as elites did. Beder rightly underscores the "clear social message" here: "Antagonistic envy of the rich was unseemly; programs to redistribute wealth were unnecessary. The best things in life were already available to all at reasonable prices." Incessantly and enticingly repeated, "visions of fellowship in a Democracy of Goods encouraged Americans to look to similarities in consumption styles rather than to political power or control of wealth for evidence of significant equality." In this way, "advertising and consumerism played a major role in the acceptance of the capitalist vision and its associated inequalities." Reconfiguring democracy—and livelihood—as inclusive access to "the goods life" helped displace desires for social change with "desires for more and better commodities." It also fostered the equation of political freedom with consumer choice, and "political citizenship with participation in the market through consumption."[23]

Assessing the state of things in 1956, sociologist Daniel Bell concluded: "If the American worker has been 'tamed' it has not been through the discipline of the machine, but by the 'consumption society,' by the possibility of a better living which his wage, the second income from his working wife, and easy credit all allow." Vance Packard's 1959 book *The Status Seekers* depicted consumer goods' rise as status symbols, fomented by advertisers—the "merchants of discontent"—who incited, then exploited customers' desires for the new and improved, aiming their messages of status through consumption "especially at people who had little chance of raising their status through their work." Historian Ely Chinoy shows that among midcentury US auto workers, advancement had indeed come to mean accumulating things and increasing one's capacity to consume. If one could buy a new car every few years, or make a major purchase for the household, then one was "getting ahead."[24] With status-conscious consumption now arguably the defining symbolic indicator of inclusion and achievement, the country had gone a long way toward becoming, as Arendt feared, no longer a nation of citizens but a society of jobholders and consumers.[25]

JOHN A. RYAN'S CATHOLIC CRITIQUE

In the 1910s and 1920s Monsignor John A. Ryan joined those swimming against the rising consumerist tide, championing a universal-livelihood, shorter-hours, moderate-consumption regime. Ryan's Catholic vision, recalls economist Martha Starr, entailed "reorganizing economic activity around a concept of human welfare that emphasizes material comfort, social involvement, and time for higher pursuits, rather than high material living standards for their own sake." And it included key distributional dimensions—not only living wages, Ryan argued, but "moderate consumption and reasonable work hours are rights due to all workers and families."[26]

To this end Ryan "sought to wed a norm of limited work with norms of ample but limited material consumption and resistance to competitive status-seeking."[27] Alongside likeminded social critics he argued that "work hours could and should decline in order to favor social, cultural and religious endeavors outside the commercial realm." Optimally, people would use the time gained by fewer hours of paid work not primarily for increasingly sophisticated consumption but to develop their "higher faculties and potentialities," to fulfill family and communal responsibilities, and to foster their spiritual vocation and relationship with God. This, Ryan contended, was the path to "industrial sanity, social wellbeing, and desirable human life."[28]

Ryan recognized that enormous modern productive capacities made a decent livelihood for all US families, with shorter hours of work, a realizable goal. The emerging mass-consumerist culture, he feared, would not only undercut that goal but undermine individual character and collective flourishing. Absorbing consumerism's message that "the highest good is to be found in material enjoyment and emotional satisfaction" led people to perceive life and welfare "in terms of quantity rather than in terms of quality." Consumerist materialism and its "culture of enjoyment" constituted a "false, deadening, and delusive" creed that ultimately led not to happiness, but to "a maimed and partial life" chained to one's "lower nature" and desires.[29]

Consumerist culture, moreover, devalued traditional virtues like temperance and self-control; removed needed restraints on desires for "more, better, and newer"; and dismantled stable benchmarks for sufficiency. Over time, the resulting hedonism harmed individuals' and communities' capacities for industry and achievement by eating away at "the very foundation of the power to do: the power to do without."

Early on, Ryan also recognized competitive consumption's power to trap people in frustrating "squirrel cages" of working and spending, in endless pursuit of the latest, most fashionable and status-conferring products and services.[30] In 1923 he observes that most families nowadays "find it possible and practically inevitable to expend substantially all their income and all the increases in their income" on purchasing commodities that can deliver more, new, or better "physical and emotional sensations." And to continue to acquire these, increasing their incomes becomes people's "principal and constant endeavor." [31]

Against this Ryan declares, church teaching, " right reason" and common experience all confirm that a life based on pursuing material enjoyment is self-defeating: it deprives one of the freedom and happiness it purports to deliver.[32] True happiness can be found only by those who accept "a rational halting place in the pursuit of material comforts," and recognize that "there is an upper limit, just as certainly as there is a lower limit, to the material goods and enjoyments that are consistent with right and reasonable human life." People coming to adulthood without learning these lessons, Ryan concludes, have had their educations stunted, even "radically perverted."[33]

To ensure work and livelihood for everyone and to guard against extreme inequality, Ryan called for setting reasonable ceilings on material standards of living. To enforce these upper limits would require both moral (moderate consumption and surplus distribution) and legal (policies and taxation) strategies. Citing Thomas Aquinas, Ryan distinguished three levels of wealth: (1) sufficient to provide the necessities of life; (2) sufficient to provide the conventional necessities and comforts of one's own social plane or station in life; and (3) superfluous to maintaining the standards of decent livelihood or one's station in life. Everyone, he held, has a natural right to the first level of wealth, an estimation of which provided the norm for a basic living wage.[34] The second level was legitimate insofar as it was needed to fulfill the duties of one's station, and to maintain social dignity and respect. Most countercultural was Ryan's Catholic claim that all material wealth at the third level, beyond definable upper limits, ought to be put wholly at the service of alleviating the personal and institutional conditions that cause others to suffer deprivation.[35]

But in modern consumerist culture, traditional moral limits on wealth and spending were vanishing. People "of every class" were succumbing to the illusion that a worthwhile life requires "a continuous and indefinite increase in the number and variety of wants, and a corresponding growth and variation in the means of satisfying them." In this milieu, for all practical purposes, sufficiency—"enough"—loses its meaning. The categories of surplus or superfluous goods, which historically Christians have been obliged to distribute to needy neighbors, effectively disappear.[36] Ultimately, consumerism's "working creed of materialism" jeopardized people's earthly and eternal happiness; for what forms or deforms human character, Ryan warned, does the same for spiritual character.[37]

Undergirding Ryan's case for a moderate-consumption, moderate-growth economy are several key Catholic social-ethical convictions. First, human flourishing, virtue, and beatitude are best served by social arrangements that enable all to enjoy ample sufficiency, not individualistic excess. Second, for families in each social stratum, it is possible to identify, at least roughly, what is amply sufficient and what is superfluous. Third, upward socioeconomic mobility is neither automatically valuable nor always morally unproblematic. Fourth, for all social classes, property ownership and access to resources come with responsibilities to the common good. The affluent are obliged to use their superfluous wealth to meet the needs and enable the economic welfare (via employment and other resources) of vulnerable neighbors.

While Ryan's Catholic economic ethic condemned rampant consumerism and greed, it was neither antimaterialist nor ascetic. As we have seen, he argued that workers were due not just the "ethical minimum" that a living wage entailed but, in a productive and successful economy, more than that minimum. Also tempering Ryan's skepticism about consumerism was his conviction that unemployment and underconsumption, specifically among non-elite households, were crucial problems in the otherwise booming economy of the early 1920s. One desired outcome of universal access to decent, justly remunerated employment would be ample consumption among the working classes. At the same time, since "the priority of an industrial economy should be to free people from toil, struggle, and want, so that they are able to pursue those activities that make human lives worthwhile," moderate levels of consumption ought to contribute to authentically good living, which, for Ryan, consists, as noted earlier, "not in the indefinite satisfaction of material wants, but in the progressive endeavor to know the best that is to be known, and to love the best that is to be loved."[38]

Ryan was not alone in critiquing burgeoning twentieth-century consumerism. Sociological pioneer Thorstein Veblen famously studied conspicuous consumption by the leisure classes and its societal effects.[39] Economist Hazel Kyrk, a strikingly compatible Ryan contemporary, described standards of consumption as social constructs that create ever-changing benchmarks and standards that make people feel pressured to compete with one another to meet them. But she also recognized that because standards of consumption are social constructs, when circumstances call for it, these standards can be reconstructed—for instance, by lowering rather than raising standards for consumption—to better serve the common good. Peer pressure to conform can be put to work in a different way. So, Kyrk writes, "if the 'simpler life,' the lowered mode of living, is known to be voluntary, or if 'everyone' else is adopting the change in question, the disagreeableness is partly removed." Anticipating behavioral economists' arguments a century later, Kyrk and Ryan refused to see consumption's upwardly competitive tendencies as wholly determinative; with communal support, hewing to differently calibrated standards is possible and becomes easier for all.[40]

CONSUMERISM AND LIVELIHOOD IN THE LATER TWENTIETH CENTURY

Driven by technical innovation, productivity, and advertising, the goods and services deemed essential to the "American standard of living," and the dollars and cents required to maintain that standard, both continued to rise during the later twentieth century. By no means was all new consumption simply hedonistic or superfluous. More people gained access to basic necessities at lower prices. And for millions, the invention and mass dissemination of recorded sound, film, and television, and later the rise of the internet and home computing, dramatically extended and lowered the costs of access to knowledge and culture.[41] Wherever one stood on its merits, no one could dispute the fact that mass consumerism was a defining feature of US economy and culture, its dispositions and practices ubiquitous and entrenched

During these decades, as well, two vast, deepening, and consequential macro changes caused rising concern: human-caused ecological degradation and economic inequality. Scholars, leaders, and activists became increasingly alarmed at mounting evidence that humans' economic activities were depleting natural resources, endangering species, polluting waters, and warming the climate. They also debated the reasons for and dangers of continuing high rates of poverty amid rising economic inequality, especially between the very richest and the very poorest, and the roles of consumer capitalism and financial markets in fostering or remediating these trends. These enormously complex and significant trajectories lent new challenges, and greater urgency, to the work of assessing how our mass-consumerist economic system impedes or fosters workers' and families' access to dignified work and a good livelihood.

Critics of consumerism during these decades tended to employ one of three interpretive frames. The first describes consumerism as a manipulative ideology that breeds and bolsters an economic culture that favors the interests of the rich and powerful. A second, structural frame emphasizes the consumerist economy's institutional, legal, and systemic dimensions. A third—which we will take up later in the chapter, using Catholic examples—approaches consumerism through the lens of virtue ethics, focusing on the habituated dispositions consumerism inculcates, and the individual and communal practices by which these dispositions are expressed. Though not mutually exclusive, each frame sheds different light on consumerism, and each suggests distinctive prescriptions for addressing its negative impacts.

Ideology- and Culture-Focused Critiques

A range of later-century critics examined consumerism as an ideology or worldview, highlighting its formative power and interest-promoting dimensions. Christopher Lasch's widely read *The Culture of Narcissism* (1974), for instance, discusses "the propaganda of commodities." Post–World War I capitalists began to see that workers "might be useful to the capitalist, not just as a producer but also as a consumer."[42] Advertising touted "consumption as the answer to . . . the malaise of industrial civilization. Is your job meaningless? . . . Is your life empty? Consumption promises to fill the aching void."[43] On Lasch's account, high-production industrial capitalism deliberately generates its own supporting ideology and culture. This consumerist culture "encourages the tired worker to despair of the possibility of changing the conditions of work" and to seek renewal instead "in the consumption of new goods and services."[44] Ingeniously, it also "turns alienation itself into a commodity. It addresses itself to the spiritual desolation of modern life and proposes consumption as the cure."

Simultaneously, by "manufacturing new 'pseudo needs'" and offering products that promise to allay them, marketers specialize in "selling dissatisfaction as a means to create expanding markets."[45] Intimating the significance of competitive mimesis that René Girard would later elaborate, Lasch writes: "Consumerism not only promises to palliate all the old unhappiness to which flesh is heir; it creates or exacerbates new forms of unhappiness—personal insecurity, status anxiety, anxiety in parents about their ability to satisfy the needs of the young. Do you look dowdy next to your neighbors? Do you own a car inferior to theirs? Are your children as healthy? As popular? Doing as well in school?"[46] Lasch further observes the devious ways that consumerist culture aligns and cloaks itself with the liberative impulses of "the progressive forces of modern society," and "the cult of the avant-garde, with the continual desire for what is new."[47]

Kathleen Vandenberg, drawing on the works of Jacques Ellul, René Girard, and Kenneth Burke, offers a rhetorical perspective on consumerist ideology and culture. Consumerism, Vandenberg proposes, is a "particular form of rhetoric, which is generated and propagated by mimetic contagion." Vandenberg employs Ellul's category of "sociological propaganda" to illuminate consumerism's distinctive rhetorical force. Unlike political propaganda, "sociological propaganda often springs up spontaneously," encompassing social behaviors that are "much more vast and less certain." Through these social behaviors, ideology penetrates society with "the active participation of the masses. Sociological propaganda is created when members of a group behave in such a way as to influence the attitudes, actions, and lifestyles of others; often this behavior is unconscious, unintentional, and spontaneous."[48]

Presaging Pierre Bourdieu's treatment of ideology and habitus, Ellul argued that sociological propaganda is neither "evil [n]or avoidable." The culture it fosters comprises individual and group behaviors that function both consciously and as "an unconscious, instinctive, reinforcement of self-identity," while also promoting and reinforcing what that society holds as true. In the United States, this "unconscious, instinctive, reinforcement of self-identity" has often been achieved through "consumption of material goods," abetted increasingly by the mass media. In consumerist culture, we communicate with and guide one another by way of practices of consumption that themselves function as persuasive "rhetorical acts." Over time, as people have become more and more "audibly and visibly linked with one another through catalogues and magazines, radio, television, and the Internet, their opportunities to identify with and imitate one another [have] also multiplied."[49]

At the same time writes Gary Cross, "growing disparities in income, especially in the last two decades of the twentieth century," left people consuming more but feeling more anxious than ever. A key driver of this was a kind of media-purveyed positional inflation whereby eventually, "keeping up with neighbor Jones was transformed into emulating the millionaire Trump."[50] Efforts to "keep up" under these conditions were unlikely ever to succeed, yet the necessity of trying to keep up was continually reinforced. Besides stoking what Daniel Horowitz calls "the anxiety of affluence," these dynamics pushed the already endangered category of sufficiency, or enoughness, to the edge of extinction. And the mimetic cycles that drive and continually ratchet up consumerist behavior, while generating profits and advantages for elites, regularly had harmful effects for the less advantaged.[51]

Structural and Institutional Analyses

Ideological and cultural interpretations dwell on consumerism's extra-institutional, dispositional, and practice-based features and manifestations. Other critics foreground consumerism's systemic, institutional, and policy dimensions. Three scholars taking this systemic perspective are philosopher Michael Sandel, and behavioral economists Fred Hirsch and Robert Frank.

Sandel analyzes the effects of consumer capitalism on US political institutions, especially its encroachment on the public sphere and its role in hollowing out democratic civic life. In the United States, according to Sandel, civic and work life have historically been distinct but deeply interdependent spheres, as "the world of work was seen as the arena in which, for better or worse, the character of citizens was formed." But the early twentieth century witnessed a significant shift as "the evolution of large retail outlets—department stores, chain stores, and mail order companies—created *consumer solidarity* in a manner similar to how large-scale production had earlier created *worker solidarity*." The movement from a political economy focused on work and producers to one focused on consumption, writes Sandel, "had major repercussions for America's understanding of democracy and citizenship." The productive-worker grounded polity envisaged by early US republicans helped to shape a democratic citizenry capable of self-government. By contrast, and problematically, "a political economy of consumerism ... views democracy not as the means of cultivating civic virtue so as to have self-government, but as a means to attain the greatest measure of material satisfaction."[52]

Like Arendt's, Sandel's claim that consumerist political economy attenuates civic institutions by replacing publicly engaged democratic citizens with privately absorbed consumers is provocative and important. On one hand, also during this period, democratic participation by women and people of color grew massively, suggesting that it is possible for citizenship and consumerism to coexist. On the other hand, if Sandel's critique is correct, advocates for economic and work justice will contend with a polity ill equipped for the civic engagement and collaborative action that pursuing these requires. Advancing inclusive livelihood will require efforts to reinvigorate the civic spaces and citizen agency on which effective action for change always depend. Sandel warns, however, that such efforts could face significant backlash from the beneficiaries of lower democratic engagement.

Behavioral economists Fred Hirsch and Robert Frank illuminate the systemic dynamics that dissolve "enough" and continually bolster standards and spending in modern consumerist regimes. Versus neoclassical economics' individualist, rationalist focus, Hirsch and Frank—like Veblen and Kyrk—treat consumerism as a profoundly social phenomenon. In modern, affluent economies, they find, people's individual consumer desires and choices become acutely context sensitive and highly comparative. Some argue that making status-based comparisons or competing for places in social hierarchies are adaptations endemic to *Homo sapiens*.[53] Whatever the cause, in modern consumerist economies, once basic needs are met, the "latest, best quality" goods and services can quickly become eagerly sought-after markers of social position and status, subject to intense competition.

In 1976, Hirsch introduced a term to describe this dynamic: positionality. In US consumerist economy, much of the value of any particular commodity—this house or that item of clothing—comes to reside in its "relative position in relation to other" kinds of housing or clothing against which we compare them. As ethicist David Cloutier explains, "many consumption goods have both positional and non-positional aspects." Housing, for instance, is something that a productive economy could make available for every family. But in our economy, houses also function as "the quintessential positional good—not everyone can have the mountain view, the park across the street, or the 'best' schools." In positional economic culture, people no longer want simply a decent place to live—which, in principle, could be accessible to all—"but a 'quiet, tranquil house still connected to the city' (a good that is scarce by definition and lost if too many others want it)."[54]

Hirsch saw that positional goods, services, and social relationships are by their nature scarce; "everyone cannot have them since their value is based on some kind of 'getting ahead.'" And as modest affluence becomes widely accessible, competition for positional advantage tends to become keener. "More wealth of the kind attainable by all paradoxically means an increased scramble for the kind of wealth attainable by some." As people devote more time, energy, and money to competing for positional goods, a further systemic paradox emerges: the outcome of all this striving and competing "is largely 'zero-sum'—everyone spends more, with the effect that everyone [simply] maintains position." Indeed, because such competition "involves additional resource costs," positional goods may end up being, in fact, "negative-sum." An economy may produce more stuff overall, but insofar as people work and spend in competition for continually recalibrating positional goods, there is likely to be no advance in overall social well-being, a rising gross domestic product notwithstanding.[55]

Robert Frank identifies another effect of consumerist positional competition that he names "expenditure cascades." Exposed through media and marketing to the ever more luxurious and higher-quality goods and services available to our financial betters (who themselves seek out these goods and services in order to signal and secure their socioeconomic positions), we who are relatively less affluent are encouraged to emulate the rich on comparatively smaller, but still inflated, scales. I can't afford and could never imagine buying an $8,000 Rolex watch or a $1,600 pair of Manolo Blahnik boots. But with these as my comparison points, I can easily feel free, or even pressed, to trade up to relatively more luxurious watches and shoes than those I might buy for $100 or less. This cascading leads to higher consumer expenditures at all income levels and a continual ramping up of the quality and types of consumer goods and accoutrements deemed necessary to maintain one's credibility within one's social position. Systematically, the line blurs between consumption sufficient to maintain dignity and respect in what Ryan called "one's station in life" and endlessly competitive positional consumption.[56]

This counterproductive process, which Frank dubs "the positional arms race," diverts individual and communal energies away from tending to important nonpositional goods (like education or the natural environment) whose enjoyment by one person does not vary according to the degree to which others are also enjoying them. As socially educed feelings of scarcity and mimetic desire push and pull people toward working for positional goods. nonpositional goods fundamental to personal and family well-being are often neglected.[57] Jennifer Lambert's craving for a Barbie Dream House as a five-year-old illustrates this problem. Lambert's mother traded time with her daughter, and her grandmother traded lower levels of credit card debt (both nonpositional goods), to acquire the positional goods their little girl so ardently desired. Lambert's story also shows how young children get sucked into this positional race, dragging their loved ones with them. For decades, stories about parents furiously competing to acquire the (seemingly) scarce, currently "hottest" toy for their children have been a fixture of the holiday season news cycle: Cabbage Patch Dolls, Beanie Babies, Tickle-Me-Elmos—the list goes on. The squirrel cage of the work-spend cycle is both a function and an outcome of the urgency we feel to assure our families' access to ever-changing, highly context-sensitive positional goods.[58]

A culture shaped by positional competition distorts people's expectations, then disappoints them. "Our consumerist ambiance leads us to expect both never-ending social [and technical] advance" and the continual happiness it promises. When neither materialize, ironically, "individual competition and frustration actually intensify despite the general affluence." The disappointments of affluence, combined with the "paradoxical increase of individual competition to get and stay ahead" and "keep what is mine," further erode "the social morality of cooperation." People "become more ruthless in their competition for the inherently limited 'ahead' spots because they have been taught that self-interested behavior produces better outcomes for all . . . though in reality it doesn't." Cloutier commends Hirsch's blunt conclusion: "Thus, to see total economic advance as individual advance writ large is to set up expectations that cannot be fulfilled, ever."[59]

Hirsch here alludes to a final systemic problem with our consumerist regime, a consequential social dynamic that Frank calls "smart-for-one, dumb-for-all."[60] The phrase denotes scenarios in which I, an individual, am led to make choices that are rational for me but that in the aggregate result in everyone (including me) being less well-off. Hirsch explains that "individual behavior on the basis of given preferences produces a chain of reactions that works itself out only after culminating in a pattern that no single individual would himself choose." So, writes Cloutier, "it is smart for one person seeking the good of their children to pay a considerable premium for housing in order to move into a 'better' school district, but it is dumb for everyone to do it because doing so simply pushes up the price of housing overall," leaving no one positionally better off than before prices rose. Analogous to treading water, spending becomes "simply 'defensive' and an attempt to hold relative position."[61] This dynamic occurs in many everyday experiences, as in an audience when "everyone stands up to get a better view."[62]

Hirsch detected this pattern in racially diversifying 1960s US urban neighborhoods. "Many residents may have wanted integrated neighborhoods," but choices that seemed rational for individual white families—to move based on realtor-stoked fears of falling property values as people of color moved in—started chain reactions that "culminated in a complete 'tipping' of the neighborhood," an outcome that in most cases proved harmful for all, as housing prices did in fact plummet, banks and other anchoring institutions left, and general neighborhood decline ensued. Other literatures have described this perplexing dynamic as the "tragedy of the commons," with a common ecological example being the tendency for communal fishing stocks to be depleted in the absence of limits binding all individual fishers.

These problems occur because "in practice, the individual is confronted with choices only on a piecemeal basis," and each of us makes decisions based on what seem to be our immediately relevant circumstances.[63] Put differently, "individual market choices do not present us with the choice of the actual state of affairs that we would most desire—though collective action could do so." In consumerist economies, many of the beneficial goods that people seek "turn out to be achieved only through some common restraint." But, crucially, "this restraint is not in any individual's particular interest to heed unless others also restrain themselves."[64]

A contemporary agenda for work justice champions families' access to goods and services considered necessary for a decent and dignified livelihood, including consumer goods and services that productive markets can most efficiently provide.[65] Indeed, Frank points out, modern markets have generated spectacular gains in both the quantity and quality of available goods and services. With "the additional wealth generated by technical change," markets are producing "more than enough to reinvigorate our schools, fix our roads and bridges, provide universal health insurance, clean up the environment, and more generally to boost all those consumption categories that the evidence suggests are getting short shrift at the moment."[66]

But here is the critical problem: insofar as legitimately necessary goods become perceived positionally and pursued competitively, they become impossible to provide for everyone. Our investment in positional competition flies in the face of ample evidence suggesting that "we would be happier if we *all* bought smaller houses and cars," or all updated our wardrobes and digital devices on a much less-frequent basis, freeing time and money for other purposes.[67] Everyone can have clothing and education, but not everyone can have the "latest" clothes or the "best school" for their kids, for both are by definition scarce.[68] In a generally affluent society like the United States, "everyone can in theory have a 'good school' or 'decent clothes'"—but, as Ryan and Kyrk saw in the 1920s, in order for this to be possible there must be consensus established around "basic standards" for sufficiently good housing and clothing "that are identified in non-comparative [that is, nonpositional] ways."[69]

Because this problem is structural, workers or families who wish to opt out of the positional spending race find doing so difficult and risky; it can be "dangerous for the individual to eschew the competition because of the potential to suffer real loss."[70] Even modest efforts to disinvest in a consumption-conferred social position may diminish a family's access to important goods and benefits like better schools, lower-crime neighborhoods, advantages in the job market, or social respect and opportunities.

Nonetheless, Frank contends, runaway positional spending is susceptible to change through collective, systemic action. If citizens can be educated concerning competitive consumerism's counterproductive effects, public support could build behind institutional moves to "put the positional consumption beast on a diet."[71] Much like Kyrk, Frank emphasizes that shifting our spending patterns to put the brakes on positional competition "would entail little or no psychological penalty, *if we all did it.*" Moving away from "smart for one, dumb for all" individual choices to foster practices and policies that are "smart for all, good for each" can happen in many ways. One example of this, familiar to many US Catholics, is the tamping down of positional competition that is accomplished when parochial schools require all students to wear the same uniforms. In wider culture, Frank argues, releasing resources currently sunk into competitive consumption and expenditure cascades would not require the rich to give up their wealth or non-elites to forgo all consumerist satisfaction. "All it would entail is postponing the upgrade of the mansion to the next larger size, postponing the upgrade from the five-thousand-dollar grill to the next larger size, and so on."[72]

But absent communal, institutionally supported commitments to move in this direction, "what's in store for us is more of the same. As incomes continue to grow at the top and stagnate elsewhere, we will see even more of our national income devoted to luxury goods, the main effect of which will be to raise the bar that defines what counts as luxury."[73] As a start, scholars like Juliet Schor and Frank urge grassroots changes in people's practices around luxury and positional competition; policy changes such as the enactment of a progressive consumption tax; and concerted educational efforts to inform the public of the positive benefits that can accrue if we face the "smart for one and dumb for all" problems besetting consumerist economies—and driving many of their negative ecological effects—and address them together.[74]

CATHOLICS AND CONSUMPTION
IN THE LATE TWENTIETH CENTURY

Later-century social Catholics mounted their own cultural/ideological and structural/institutional critiques of consumerism, providing, in addition, virtue-based analyses and strategies for addressing consumerism's harmful hold on contemporary thought and practice. During and after the tumultuous 1960s, many US Catholic families enjoyed growing affluence, but simultaneously, many were becoming more aware of the material and social insufficiencies afflicting large percentages of their neighbors at home and abroad. Latin American liberation theologians made grappling with Christian responses to the paradox of poverty amid abundance their special focus. And later-century Catholic social teaching evinced greater attention to structural contributors to poverty and economic injustice. As we have seen, official teaching began slowly to incorporate emphases on duties to a "preferential option for the poor" and active solidarity with—versus simply charity toward—vulnerable and marginalized people in their struggles for betterment. Post–Vatican II popes also gave increasing attention to the moral challenges posed by consumerism and consumer culture, particularly in light of inequality and poverty and, after 1990, in light of the growing ecological crisis.

By the early twenty-first century a range of new US Catholic critiques of consumerism had emerged.[75] With their secular counterparts, they engaged interdisciplinary sources and varied in their respective emphasis on ideological/cultural, systemic/institutional, and virtue/vice approaches. John F. Kavanaugh, SJ, Vincent Miller, David Cloutier, and official Catholic social teaching offer examples of each of these foci.

Catholic Ideological/Cultural Critiques

First published in 1981, with updated editions appearing in 1991, 2001, 2006, and 2014, Jesuit philosopher John F. Kavanaugh's *Following Christ in a Consumer Society* subjects consumerism to a stinging Christian cultural critique. Kavanaugh exposes consumerist ideology and culture as both pervasive and idolatrous and holds up communities of virtue and discipleship as key sites for resistance. Theologically, Kavanaugh draws on a prophetic reading of scripture and on modern Catholic social teaching, especially the writings of Pope John Paul II. His analysis of ideology and commodity fetishism, replete with examples from popular culture, is influenced by Marxian thought.

Kavanaugh acknowledges that modern economic developments, including commoditization and consumption, have served people and their noncommodifiable human dignity and relationships in myriad ways. Material goods, along with "scientific and technical intelligence . . . when placed at the service of human dignity, actually exalt and enhance the lives of men and women." But, like Ryan, he warns that a fundamental distortion occurs when economic profits and products, their possession and consumption, are accorded primary, or absolute, value. In a perverse reversal of ends and means, instrumental economic goods become goals in themselves, displacing other, more primary human ends. Profits are valued over persons, having over being, surfaces over substance. Alienated from their people-serving purposes, consumerist economies and cultures reduce persons to commodities and relationships to transactions, distorting and diminishing both. "Possessions which might otherwise serve as *expressions* of our humanity, and enhance us as persons, are transformed into ultimates. Our being is in having." Over time, "our drive to consume, bolstered by an economics of infinite growth, becomes addictive: it moves from manipulated need to the promise of joy in things, to broken promises and frustrated expectations, to guilt and greater need for buying."[76]

Kavanaugh describes consumerism as a pervasive and dominating ideology that funds a totalizing worldview and way of life he calls the Commodity Form. In so doing, consumerism functions not just as a set of economic practices but as "a system of reality (a philosophy of what is most real and valuable) and a religion (a belief in what saves us and gives us ultimate meaning)." Filling spaces and roles historically held by religious traditions, consumerist ideology and culture form "an integrative unity which penetrates and unites the seemingly separate dimensions of our life-world." In the contemporary United States, Kavanaugh contends, "the producing, purchasing, and consuming of objects provides the ultimate horizon of meaning for persons. Its 'lived' gospel, its 'real world' is the Commodity Form." In this all-pervading life-world, everything is subject to commodification, and a reductive trio of values—"producing, marketing, and consuming"—come to constitute "the ethical lens through which we are conditioned to perceive our worth and importance," and to serve as the measures of human behavior, knowledge, and affectivity.[77]

Kavanaugh paints consumerist culture's influence as deep, insidious, and transgressive.[78] Kudzu-like, its perceptions, values, and practices invade non-market spheres, threatening to overrun or displace the values and practices on which those spheres—the familial, the political, the religious—depend.[79] Filtering every experience, "cutting across every human activity," insinuating itself into the human psyche and spirit, the Commodity Form's impact is systemic. Its cumulative impact is to dehumanize. The consumerist lens warps our perceptions of humanity, "revealing" people—including ourselves—as replaceable objects whose value hinges on "how much [and how well] we market, produce and consume." Moreover, by stimulating desires it is incapable of fulfilling, the Commodity Form functions addictively, breeding frustration and disappointment, which it then draws people to assuage through ramped-up marketing, producing, buying, and consuming. And to numb our unhappiness "hedonism and escapism"—two commodities that consumer economy offers for sale 24/7—"serve as opiates."[80]

Kavanaugh underscores one further way that the Commodity Form dehumanizes: it trains us to fear, to detest, and to recoil from vulnerability and frailty both in ourselves and in others. We ignore, regard with repugnance, or avoid the elderly, the poor, or disabled. Conversely, we admire and are drawn to people who seem unafflicted by the creaturely vulnerabilities we so fear: the powerful, the beautiful, the wealthy, those who are strong and in control. Underlying this dynamic, Kavanaugh detects "a hidden rejection of our very selves, our personal limits, our deficits of mind and body." This self-rejection "inhabits and covertly motivates the addictive patterns of our lives," including the consumerist strategies by which we soothe or distract ourselves.[81]

The system has little use for certain types of people and activities. From the point of view of the Commodity Form, Kavanaugh explains, "If you like to pray in solitude, if you just like talking to people, visiting them, spending time in conversation with them, if you enjoy living simply, if you have no sense of competition with your friends or neighbors—*what good are you economically* in terms of our system? You haven't spent a nickel yet." Instead, the consumerist lifestyle breeds, needs, and at least purports to reward another type of person:

> [I]f you are unhappy and distressed, if you are living in anxiety and confusion, if you are unsure of yourself and your relationships, if you find no happiness in your family or sex life, if you can't bear being alone or living simply—you will crave much. Our lack of intimacy, community, personally enduring relationships, our sense of competiton and lack of solidarity nudge us into possessing and accumulating things [or experiences, including experiences of consuming itself] in order to fill up the lack we experience by missing persons in our lives.[82]

People consumed by consumerism have little energy or ability to resist the harms or question the terms of the Commodity Form's status quo.

Theologically, Kavanaugh depicts the triumph of consumerism as an instance of idolatry, wherein the dynamics of producing (how I view my work), consuming (what I can buy, possess, use, and discard), and marketing (how I present myself) become, in effect, absolute values pursued with a devotion due only to God. Here, for Kavanaugh, is the root of the problem. Right-relationship with God enables us to thrive as beings made in God's image; but entangled in the Commodity Form, we are ruled by, and even come to resemble, the false absolutes on which we vainly pin our hopes. We become "possessed by our possessions, produced by our products. Remade in the image and likeness of our own handiwork, we are revealed as commodities."[83]

To escape the Commodity Form's thrall is possible, but to do so requires conversion to a more authentic, personal worldview and form of life, "a mode of perceiving and valuing men and women as irreplaceable persons whose fundamental identities are fulfilled in covenantal relationships." For Christians the full meaning of the "Personal Form" is encountered in the revelation of God in Jesus. Yet this "form of life is revealed and manifest, at least in some way, whenever and wherever human beings are faithful to their personhood."[84]

Kavanaugh's Christian and humanist perspective ascribes to humanity ineluctable freedoms and dependencies, and virtually inexhaustible desires for truth, value, and life, yet limited resources for attaining them. As Protestant theologians like Søren Kierkegaard and Reinhold Niebuhr have observed, living amid these tensions evokes uncertainty, ambivalence, and anxiety. Too often, rather than accepting ourselves as "precariously contingent and unfinished," we attempt "to ground, finish and fill ourselves by *running away from the fragility of our personhood*." The Personal Form invites another, countercultural path: to accept and to embrace courageously the vulnerability and risks that relational, open-hearted and open-handed living demand.[85]

Catholic theologian Vincent Miller's analysis of consumerist culture and economy, published in the early 2000s, sharpens and advances several aspects of Kavanaugh's treatment. Miller unpacks the abstracting and coopting power of commodification—the process by which goods and services are rendered objects suitable for exchange. Because a commodity must be "acceptable for exchange by as many people as possible," commodification abstracts things from their embodied, communal and cultural contexts, so that they enter the market "shorn of the communal references that would grant them [their particular identity and] significance." Detached from their material origins and enculturated particularities, commodities can be reclothed with whatever meanings mass consumer audiences might desire. Commodification also obscures the social conditions under which marketable goods are produced, thereby contributing to conditions in which worker exploitation occurs.[86]

Like Kavanaugh, Miller argues that consumerism's "commodity logic" has gained a near-stranglehold on the habits and the daily lives of everyone in our society, from richest to poorest. But for addressing this problem, Miller finds personhood-focused critiques of consumerism—prominent in official Catholic social teaching—insufficient. Seeking to more adequately understand the dynamics at play, Miller draws on critical historical, cultural, economic, and social-structural scholarship to produce an analysis of consumerism that augments Kavanaugh's in several key ways.

First, Miller adds nuance to Kavanaugh's discussion of consumerism's power to coopt and reshape our values and desires. Under consumerism's sway, all our "beliefs, creeds, hopes, fears, values"—including religious beliefs and values—are subject to being "reduced to sentiments that function only to flavor consumption."[87] In addition, our desires become refocused not only on acquiring or possessing commodities but on the experience of consuming itself. We are conditioned to crave above all the moment of consumption. But that moment quickly passes, pressing us to seek another moment, then another. "Consumer desire is not focused on particular things; it is constantly enticed to go beyond what has been acquired to consider something new." The unquenchable restlessness of the consumer heart is spiritually dangerous, for it mimics religious desire for the infinite God. The fact that it does this subtly and indirectly makes it even more insidious.

Second, Miller stresses that in contemporary consumerist culture, culture itself, including religious culture, has become commodified. Like a vacuum that sucks up everything in its path, our late-capitalist economy inhales cultural products, processes, and traditions. These are ingested, parsed, and repackaged as appealing commodity versions of their former selves, thin and exchangeable. Image and surfaces come to matter more than substance as cherished communal art, beliefs, and traditions are reduced to easily consumable products.

Miller identifies a third, especially troubling feature of the consumerist system: its uncanny power to absorb and domesticate attempts to critique, resist, or build alternatives to it. In a culture saturated with consumerist logics, even serious social and religious challenges to the status quo are subject to commodification's power to absorb, repackage, and return everything for sale or consumption, largely evacuated of content and efficacy. Political protest becomes a twenty-five-dollar T-shirt. Work against poverty and injustice is retooled to fit into a two-week "service experience" that, once ended, has no way of being embedded in ongoing practices of daily life. This process is abetted, Miller continues, by two of consumer culture's key tactics: *misdirection*, "the systematic association of other needs and desires for love, acceptance, community involvement, etc. with commodity objects and the resultant channeling of the drive to fulfill these needs into acts of consumption," and *seduction,* "consumer culture's capacity to entice by evoking the promise of dispersed pleasures," and the "vast, undifferentiated horizon of *potential* fulfillments." These tactics help blunt or fend off challenges to the status quo. Consumers' economic dependence on this system for their livelihoods further dampens resistance.[88]

US liberationist and feminist theologians like Gloria Albrecht echo and amplify many of these concerns. Albrecht underscores cultural ideology's capacity to blind more-advantaged US Christians to the oppressive dynamics that interlace our contemporary economic system. "The power of a dominant ideology," she writes, lies in the way it inscribes itself in people's psyches and practices, until they become an "embodied expression of that to which a dominant group is actually committed" in its social life. "We learn that ideology simply by learning to live properly within our culture." For people in consumerism's ideological grip, "good intentions are not sufficient. Within our own horizons, what does not fit will remain unseen, be ignored, or be considered abnormal." For Albrecht, Amata Miller's phrase "cruel innocence" conveys "the sense of moral self-assurance that characterizes a dominant ideology with its power to limit the view of good people. Assured of their innocence, members of a dominant group never see, much less question, the harm they bring to others."[89]

In the early twenty-first century, Albrecht contends, "Christian faithfulness is still most threatened by the acquiescence of those Christians in overdeveloped social locations to the powers that sustain our privileges," at great cost to vulnerable peoples and to nature. Change is possible only if enough people awaken, and shake off that acquiescence. "In ways that provoke our own action, we need to lament the loss of so much of humanity to the deprivation of poverty and the despair of exploitive work. We need to interrogate the *savagely innocent materialism* of the affluent. And we need to ask why women, mothers, children, and especially families of color bear such a disproportionate share of suffering."[90]

Though their prophetic style differs in sweep and tone from more measured treatments typical of Catholic social ethics, critiques like Kavanaugh's, Albrecht's, and Miller's are in line with radical denunciations of idolatry and injustice found in Christian scriptures. Their challenging treatments highlight issues and raise questions that a twenty-first-century livelihood agenda must take seriously.

Virtue-Focused Catholic Critiques

Other contemporary Catholic critics argue that counteracting consumerism requires individuals and communities imbued with virtues conducing to sufficiency. Moral theologian David Cloutier takes this tack in his 2015 book, *The Vice of Luxury: Economic Excess in a Consumer Age*, arguing that if contemporary Christians are to effectively address poverty and economic inequality they must confront the vicious "disposition to luxury that has become commonplace among middle-class and wealthy Americans."[91]

Cloutier's treatment bears resemblances to those of Ryan and other early twentieth-century ethicists and institutional economists. With Ryan, Cloutier decries consumerism's corrosive impacts on character and virtue. But, he argues, to fight consumerism Christians must overcome not only intemperance and imprudence but a further, entangling vice that the ancients called *luxuria*, or luxury. Luxuria is a disposition to use "surplus resources for inordinate consumption of private goods and services in search of ease, pleasure, novelty, convenience, or status."[92] In a sly alchemy, modern consumerism has recast this traditional vice as an innocent, even virtuous disposition and practice.[93] By discouraging economic moderation or constraint, our enculturation to luxuria keeps the wheels of our high-consumption, high-growth, high-work economy greased. Steeped in luxury culture, we neither see nor can name the harmful consequences of our deep attachment to comfort, novelty, and convenience. "By eliminating this vice as vice from our language, we open the door to the unlimited pursuit of a certain way of life that is deeply corrosive but which cannot be identified as such," much less resisted.[94]

Perhaps more subtly than selfishness, intemperance, or greed, luxuria helps propel and sustain consumerist economies by cultivating people who are "captured by comfort and delight in material things." Extending points made by Miller, Cloutier asserts that "consumer society makes a religion not out of accumulation and attachment"—that is, greed—"but of constant detachment through the process of continual acquisition and discarding—that is, shopping." Frequently, in fact, greed is parasitical on, and injustice flows from, "the more fundamental preoccupation with luxury."[95]

Cloutier details ways in which US-style, luxury-focused consumerism undermines the human flourishing it purports to enhance.[96] First, a culture disposed to luxury trains people's energies on attaining and enjoying "excessive, disproportionate quantities of external goods," rather than the goods inherent in excellent or virtuous human practices. Because sought-after "external" goods tend to be scarce and positional—"only one person can have the corner office"—a life devoted to luxuria requires inordinate attention to what Pope Francis calls "private interests and individualism." Meanwhile, "internal" goods and practices—such as creating art, fostering friendships, or playing sports—which are more inherently cooperative, less positional, and less commodifiable, get short shrift.[97]

On this Aristotelian-Thomistic view, forming our desires to focus primarily on internal goods is constitutive to growth in virtue and, hence, genuine flourishing.[98] Maturing within formative moral communities, one moves beyond doing good merely for external rewards, and one's desires are redirected to goods valuable in themselves, and to the common goods these generate and sustain. To prioritize internal goods, persons and communities must practice "a kind of 'asceticism'" with respect to instrumental goods like money, material comforts, or luxuries. People motivated by luxuria's extrinsic rewards, conversely, more easily put aside (or merely simulate) virtue in order to get what they want.[99] When one prioritizes luxury over virtuous practice, the latter becomes a casualty of the former.

Second, notwithstanding well-pedigreed claims that affluent economies foster social peace and cooperation, a disposition to luxury undermines both.[100] Pursuing luxury, by definition positional and scarce, creates zero-sum competitions whose standards are subject to the continual ratcheting-up Hirsch and Frank described. Paradoxically, this problem becomes more severe in our affluent society where mass production, media, and marketing conspire to encourage non-elites to envy and seek to emulate elites' luxurious lifestyles. As "more and more activity is devoted to pursuing goods that go beyond necessity" across social classes, competition increases, as does the potential for social division. Further, as Sandel argued, by fostering focus on private interests, consumerism drains political support for public or common goods, and steers citizens away from commitments to redistributive and social justice. Thicker bonds of solidarity and citizenship fray, and our primary social bonds become consumeristic and thin. In this milieu, "'More' is taken to be a universal aspiration, perhaps one of the few we are all supposed to share in our multicultural society. . . . Whatever else we may disagree about, we agree that if you can have nicer things, you should have nicer things."[101]

Third, as Ryan saw, ever-changing standards for what counts as sufficiency or luxury corrode people's incentives and abilities to distinguish between necessity and surplus. Historically, ethicists and economists sought to delineate necessities, comforts, and luxuries; modern mass consumerism strips these distinctions of their salience.[102]

Fourth, luxury-focused consumerism blinds or inures participants to the system's impacts on those who are economically disadvantaged or vulnerable. Cloutier uses the mundane example of regular restaurant dining to illustrate how luxuria becomes intertwined in the daily lives of even the moderately well-off, and the moral blinkers that accompany the delivery of an abundance that is only apparently innocent. Invoking what Peter Brown called the ancients' "luxury self," epitomized by the rich in their villas who enjoyed servant- and slave-supplied lifestyles of seemingly innocent abundance, "Today," Cloutier writes, "at any Olive Garden Restaurant you will get innocent abundance of 'ancient villa life' reproduced for the masses, right down to the unlimited salad and breadsticks."[103] But then and now, Edenically guiltless consumption is a dangerous illusion. It conceals injustices to vulnerable workers endemic to systems that deliver the goods we consume, teaching us to "pay no attention to the men and women behind the curtain," and thereby to ignore both the wrongs perpetrated by those who pull the levers and the harms suffered by those who labor to keep our illusions alive. In our vincible ignorance, ensconced in "soap bubbles of indifference," we implicate ourselves in what Albrecht names "the savagely innocent materialism of the affluent."[104]

Fifth, as earlier discussed, across the past century consumerism has had certain democratizing effects: today, luxury of some sort is accessible to anyone with a little discretionary income. But the consumptive lifestyles of the affluent "create norms for success that infect the rest of the population," triggering expenditure cascades as the rich seek to distinguish themselves from the prosperous, the prosperous emulate the rich, and the middle- and working-classes emulate the prosperous.[105] Luxury-focused positional consumerism also exacerbates socioeconomic inequality. Though "a wealthy society need not be a luxury society," a luxury society, premised on positionality, undermines equality.[106] The entanglement of positional and non-positional spending involved in consumption inequality—e.g., the fact that affluent families in more luxurious zip codes spend more on children's educational enrichment and education, and on "security" expenditures like life insurance—further contributes to income and wealth gaps.[107]

Finally, luxury-focused consumerism contributes to human and environmental degradation by diverting attention from the ways our devotion to "ever more" drives excess, exploitation, and waste, harming both the vulnerable poor and a vulnerable ecosphere. Cloutier cites recent papal expressions of these concerns, particularly by Pope Francis.[108]

Versus anticonsumerist arguments that "critique social structures rather than personal desires," Cloutier's prescriptions for combating luxury-focused consumerism intentionally place persons, as citizens and as disciples, center stage.[109] Addressing problems like economic precarity, inordinate debt burdens, and structural inequality "requires attention to more than justice alone; it also requires restraining the vice of luxury" and cultivating virtues of moderation or temperance.[110] North Americans' habituation to cheap imported goods and reliance on imported oil, for instance, "are matters of ease and convenience that could be otherwise if we—rich and poor alike—had not accustomed ourselves to a pattern of consumption that we are loathe to break."[111] Indeed, for many complex justice problems "the best social outcome turns out to require cooperative, collective restraint—that is, a disposition against luxury."[112]

Cloutier therefore underscores shared "informal social norms" as key to restraining luxury within what Daniel Finn calls "the moral ecology of markets." Far more than laws, widely shared informal norms are the mainstay of cultures wherein "most of us, most of the time, can count on our neighbors, co-workers, and friends to be generally truthful, to offer help when needed," and where civility, cooperation, and necessary forms of economic restraint are mutually accepted practices. To some extent, the need for legal constraints on consumption signifies the failure of this crucial moral ecology, for which laws can never fully substitute.[113]

Highlighting Catholicism's incarnational sensibilities, Cloutier concludes by proposing directions toward virtuous practices of consumption and a Christian spirituality of possessions.[114] Theologically, he calls for "attention to the disciplined use of wealth in the world as an aspect of the universal call to holiness." Eschewing *luxuria*, disciples will direct surplus wealth to a range of uses "that can be called 'sacramental.'"[115] To this end, Cloutier attempts to construct "a positive moral language to specify our prudent use of excess resources," in part by distinguishing between necessary goods, shared goods, festival goods, vocational goods, and enrichment goods.[116]

Catholic Social Teaching and Consumerism

In a 2004 essay economist Charles Wilber divided treatments of consumerism in modern Catholic social teaching into two periods. In the first, Popes Leo XIII through Pope John XXIII (1891–1963) foregrounded the problem of "too little consumption by the poor." In the second, from Pope Paul VI forward, popes have highlighted the problem of "too much consumption by the rich."[117] Underlying recent papal attention to overconsumption and consumerism, Wilber detects three important sets of concerns, which frame our brief analysis here: *anthropological concerns* about deleterious impacts on people for whom "consumption has become the primary goal to the detriment of their own well-being"; *distributional concerns* about excessive consumption by some while others suffer poverty and want; and *environmental concerns* about the destructive ecological impacts of overconsumption and waste.[118]

Anthropological Concerns

Pope Paul VI's 1967 encyclical *Populorum progressio* (On the development of peoples) emphasizes the harmful anthropological consequences of a singular focus on obtaining more and better material goods. "The pursuit of life's necessities is quite legitimate," Paul writes, but becoming absorbed in "the acquisition of worldly goods can lead . . . to greed, the unrelenting desire for more." Economic and material progress are genuine goods, but they can enslave and dehumanize people who come to regard them as supreme goods. Both rich and poor are susceptible to falling into "avarice and soul-stifling materialism."[119] These stunt authentic human development by upending the proper scale of values that prioritizes "the higher values of love and friendship, of prayer and contemplation" that enable people "to find themselves."[120]

More than technical experts and know-how, development requires a "new humanism" that keeps these higher values to the fore. Embracing this humanism can help individuals and nations to overcome avarice—"the most obvious form of stultified moral development"—and pursue authentic development, whose mark is "transition from less than human conditions to truly human ones." Among these less-human conditions are "the material poverty of those who lack the bare necessities of life" but also "the moral poverty of those who are crushed under the weight of their own self-love" and the exploitative structures that greed and selfishness help sustain.[121]

Twenty years later, in addition to reiterating underdevelopment's dehumanizing effects, Pope John Paul II criticized the phenomenon of "super-development" typified by "an excessive availability of every kind of material goods for the benefit of certain social groups." Superdevelopment makes people "slaves of 'possession' and of immediate gratification, with no other horizon than the multiplication or continual replacement of the things already owned with others still better."[122] Elsewhere, John Paul links superdevelopment with a dehumanizing "civilization of 'consumption' or 'consumerism,' which involves so much 'throwing away' and 'waste.'"[123]

Among consumerism's negative consequences on persons, John Paul underscores "crass materialism," and "radical dissatisfaction": the more one has, the more one craves. Both are emblematic of consumerism's inability to satisfy "the deeper aspirations" that "remain unsatisfied and perhaps even stifled." For everyone in a consumerist culture, "having" takes precedence over "being." But for the poor, "being"—the ability to flourish as a human being—is threatened by a lack of essential goods, whereas for the affluent, it is undercut by an excess of nonessential goods. In both cases, having per se is not the problem, but rather, having "without regard for the quality and the ordered hierarchy of the goods one has."[124] Impoverished underdevelopment and consumerist superdevelopment are "equally unacceptable and for the same reason: [they work] against what is good and leads to true happiness."[125]

This anthropological focus is even more explicit in the 1991 encyclical *Centesimus annus*. "The manner in which new needs arise and are defined is always marked by a more or less appropriate concept of the person and his true good." Much like Ryan, John Paul insists that practices of consumption must "be guided by a comprehensive picture of the human person which respects all the dimensions of his being and which subordinates his material and instinctive dimensions to his interior and spiritual ones."[126]

Distributive Justice Concerns

Initial references in modern social teaching to the links between disordered consumption, distributive injustice, and environmental harm appear in the 1971 World Synod of Bishops' document, *Justicia in mundo*. Criticizing richer nations' disproportionate resource and energy use, and the environmental damage caused by their dumping waste into the atmosphere and sea, the bishops sound a strong distributive chord: "Irreparable damage would be done to the essential elements of life on earth, such as air and water, if their high rates of consumption and pollution, which are constantly on the increase, were extended to the whole of humanity."[127] The bishops call both church and society to an "examination of conscience" regarding material lifestyles. Among Christians, "faith demands of us a certain sparingness in use, and the Church is obliged to live and administer its own goods in such a way that the Gospel is proclaimed to the poor. If instead the Church appears to be among the rich and the powerful of this world its credibility is diminished."[128] As for affluent societies "enjoying a higher level of consumer spending, it must be asked whether our life style exemplifies that sparingness with regard to consumption which we preach to [other, less affluent nations] as necessary in order that so many millions of hungry people throughout the world may be fed."[129]

The United States bishops' 1986 pastoral *Economic Justice For All*, discussed in the previous chapter, also decried excessive consumption by some while others lack access to "the floor of material wellbeing" that basic justice demands.[130] It ensures everyone that this economic minimum is a duty "of the whole society," but it especially obliges those with greater resources. Given widespread poverty and "extreme inequalities of income and consumption when so many lack basic necessities," the bishops conclude that "Christian faith and the norms of justice impose distinct limits on what we consume and how we view material goods."[131] Everyone is obliged to examine their "way of living in light of the needs of the poor," and "Americans are challenged today as never before to develop the inner freedom to resist the temptation constantly to seek more."[132]

In a just economy, "meeting fundamental human needs must take priority" to fulfilling desires for "luxury consumer goods, for profits not conducive to the common good, and for unnecessary military hardware."[133] Communities and governments may legitimately require members to curtail some of their unnecessary consumption in order to help fund institutional initiatives and programs for ensuring economic participation and a just livelihood to those currently excluded.

Concluding, the bishops reiterate that everyone "must reflect on our personal and family decisions and curb unnecessary wants in order to meet the needs of others," asking themselves difficult questions like: "Are we becoming ever more wasteful in a 'throw-away' society? Are we able to distinguish between our true needs and those thrust on us by advertising and a society that values consumption more than saving?" But the bishops' calls to action and lifestyle change tended to remain hypothetical, indirect, nonimperative. Their tone in the 1971 synod document is typical, as they mildly suggest that "all of us could well ask ourselves whether as a Christian prophetic witness we are not called to adopt a simpler lifestyle, in the face of the excessive accumulation of material goods that characterizes an affluent society."[134]

Environmental Connections and Concerns

As noted, the 1971 Synod document alluded to links between consumerism and environmental harm. But only during John Paul II's papacy did "the ecological problem" and its connections to overconsumption and waste begin to be referenced regularly in official social teaching. In his 1990 World Day of Peace message, the first papal document devoted to the subject of environmental responsibility, John Paul contends that "the seriousness of the ecological issue" exposes "the depth of humanity's moral crisis." Modern society will find no solution to the ecological problem, the pope stresses, "unless it *takes a serious look at its life style*," including at consumerism and its moral and environmental consequences. "Simplicity, moderation and discipline, as well as a spirit of sacrifice, must become a part of everyday life, lest all suffer the negative consequences of the careless habits of a few."[135] Connecting the dots between "the ecological question" and consumerism, John Paul condemns the many ways that humankind today "consumes the resources of the earth and [our] own life in an excessive and disordered way."[136]

Pope Benedict XVI also pointed to close connections between environmental degradation and rampant consumerism. Like his predecessor, he traced direct lines between the disordered desires and values—both moral and spiritual—that consumerism fosters and the environmental damage caused by humans' exploitation and overuse of natural resources. Speaking in Australia for World Youth Day 2008, Benedict likened consumerism to the lure of "false idols" and pointed to its destructive effects visible in the "scars which mark the surface of our earth: erosion, deforestation, the squandering of the world's mineral and ocean resources in order to fuel an insatiable consumption." Exhorting his young audience to resist consumerism's reductive anthropology, Benedict urged them, "Do not be fooled by those who see you as just another consumer in a market of undifferentiated possibilities, where choice itself becomes the good, novelty usurps beauty, and subjective experience displaces truth."[137]

In 2007, Kenneth Himes noted that modern Catholic social teaching to date, while not ignoring links between consumerism and poverty, or more recently, ecological sustainability, had grounded its criticisms of consumerism primarily in anthropological convictions about genuine human flourishing.[138] During Francis's pontificate (2013–), critiques of consumerism became tethered more explicitly and firmly to all three of these concerns: the environmental, the anthropological, and care and justice for the poor.

With striking bluntness, Francis has frequently denounced what he deems negative features of the economic status quo. His declamations, of which this one is representative, often target consumerism and its invasive, destructive impacts:

> Today consumerism determines what is important. Consuming relationships, consuming friendships, consuming religions, consuming, consuming... whatever the cost or consequences. A consumption which does not favor bonding, a consumption which has little to do with human relationships. Social bonds are a mere "means" for the satisfaction of "my needs."... The result is a culture which discards everything that is no longer "useful" or "satisfying" for the tastes of the consumer. We have turned our society into a huge multicultural showcase tied only to the tastes of certain "consumers," while so many others only "eat the crumbs which fall from their masters' table." This causes great harm.[139]

A principal theme of Francis's 2015 *Laudato si'* is the intrinsic connection between the survival and thriving of persons—especially the poor and vulnerable—and the well-being of a vulnerable ecosphere. "When we fail to acknowledge as part of the reality the worth of a poor person, a human embryo, a person with disabilities—to offer just a few examples—it becomes difficult to hear the cry of nature itself; everything is connected."[140] Echoing

Benedict, Francis stresses that "the human environment and the natural environment deteriorate together; we cannot adequately combat environmental degradation unless we attend to causes related to human and social degradation."[141]

An adequate ecological approach, therefore, must also be a social approach; "it must integrate questions of justice in debates on the environment, so as to hear *both the cry of the earth and the cry of the poor*."[142] Pressing consumption's connections to distributive justice, Francis declares that blaming the plights of the poor and the earth on other factors while leaving unquestioned the "extreme and selective consumerism on the part of some" is a dishonest dodge. "It is an attempt to legitimize the present model of distribution, where a minority believes that it has the right to consume in a way which can never be universalized, since the planet could not even contain the waste products of such consumption."[143]

Further, neither environmental protection nor just livelihood for all can be assured "solely on the basis of financial calculations of costs and benefits." Markets on their own are inadequate to these tasks.[144] Echoing social and ecological economists, Francis rejects a "magical notion of the market" and treats the present high-growth, high-consumption economic model as neither natural nor sacrosanct. Instead, he dares to propose that we pursue slower and different kinds of growth; for "a decrease in the pace of production and consumption can at times give rise to another, [more authentic] form of progress and development." To this end, Francis advocates expanding economic imaginations, and "openness to different possibilities which do not involve stifling human creativity and its ideals of progress, but rather directing that energy along new channels" in order to (sounding the three-note thematic chord): "promote a sustainable and equitable development within the context of a broader concept of quality of life."[145]

New approaches to sustainable development must also offset harms caused by "insatiable and irresponsible growth produced over many decades." The issues at stake are both ethical and practical. For Francis, today's social inequities and ecological vulnerabilities make it clear that "the time has come to accept decreased growth in some parts of the world, in order to provide resources for other places to experience healthy growth." Those with the most must consume less. "Technologically advanced societies must be prepared to encourage more sober lifestyles, while reducing their energy consumption and improving its efficiency."[146]

More fundamentally, forging just and sustainable ways forward requires rethinking economy's meaning and purposes "with an eye to correcting its malfunctions and misapplications." Half measures will not do. "Put simply,"

Francis declares, "it is a matter of redefining our notion of progress. A techno-logical and economic development which does not leave in its wake a better world and an integrally higher quality of life cannot be considered progress."[147]

Making these changes will not be easy. Like other critics discussed in this chapter, Francis recognizes that the dynamics of consumerist society are entrenched and self-perpetuating: "Since the market tends to promote extreme consumerism in an effort to sell its products, people can easily get caught up in a whirlwind of needless buying and spending. . . . This paradigm leads people to believe that they are free as long as they have the supposed freedom to consume."[148] But affluent consumerist societies, by offering "too many means and only a few insubstantial ends," can leave members confused, disoriented, and anxious. Widespread feelings of "instability and uncertainty" then become "a seedbed for collective selfishness," and as people become more "self-centered and self-enclosed, their greed increases."[149]

Francis underlines the spiritual dynamics at play: "The emptier a person's heart is, the more he or she needs things to buy, own and consume." Over time, immersion in consumerism distends and distorts judgment until "it becomes almost impossible to accept the limits imposed by reality." Satiation and sufficiency become elusive; significantly, "in this horizon, a genuine sense of the common good also disappears."[150] Obsession with a luxury-focused lifestyle among the minority capable of attaining it exacts ecological, per-sonal, and social costs, and, over time, fosters division and social unrest that, in the extreme, portend "catastrophic consequences."[151]

Quoting bishops' conferences in many regions of the world, Francis reiterates that "the issue of environmental degradation challenges us"—as individuals, families and nations—"to examine our lifestyle." Echoing Ben-edict, he declares that "purchasing is always a moral—and not simply eco-nomic—act."[152] Successful education in "ecological citizenship" will not simply inform; it must also form, instilling new ways of seeing, of valuing and acting in relation to our selves, neighbors, and natural environment.[153] New awareness must lead to transformed habits; we must move from intellectual to moral conversion and action.

Ecological and economic conversion entails transforming patterns in both our culture and institutions, and in our daily lives. Here, Francis emphasizes the significance and nobility of caring for creation "through little daily actions such as avoiding the use of plastic and paper, reducing water consumption, separating refuse, cooking only what can reasonably be consumed," reusing and conserving, and more.[154] Though small and local, "we must not think that these efforts are not going to change the world. They benefit society, often unbeknown to us, for they call forth a goodness which, albeit unseen, inevitably tends to spread. Furthermore, such actions can restore our sense of self-esteem; they can enable us to live more fully and to feel that life on earth is worthwhile."[155]

But institutional action, laws, and regulations are also urgently necessary. "Because the stakes are so high, we need institutions empowered to impose penalties for damage inflicted on the environment."[156] More fundamentally, our currently dominant consumerist ideologies and cultures need to be questioned, reevaluated, and reformed. At the personal, institutional, and cultural levels, "a new way of thinking about human beings, life, society, and our relationship with nature" must be promoted. "Otherwise, the paradigm of consumerism will continue to advance, with the help of the media and the highly effective workings of the market."[157] Laws are needed, but for laws to bring about "significant, long-lasting effects, the majority of the members of society must be adequately motivated to accept them, and personally transformed to respond."[158]

Finally, Francis encourages Christians to cultivate an "ecological spirituality" capable of grounding and sustaining ardent concern for our personal, social, and natural worlds.[159] Christianity "proffers an alternative understanding of the quality of life, and encourages a prophetic and contemplative lifestyle, one capable of deep enjoyment free of the obsession with consumption." Whereas "a constant flood of new consumer goods can baffle the heart and prevent us from cherishing each thing and each moment," Christian spirituality proposes a different approach "marked by moderation and the capacity to be happy with little." We are invited to cultivate a "simplicity which allows us to stop and appreciate the small things, to be grateful for the opportunities which life affords us, to be spiritually detached from what we possess, and not to succumb to sadness for what we lack." Avoiding "the dynamic of dominion and the mere accumulation of pleasures," a spiritually attuned lifestyle refocuses our attention on the value of nonpositional goods and relationships, and on the richness of the present.[160]

To this end Francis commends humility, along with a liberating sobriety that is "not necessarily sacrifice, but the ability to savor the essence, to share; the ability to renew every day the wonder at the goodness of things, without being weighed down in the obscurity of voracious consumption."[161] Freely embraced, such sobriety "is a way of living life to the full" insofar as "happiness means knowing how to limit some needs which only diminish us, and being open to the many different possibilities which life can offer."[162]

Again sounding the triadic chord of human flourishing, care for the earth, and justice for the poor, Francis describes the ecologically converted life as marked by an "inner peace" that itself is "closely related to care for ecology and for the common good." This peace, at root, is "an attitude of the heart, one which approaches life with serene attentiveness, which is capable of being fully present," after the example of Jesus in the Gospels, who was "completely present to everyone and to everything," modeling "the way to overcome that unhealthy anxiety which makes us superficial, aggressive, and compulsive consumers."[163]

CONCLUSION

Our consumerist milieu poses sharp challenges to a twenty-first-century livelihood agenda centered on radical sufficiency; challenges that entwine the ecological, anthropological, and social equity problems that beset us today. Our reigning, neoliberal economic paradigm functions in ways that deny scarcity, ignore maldistribution, and overlook ecological limits and impacts. Premised on unceasing growth, its macroeconomic models erroneously assume the endless abundance or substitutability of the planet's resources.[164] While promising "always more," consumerist culture locks people into the work-spend cycle by imbuing its participants with a chronic sense of scarcity—of needing or wanting what one currently does not have. US-style consumerism perpetrates harms that affect poor and economically vulnerable people disproportionately. These include stimulating the production of luxuries and novelties while reducing market incentives to produce and improve the delivery of necessities. And by masking or ignoring maldistribution while continually upping the ante for positional sufficiency, the consumerist way of life helps sustain and exacerbate economic inequalities.

Consumerism, we have also seen, is anthropologically reductive, socially incursive, and self-perpetuating. It rewrites human nature and flourishing in its own terms. Especially insidious for our livelihood agenda is consumerism's capacity to hijack and remake economic sufficiency, security, and status in its own image and likeness, while obscuring issues surrounding inequality, poverty, and ecological sustainability.

I have devoted considerable attention to the writings and teachings of Pope Francis on consumerism, economic equity, and ecology. This is intentional. Francis, in my view, is attempting a decisive turn in papal social teaching: to require that, henceforth, no Catholic economic agenda can champion "sufficiency, security, and status" for workers and families (though these goals remain crucial) without also incorporating a fourth S—ecological sustainability. For most of the history explored in this book, the concerns of Catholic social teaching and US social Catholics were firmly fixed on people, not the planet; environmental or ecological issues received scant to zero attention. Only in the 1990s did this begin to change in papal teaching, and thereafter, in the US bishops' conference.

Francis's campaign for an integrated, social-economic-ecological Catholic teaching gained unprecedented momentum with his 2015 issuance of *Laudato si'*, the first social encyclical devoted to "care for our common home." In the wake of *Laudato si'*, Catholic agendas for work justice can no longer allow the fourth *S* to remain silent; in an inclusive-livelihood political economy, ecological sustainability must be a constitutive goal.

These advances notwithstanding, a glance at both the US bishops' and the Vatican's websites in 2020 confirmed that integrating ecological and economic justice concerns in Catholic teaching and practice was far from a fait accompli. And to make further progress toward the ecologically sustainable, inclusive-livelihood US political economy that social Catholicism adumbrates, we urgently need to find ways to loosen and break consumerism's cultural and economic grip.

The final chapter of this book discusses civic groups and religious communities who are generating spaces for deconstructing consumerist narratives and for crafting a different, truer story built on democratic participation and inclusive, sustainable livelihood. As Sharon Beder wisely observes, one important piece of this reconstructive project will involve decoupling status from positional consumption. "What people really want," she argues, "more than the multitude of goods on offer, is status, and history has shown that the determinants of status can change." If we hope to live in an economically and ecologically sustainable society, then we need to award greater status to those who are happy with a basic level of comfort rather than to those who accumulate possessions. "If, as a community, we admired wisdom above wealth and compassion and cooperation above competition, we would be well on the way to undermining the motivation to consume" in the competitive and luxury-beholden ways that are the trademarks of our current economic culture.[165]

NOTES

1. Anthropologist Daniel Miller emphasizes that consumption, embedded in different market and political contexts (e.g., Norway versus the United States) does not inevitably exhibit the extreme moral and religious distortions described by North America–focused critics. Miller, "Consumption as the Vanguard of History," 27; on myths concerning consumption, 20–30.

2. For Pierre Bourdieu, *habitus* names pervasive and formative "systems of durable, transposable dispositions, structured structures predisposed to function as structuring

structures, that is, as principles which generate and organize practices and representa-tions that can be objectively adapted to their outcomes without presupposing a con-scious aiming at ends or an express mastery of the operations necessary in order to attain them." *Logic of Practice*, 53.

3. Arendt, *Human Condition*, 125–26.

4. Excerpted from Lambert, "Beyond the 'Goods Life,'" 103, 106–7.

5. Muller, "Capitalism and Inequality," 33.

6. Jan de Vries, "Industrial Revolution," 249.

7. De Vries, 249. See also de Vries, *Industrious Revolution*.

8. Beder, "Consumerism," 42, citing Cherrington, *Work Ethic*, 37; Cross, *Time and Money*, 7–9, 38. Cf. Clapp, ed., *Consuming Passion*.

9. Beder, "Consumerism," 42, citing Cross, *Time and Money*, 7–9, 39; see also Hunni-cutt, *Work without End*, 42, 67.

10. Beder, "Consumerism," 42, citing Cross, *Time and Money*, 7–9, 16, 28, 39; see also Hun-nicutt, *Work without End*, 41, 42 47; Schor, *Overworked American*, 74.

11. Starr, "Consumption, Work Hours, and Values."

12. By the 1990s, the "US model" of this system presumed and normed low unionization, lower minimum wages, lower taxes, and less generous social benefits. Mishel, Bernstein, and Allegretto, *State of Working America*, ch. 8. Cf. Baum, "Social Economy."

13. Beder, "Consumerism," 43.

14. Beder, 42, citing Hunnicutt, *Work without End*, 42.

15. Beder, "Consumerism," 44, citing Ewen, *Captains of Consciousness*, 54.

16. Beder, "Consumerism," 43, citing Ewen, *Captains of Consciousness*, 43–45.

17. Beder, "Consumerism," 43–44, citing Ewen, *Captains of Consciousness*, 77–78, 85–86, 109. Cf. sweatshop worker Sadie Frowne's story in ch.1; also Peiss, "Gender Relations."

18. Beder, "Consumerism," 43; Cross, *Time and Money*, 41n7. Hirsch and Frank would later "point toward the ultimate problem . . . in marginalism: the ongoing need to manufacture artificial scarcity in a situation of apparent affluence." Cloutier, *Vice of Luxury*, 165, citing Clark, "Wealth as Abundance and Scarcity," 43–44.

19. See, e.g., Miller, *Consuming Religion*, 41, 43.

20. This April 1931 *Ladies Home Journal* advertisement is referenced in Marchand, *Advertis-ing the American Dream*, 162, 222.

21. Glickman, *Living Wage*, ch. 4.

22. Vandenberg, "René Girard and the Rhetoric of Consumption," 263.

23. Beder, "Consumerism," 44, citing Marchand, *Advertising the American Dream*, 218, 220, 222; Ewen, *Captains of Consciousness*, 89, 91.

24. Bell, *Work and Its Discontents*, 32; Packard, *Status Seekers*, 269–70; Chinoy, *Automobile Workers and the American Dream*, 126.

25. Arendt, *Human Condition*, 46, 219, 122–26.

26. Starr, "Consumption, Work Hours, and Values," 22.

27. Hunnicutt, "Monsignor John A. Ryan," 88–91.

28. Starr, "Consumption, Work Hours, and Values," 10, citing Ryan, "Experts Look at Unem-ployment," 636. Cf. Horowitz, *Morality of Spending*, xvii–xix.

29. Ryan, baccalaureate sermon, Trinity College, June 3, 1923, p. 3, box 37, file: "Com-mencement Addresses," John A. Ryan Archives, Mullen Library, Catholic University of America, Washington, DC. See also Ryan, *Church and Socialism*, 180–216; Ryan, *Declin-ing Liberty*, 320–28.

30. "Squirrel cage" is used by Juliet Schor, but Starr, "Consumption, Work Hours, and Values," 18, notes Ryan's much earlier description of high-production consumerist economy as "a squirrel cage concept of progress unenlightened by considerations of the other ethical and human claims of the individual or the church. It has produced a culture sunk in materialism without a transcendent vision." Cf. Hunnicutt, *Work without End*, 90.

31. Ryan, baccalaureate sermon, 3.

32. Ryan, *Church and Socialism*, 190–91.

33. Ryan, baccalaureate sermon, 6; Ryan, "Minimum and Maximum Standards of Living," in *Declining Liberty*, 315–29.

34. See Ryan, *Living Wage*, ch. 7; Ryan, *Distributive Justice* (1942), ch. 18, esp. 242–45, ch. 21; also "The Fallacy of Bettering One's Position," *Catholic World*, 1907, and "False and True Conceptions of Welfare," in Ryan, *Church and Socialism*.

35. Ryan, *Distributive Justice* (1942), 233–48. Cf. Cloutier, *Vice of Luxury*, 210.

36. Ryan, "True Welfare," 192–97.

37. Ryan, 192–97. Cf. Ryan, *Distributive Justice* (1942), 243.

38. Starr, "Consumption, Work Hours, and Values," 14. For Ryan, rights to livelihood ordinarily entail obligations to work. Starr, "Consumption, Work Hours, and Values," 14, citing Ryan, *Distributive Justice* (1927), 395. Ryan, *Declining Liberty*, 323; Ryan, *Distributive Justice* (1942), 244.

39. Cloutier, *Vice of Luxury*, 78, 80.

40. Kyrk, *Theory of Consumption*; Cloutier, *Vice of Luxury*, 233, citing Kyrk, 225, 202–3, 229.

41. Muller, "Capitalism and Inequality," 30–31.

42. Lasch, *Culture of Narcissism*, 73, cited in Beabout and Echeverria, "Culture of Consumerism," 347.

43. Lasch, *Culture of Narcissism*, 72.

44. Beabout and Echeverria, "Culture of Consumerism," 347, citing Lasch, *Culture of Narcissism*, 73.

45. Beabout and Echeverria, "Culture of Consumerism," 347.

46. Lasch, *Culture of Narcissism*, 74.

47. Lasch. Himes cites Gary Cross's "less critical assessment" of consumerism as providing "a more dynamic and popular, while less destructive, ideology of public life than most political belief systems in the twentieth century." Himes, "Consumerism and Christian Ethics," 135, citing Cross, *All-Consuming Century*, viii. For Cross, "consumer culture is democracy's highest achievement, giving meaning and dignity to people when workplace participation, ethnic solidarity, and even representative democracy have failed."

48. Vandenberg, "René Girard and the Rhetoric of Consumption," 260, citing Ellul, *Propaganda*, 62.

49. Vandenberg, "René Girard and the Rhetoric of Consumption," 266, 270. Cf. Bourdieu, *Logic of Practice*.

50. Cross, *All-Consuming Century*, 223, cited in Vandenberg, "René Girard and the Rhetoric of Consumption," 267.

51. Vandenberg, "René Girard and the Rhetoric of Consumption," 263.

52. Himes, "Consumerism and Christian Ethics," 134–35, citing Sandel, *Democracy's Discontent*, 222, 224.

53. Frank, *Falling Behind*, 79.

54. Cloutier, *Vice of Luxury*, 162, 163, citing Hirsch, *Social Limits to Growth*, 23–24. I follow here Cloutier's insightful discussion of Hirsch and Frank in *Vice of Luxury*, ch. 2.

55. Cloutier, *Vice of Luxury*, 162, citing Hirsch, *Social Limits to Growth*, 52. Recall our discussion of competition in chapter 5.

56. On "expenditure cascades," see Frank, *Falling Behind*, xi–xii.

57. Frank, *Falling Behind*, 67, 103. For positional goods, relative consumption matters. For nonpositional goods, absolute, more than relative, consumption levels matter.

58. Cf. Juliet Schor's troubling study of the industry of child-focused marketing, *Born to Buy*.

59. Cloutier, *Vice of Luxury*, 165. "Frank levels one of the basic critiques against the marginalist model of consumption: In traditional economic models, *individual utility depends only on absolute consumption*." Newer models that take relative consumption into account expose "a fundamental conflict between individual and social welfare" Cloutier, 162–63.

60. Cloutier, 236; see Frank, *Falling Behind*, ch. 9.

61. Cloutier, *Vice of Luxury*, 163–64, citing Hirsch, *Social Limits to Growth*, 89.

62. Frank, *Falling Behind*, 93.

63. Frank, 90.

64. Cloutier, *Vice of Luxury*, 163.

65. Cloutier, 198.

66. Frank, *Falling Behind*, 101.

67. Frank, *Luxury Fever*, 94, inter alia.

68. Cloutier, *Vice of Luxury*, 164. "Frank states that status purchases can sometimes be even more attractive to the poor, because the 'gain' in esteem is so large, relatively speaking." Cloutier, 21, citing Frank, *Choosing the Right Pond*, 144.

69. Cloutier, *Vice of Luxury*, 198.

70. Cloutier, 162.

71. Frank, *Darwin Economy*, ch. 5.

72. Frank, *Falling Behind*, 101.

73. Frank, 102.

74. E.g. Schor, *Overspent American*, chs. 5, 6. Catholic business scholar Andrew V. Abela (erroneously, in my view) contrasts Catholic social teaching's focus on families and civil society with "secular critics of consumerism" like Schor and Frank, "who tend to place the responsibility on individual consumers themselves and on the government." Abela, "Price of Freedom," 15.

75. See, e.g., Himes, "Consumerism and Christian Ethics"; Beabout and Echeverria, "Culture of Consumerism"; Yuengert, "Free Markets and the Culture of Consumption"; Nixon, "Satisfaction for Whom"; and studies by Thomas Beaudoin, John Kavanaugh, David Cloutier, and David Matzko McCarthy.

76. Kavanaugh, *Following Christ* (2006), 66, 27.

77. Kavanaugh, 38–39, 62.

78. Beabout and Echeverria, "Culture of Consumerism," 342, citing Kavanaugh, *Following Christ* (1991), 38, 109. Cf. Himes, "Consumerism and Christian Ethics," 141–43, quoting McCarthy, *Good Life*, 54–55, 76. Himes critiques McCarthy's proposed "middle-class asceticism," 142.

79. Kavanaugh, *Following Christ* (2006), 46, 64.

80. Kavanaugh, 64, 71, 60.

81. Kavanaugh, 39.

82. Kavanaugh, 71.

83. Kavanaugh, 45.

84. Kavanaugh, 76, 78.

85. Kavanaugh, 78, 79, cf. 80. Beabout and Echeverria, "Culture of Consumerism," 344, offers a summary critique.

86. Miller, "Taking Consumer Culture Seriously," 284, 286.

87. Miller, 294.

88. Miller, *Consuming Religion*, 141, 119, 117.

89. Albrecht, *Hitting Home*, 24–25.

90. Albrecht, 29.

91. Reimer-Barry, review of *Vice of Luxury*, 211.

92. Cloutier, *Vice of Luxury*, 180.

93. Reimer-Barry, review of *Vice of Luxury*, 211; cf. Cloutier, *Vice of Luxury*, 13.

94. Cloutier, *Vice of Luxury*, 183, 96.

95. Cloutier, 31, 35.

96. Cloutier, 67, 86.

97. Cloutier, 90, 91. However, today, Catholic historian Catherine Osborne observes, "we are finding plenty of ways to make [these activities] less cooperative, more positional, and more commodifiable." Osborne, email message to author, July 10, 2019.

98. Cloutier, *Vice of Luxury*, 86–87.

99. Cloutier, 86, 92. Following MacIntyre, Cloutier distinguishes internal and external goods, later applying them to "enrichment" versus "luxury" goods, respectively. Cloutier, 269, 92.

100. Cloutier, 90.

101. David Cloutier, "Sending the Wrong Signal: How Luxury Comprises Christian Witness," *Commonweal*, December 9, 2013, https://www.commonwealmagazine.org/sending-wrong-signal.

102. Cloutier, *Vice of Luxury*, 178.

103. Cloutier, 7–8.

104. Albrecht, *Hitting Home*, 29; Francis, homily, Lampedusa, Italy, July 8, 2013, http://w2.vatican.va/content/francesco/en/homilies/2013/documents/papa-francesco_20130708_omelia-lampedusa.html.

105. Cloutier, *Vice of Luxury*, 204.

106. Cloutier, 204, and 180, citing Arbo, *Political Vanity*, 43.

107. Niki Bunker, "How Does Consumption Impact Inequality?" World Economic Forum, April 13, 2015, https://www.weforum.org/agenda/2015/04/how-does-consumption-impact-inequality/.

108. Cloutier, "American Lifestyles," 215–35; Francis, *Laudato si'*, §49, cf. §117.

109. Cloutier, *Vice of Luxury*, 96. "The language of luxury focuses on personal desire in a way that consumerism may not; like racism or sexism, consumerism suggests a kind of victimhood that creates a stereotypical dichotomy—the lazy corporate rich and the indolent struggling poor—which distorts the actual problems." Cloutier's point about "victimhood" demands further critical discussion.

110. Cloutier, *Vice of Luxury*, 96, 203. "Justice does matter, but so do the luxurious spending patterns of both rich and poor in a consumer society." Addressing inadequate wages and "improvident spending" should be a both-and proposition.

111. Cloutier, 203–4.

112. Cloutier, 91.

113. Cloutier, 165. "As luxury increases and informal norms of frugality diminish, a tipping point is reached" after which norms "end up having to be legislated or contested legally."

114. Cloutier, 6.

115. Cloutier, 11. Christians' virtuous use of surplus wealth, I would add, must also be solidary and transformative.

116. Cloutier, 254–68, cited by Reimer-Barry, review of *Vice of Luxury*, 210–11.

117. Himes, "Consumerism and Christian Ethics," 149, citing Wilber, "Ethics of Consumption," 404.

118. Himes, "Consumerism and Christian Ethics," 149, citing Wilber, "Ethics of Consumption," 404, 405.

119. Paul VI, *Populorum progressio*, §18.

120. Paul VI, §19, 20.

121. Paul VI, §19, 20, 21.

122. John Paul II, *Sollicitudo rei socialis*, §28.

123. Himes, "Consumerism and Christian Ethics," 151, citing John Paul II, *Sollicitudo rei socialis*, §28.

124. John Paul II, *Sollicitudo rei socialis*, §28.

125. Himes, "Consumerism and Christian Ethics," 151–52.

126. John Paul II, *Centesimus annus*, §36, cf. Himes, "Consumerism and Christian Ethics," 151–52.

127. World Synod of Catholic Bishops, *Justicia in mundo*, §28.

128. World Synod of Catholic Bishops, §47.

129. World Synod of Catholic Bishops, §48.

130. World Synod of Catholic Bishops, §74.

131. World Synod of Catholic Bishops, §75.

132. World Synod of Catholic Bishops, §76. "The concentration of privilege that exists today results far more from institutional relationships that distribute power and wealth inequitably than from differences in talent or lack of desire to work. These institutional patterns must be examined and revised if we are to meet the demands of basic justice."

133. World Synod of Catholic Bishops, §90.

134. World Synod of Catholic Bishops, §334.

135. John Paul II, "Message of His Holiness Pope John Paul II for the Celebration of the World Day of Peace," January 1, 1990, §13, https://w2.vatican.va/content/john-paul-ii/en/messages/peace/documents/hf_jp-ii_mes_19891208_xxiii-world-day-for-peace.html.

136. John Paul II, *Centesimus annus*, §37.

137. Benedict XVI, "Address of His Holiness Benedict XVI: Welcoming Celebration by the Young People," World Youth Day, Barangaroo, Sydney Harbour, July 17, 2008, https://w2.vatican.va/content/benedict-xvi/en/speeches/2008/july/documents/hf_ben-xvi_spe_20080717_barangaroo.html.

138. Himes, "Consumerism and Christian Ethics," 153.

139. Francis, address to bishops at the World Meeting of Families, Philadelphia, September 27, 2015, https://m.vatican.va/content/francesco/en/speeches/2015/september/documents/papa-francesco_20150927_usa-vescovi-festa-famiglie.html.

140. Francis, *Laudato si'*, §117.

141. Francis, §48. Benedict highlights the moral aspects of social ecology; Francis foregrounds the billions of poor in the "majority world" who are most vulnerable to the effects of social and environmental deterioration.

142. Francis, §49.

143. Francis, §50.
144. Francis, §190.
145. Francis, §§191–92.
146. Francis, §193, citing Benedict XVI, "Message of His Holiness Pope Benedict XVI for the Celebration of the World Day of Peace," January 1, 2010, http://w2.vatican.va/content /benedict-xvi/en/messages/peace/documents/hf_ben-xvi_mes_20091208_xliii-world -day-peace.html.
147. Francis, *Laudato si'*, §194. "Frequently, in fact, people's quality of life actually diminishes . . . in the midst of economic growth. In this context, talk of sustainable growth usually becomes a way of distracting attention and offering excuses. . . . and the social and environmental responsibility of businesses often gets reduced to a series of marketing and image-enhancing measures."
148. Francis, §203.
149. Francis, §204.
150. Francis, §204.
151. Francis, §204.
152. Francis, §206.
153. Francis, §§210–11.
154. Francis, §211.
155. Francis, §212.
156. Francis, §214, cf. §212. Francis also stresses "the relationship between a good aesthetic education and the maintenance of a healthy environment. . . . By learning to see and appreciate beauty, we learn to reject self-interested pragmatism." Francis, §215.
157. Francis, §215.
158. Francis, §214. "Only by cultivating sound virtues [including 'self-control and willingness to learn from one another'] will people be able to make a selfless ecological commitment."
159. Francis, §216.
160. Francis, §222.
161. Francis, Angelus, Vatican City, January 29, 2017, http://w2.vatican.va/content/francesco /en/angelus/2017/documents/papa-francesco_angelus_20170129.html.
162. Francis, *Laudato si'*, §§223, 225.
163. Francis, §§225, 226. Cf. Francis, Angelus.
164. A point frequently made by ecological economists; see, e.g., Herman Daly, "Three Limits to Growth," Center for the Advancement of the Steady State Economy, September 4, 2014, https://steadystate.org/three-limits-to-growth/.
165. Beder, "Consumerism," 46.

CHAPTER 7

Toward a Radically Sufficient
Economic Order

For non-elite working families, small changes can have outsize effects. When resources are chronically too thinly stretched, "a small setback" like a missed rent payment or a car breakdown "can quickly spiral into a major trauma," like unpayable late fees, a job loss, even eviction or jail time. Living in tight economic straits also burdens people emotionally and psychically. Poverty or working poverty, writes Harvard researcher Matthew Desmond, can be "unrelenting, shame-inducing and exhausting." Decades of studies confirm that most US workers find low wages "an affront to basic dignity. They make people feel small, insignificant and powerless."[1] Habitually experiencing such feelings contributes to negative health consequences in addition to material hardships.

The stress of economic insufficiency "can also burden the mind, causing us to make worse decisions and ignore our health." Scarcity researchers Sendhil Mullainathan and Eldar Shafir call this "the bandwidth tax." Grappling with chronic economic insufficiency and its side effects, their studies show, "reduces a person's cognitive capacity more than going a full night without sleep." When we are preoccupied by economic precarity or poverty, "we have less mind to give to the rest of life," including caring for self and loved ones, or creating long-term strategies for improving our job or financial circumstances.[2] But while small setbacks can produce big negative consequences for low-wage workers, researchers also find that "modest wage increases have a profound impact on people's well-being and happiness."[3]

Consider Julio Payes, a Guatemalan immigrant and permanent US resident, living in the small Bay Area community of Emeryville, California, which has a population of twelve thousand. In 2014 Payes, age twenty-four, was putting in eighty-hour weeks at two full-time, minimum-wage jobs. "I felt like a zombie," Payes told Desmond. "No energy. Always sad." Just to afford basic necessities, he often worked sixteen-hour days or seven-day weeks. Often sleep-deprived, he guzzled coffee and Cokes to keep going. He, his mother, and two siblings all shared a tiny apartment, but Payes was rarely there. Alexander, his eight-year-old brother, once brought Payes to tears when he told him he was saving up money to buy an hour of Payes's time. "How much for one hour to play with me?" At one point that year, Payes fainted from exhaustion in the aisle of a grocery store.

But in 2014 the Emeryville City Council began to reconsider the city's minimum wage, and Payes began to pray. "God, he believes in justice," he told Desmond. "I have faith. But I also have politics." Hesitant at first, Payes became active in the Fight for $15 campaign, participating in marches and other shows of collective force. "'The first time we did a strike, I felt very nervous,' he said. But when he showed up in his work uniform and saw a mass of fast-food workers, thousands strong, he found his voice. It felt like church."

In 2015, amid contentious debate, Emeryville's City Council did something remarkable: it mandated raising the minimum hourly wage for all businesses in the town to $16.30 by 2019, making Emeryville's the highest minimum wage rate in the nation. Employees were also guaranteed a minimum of forty-eight to seventy-two hours of annual paid sick leave. On posters distributed throughout town in six different languages, a bright red box gave notice that "Employees can File a Complaint with the City if They: Do Not Receive the Minimum Wage—Do Not Receive Paid Sick Leave—Experience Retaliation."[4]

Emeryville's living wage ordinance, Payes reports, "had a big impact on my life." By 2018, he was making $15 an hour at a Burger King and $15.69 at a large hotel, working as a room attendant. He could now afford to work less, logging around forty-eight hours weekly. He opened a small savings account. Since his wages increased, Payes had been able to eat more healthily, get more sleep, and exercise by walking in the park. He told Desmond, simply, "I feel better." And "he now gets to spend more time with Alexander, often picking him up from school." Payes reflected, "'Before, I felt like a slave,' ... 'But now I feel, ¿Cómo se dice, más seguro?' Safer, he said. 'I feel safer.'"[5]

As Payes's story attests, "a living minimum wage buys prescriptions and rest and broccoli, yes; but it also provides something less tangible"—more of the sufficiency, security, and status that mark a dignified livelihood. Payes's engagement in the living wage movement and his still modest, but more livable wages and working conditions have increased his sense of efficacy, dignity, and well-being as a person, a worker, and a community member. Studies now correlate decent pay and working conditions with so many positive effects for people like Payes that Desmond declares: "A living wage is an antidepressant. It is a sleep aid. A diet. A stress reliever. It is a contraceptive, preventing teenage pregnancy. It prevents premature death. It shields children from neglect."

Minimum-wage laws remain controversial, and on their own will not fully eliminate working poverty or working-class distress. "But this truth," as Desmond writes, "should not prevent us from acknowledging how powerfully workers respond to relatively small income boosts."[6] Something similar can be said about the relatively small power boosts generated when workers, community groups, unions, and religious communities join forces in efforts like living wage campaigns. These and other initiatives for worker justice across the country, beyond their own immediate impacts, offer empowering resources and lessons for the broad-based, democratic movement toward an inclusive livelihood US political economy being advocated here.

In this final chapter, I first take stock of where things stand for US working families in 2019. Building on previous chapters' analysis, I then discuss the fundamental changes in orientation, goals, and priorities that an inclusive livelihood economy requires; the kinds of virtues and communities we need to cultivate to get there; and several examples of policies, initiatives, and practices that can contribute to advancing inclusive livelihood. I conclude by reflecting on what we can learn from broad-based civic efforts for work justice going on today about how a radical vision joined to a strategic, transformationist approach can help us move the needle toward the larger shifts in paradigm and practice that building a truly inclusive, sustainable political economy will require.

As this book went into production in spring 2020, the COVID-19 pandemic and associated economic shutdowns had begun to threaten the health, jobs, and livelihoods of millions of non-elite workers and families in the United States and globally. Amid a national climate of palpable fear, uncertainty, heartbreak, and grief, two things relevant to this project came into sharp relief. First, vast numbers of the those whose continued labors were deemed essential to keeping quarantined Americans safe, cared for, and supplied during the pandemic were non-elite workers, from vulnerable small business owners to people performing minimum- and lower-wage jobs, many without health insurance or benefits.[7] With schools and businesses shut down and millions of families sheltering in place in an effort to halt the virus's spread, the country received an object lesson concerning our dependence on non-elite working people, who left the safety of their homes daily to provide frontline emergency services, to tend to and bathe our hospitalized, aged, or frail loved ones, to pick up our trash, to deliver our mail and packages, to cook and deliver our food, and more. Second, amid so much unpredictability, one sadly predictable outcome was already coming into view: both during and after the crisis, the negative health and economic impacts of the pandemic would fall disproportionately on already-struggling, non-elite—and disproportionately on women and non-white—workers and their families.[8] This most recent calamity, and the waves of anti-racist protest that soon accompanied it, further underscore the need to reorder our economic priorities and policies around a sustainable, radical-sufficiency agenda for ensuring good work and a just and dignified livelihood to every US household and family.

WHERE THINGS STAND

"To compel a man to work for less than a Living Wage is as truly an act of injustice as to pick his pocket. In a wide sense it is also an attack upon his life."[9] So wrote John A. Ryan in 1906. But today, more than a century later, the sufficiency, security, and status of a dignified livelihood as Ryan understood it, also outlined in the 1948 United Nations Universal Declaration of Rights, still elude a majority of workers and families, even in the relatively affluent United States.[10]

For one thing, pay is insufficient. "Despite a long streak of economic growth, low unemployment, and some increases in average wages and new job creation," reports Tim Sandle, "of the 130 million people employed in the United States in 2018, 18 million earned less than $10 per hour."[11] That year, nearly half of working Americans, 42.4 percent, were making less than $15 per hour, a pay rate that would supply a full-time worker a $31,200 income. According to two respected living-wage calculators, this was just under the $33,400 annual wage required to support one single person in the median-cost US city of Des Moines, Iowa. In Emeryville, Payes needed an income of at least $36,000 to meet this mark.[12]

Jobs and social benefits are increasingly insecure. Of the top ten jobs employing the most people in the United States in 2019, the vast majority were lower-paying service jobs; growing numbers were nonstandard "gig" jobs.[13] In addition, between 1980 and 2010 the percentages of US workers in larger, private sector companies with pensions fell from 80 percent to 33 percent; workers with employer-provided health insurance fell from 70 percent to 55 percent; the minimum wage lost significant buying power; and real wages were all but stagnant, declining for men by 5 percent.[14] Low unemployment hides these realities. As Robert Reich puts it: "We don't have a jobs crisis; we have a good jobs crisis."[15] Scholars and workers lamented the growing prevalence of precarious, nonstandard job arrangements: the "permatemp economy" (Erin Hatton), "spot labor market" (Julia Heath, David H. Ciscel, and David C. Sharp), "permanent underemployment model" (Ulrich Beck), or "on-demand employment."[16] These subcontracted, temporary, on-call, on-demand, or freelance jobs are wage, benefit, and security deficient compared to standard job arrangements. Nonstandard workers are disproportionately female and nonwhite; and nearly half would prefer standard, full-time employment.[17] Many predicted that the twenty-first-century digitalized and information-based economy will continue to foster a dual labor market "composed by on the one hand a core labor force . . . and on the other hand a disposable labor force which can easily be automated and/or hired and/or dismissed depending on the demands of the market and the labor costs."[18]

Meanwhile, prices for necessities have risen, along with consumer spending and household debt. As the cost of living continued to rise after 2000, the inflation-adjusted capacity of the dollar to keep up with those costs fell behind. By 2019, after accounting for inflation, the average worker was still making the same amount of money as in 1980. During those four decades, however, consumer spending consistently outpaced wages.[19] Higher costs for necessities such as housing, medical care, childcare, and education—not frivolous consumerist purchases—accounted for these spending and debt increases for all but the top 10 percent of households.[20]

The nonwaged economy is also under strain and stress. To keep up with rising costs, non-elite families have devoted more weekly hours to wage earning, contributing to scarcities of time, attention, and energy for childcare and the work of the home, for rest and leisure, and for involvement with neighbors and in civic life. Under current policies, most families must operate "in an environment devoid of institutional support" for these crucial, nonmarket activities.[21]

Systemic, group difference-based inequities persist, along with wealth and income gaps. Previous chapters have probed key social dynamics that accompany wage and employment numbers and conditions. We have discussed the asymmetrically gendered ways that waged and unpaid household work are distributed and rewarded. We have also seen how differentials in economic opportunities, outcomes, status, and power get etched along racial and class lines. In particular, our country's long, ugly history of creating ingroup economic and social advantage by "othering" and exploiting racialized outgroups continues to haunt the present, feeding inequities that impede livelihood for non-elite families of color. Growing income and wealth inequalities, along with policies that cement and compound these inequalities, have also constrained social mobility and widened social divisions.

Our identities and agency as consumers may be superseding our identities and agency as citizens. Over the past several decades, maintaining

Americans' freedom and power to consume has become a focus of economic culture and policies. In daily life, our identities and agency as consumers can feel more potent than our identities and agency as either workers or citizens. For many non-elite families, credit for consumer goods like flat-screen TVs and cell phones is within reach, while secure, decently paying employment or affordable health care are not. Many opt for social participation as consumers who are able to procure and enjoy the latest goods and gadgets, just like everyone else. Their incentives to do so combine continually rising and changing expectations for consumption, easily available credit, and the fact that items that would actually lift families into a higher socioeconomic location—such as a college education, or housing in a neighborhood with low crime and excellent schools—are priced completely beyond their reach.[22]

For decades, the system underwritten by neoliberal economic orthodoxy has excelled at delivering Americans high standards of living via consumption. But "to the extent that one values non-consumption quality of life, the system is not highly successful. Jobs are comparatively precarious, work-life balance is poor, schools do not perform well, crime is high, and life expectancy is low."[23] These factors help explain why, whatever the GDP or stock market numbers, life for a majority of US families today fails to measure up to the American dream.

In addition, working families are navigating these challenges in an era of keenly felt societal divisions. Today's cultural landscape is riven by sharp, often hostile disagreements over what is important, what is amiss, why, and what should be done to improve conditions for ordinary people and families. Political disagreements frequently get framed as clashes between groups' core identities and cherished values.[24] Partisan mass media and social media work as digital accelerants, inflaming emotions and further cementing divisions.[25] People experience deep cognitive, moral, and affective dissonances between their own views and (what seem to be) the patently false beliefs or pernicious values held by those they oppose. In this climate, even dialogue or attempts to collaborate on shared concerns can appear not only a waste of time but morally dangerous.

Across sharp divisions, most Americans *would* likely agree on two things: everyone is not thriving, and it is hard to figure out how to make things better. Impersonal forces, whether big government or big business, economic globalization, environmental deterioration, or global pandemics, threaten our own well-being and that of our children and grandchildren. In response, non-elite Americans reported increasing "fatalism and pessimism," reflected in diminished civic engagement among some and attraction to protest populism among others. In 2017, for the first time, a majority of Americans without a college degree reported that for them the American dream—that if you work hard and play by the rules, you can get ahead—no longer held true.[26]

Facing complex and seemingly intractable economic, social, and ecological problems, our daily time and energies already stretched thin, it is tempting to throw up our hands and retreat into tribalism, cynicism, or apathy.[27] Many of us feel that the system is rigged and are skeptical that efforts to fix things can have significant impact.[28] Demoralized, we find it hard to envision what organizer Marshall Ganz calls "the plausibility of the possible rather than the inevitability of the probable." But for the sake of all families struggling for livelihood today, we badly need to find ways to do so.[29]

WHERE WE NEED TO GO

This book advocates a US Catholic radical sufficiency agenda that embraces inclusive, sustainable livelihood as its *concrete historical ideal*—a compelling social vision appropriate to the needs of our twenty-first-century context.[30] It envisages work and economic livelihood as parts of a holistic, flourishing life that eschews both workaholism and the work-spend squirrel cage, and includes time and resources for rest, leisure, self-development, family and personal relationships, and community and civic participation. This agenda reframes US economic priorities and policies around a focal commitment to making available, and adequately supporting, ample amounts and kinds of socially useful work, including for the majority of people who do not have or want traditional college or graduate degrees. And, recalling but superseding the twentieth century's aspirational "era of the common man," the ordinary workers and families spotlighted in this new livelihood agenda comprise a wide diversity of gendered, racial-ethnic, and cultural faces and forms.

Guided by social Catholicism's normative understanding of economy's participative, productive, and provisioning purposes, and extending Ryan's "sufficiently radical" frame, this twenty-first-century agenda is impelled by a more explicitly critical and encompassing vision and aim that I have called *radical sufficiency*. A radical sufficiency livelihood agenda presses those struggling for work justice to take into account and responsibly address both the inequities of gender, race, and class, and the looming ecological crisis. Its stipulations for a properly functioning economy are radically inclusive: everyone must be enabled to participate, and everyone must be able to gain access to enough. And while it is dedicated to actionable strategies for incremental reform, it is radical in both its critical analysis of the economic status quo and its recognition of the deep changes—the root-level reorientations—that an inclusive livelihood political economy requires.

Shifting the Economic Axis and Narrative

The first order of change is one of the most fundamental. We need what Robert Lane calls an "axis shift," from the currently dominant economic orthodoxy to a different descriptive and normative axis, centered around economy's provisioning purposes, on markets as embedded within larger institutional and moral ecologies, and on the participation and well-being of non-elite working people as the key metric for gauging the economy's success.[31]

Recall the reigning paradigm's assumption that maximizing markets' allocative efficiency and productivity requires that they operate according to their own internal logics, with minimal tinkering or government interference. Economic performance is measured primarily by annual growth in gross domestic product and in overall income. This orthodoxy's core premise is that unfettered markets and a growing economic pie provide maximal opportunity for gain and financial improvement, with more money, goods, and services for everyone. Its ideological effects tend to naturalize existing economic relations, conceal the ways business as usual can disproportionately benefit sectional interests, and discourage efforts to try or even imagine anything different. A radical sufficiency economic paradigm, by contrast, makes its central focus and concern the work, livelihood, and well-being of flesh-and-blood people and families, no one excluded. Given this descriptive and normative axis, the chief criterion for evaluating an economy's performance becomes the extent to which all people and families can participate in it, accessing a dignified livelihood through work that is honest, contributive, and adequately remunerated and supported.

Modern social Catholicism has not been alone in questioning the reigning neoliberal economic frame. Today, critiques of and proposals for alternative market-economy paradigms are coming from an array of voices and communities, including conservative and progressive scholars; feminist, behavioral, and ecological economists; religious congregations; organizations and movements of varied class, gender, and racial/ethnic compositions and perspectives. This diversity holds potential for building cross-group support for the kind of axis change I am advocating here.

Conservative scholar Oren Cass, for instance, highlights the differences between a work- and family-centered economic agenda and current US "economic piety," which, he contends, "represents a truncated and ultimately self-undermining concept of prosperity." In the dominant paradigm, "workers have no standing," and "neither do their families or communities." Expanding the economic pie is the main goal; "maintaining a healthy, inclusive society is a hoped-for by-product, not an end in itself."[32] Cass criticizes US policies that privilege an "access-to-consumption" versus "productive-work" economic culture. "What if," Cass asks, people's ability to be productive workers and contributors "matters more than how much they can consume?" Further, "what if smaller losses for those at the bottom of the economic ladder are much more consequential," both to those families and to the overall health of our society, "than larger gains for those who are already at the top? Under those conditions, rising GDP will not necessarily translate into rising prosperity," no matter what the numbers say.[33] Current economic and labor policy have steered the nation off course by failing to recognize that neither GDP growth nor redistribution, but rather "a labor market in which workers can support strong families and communities" is the key to genuine and sustainable prosperity. Cass argues that building and sustaining this inclusive labor market should be public policy's central focus.[34]

Calls to reorient our economic paradigm are also coming from radical and progressive corners. Economists like Herman Daly and Kate Raworth, for instance, make an urgent case for a renovated, ecologically and ethically responsive political economy. Raworth argues that present-day economic orthodoxy's "narrative about the efficiency of the market, the incompetence of the state, the domesticity of the household and the tragedy of the commons," while yielding financial gain for some sectors, "has helped to push many societies towards social and ecological collapse." Echoing growing numbers of economists and religious leaders including Pope Francis, Raworth stresses that "it's time to write a new economic story fit for this century—one that sees the economy's dependence upon society and the living world." This story does not impugn or reject markets but insists that they, along with money, work, and the economy overall, serve people and sustain the planet, not the other way around.[35] Raworth and Cass represent very different political perspectives, and their proposals differ in key respects. But, along with contemporary social Catholicism, they are among a growing chorus of voices calling for recentering our economy's attention and priorities around ecologically sustainable, community-friendly work and livelihood for all.

By Way of the Existing System . . .

Does inclusive livelihood require that the existing US political economy be scrapped, abandoned, or completely replaced? Recalling Ryan's prediction that a fully adequate political economy would look like "the present system," but "greatly, even radically modified," it is important to stress what Catholic inclusive livelihood advocates value and would build upon in our current US political and economic institutions.[36]

Politically, inclusive livelihood advocates share strong commitments to democratic principles, promoting individual rights and freedoms within a robust, multiassociational civil society where power and participation are widely shared, and average people are afforded voice, agency, and opportunities for growth and improvement. They embrace central US political and legal institutions and honor working people's values such as the dignity of labor; self-reliance and responsibility; honesty, reciprocity, and pulling one's weight; and dedication to family and local communities.

On the economic front, US livelihood advocates value markets, market structures, and market activities. They take seriously mainstream economic concerns like efficiency, scarcity, price signals, allocation, incentives, supply and demand, and marginal utility. But in an inclusive livelihood paradigm, "all of these are understood as directed toward maximizing provision for actual people and their households."[37] As feminist economist Julie Nelson writes, provision- and livelihood-centered economics affirm the key human goods that capitalist free markets provide, in particular, "the production of goods and services that support survival and flourishing; creation of employment opportunities; promotion of self-support and financial responsibility; and opportunities for creation, innovation, and growth in the enjoyment of life."[38]

" . . . Greatly, even radically, modified."

An inclusive livelihood political economy also substantially reorders and in some cases reverses neoliberal market orthodoxy's key priorities. Specifically, in a democratic political economy centered on inclusive, sustainable livelihood:

- Relational, well-being-promoting and "satisficing" *Homo solidarietus* takes priority over individualist, profit-maximizing, insatiable *Homo economicus*.[39]
- Markets depend on, and principally serve the sustenance and well-being of, households, families, and local communities.
- Efficiency serves, and cannot substitute for, inclusive and sustainable sufficiency.
- Profit and growth depend on, and may not exploit or undermine, sustainability and inclusive sufficiency.

- Economy's obligation to serve the dignity and well-being of all members precludes arrangements that constrain or reward persons or groups based on asymmetrical valuations attached to gender/sexual, race/ethnicity, class, or other group differences.
- Work, and the wealth it produces, must not compromise or take precedence over the dignity and well-being of persons, families, and communities.
- Competition for individual gain depends upon, and may not exploit or undermine, collaboration for inclusive provisioning.
- Consumerist, *Homo economicus* behaviors are instrumental to, and may not supersede or crowd out, inclusive, provisioning behaviors and goals directed to advancing the civic and political common good.
- Likewise, desires for "more, new, and better" are secondary to and may not supersede or crowd out "satisficing" choices that respect ecological and social floors and limits.
- Inequalities in income and wealth must be buffered by policies that secure access to livelihood and to meaningful political and economic power and participation for all citizens.[40]

This list augurs significant—even radical—changes in economic and societal business as usual. Recognizing this, Ryan declared in 1913 that "to a Catholic who knows something of economic history, and something of the economic aspects of Catholic teaching, the attempt to chain the Church to the car of a plutocratic Capitalism is impudent and sickening." Attaining universal worker justice, he saw, required not only raising wages but significant, systemic change: "Subnormal conditions of life and labor must be abolished; excessive gains on privileged capital must be made impossible; and ways must be found through which the majority of the workers will gradually become owners at least in part, of the instruments of production."[41]

But even as his vision intimated radical change, Ryan endeavored to approach social reform scientifically, morally, and practically: identifying and advocating what he concluded to be the wisest, most prudent, and timeliest courses of action in light of Catholic social principles, the circumstances at hand, and the best possible grasp of "economic and industrial facts."[42] The contemporary livelihood agenda developed in this book seeks to honor Ryan's legacy on all these counts. Its aims, I am convinced, will be most effectively refined and advanced in the dialectical space between (so-called) reformist and radical approaches to social change, in the alchemic contention between radical diagnosis and transformative vision on one hand, and diligent research and practical reformism on the other.

The twentieth-century US civil rights movement for racial justice illustrates well the arc of this radical-transformationist approach: Reformist steps, once accomplished, raised people's standards and expectations. Over time, critical masses of people came to recognize the shortcomings of these incremental advances, sparking dissatisfaction, protest, and debate among leaders and communities concerning avenues to further, more thoroughgoing changes.[43] By the mid-1960s, Martin Luther King Jr. and other civil rights advocates were advancing deepening critiques of militarism and economic inequality and their connections to racial injustice.[44] The 2020s may prove to be another such inflection point. Variously articulated by contemporary theorists, leaders, and movement activists, this radical-transformationist approach to social change honors both the realism about human limits and the profoundly transformative hope that lie at the heart of modern social Catholicism's Gospel-inspired labors for social and economic justice.[45]

WHAT WE NEED IN ORDER TO GET THERE

If a sustainable, inclusive livelihood political economy is indeed the destination toward which this historical moment points, what "new things" must US Catholics and citizens cultivate in order to move in this direction? Three things top the list: new virtues and practices; a corresponding political-economic imaginary anchored in participative civic and faith communities; and a stalwart commitment to acknowledging and undoing the harms and impediments to inclusive livelihood and citizenship wrought by systemic, difference-based power asymmetries, historically and today.

Virtues and Practices of Solidarity and Sufficiency

Effecting a large-scale economic reorientation means changing cultures and institutions, and for this we need people with changed imaginations, values, and practices. Putting aside the perceptions and motivations of individualist, self-maximizing *Homo economicus*, such people will engage polity, work, and economy through the eyes, mind, and heart of *Homo solidarietus*, the solidary person and citizen. *Homo economicus* perceives the economic arena as an impersonal field of individual striving where each of us competes for our own maximum material aggrandizement. Wants and needs are limitless, and sufficiency, security, and status are constantly under threat and in need of shoring up. *Homo economicus* is in the game to win, which means minimizing vulnerabilities and maximizing power and control over, and, when necessary, against one's fellow strivers. While requiring workers to seek their sustenance by way of the competitive and impersonal rules of the market involves tradeoffs and costs, doing so is—according to this way of thought—the surest and most efficient path to the best economic outcomes for the most people.

For *Homo solidarietus*, on the other hand, each person is unique in worth and dignity, but no one is on their own. In economic thinking and activity, one's holistic, relational identity as neighbor, friend, family member, colleague, and citizen comes into play, and is not replaced or overridden by one's identity as gain-seeking worker, spender, or consumer. For *Homo solidarietus*, market economy and market competition are always embedded in and answerable to cooperative and reciprocal relationships and communities. In particular, the waged economy depends upon and exists to support family and household economies, as well as the larger common and public good. Recognizing that sufficiency, security, and status entail and require a web of interdependent relationships, *Homo solidarietus* experiences these "three S's" as less dependent on individual achievement and self-protection. Because personal and common goods are seen as intertwined, not zero-sum, this mindset is also more receptive to political and economic policies that advance shared economic well-being and inclusive livelihood, giving particular attention to those who are most vulnerable or in greatest need. And whereas *Homo economicus* makes a virtue of competitive individualism and ever more increase, hallmark virtues for *Homo solidarietus* are solidarity and sufficiency.

Solidarity shifts the way one sees, values, and must approach strangers, the marginalized, and vulnerable others. While connoting bonds among likeminded communities, solidarity also has a universal, "catholic" reach—solidary people perceive and respond to the fundamental human interdependencies and interrelations that prompt Pope Francis to repeatedly affirm that everyone, and indeed, everything, is connected.[46] This creates a strong rationale and motive for reaching beyond the boundaries of one's own communities or social locations to construct links of communication, respect, and collaboration, building what Putnam called bridging social capital. Practicing solidarity, Francis urges, means breaking out of "soap bubbles of indifference" to encounter and connect with people outside our circles of comfort or familiarity, especially people who are poor, vulnerable, marginalized, or otherized.

In this commitment to the excluded, solidarity in practice becomes preferential, in the service of inclusivity. While animated by a vision of peace and right-relatedness that ultimately includes all, under finite and fallen historical conditions solidarity leads justice seekers to exercise partiality toward the less powerful and more vulnerable.[47] Given this, practicing solidarity entails a more critical and dialectical relationship to the status quo, and educes more love-motivated confrontation, conflict, and sacrifice, than modern Catholic social teaching has tended to acknowledge. For advantaged groups, this means stepping away from self-protection and into "risk solidarity": getting skin in the game, for instance by supporting policy changes or engaging in practices that expose us to hazards or losses from which we are typically insulated.[48] Cristina Traina reminds privileged people that we need to "distinguish sharply between the genuine and appropriate feeling of vulnerability [that arises when the privileged begin to experience or practice solidarity] and actual victimization by structural evil." Too often, she writes, "When structures shift to dislodge the veneer of predictability, security, and control that seems normal and even natural to privileged people, they do not cry 'vulnerable' they cry 'victim.' They are not victims. They have not been wronged.... The feeling of security that they are losing is an unjust privilege." However, she adds, "The good news is that giving up the myth of control and shedding the privilege of relative security is the prerequisite for making common cause with everyone who never had the luxury of either."[49] Vulnerability, something that only the advantaged have the privilege of deciding whether to acknowledge or practice, is the indispensable "door to compassion, solidarity, and community, and therefore to justice. If I am not vulnerable, solidarity is impossible; I can at best be a philanthropist."[50]

Undertaking solidarity in the concrete is difficult, messy, and at times scary work, and it is always liable to the blinding and corruptive effects of bias and selfishness.[51] But the vanguard and lifeblood of any movement for inclusive livelihood will be critical masses of people across classes, cultures, religions, and social locations who have the courage to commit themselves to risking the long-haul, always incomplete process of conversion to *Homo solidarietus.*

Sufficiency is a second habituated disposition that advancing a sustainable, inclusive-livelihood economy will require. Our current US economic culture fosters consumerist insatiability, individualist self-protection, and the sense that one's economic sufficiency, security, and status are chronically at risk. Advancing an inclusive livelihood culture means pushing against all these currents. Anxieties about material, relational, or psychological scarcities, or fears that our basic needs are in zero-sum competition with the basic needs of others, pose serious obstacles to solidarity. To overcome these obstacles, people need, among other things, reassurance that the common good to which the virtue of solidarity points is one in which they, too, will have enough. And this in turn requires people and communities who can recognize, and be satisfied with, what "enough" entails in specific contexts and circumstances.

Along with solidarity, therefore, an inclusive livelihood political economy requires formation in a second virtue: sufficiency. This is the disposition to discern, in particular economic circumstances, what is enough; asking, as John Bogle puts it, "Enough of what? And to what avail?" It is also the cultivated capacity to recognize and to be satisfied with what is "good enough," or what "satisfices."[52] People disposed to sufficiency are more able to limit acquisitive or consumerist excess when justice or love—for self, family, near and far neighbors, or the earth—requires it. While still valuing a strong work ethic, productive markets, and the goods and services markets supply, their embrace of this *habitus* of sufficiency tempers participants' drives for "ever more" in their personal, community, and institutional lives.

Describing this solidary and sufficient way of living, Pope Francis writes that "Christian spirituality proposes an alternative understanding of the quality of life," and a lifestyle "capable of deep enjoyment free of the obsession with consumption." "Joy and peace" come from recovering "that simplicity which allows us to stop and appreciate the small things, to be grateful for the opportunities which life affords us, to be spiritually detached from what we possess, and not to succumb to sadness for what we lack." A life freed of consumerist excess, "when lived freely and consciously, is liberating . . . a way of living life to the full." People of solidarity and sufficiency learn to attend to, appreciate, and enjoy "each person and each thing"; they are energized and freed by the discovery that "happiness means knowing how to limit some needs which only diminish us, and being open to the many different possibilities which life can offer."[53]

On political and policy levels, advocates for inclusive livelihood require data-backed, credible strategies for distinguishing the (quantitative and qualitative) elements that constitute ample sufficiency for individuals, households, and communities; as well as sufficiency's upper and lower boundaries in light of others' unmet needs, and in light of limits to natural resources and ecological sustainability. To sort this through, Catholic economist Albino Barrera, OP, invokes social Catholicism's "universal access principle" to affirm every person's rights to sufficiency but also to delineate responsibilities for limiting acquisition and consumption for the sake of fulfilling the unmet basic needs of others. Barrera specifies scarcity and sufficiency in terms of three kinds of needs: survival/constitutive needs (necessary for basic subsistence); determinative needs (necessary to enable minimum access to dignified social and economic participation, such as schoolbooks and educational opportunities); and life-enhancing needs (connected, for example, to legitimate development and use of talents and gifts, such as music lessons or specialized tools). Each has material, social, and psychological dimensions.

Taking a position similar to that of Nobel laureate economist Amartya Sen, Barrera uses "capacities for dignified social participation" as an important metric for determining people's rights-bearing needs.[54] And when some people's needs are going unmet, "claims for economic resources" should be "weighed according to the unmet needs of the contending parties, prioritizing constitutive needs over determinative, and determinative over life-enhancing."[55] This ethical formula makes a challenging—and traditional Christian—claim: when my neighbors' survival or constitutive needs are unmet, fulfilling those needs takes precedence over fulfilling my own life-enhancing needs, and even more, over my right to acquire luxuries.

In this Catholic economic view, consumption serves what recent popes have called "integral human development"—but only up to a point. Just as human development requires establishing "a floor to consumption below which human survival is not possible, it also defines a ceiling, an upper limit."[56] This puts the onus on individuals, households, and communities to figure out and pursue livelihoods and lifestyles calibrated within "an optimal band in consumption levels bounded by underdevelopment and superdevelopment, by destitution and overindulgence."[57] Here Barrera echoes ecological economists like Raworth, whose widely used image of "doughnut economics" visualizes the "safe and just" space for "inclusive and sustainable economic development" as residing between a minimum "social foundation," with everyone's material and social needs sufficiently met, and a maximum "environmental ceiling" beyond which human activity becomes what Daly calls "uneconomic" by eroding its own ecological prerequisites.[58]

Our dominant economic culture exercises strong, distorting influences on our collective assumptions about sufficiency, security, and status, and how to attain them. Recall Pope Francis on this misalignment of values and priorities: "Today consumerism determines what is important." The consumerist habitus "does not favor bonding," and has "little to do with human relationships," but rather focuses on our own satisfactions. Echoing Jesuit superior Adolfo Nicolás's concerns about a "globalization of superficiality," Francis worries that "we have turned our society into a huge multicultural showcase tied only to the tastes of certain 'consumers,'" while the majority are left with crumbs. This, he says "causes great harm" for the poor. It also harms the wealthy, by feeding "a kind of impoverishment born of a widespread and radical sense of loneliness," wed to "a fear of commitment in a limitless effort to feel recognized."[59]

To resist these dynamics and reorient political economy toward inclusive livelihood, we need, instead, to cultivate the antidote habits of solidarity and sufficiency. Families and intermediate communities and associations, both civic and faith-based, have integral parts to play in forming people with the freedom, hope, and strength—what organizer Ganz calls "the self-esteem and the self-confidence"—to say yes to solidarity's demands.[60] With the support of constituencies committed to solidarity and sufficiency, policymakers can address scarcity more realistically and ethically, putting aside models predicated on endless "more" to build a political economy dedicated to ensuring access to ample sufficiency for everyone, within the ecological and social bounds necessary for securing sufficiency both now and for future generations.

Imagination and Community

In forming people and communities of solidarity and sufficiency, imagination plays a constitutive role. For novelist Marilynne Robinson, "the glue that bonds a community, at least a community larger than the immediate family, consists very largely of imaginative love for people we do not know or whom we know very slightly." Resonating with Catholicism's sacramental imagination, Robinson lifts up the disciplined, continually refreshed expansion of mind and heart—the solidary spirituality—that building and sustaining communities requires. Cultivating solidarity both within (bonding) and beyond (bridging) our insular group borders always involves this work of the imagination, and "the more generous the scale at which imagination is exerted, the healthier and more humane the community will be."[61]

Christians anchor their practices of solidarity and sufficiency in an encompassing religious imaginary, a vision that affirms a Divine who connects humans to one another and to creation; and who calls forth human communities, agency, and work. This God promises and orients human endeavors toward an eschatological completion biblically symbolized as God's reign, kingdom, or household (*oikos*), where everyone will have a place at the table, with more than enough for all. Yet while steadfastly trusting in the power and ultimate victory of God's redeeming love in Jesus and the Holy Spirit, Christians also live in the shadow of the cross: they struggle with the mysteries and miseries of suffering, grief, and perplexity that mark our finite human condition, and with the sin and moral evil reflected in our species' stunning capacities for selfishness, cruelty, and violence. Facing the realities of evil and suffering lends Christian hope sobriety and realism, and counsels justice seekers to humility marked by attentiveness to our own sinful tendencies and biases.

At their best, spiritual and religious communities help people to confront, delve deeply into, and learn to live and act amid and beyond their deepest flaws, vulnerabilities, and fears. When believers resist facile theologies that merely "gloss the surface of the fractured and wounded narratives of the human soul," religious communities can offer wisdom, rituals, and language for "digging down into the depths of the crises we face today," and for "reflection on the nature of sin and desire, of vulnerability and violence, of identity and otherness rooted in prayerful contemplation of the mystery of divine love, mercy and justice."[62] These spiritual dynamics and connections provide vital nourishment to the worldly work of providing good work for all. And by fostering deep-level trust in our secure belonging and inviolable worth, faith and spirituality can help us to calm down, to unclench our hearts and hands, and to navigate more freely and bravely the risks and insecurities that pursuing an inclusive livelihood economy will inevitably entail.

Participative, Democratic Polities

Robustly communitarian, pluralist, and democratically participative polities are another key to advancing a US economy centered on sustainable livelihood for all. People need and deserve communities of identity and belonging, but solidary citizens and believers do not cling exclusively to the familiarity of a closed-in "us." Moving toward a future where all families have access to livelihood requires wide, cross-community buy-in and collaboration. And for building solidary, intra- and intercommunity connections and power, especially among non-elite and vulnerable workers and citizens, bridging as well as bonding labor will be ongoing needs.

For US Catholics, democratic engagement is further informed by their modern social tradition's emphasis on promoting personal rights and freedoms within a robust, multiassociational civil society where power and participation are widely shared, and average people are afforded voice, agency, and opportunities for growth and improvement. Catholics champion the people-serving purposes of US economic and political institutions, and affirm US values like the dignity of work; self-reliance and responsibility; honesty, reciprocity, and pulling one's weight; and dedication to family and local communities. Catholics also envisage and promote a vibrant, multigroup democratic polity wherein power and authority are widely dispersed, and state and federal governance serve local units by overseeing the common good and performing functions that require higher levels of organization.

Minding the Power and Equity Gaps

As earlier chapters have detailed, advancing a truly inclusive US political economy requires addressing historic divisions, inequities, and denials of livelihood to members of groups deemed lesser or other, whether on grounds of gender, race/ethnicity, or socioeconomic class.

Gender Equity and the Household/Care Economy

Testifying to the complex ways that gender continues to thread through the story of Americans' pursuit of livelihood, dismantling ideal-worker job standards and reorganizing labor markets around equitable, universal-caregiving policies are goals that current US work-family policies reflect dimly at best. To make progress toward inclusive livelihood, we need a new, effective agenda for justly supporting the work of both the waged/formal and unpaid/domestic or care economies; and on this point, feminist scholars, social conservatives, and modern social Catholics share some important common ground.

Recall, for instance, that feminist Nancy Fraser's critique of the two-earner family norm, discussed in chapter 3, takes aim at more than the inequity of women's typically greater responsibilities for household work. Fraser argues that assuming two full-time earners per household impedes access to economic sufficiency for single parents and people living alone. For all families, valorizing a dual-earner norm provides cover for "the steep rise in the number of hours of paid work now required to support a household, and if the household includes children or elderly relatives or people who are sick or disabled and cannot function as full-time wage earners, then so much the worse."[63]

What results is a "crisis of care" that is structured into the current social and economic regime. By requiring more hours of work per household and cutting back family-supporting public services, the present political economy "is systematically depleting our capacities for sustaining social bonds" and "stretching our caring energies to the breaking point." This system also exacerbates class-based income inequality by creating "a dual organization of care work in which those who can afford domestic help simply pay for it, while those who cannot scramble to take care of their families, often by doing the paid care work for the first group, and often at very, very low wages with virtually no protections."[64]

Currently, in 70 percent of households with children, all adults are also wage earners. The standard full-time work week, shaped by the traditional male breadwinner model, plus the long commutes bred by the spatial arrangement of cities and suburban sprawl, deplete time for family care.[65] Two-parent households may adapt by reducing the employment hours of one parent, typically the mother; but part-time pay is penalized. Meanwhile, "single mothers inhabit the cutting, bleeding edge of social change."[66] The inequities that mar the present setup point to an urgent need both for "some new way of organizing social reproduction" and for organizing livelihood as a whole.[67]

In short, a work-justice program that focuses only on one side of the waged/household economy dyad will fail. To make a good living available to all, new social norms, employment policies, and labor laws must enable men and women across race and class lines to equitably share and fulfill responsibilities for supporting their households through work, both domestic and waged.[68] Family-work policies must "provide increased support for both unpaid and paid care work, helping individuals gain the flexibility they need to balance family responsibility with paid employment," according to families' different and changing needs and circumstances.[69]

A reorganized, equitable US labor system would guarantee non-elite wage earners many of the supports (schedule and time flexibility, paid health insurance, and sick, parental, and family leave) now common in other wealthy (and many less wealthy) nations. And because, in addition, one or both parents in a family—particularly female parents—are likely to hold a service- or care-related job, work justice campaigns must target improving the status, remuneration, benefits, and working conditions in these burgeoning job categories.

As forebears like Ryan well knew, hammering out such policies in the political and economic trenches requires intelligence, negotiation, persistence, and trial and error. In 2019 two proposed paid family leave bills illustrated this, as well as the importance of attending to both solidarity and subsidiarity in crafting family-supportive policies. David Cloutier observed that the Republican-backed family-leave legislation, which entailed a "self-funded" plan (one would pay for one's own family leave by deducting the cost from future Social Security benefits) stressed subsidiarity, but evinced little solidarity with financially vulnerable poor and working-class families. Alternatively, Democrats had proposed a federal-government-mandated family leave policy, funded by higher taxes. Their "one-size fits all law" covered everyone, but lacked the flexibility and self-correcting potential of a plan where more power and authority to adapt and implement were accorded to local communities and employers.[70]

Resistance to government-sponsored paid family care has also been fueled by worries about commodifying or unintentionally "crowding out" the socially valuable, unpaid care work performed in homes. Feminist economist Nancy Folbre acknowledges these concerns, but worries equally that "increasing the cost of fulfilling family obligations"—which the current setup does—"will discourage family and community commitments."[71] Tragically

illustrating this latter problem is the plight of poor immigrant women participating in "global care chains," who relinquish the care of their own children
to others in order to financially support them by caring for the children of
wealthy families in distant countries. The contributions and predicaments
of these caregivers and of other immigrant laborers also remind us that a
Catholic inclusive livelihood ethic cannot restrict its attention to US citizens,
but must take into account all vulnerable workers and families on whom
we depend and to whom we are economically connected, both inside and
beyond national borders.[72]

Addressing Racial/Ethnic and Class Divides

Race and class, frequently intersecting with gender, continue to be implicated
in the structuring of work and the labor markets.[73] Between 1980 and 2018
income growth was stagnant for all non-elite workers and families. Measured across demographics, wealth levels were dismal for working-class families regardless of race, even among the highest-earning households in both
groups.

Yet important gender- and race-correlated distinctions persisted, especially in hourly wages and income. In 2014, about half of all US households' earnings fell below basic family needs thresholds. In 2016, non-elite
white men still out-earned all other demographic groups. On average, white
working-class families consistently out-earned Black, Hispanic, and Native
American households of the same size and worker education levels. And
across all family types, families of color were less likely to earn a living wage.[74]
But among white working-class men, any statistical income advantage over
nonwhite neighbors since the 1980s was overshadowed by the more viscerally felt experience of a five-dollar-per-hour decline in average real wages.[75] As
working-class wages stagnated overall, women as a group made modest gains,
but men's wages saw "only significant declines."[76]

The working-class frustrations and anxieties behind these numbers contributed to the cultural and political turmoil that surrounded the 2016 presidential election and its aftermath. But rather than sparking solidarity and
concerted action for change, these economic discontents more often seemed
to stoke complicated, group-based resentments and divisions. In the even
further fragmented political and cultural landscape that resulted, non-elite
working families remained separated and disempowered. In these circumstances, creating coalitions that can advance an inclusive livelihood agenda
in these circumstances will require efforts on two fronts: first, to bridge often
toxic class- and race-related social divisions; and second, to identify and act

to redress systemic factors that contribute to the opportunity, income, and wealth deficiencies and disparities that undermine the livelihoods of so many non-elite working families in the United States today.

On the first front, political scientist Marc Howard Ross observes that systemic inequities and conflicts of economic interest often crystallize and coagulate around issues of group identity, including racial identity.[77] For addressing such group-based divisions, Ross argues that understanding the "political psychology of competing cultural narratives" is key. Bonding cultural narratives heighten a group's internal unity; they often also sharpen us-versus-them intergroup enmities. To offset these divisive side effects, differently framed, bridging cultural narratives can help foster peace and open doors to collaboration between those same groups. In a large, diverse urban center, for example, a bridging storyline, like "We are different, but people treat each other with respect and civility here," can act as a civic glue that helps preserve public safety, civility, and peace. Nationally, the presence of multiple, evolving, and often conflicting articulations of American identity and values testify to the fact that adjudicating competing cultural narratives, and constructing shared stories of varying types and scopes, are complex, ongoing processes.

Practices of listening and learning to appreciate others' distinctive, sacred stories, while also striving to tell a unifying meta-story are endemic to race, class, and cultural literacy in the United States. Such literacies, moreover, can be taught, fostered, and learned. Civil rights lawyer Lani Guinier, for instance, calls for a new kind of civic education that cultivates "the capacity to conjugate the grammar of race in different contexts and circumstances" as racism takes on changing expressions and forms. Such literacy education can better equip citizens to recognize and address the wide range of group-discriminatory practices that "affect blacks and Latinos first and most acutely, but . . . also disempower poor and working-class white people," particularly poor or working-class rural white men.[78] Betsy Leonard-Wright and Joan Williams describe a similarly urgent need for education to combat "class cluelessness" and to improve cross-class literacy and understanding.

Class and racial reeducation do not occur simply by putting people from different groups into contact with one another. But when people join in cross-group efforts to address shared social and economic concerns, opportunities for learning more naturally arise, and participants frequently find themselves becoming active participants in the difficult work of constructing bridging discourses and practices that strengthen bonds of unity amid real and continuing differences.[79] It is messy work, requiring honesty, patience, and realistic expectations. Building cross-group coalitions, notes Carla Murphy, involves promoting leaders from among the community "who value inclusion *and* who will address racial [along with class and cultural] divides." It also means accepting that joining forces for achievable change "requires the low but reachable standard of common interest, not the higher bar of absolute purification."[80]

Today, new work justice initiatives show promise for spanning divides between class- and race-based change agendas, and for combining narrowly targeted with more broadly socially beneficial strategies for advancing inclusive livelihood. One example is a coalition among labor unions and racial justice activists in a movement known as "Bargaining for the Common Good" (BCG).[81] With roots in contemporary social movement unionism, BCG seeks to build citizens' power by broadening and deepening unions' ties with likeminded grassroots communities and movements. In national summits and regional initiatives, BCG is connecting unions, community organizations, and racial justice advocates, and expanding labor bargaining campaigns to include racial justice demands. Forming alliances and creating shared plans is enabling BCG coalitions "to win intersectional victories for their members and communities."[82]

To be effective, inclusive livelihood initiatives must also address systemic ways that sexist, racist, and class-based power relations affect economic theorizing, institutions, and practices, including within change seekers' own ranks. We must never forget, stresses Michael Zweig, how tightly race, culture, and economy are intertwined.[83] Given this, livelihood-focused policies like wage increases or tax reforms must incorporate, or be augmented by, intentional strategies for addressing longstanding patterns of exclusion or discrimination and their compounding effects on the poor, women, and people of color.

Recent attention to the ugly, persisting saga of antiblack racism and white supremacy in the United States has sparked fierce public debate over how to do right by groups historically subjected to systemic, racist social and economic oppression.[84] By 2019, author Ta-Nehisi Coates's forceful appeal to open a serious national conversation on reparations, and for Congress to finally pass a long-tabled bill (HR 40) mandating its study, had generated some significant responses. Jesuit institution Georgetown University had undertaken an investigation into and public reckoning with its slaveholding and slave-selling history, and was developing programs to offer education and other benefits to descendants of persons whom nineteenth-century Jesuits had enslaved and later sold to raise funds for maintaining their schools.[85] And several serious contenders for the 2020 Democratic presidential nomination published detailed proposals and plans for, as one put it, "proactively addressing the aftereffects of generations of racist inequity."[86]

Racial reparations' rationale, form, scope, and implementation all remained hotly contested. In general, economic policies perceived as benefiting "all" have been strongly preferred by voters—especially white and working-class voters—over policies benefiting "some." Noting this, Cindi Suarez observes that "for those concerned with the US mainstream, the key challenge appears to be how to confront the enormous debt to Black Americans while addressing the very real economic challenges other Americans are facing. (Not that these are mutually exclusive.)" Meanwhile, for Black Americans, the challenge is "how not to make black reparations just about a financial debt and forget about white supremacy," insofar as slavery and its long aftermath have never been simply about economic domination "but also about racial domination"—domination inflicted in different ways on Native Americans, and on other peoples deemed "not white." [87] Those working to build a political economy that delivers livelihood for everyone will need to seriously engage with both of Suarez's challenges.

WHAT, THEN, SHOULD WE DO?

In the Gospel of Luke, John the Baptist's disciples respond to his call to "prepare the way of the Lord" by asking, "What, then, should we do?" John's answers, directed to different groups, are striking in their specificity, and in their economic focus: Whoever has two tunics—or extra food—should share it with the person who has none. Tax collectors should stop skimming off money by overcharging. Soldiers should not extort or falsely accuse people, and they should be satisfied with their wages.[88] This text is one of many that testify to the inextricable links in biblical religions between one's standing before God and one's responsibilities to neighbors in matters of wealth and possessions, work, and economy.[89] For twenty-first-century Christians, gospel-based solidarity requires, in addition to personal economic integrity, collective efforts to reform institutions. To act in solidarity, Pope Francis declares, "is to fight against the structural causes of poverty, inequality, lack of work, land and housing, the denial of social and labor rights. It is to confront the destructive effects of the empire of money."[90] Solidarity, seriously practiced, leads to "a global rethinking of the whole system, and a quest for ways to reform it and correct it in a way consistent with the fundamental human rights of all human beings."[91] But how, in our contemporary context and circumstances, does any of this actually begin to happen? What are people doing to make it happen? And what should, or can, each of us do?

Building an ecologically sustainable economy centered on dignified work and a good livelihood for all requires action on multiple levels—from household and local, to national and even global economies, and in multiple forms, from changes in personal and family practices to changes in policies, laws, and institutions. What Pope Francis calls the polyhedric (locally diverse but widely interconnected) nature of our society and economy opens myriad opportunities to design and execute contextualized initiatives for addressing the exclusions and inequities that afflict our social and economic status quo.

Recalling Ryan's admonition that "obviously we shall make mistakes," but that "until the attempt is made, and a certain (and very large) number of mistakes are made, there will be no progress," effective change seekers will be inventive and resilient, experimenting and initiating, often failing or succeeding only partially, learning to do better.[92] Today as in the past, people with this kind of long-view perspective and dedication, most working in the background with little public notice, are creating prototypes for and making inroads toward a renovated US political economy that includes, and serves, everyone.

The people, communities, and organizations making these efforts are highly diverse, but they share values, priorities, and practice that give them instructive family resemblances. These include an embrace of *economic citizenship* as entailing rights and duties pertaining to solidarity, sufficiency, and sustainable livelihood; fostering both *bonding social capital* in thick communities of belonging, and *bridging social capital* via cross-group connections and coalition building; creating and adapting unifying interpretive *frames* to crystallize shared moral commitments and energize action; cultivating personal and communal *agency*, voice, and power through engagement in *participative democracy*; establishing dynamic *grassroots coalitions* and *grassroots-elite partnerships*; and engaging the energies and resources of *religious, spiritual, and ethical traditions* and communities.

A brief set of examples suggests the great number and variety of ways in which people, communities and institutions are contributing to the urgent work of building the sustainable, inclusive-livelihood political economy that we and our neighbors, our country, and our planet need.

Paying Living Wages

A century ago, US Catholics joined unions and social activists to champion all workers' rights to livable wages. Today this same impetus drives renewed support for policies and legislation to guarantee wages and working conditions commensurate with a dignified livelihood. By 2019, local and state efforts to increase minimum wages to fifteen dollars per hour had reached the halls of Congress, where vigorous debate ensued over a "Raise the Wage" bill that would mandate a new federal hourly wage of fifteen dollars by 2024. Supporters argued the proposed law would raise the pay of nearly forty million workers, with benefits accruing disproportionately to Black and Latinx wage earners—an example of how policies that benefit everyone can especially help more vulnerable groups. Nearly 20 percent of the nation's children would be positively affected, and 67 percent of workers in the lowest income deciles would get a raise.[93] Detractors argued that by increasing unemployment and hurting small businesses, such a law would ultimately harm vulnerable workers.[94] We will circle back to this issue when we examine grassroots organizations in contemporary living wage campaigns. But first I will briefly survey other policy proposals and some practical experiments currently under way, each of which aims to push the needle closer to the goal of a renovated US culture, polity, and economy centered on delivering an ecologically sustainable and dignified livelihood for all its workers and families.

Reducing Financial Burdens, Providing Resources

One set of initiatives focuses on changing policies and expanding programs to help non-elite families experiencing underemployment, job insecurity, and steeply rising housing, education, childcare and healthcare costs. Desmond denounces current US policies such as tax deductions for mortgage interest, which "continue to give the most help to those who least need it—affluent homeowners—while providing nothing to most rent-burdened tenants," and perpetuating economic inequality and precarity for vulnerable working families. He illustrates with one achingly sad story, that of a hardworking single mother of two in Braintree, Massachusetts, Crisaliz Diaz, who, despite her indefatigable efforts, faces eviction from her small apartment. When Desmond asks her, "What would you do if you only had to pay 30 percent of your income for housing?" Diaz replies, with a poignant sigh: "That would be life." Desmond's research shows that "more than half of all poor renting families in the country spend more than 50 percent of their income on housing costs, and at least one in four spends more than 70 percent." In a nation that cared about giving everyone a chance at economic sufficiency, he argues, advantaged citizens would support reforms that might lessen their housing deductions but help neighbors like Diaz and her children.[95]

Feminist economists, we have seen, propose a range of policies for better supporting working families with care responsibilities for children, the frail, or the elderly.[96] Gregory Squires underlines the need to rebuild the social-institutional supports that ensured broad middle-class prosperity during the postwar years.[97] Joel Cohen advocates stronger, European-style social programs to take the financial pressure off non-elite households, enable savings, and make daily well-being "less contingent on having enough money."[98] If we were to muster the political will, he continues, "the United States has the resources to create a quality educational system that serves children from birth to the moment they are ready to assume a meaningful role in the economy"; "to ensure access to quality healthcare"; and "to make every neighborhood—even the poor ones—completely acceptable places to maintain livelihoods and raise children." With so many families struggling for livelihood in our affluent country, Cohen concludes, "we aren't fated to do nothing. Governments do have the capacity to at least ease the burden of these problems, and other countries offer ideas about how this can be done."[99]

Guaranteed or Universal Basic Income

Amid current and projected shrinkages in numbers of available jobs, another proposed government-administered program has sparked fresh interest and debate: the guaranteed or universal basic income (UBI). The UBI is a monthly cash transfer provided by the government to all (usually, adult) citizens, with no strings attached. In most proposals, the income envisaged is quite spare, with funding coming from the shrinkage or elimination of other poverty-mitigating programs. Critics like Cass contend that a UBI would deincentivize work and breed dependence. Supporters counter that, since any basic income will fall below a level most people can or want to live on, almost everyone will continue to seek and perform paid work, whose taxation in turn will help support the UBI.[100] Additionally, a UBI could free adults formerly required *not* to work in order to qualify for poverty-level welfare benefits to join the paid workforce and augment their basic income without penalty.[101] A UBI also enables people to forgo or limit waged work in particular life stages or circumstances; most often, experiments have shown, in order to study, or to perform urgently needed, familial care work.

Many regard UBI policies as *distributively* unjust: taking money from those who labor for their wages and giving it to able-bodied adults who do not or will not work seems patently unfair. But thoughtful proponents like Philippe Van Parijs and Yannick Vanderborght point out that a UBI can increase *reciprocal* or *social* justice, and reduce inequality, because it "strengthens the bargaining power of the most vulnerable participants in the labor market and would therefore mean that the irksomeness of a job, its lack of

intrinsic attractiveness, would be better reflected in the pay it commands."
Agreeing, Danny Dorling adds, "once a basic income is high enough, people
are free to choose not to do inadequately paid work, or even better-paid work
that they do not see a value in doing, and so the labor market begins to function properly: people can exercise choice."[102] A UBI can also help address two
sorts of economic free riding that usually go unnoticed: first, that of family
members dependent on the unpaid labor being done in their households, and
second, a systemic form of exploitation by higher earners who, thanks to their
superior bargaining power, "can do jobs they enjoy while benefiting from the
toil of people who have no option but to accept low-paid jobs that the better
paid would hate doing."[103]

One last pro-UBI argument, resonant with Catholic social teaching on
the universal destination of created goods, points out that many of the material benefits we enjoy today are ours only thanks to the collective legacy of the
technology, political framework, science, inventions, and so on that our forebears have bequeathed us. As much as 90 percent of what is earned in richer
versus poorer countries, Nobel laureate economist Herbert Simon avers, is
due not to our superior abilities or efforts but to the "social capital" to which
people in richer countries have disproportionate, unearned access. These UBI
supporters underscore "the extent to which our economy [already] functions
as a gift-distribution machine, as an arrangement that enables people to tap—
very unequally—our common inheritance."[104]

UBI debates highlight the importance of gathering and considering all relevant economic data, and carefully considering possible unintended effects
of proposed policies for ensuring work and livelihood. Surveying available
research, Canadian economist Mario Seccareccia concludes that on their
own, UBI policies are likely to hurt vulnerable workers not by making them
lazy but by incentivizing employers to further lower wages for jobs that are
already the least paid. Especially in times of labor surplus, a UBI program
must be joined with a commitment to full employment and "other floors to
market wage deflation (such as a comprehensive minimum wage system and
unemployment insurance)," or it risks becoming "an institutional mechanism
to spread low-wage employment." Unlike Cass's concern with a UBI eroding
people's work ethic, Seccareccia's systemic analysis focuses on the need to offset its potential negative (for workers) incentives to capitalist labor markets.[105]

Prioritizing Productive, Fairly Remunerated Work

Campaigning for jobs with living wages, just working conditions, and secure
benefits has been a central strategy for work justice advocates from Ryan's day

to our own. A different approach is Cass's agenda for "productive pluralism," which pivots on a "holistic conception of the American citizen" as productive contributor rather than as consumer, and "seeks to put the fundamental dignity of working and family life first." His proposals center on the "working hypothesis" that a "labor market in which workers can support strong families and communities is the central determinant of long-term prosperity," and therefore should be the central focus of economic policy.[106]

Current economic orthodoxy, Cass contends, leads the US to pursue growth in ways that erode the labor market's health and subsequently to redistribute funds to losers in the job market via consumption-focused welfare programs. But as job-starved, deteriorating cities and towns across the country bear witness, the current approach is systematically undermining sustainable prosperity by neglecting to provide for its human prerequisites in families and communities. Instead of economic growth for its own sake, strengthening labor markets and local communities by cultivating livelihood-supporting jobs should be policymakers' main target. Effective labor market boosting policies will incentivize citizens to work and reward businesses that invest in secure, labor-intensive working- and middle-class jobs.

Cass's palette of proposals pushes against both Democratic and Republican Party pieties and illustrates the benefits of replacing a growth and consumption economic policy axis with one centered on family- and community-supporting labor markets. Cass proposes that instead of mandating higher minimum wages—he believes they unduly penalize employers—governments should provide a taxpayer-funded wage subsidy to bring low-paid workers' pay up to an agreed-upon level. Wage subsidies would improve on the popular earned income tax credit with a simpler formula and delivery system (a "federal work bonus" would appear in each paycheck, along with regular deductions) and incentivize work by making transparent the direct link between hours worked and money—including subsidies—received each pay period.

Cass argues that policies that cut corporate taxes to encourage capital investment, but levy heavier employer taxes per worker, send businesses the implicit message, "Try to grow rapidly with as little as possible."[107] A better corporate tax code would "lower the tax burden of firms with relatively more workers." To maintain revenues for this, the corporate tax rate would need to rise, "yet firms that generated profits through the productive employment of workers would benefit at the expense of firms that did so through other means." When "work, rather than unemployment, draws government support, and that support can flow to a fuller range of productive activities in the community," positive economic and social effects will proliferate.[108]

Cass's reorientation of economic policy around productive, stable, living-wage-paying jobs for all workers and their families jibes with key premises of our inclusive livelihood agenda. His agenda also has limits. He gives no attention to how productive pluralism incorporates or ensures support for the vast unpaid sector of the household and care economy. Issues of gender, racial/ethnic, or other group-based wage and work discrimination are also left aside. At times Cass expresses more concern about deterring individuals from being idle "takers" than about curtailing incentives to employers and businesses to raise their profits by keeping wages low. But Cass's labor agenda suggests the potential of an inclusive-livelihood agenda to generate support across current political and ideological divides, around shared commitments to the economic well-being of ordinary workers, families, and their communities.

Businesses Serving the Common Good

For improving workers' situations and moving toward a sustainable, inclusive livelihood economy, participation by employers and business leaders is key. In this direction, one significant US trend is a growing interest in community-benefit-oriented "social entrepreneurship," including the rise of a network of businesses that intentionally embrace a social and environmental mission. "Benefit Corporations," or B Corps, are for-profit corporations whose legally defined aims include not only profits but beneficial impacts on workers, the community, and environment. Being certified for Benefit Corporation status legally mandates a corporation "to balance the impact on their stakeholders in addition to their shareholders in their decision-making."[109] Beginning with Maryland in 2010, by 2018 thirty-five states had passed legislation establishing Benefit Corporations as recognized business models. By 2019 the cohort of more than 1,800 certified B Corps spanned 130 industries, ranging from small local companies to large corporations like Ben & Jerry's, Patagonia, and Eileen Fisher.[110]

Experiments in Economic Democracy

In 1909 Ryan laid out a two-part US Catholic agenda for social and economic reform. The first part focused on labor legislation and included a legal minimum wage, an eight-hour law, and protective labor legislation for women and children. The second concerned establishing "industrial democracy," in which workers would become copartners or cooperators in all levels of the modern industrial order. By 1920 Ryan was describing industrial democracy more specifically as entailing a threefold sharing among workers and owners: in management, profits, and ownership.[111]

A century later, political economist Gar Alperovitz and his colleagues in The Next System Project's Democracy Collaborative were encouraging a range of efforts to chart a path beyond rigid capitalist-socialist binaries by contributing to "*evolutionary reconstruction*—systemic institutional transformation of the political economy that unfolds over time."[112] For generating effective responses to the "challenges being created by issues of political stalemate, of scale, and of ecological, resource and climate change," Alperovitz and Dubb are promoting and documenting diverse institutional and community experiments geared toward building a different political economy, one that "emphasizes sustainable, economically and democratically healthy local communities that are anchored by wealth-democratizing strategies, policies and institutions."[113] Their long-term goal is a "pluralistic commonwealth" or "community-sustaining system" that rests on four axioms: democratization of wealth; community as a guiding theme; decentralization; and democratic planning to support community and longer-term economic, democracy-building, and ecological goals.[114]

Dovetailing with Catholic emphases on multigroup participation and the common good, the Next System agenda closely connects building an inclusive economy with "reconstituting a culture of community—the sense that 'we are all in it together.'" We need a culture "that understands that collective community-building solutions—grounded in hard effort, compromise, and even sacrifice—are necessary if we are to aspire to anything beyond the continuing hollowing out of our democracy and the degradation of our shared environment." Also in line with our livelihood agenda, The Next System project's constituencies and loci extend beyond formal workplaces and economic institutions to include neighborhoods, families, and households. And striking chords of solidarity, Alperovitz invites change seekers to undertake "self-conscious efforts to reach out, to include, to understand difference, and to personally cultivate new relationships that recognize our mutual interdependence and that move beyond politics and institution building."[115]

Finally, evincing an incarnational sensibility, Democracy Collaborative leaders recognize that "building a system which values the community as a whole requires a commitment to place." This means that "what is done regionally or nationally has to nurture the space for community and its institutional matrix to grow and develop." It also means that efforts to advance democratic economic institutions must respect US culture, and appeal to communities' values. In places like Cleveland and the Bronx, initiatives that keep in mind Americans' wariness about "big government" and appreciation for "localism and decentralization" are focusing on "multiple and pluralist forms of enterprise," the majority of them—as is the case in the United States today—small to medium-size businesses.[116] And given Americans' deeply ingrained appreciation for entrepreneurialism and self-reliance, efforts to build "systemic alternatives" to economic business as usual are likely to be more successful when they are grounded not in abstract theories or grand historical visions but "in pragmatic, practical problem solving."[117]

To the question "What then can we do?" Alperovitz and collaborators answer, "In fact, a great deal." They point to cross-institutional experiments already under way on Main Streets across the country, that are constructing scaffolding for a new, ecologically sustainable, locally empowered, and inclusive political economy.[118]

Since 2008, for example, one struggling urban neighborhood in Cleveland has been home to a major experiment in "an innovative approach to economic development, green job creation, and neighborhood stabilization," using a strategy pioneered by the Democracy Collaborative called "community wealth building." Municipal government, the collaborative, and other nonprofit corporations; "anchor institutions" including hospitals and universities; and local community residents have partnered to build the Evergreen Cooperatives, a series of environmentally positive worker-owned businesses that employ local community members at fair pay. Anchor institutions commit to purchasing goods and services produced by the local cooperatives, and make investments in the local community. By building a self-sustaining cooperative system, the "Cleveland model" puts wealth and economic power in the hands of local community members, reducing reliance on unequal relationships with distant, wealth-extracting corporations or chain retailers, and basing economies on local, more socially conscious businesses instead.[119] Documented at the collaborative's website, CommunityWealth.org, community wealth building initiatives are under way in dozens of other economically distressed urban communities from the Bronx to Kansas City, Denver, and Seattle.[120] Community wealth building, says Democracy Collaborative cofounder Ted Howard, aims to "stop the leakage of money out of our community" while concretely demonstrating "that economic decisions can be based on more than neoliberalism's narrow criteria."[121]

Alongside ambitious projects like these are a panoply of less-flashy sites of sprouting economic democracy. Many are advancing Ryan's vision of workers' sharing in management, profits, and ownership. Some groups, including some Catholic congregations of religious sisters, are pursuing socially responsible investing or shareholder activism, pressing corporations to mend unjust economic and harmful ecological practices.[122] Since the 1990s, worker-owned businesses have also increased in number and type. By 2009 ethicist Gary Dorrien counted twelve thousand "worker-owned firms in the United States, including large enterprises such as Republic Engineered Steels, Publix Supermarkets, and Northwestern Steel and Wire." Such ownership schemes have many limitations, but they are potential building blocks for a future, more fully developed economic democracy.

All of these leaders champion local experimentation and warn against a "blueprint mentality" that reifies any particular theory or model. In the US setting, Dorrien argues, we need a patient, ground-up approach toward economic democracy that is "organic, pluralistic, pragmatic, and voluntary." Strategies like producer cooperatives, community land trusts, community finance corporations, and planning agencies that direct investments into community-identified areas of need contribute by providing alternatives to private corporations and widening the base of social and economic power.[123]

All of these are sites for crafting principles and protoypes for a new political economy, centered on "building egalitarian wealth, nurturing democracy and community life, avoiding climate catastrophe and fostering liberty through greater economic security and free time."[124] As happened in New York prior to the New Deal, experiments at state and local levels may offer direction for "new democratizing approaches for larger-scale system-defining institutions when the appropriate political moment occurs."[125] In the shorter term, such initiatives are "opening new choices, creating more democracy, building an economic order that allows for social contracts, common goods, and ecological flourishing."[126]

Stoking People Power in Community Organizations

Community- and faith-based organizations, often collaborating with social-movement-focused labor unions, are playing roles in most of the initiatives just discussed. These civic associations exemplify many of the commitments, competencies, and practices that people working toward a reconstructed, livelihood-focused economy require.[127] Beyond targeted campaigns for work justice, these groups dedicate themselves to a crucial form of asset building: strengthening the capabilities and conditions for action among ordinary citizens. They do this by building strong communities of belonging, cultivating alliances and collaborations, and activating community and citizen agency through hands-on, participative democracy.

Religious congregations and their members are important participants in these associations and networks, and in 2013 Catholics gained a vocal papal supporter of popular and grassroots movements in Pope Francis. At numerous international gatherings, Francis has praised and encouraged grassroots popular movements; for him, they represent "in the panorama of our contemporary world, a seed, a renewal that, like the mustard seed, will bear much fruit—the lever of a great social transformation." The future of humankind, he affirms, "is not only in the hands of the great leaders, the great powers and the elites. It is fundamentally in the hands of the people, in their capacity to organize themselves. It is in their hands, which can guide with humility and conviction this process of change." Francis also emphasizes the power of ground-level, democratic participation to generate the crucial resources of vision and hope for a different future. He praises "the efforts of organized citizens, particularly those who create in their daily lives . . . fragments of other possible worlds," from which "large trees will grow, thick forests of hope will arise to oxygenate this world." By enfleshing solidarity in action, people's movements "express how the 'force of us' is the answer to the 'culture of the self' that looks only at the satisfaction of one's own interests, cultivating—despite its own precariousness—the dream of a different and more humane world."[128]

Francis recognizes what community-organizing leaders have also learned: that political alienation, apathy, and despair can be counteracted in bonded, publicly engaged communities, where what Bruce Levine calls the psychological building blocks of "individual self-respect" and "collective self-confidence" are nurtured, and transformative agency is generated and renewed.[129] In the United States, much has been written, and rightly so, of the work and accomplishments of legendary community organizer Saul Alinsky in this regard. A less-celebrated but equally precious source for understanding how democratic agency is sparked and sustained is the legacy of civil rights organizer Ella Baker, who spent her life fostering community organizations that prioritized group-centered leadership, sustaining long-haul commitment to social justice work, and members' active engagement in hands-on participatory democracy.

Baker's approach to participative democracy emphasized three core tenets: "organizing," bringing people together at local levels to engage actively in the decisions that affect their lives; a commitment to "group-centered leadership" that minimizes hierarchy and overreliance on experts or professionals; and strategic, direct action—"mobilizing"—as an antidote to fear, alienation, and intellectual detachment. Baker distinguished mobilizing, which involves attention-grabbing public actions, from organizing, the slow, less glamorous, but in her view crucial work of building strong and lasting community bonds. Passionate about the indispensable role of community organizing and organizations, Baker also recognized that work for social and economic justice needed different types and levels of engagement. So, while she criticized the

National Association for the Advancement of Colored People (NAACP) for failing to establish self-directed local chapters and leaders, Baker also recognized the invaluable contributions made by NAACP lawyers's work in the courts to realizing historic civil rights gains for African Americans.[130] As they carried Alinsky's organizing legacy into the later twentieth century, leaders like Ed Chambers and Ernesto Cortez built community organizations and networks that also embraced Ella Baker–style, participative-democracy organizing models.

Ganz, a veteran community organizer who spent years working with Baker, and later with Cesar Chavez's farmworkers' union, highlights the critical importance of empowering narratives for uniting and mobilizing people to act for the common good.[131] Ganz believes it is through narratives that people learn to access the moral and emotional resources we need to respond with agency in the face of danger, challenge, and threat. Like Ross, Ganz recognizes the special need for public narratives that can draw people together across today's fractured political and social landscape. To succeed, change-seeking communities need strong, reality-grounded, action- and hope-inducing narratives "of self, of us, and of now." These meaning-shaping narratives are inevitably particular, writes James Hoggan, yet they nurture the confidence to connect with others: we actually have a better chance of avoiding getting trapped in defensiveness or in blindered advocacy for our narrow positions when "we stay strongly rooted in the values that emerge from our own story."[132] This wise perspective encourages economic-justice-seeking people of faith to tap their own traditions' narratives, both for their morally energizing and action-galvanizing powers and for their power to spark dialogue and to make connections with their neighbors' own cherished, formative narratives.

To muster action for change, organizers also work "to mobilize the emotions that make agency possible."[133] In contrast to Alinsky's central focus on self-interest, organizers like Baker and Ganz regard moral and spiritual values as primary motivators for social and economic justice campaigns.[134] To overcome "action barriers" like inertia, apathy, fear, isolation, and self-doubt, good leaders cultivate emotions that become "action catalysts": urgency and indignation at injustice, combined with the crucial trio of hope, solidarity, and efficacy.[135] Hope, a key mobilizing emotion, is sparked and sustained by "direct experiences of credible solutions," small successes and victories, and leaders able to inspire hope in others.[136] Religious scholar Jeffrey Stout also highlights community-based coalitions' power to create renewable energies for long-haul transformative work.[137] Where community connections and an ethos of "belovedness" nourish group solidarity, the legacy of Baker continues. Efficacy, the all-important sense that "you can make a difference," is stoked by focusing on "what we *can* do," by recognizing and celebrating accomplishments, and by practices of accountability.[138]

Since the late nineteenth century, US Catholics have supported labor unions as an avenue for expressing faith-based commitments to worker justice. Beginning in 1930s Chicago, Catholics also began to join citizens of many faiths and walks of life in broad-based community coalitions. Over eight decades, congregation-anchored community organizations have harnessed the energies of diverse constituencies in activist coalitions dedicated to improving the economic, health, and civic well-being of their neighborhoods, cities, and regions. The largest and oldest of these organizations, the Industrial Areas Foundation (IAF), now an international community-organizing network, was established in 1940 by Alinsky with founding board members who included Chicago Roman Catholic bishop Bernard James Sheil, businessman Marshall Field III, and Kathryn Lewis, daughter of John L. Lewis, president of the United Mine Workers.[139]

After Alinsky's death in 1971 his longtime associate Ed Chambers, a Catholic, became IAF's executive director. Chambers helped create the institutional structures and systematic training of local leaders and organizers that would assure the IAF's long-term viability.[140] During the 1970s and 1980s, Chambers worked with another Catholic organizer, Ernesto Cortez Jr., to reshape "the modern IAF" on the model of the interfaith, congregation-based community organizing that Cortez had developed for the San Antonio, Texas, coalition, Communities Organized for Public Service (COPS).[141] Today the IAF comprises more than sixty-five "multi-racial, broad-based organizations spanning metropolitan areas, and including African American, Latino, and Anglo churches," which, as "organizations of organizations," join forces to influence local, state and national government and policy.[142] Working in partnership with labor unions and other civic organizations, and hewing to their "Iron Rule"—"Never do anything for others that they can do for themselves"—the IAF, COPS, and its affiliates have made justice for workers and economic empowerment for ordinary people central priorities.[143]

Like their early twentieth-century counterparts, twenty-first-century Catholic church leaders like Pope Francis and Chicago's Cardinal Blase J. Cupich, Catholic labor leaders like John Sweeney and Maria Elena Durazo, and Catholic community organizers like Ernie Cortez in San Antonio, Greg Galluzzo in Chicago, and Sisters Maribeth Larkin in Los Angeles and Christine Stephens in Houston, have all grasped the deep resonances between the animating missions of these civic organizations, and their faith tradition's teachings about the dignity and rights of workers and the economically vulnerable.[144] Partnering with these organizations enables religious congregations and their members to channel faith-based convictions about justice into concrete action. Community coalitions draw members beyond comfortable insularity into purposeful, at times challenging relationships with diverse people and groups. Participants learn about and experience the bonds and practices that make economic solidarity, and active democracy, a reality. For Catholics, in particular, community organizations offer experience in grappling with social power, community self-interest, and conflict.[145] And as generators of social capital of both the bonding and bridging variety, these associations strengthen and enrich the fabric of the neighborhoods and communities that religious congregations inhabit and serve.

For their parts, labor leaders and community organizers have long recognized that religious congregations also have much to offer them. Formation in a faith tradition can foster in members orientations to solidarity, service, and hope with realism that civic organizations depend and thrive upon. And as leaders like Martin Luther King Jr. and Chavez have shown, aptly engaging religious symbols, stories, and practices can powerfully enrich movement leaders' efforts to connect with, unify, and motivate their constituencies to act for social and economic justice.[146]

Fighting for Dignified Livelihood in Latter-Day Living Wage Campaigns

This brings us back to the living wage struggles that have engaged and benefited ordinary people like Julio Payes and his family. Though not a panacea, solid research suggests that, in addition to the measurable improvements in workers' personal and family lives that Payes's experience reflected, raising basic wages can help reduce poverty, reduce income inequality, and lessen gender and racial pay gaps.[147]

In 1994, ending a period during which living-wage discourse and organizing had receded from the US public stage, IAF affiliates in Baltimore designed and successfully executed a campaign to pass the nation's first municipal living wage law. Subsequently, similar campaigns were mounted in other metropolitan areas. Fueling these efforts have been living wage coalitions whose members have engaged in participatory democracy to advance economic rights and inclusive livelihood values. These coalitions and campaigns have also cultivated solidary and transformative practices; in particular, political activation around powerful, unifying action "frames."[148] Social movement theorists identify "framing" as a key strategy for unifying coalitions' diverse constituents, for focusing and motivating action, and for creating power-enhancing bridges among groups and organizations. By succinctly capturing a morally persuasive snapshot of what is wrong, why it is wrong, and what needs to be done about it, an effective frame can bring people together and motivate them to act for change. For movement leaders and members, framing is thus an important exercise in imaginative group meaning making.[149] In campaigns for living wage legislation, frames like "No one who works full time should be in poverty," or "A job should bring you out of poverty, not keep you in it," performed powerful bonding, bridging, and action-motivating work.

Theologian-activist Melissa Snarr has participated in and researched contemporary municipal living wage campaigns in a number of US cities. She finds that religious communities bring particular competencies and make distinctive contributions to these diverse coalitions.[150] In grassroots coalitions in Baltimore, Nashville, and elsewhere, for instance, "religious organizations are major players in connecting economic and racial justice issues within living wage campaigns." Further, "religion provides a space for confronting and mediating . . . divisions that could conceivably divide this economic justice movement." Religiously identified living wage activists often shared an ethos centered on a "preferential option for the poor/vulnerable," "being reconcilers of humanity," and "welcoming the stranger," which spurred and energized their work for racially inclusive economic justice.[151]

Within racially and economically diverse community coalitions, Snarr observed religiously affiliated members performing two important tasks: bridge building and political activation. Often, the worldviews, values, and practices absorbed in their religious communities made these members skillful at "essential bridging tasks." One of these, "ideology translation," involves "interpreting the frameworks, values, and strategic repertoires of one movement to another in order to foster better collaboration and respect for differences."[152] Religious affiliations also created "important alternate pathways for trust cultivation." This was particularly important in instances when "conscience adherents" and "beneficiary adherents" of a social movement came from "dramatically different housing and employment contexts"—in other words, when members diverged sharply in class positions or cultures. When people from such different worlds come together, "the confession of transcendent belief is often one of the first foundations for trust cultivation."[153] Trust building across racial, class, and even religious lines is facilitated when people recognize each other as sharing a meta-identity as "people of faith."[154] Members of faith communities also showed facility at "relational repair," finding avenues to strengthen or rebuild trust among members and member organizations during and following conflicts, thus enabling the coalition to move forward, united in its shared goals.[155] Finally, religious activists often took the lead in what Snarr calls "inclusion monitoring," keeping an eye on the coalition's own inclusiveness by regularly asking, "Who is not at the table?" These varied bridging tasks played a significant role in a coalition's "formation, survival, and success."[156]

Religious organizations also contribute to the "political activation" of members in economic justice coalitions, especially by welcoming and cultivating "the involvement of those who are regularly left out of the dominant pathways of political engagement." With the decline of traditional labor unions, religious communities and organizations, which continue to be strong presences in working-class and poor communities, "are one of the few institutions in American civil society that mitigate political alienation based on race, low income, and limited formal education."[157] In their religious congregations, many poor and working-class people receive opportunities to learn and practice leadership skills that, in turn, can translate into more confident and effective civic and political engagement.

Snarr found living wage coalitions to be strikingly racially and ethnically diverse. Yet the particular churches, synagogues, or mosques within those coalitions were often quite homogeneous in terms of race and class. Here Snarr lifts up the benefits that some bonded "communities of the similar" can confer. Unlike workplaces stratified by roles, power, and wages, in many poor and working-class religious congregations, "skill opportunities are more equally allocated across educational, income, or racial and ethnic groups because, within the congregations, there is a more limited range of people who can be chosen—or select themselves—to be active." In these congregations, "line workers organize prayer meetings, file clerks write newsletters, and janitors lead the choir, developing important civic skills in the process."[158]

In their strengths and successes, as well as their limits and failures, these coalitions and campaigns have much to teach US Catholic inclusive livelihood advocates. One limitation, in fact, has been the frequently tepid engagement of Catholic clergy and parishioners in local faith-based coalitions and living wage campaigns. With important exceptions, the failure of pastors and parishes in mostly urban, working-class neighborhoods to embrace and promote this kind of grassroots civic involvement deprives Catholic laypersons—who are increasingly Latinx, young, and female—of opportunities for civic education and empowerment, and for connecting their faith with concrete action for the common good, that these coalitions provide. As we have noted, in most US regions and metropolitan areas, Catholics are represented in every class, racial, ethnic, and geographical category, making them potentially influential participants in the diverse membership of democratic community coalitions. But for a variety of reasons, including more affluent Catholics' retreat into privatized suburban life, this potential remains largely untapped.

A second limitation is the fact that even successful living wage campaigns have thus far fallen short of their inclusive livelihood goals. In his study of campaigns in Baltimore, Maryland, and Rochester, New York, Catholic ethicist and activist Marvin Mich laments that the genuine improvements wrought by municipal living wage laws applied only to city workers; moreover, the hard-won raises in minimum pay still failed to constitute a genuine living wage. The small percentage of workers covered by the Baltimore ordinance saw their salaries rise to 130 percent of the federal poverty guidelines. During its campaign, Rochester's Living Wage Coalition had calculated a modest living wage for families as $17.49 an hour. Realizing that achieving this wage was politically impossible, "the Coalition agreed that if a person is working full time they should at least reach the federal poverty level by their wages, which they calculated to require a wage of $8.52 in 2000. "This became the *politically feasible living wage* even though we realized that a realistic living wage would actually be about twice that amount."[159]

The limits and shortcomings Mich points out are undeniable. Yet these campaigns have also been successful at advancing a more fundamental change, well summarized by Jon Gertner: "The Baltimore campaign was ostensibly about money. But to those who thought about it more deeply, it was about *the force of particular moral propositions: first, that work should be rewarded, and second, that no one who works full time should have to live in poverty.*"[160] By eliciting broad public assent to these two propositions, living wage movements have struck a blow against the dominant economic orthodoxy by sowing the conviction that markets can, and should, be reoriented, even at the cost of some "efficiency," to make it possible for honest work to yield a decent living. By shifting mindsets in new, promising directions, this kind of reframing of public moral perceptions contributes substantively to the work of creating a transformed, inclusive-livelihood political economy.[161]

Still another lesson that community organizing campaigns and institutional experiments in economic democracy teach is that transformative work is difficult, slow, and messy. History shows that "forging a new kind of politics is not just a matter of changing the discourse in a superficial way, and hoping people will join on, but it's through long struggles and new practices with different people working and thinking and acting together to break down old barriers and forge new coalitions."[162] In this regard, philosopher Richard Rorty warns change seekers against overattachment to ideological or group "purity." Often, "in democratic countries you get things done by compromising your principles in order to form alliances with groups about whom you have grave doubts." Nor, history shows, are effective justice movements propelled only by bottom-up initiatives of grassroots groups, for all their importance. In truth, "the history of leftist [and progressive] politics in America is a story of how top-down initiatives and bottom-up initiatives have interlocked."[163]

Rorty's last point here is important in light of critics of living wage laws who assume, often on mainstream Economics 101 grounds, that higher minimum wages will inevitably cause employers to reduce hiring, raise prices, or both, thereby harming the very low-wage workers that living wage ordinances seek to assist. In fact, economists continue to debate over how best to measure the net impact of higher minimum wages on jobs, prices, and businesses, especially small businesses. On the ground, the tradeoffs between living wage laws' downsides and the benefits they yield to workers like Payes require ongoing study. To move toward a new public consensus concerning the merits of living wage legislation will require more data gathering, careful, unbiased research, and judicious analysis. In this, workers' and grassroots associations, academics, research professionals, and policymakers all have essential parts to play.

One final objection leveled at campaigns like fast food workers' "Fight for $15" brings home the influence of one's normative axis on perceptions of economic value. Some claim that such low-wage jobs, simply, "are not worth fifteen dollars an hour." As one *Wall Street Journal* reader repeatedly commented concerning the Emeryville living wage ordinances, "The real minimum wage for labor is zero, and no one can change that." From the perspective of standard economic theory, for which human work is simply one factor of production, subject to market forces and market valuation, this commenter is simply stating an unvarnished economic fact.

Yet echoing, however faintly, social Catholicism's normative construal of economy and work, most experts, leaders, and citizens across the US political spectrum do recognize that wages concern not simply the current "market value" of the labor performed but also the value of livelihood, and labor markets' role in enabling workers to support themselves and their families. And given this unvarnished, human fact, the question becomes how to set wages in ways that respect and maintain fair and dynamic markets, while also honoring and facilitating labor's capacity to yield a dignified living for all those who work. As one of an array of initiatives I have only been able to intimate here, living wage campaigns are shifting US perceptions in the direction of sustainable, inclusive livelihood; and the people and coalitions behind these multifaceted efforts have important lessons to teach Catholics and other religious and civic communities about furthering an agenda of radical sufficiency for all.

CONCLUSION

Building a sustainable, democratic political economy that prioritizes and ensures dignified work and decent livelihood for every person, family, and community is a vast, complex, and multilayered project. As I close this book, the twenty-first century, now in its third decade, is no longer so new. But the great dream of radical sufficiency—of enough community and good work to yield enough sustenance, security, and status, within the sustaining capacities of our planet and ecosphere, for all of us and our descendants to flourish; and the smaller, more local and personal dreams of livelihood we each cherish and pursue—remain fresh. These dreams, and the new obstacles that threaten their realization in 2020 and beyond, continue to cry out for new imagination, new framings, new strategies, and continually renewed, transformative action.

No scholarly book can create or substitute for that action. Yet this project—like the US and Catholic intellectual and social-change traditions that animate it—*has* aimed to inform, illumine, and encourage it. And though it is far from a GPS-like guide that at this point would confidently announce, "You have reached your destination," I hope this book does offer a kind of provision kit of resources, orientations, and inspiration to help sustain economic justice seekers on what will necessarily be a continuing journey. Along the way, each person and community will need to discern and enact our distinctive contributions to fashioning and maintaining communities, workplaces, and political economies where a dignified livelihood is within everyone's reach.

As for what specific contributions might be ours to make, we have seen that the possibilities and starting places are many. In this regard, Bishop—now Saint—Oscar Romero reminded his El Salvadoran community during a time of great turmoil and violence in that country that the "huge differences" among people in "vocations, charisms, and ways of being" make a diversity of gifts and skills available for the work of fashioning a just political and economic order. Like Pope Francis would later do, Romero encouraged those drawn to political activism to take it up as a praiseworthy calling. But he acknowledged that activism is not everyone's path: "You can't get everyone into an organization."

After all our talk of participative democracy and transformative engagement, Romero's words here sound slightly heretical. But, also like Francis, Romero recognized that if building a just political economy is a God-desired human project, then everyone, starting with their own gifts and from within their own circumstances, has something distinctive to contribute. The point, he concludes, is to discern, to participate, and to bring our varied talents and efforts to bear on the community's welfare.[164]

For advancing a twenty-first-century, concrete-historical ideal of sustainable livelihood for all, sturdy communities of care, imagination, and vision are not sufficient; but they are necessary for setting the course, for celebrating progress and weathering setbacks, and for keeping hope alive that another political economy is possible. Individual and local actions in households, families, and neighborhoods are not sufficient; but they do have impacts, and can create space for and build momentum toward wider shifts in practice and paradigms. Nor, on their own, will academic research, prophetic protests, pragmatic political strategies, policy-based efforts to amend the present system from within, or experiments with new prototypes at the margins, be enough to effect the needed changes. But all of these initiatives, and each of us in our particular vocations and capacities, have parts to play in the worthy work of crafting a renovated, radically sufficient economic order—one that excludes no person, household, or community from the mundane and fleshly, yet holistic and holy, dream of a good living.

NOTES

1. Matthew Desmond, "Dollars on the Margins," *New York Times Magazine*, https://www .nytimes.com/interactive/2019/02/21/magazine/minimum-wage-saving-lives.html. See also Victor Tan Chen, "All Hollowed Out: The Lonely Poverty of America's White Working Class," *Atlantic*, January 2016, https://www.theatlantic.com/business/archive/2016 /01/white-working-class-poverty/424341/; and Newman and Chen, *Missing Class*.

2. Desmond, "Dollars on the Margins," citing Mullainthan and Shafir, *Scarcity*.

3. Desmond, "Dollars on the Margins."

4. Minimum Wage Ordinance, Emeryville, California, http://www.ci.emeryville.ca.us /1024/Minimum-Wage-Ordinance.

5. Desmond, "Dollars on the Margins."

6. Desmond.

7. Eric Morath and Rachel Feintzeig, "'I Have Bills to Pay': Low-Wage Workers Face the Brunt of the Coronavirus Crisis." *Wall Street Journal*, March 20, 2020, https://www.wsj .com/articles/i-have-bills-i-have-to-pay-low-wage-workers-face-brunt-of-coronavirus -crisis-11584719927; also Campbell Robertson and Robert Gebeloff, "How Millions of Women Became the Most Essential Workers in America," *New York Times*, April 18, 2020, https://www.nytimes.com/2020/04/18/us/coronavirus-women-essential -workers.html.

8. David Leonhardt and Yaryna Serkez, "America Will Struggle after Coronavirus. These Charts Show Why," *New York Times*, April 10, 2020, https://www.nytimes.com /interactive/2020/04/10/opinion/coronavirus-us-economy-inequality.html.

9. Ryan, *Living Wage*, 301.

10. United Nations, *Universal Declaration of Human Rights*, Articles 22–25, https://www.un
.org/en/universal-declaration-human-rights/.

11. Tim Sandle, "More U.S. Jobs Created, but Most Pay under $20 an Hour," *Digital Journal*,
January 26, 2019, http://www.digitaljournal.com/business/more-usa-jobs-created-but
-most-pay-under-20-an-hour/article/540295#ixzz5uLsQUO5g. The EPI Basic Family
Budget Calculator may be found at https://www.epi.org/publication/family-budget
-calculator-documentation/.

12. William M. Rodgers III and Amanda Novello, "Making the Economic Case for a $15
Minimum Wage," Century Foundation, January 28, 2019, https://tcf.org/content
/commentary/making-economic-case-15-minimum-wage/. Center on Poverty and
Inequality, *Bare Minimum*, 2.

13. Cf. Hatton, *Temp Economy*; also James Manyika, Susan Lund, Jacques Bughin, Kelsey
Robinson, Jan Mischke, and Deepa Mahajan, *Independent Work: Choice, Necessity, and
the Gig Economy*, McKinsey Global Institute, October 2016, https://www.mckinsey
.com/featured-insights/employment-and-growth/independent-work-choice-necessity
-and-the-gig-economy; Mike Boro, "The Gig Economy is Bigger than US Government
Data Makes it Look." *Quartz at Work*, July 11, 2018, https://qz.com/work/1324292
/gig-economy-data-why-the-us-department-of-labor-numbers-are-misleading/; US
Government Accountability Office, "Contingent Workforce: BLS Is Reassessing Measurement of Nontraditional Workers," GAO-19-273R, February 28, 2019, https://www
.gao.gov/products/GAO-19-273R.

14. Squires, "Social Insecurity," 288. See also US Bureau of Labor, CareerOneStop, "Careers
with Largest Employment 2018," https://www.careeronestop.org/Toolkit/Careers
/careers-largest-employment.aspx.

15. Robert Reich, "Almost 80% of US Workers Live from Paycheck to Paycheck. Here's Why,"
Guardian, July 29, 2018, https://www.theguardian.com/commentisfree/2018/jul/29/us
-economy-workers-paycheck-robert-reich. Cf. investor and business owner Nick Hanauer's
reframing of "makers and takers" in "Confronting the Parasite Economy," *American Prospect*, May 16, 2016, https://prospect.org/labor/confronting-parasite-economy/.

16. Erin Hatton, "The Rise of the Permanent Temp Economy," *Opinionator* (blog), *New York
Times*, January 26, 2013, https://opinionator.blogs.nytimes.com/2013/01/26/the-rise
-of-the-permanent-temp-economy/; Beck, *Risk Society*; Heath, Ciscel, and Sharp, "Work
of Families."

17. National Employment Law Project, "Black and Latinx Workers Overrepresented in Nonstandard Work with Lowest Job Quality—Temporary Help Agency Work," June 7, 2018,
https://www.nelp.org/news-releases/americas-nonstandard-workforce-faces-wage
-benefit-penalties-according-us-data/.

18. Lesley Hustinix and Frans Lammertyn, "Solidarity and Volunteering under a Reflexive-
Modern Sign: Towards a New Conceptual Framework," working paper, Catholic
University Leuven, Belgium, 2000, https://cdn.ymaws.com/www.istr.org/resource
/resmgr/working_papers_dublin/hustinx.pdf. Hudson finds that "since the early
1970s the level of dualism in the American labor market has increased substantially,"
but that, "combined, nonstandard work and citizenship now play a greater direct role
in allocating workers to secondary and intermediary jobs than race or sex." Hudson,
"New Labor Market Segmentation," 286. See also Seccareccia, "Dualism and Economic
Stagnation."

19. Investopedia, "How Does the Current Cost of Living Compare to 20 Years Ago?" August 11, 2019, https://www.investopedia.com/ask/answers/101314/what-does -current-cost-living-compare-20-years-ago.asp; See also Derek Thompson, "Why America's Essentials Are Getting More Expensive While Its Toys Are Getting Cheap," *Atlantic*, May 2, 2014, https://www.theatlantic.com/business/archive/2014/05/its -expensive-to-be-poor/361533/; Hillary Hoffower, "7 Ways Life Is More Expensive Today for American Millennials than Previous Generations," *Business Insider*, May 28, 2018, https://www.businessinsider.com/millennials-cost-of-living-compared-to-gen -x-baby-boomers-2018-5; James Pethokoukis, "Wages Rising: The US Economy Is Now Working Best For Lower-Wage Workers, *AEIdeas* (blog), American Enterprise Institute, March 13, 2019, https://www.aei.org/economics/wages-rising-the-trump -economy-is-now-working-best-for-lower-wage-workers/.

20. Cohen, *Financial Crisis in American Households*, 10–11.

21. Heath, Ciscel, and Sharp, "Work of Families," 502.

22. Cohen, *Financial Crisis in American Households*, 12.

23. Cohen, 165. The 2020 pandemic glaringly exposed these inequitably distributed economic vulnerabilities. See Patricia Cohen, "Struggling in a Good Economy, Now Struggling in a Crisis," *New York Times*, April 16, 2020, https://www.nytimes.com/2020/04 /16/business/economy/coronavirus-economy.html.

24. Cf. Haidt, *Righteous Mind*; Hoggan, *I'm Right*. Cf. Simon Greer, "Should Progressives Demonize or Try to Find Common Ground with 60 Million People Dealing with Economic Anxiety Who Vote for Racist Politicians?" *AlterNet*, October 31, 2018, https:// www.alternet.org/2018/10/should-progressives-demonize-ignore-or-attempt-find -common-ground-60-million/.

25. For the term "digital accelerant," see Zach Goldberg, "America's White Saviors," *Tablet*, June 5, 2019, https://www.tabletmag.com/jewish-news-and-politics/284875/americas -white-saviors.

26. Daniel Cox, Rachel Lienesch, and Robert P. Jones, "Beyond Economics: Fears of Cultural Displacement Pushed the White Working Class to Trump," Public Religion Research Institute, May 9, 2017, https://www.prri.org/research/white-working-class-attitudes -economy-trade-immigration-election-donald-trump/. Cf. Cox, Navarro-Rivera, Jones, *Economic Insecurity*.

27. See Ted Nordhaus and Michael Shellenberger, "Apocalypse Fatigue: Losing the Public on Climate Change," *YaleEnvironment360*, November 16, 2009, https://e360.yale.edu /features/apocalypse_fatigue_losing_the_public_on_climate_change. Cf. Himes, "Consumerism and Christian Ethics"; Schor, *Overspent American*.

28. Bruce E. Levine, "3 Things That Must Happen for Us to Rise Up and Defeat the Corporatocracy," *AlterNet*, August 26, 2011, https://www.alternet.org/2011/08/3_things_that _must_happen_for_us_to_rise_up_and_defeat_the_corporatocracy/. Cf. Levine, *Get Up, Stand Up*.

29. Ganz, "Leading Change," 11.

30. See Maritain, *Integral Humanism*, 127–28, 132; Maritain, *True Humanism*, 121, 122.

31. Lane, *Market Experience*; Finn, *Moral Ecology of Markets*.

32. Cass, *Once and Future Worker*, 29.

33. Cass, 19.

34. Cass, 15.

35. Raworth, *Doughnut Economics*.
36. Hillquit and Ryan, *Socialism*, 13.
37. Nelson, *Economics for Humans*, 54. Aldred, *Skeptical Economist*, 2–4, connects market orthodoxy to "black box" and "veto" economics.
38. Nelson, *Economics for Humans*, 52–57, at 54.
39. "Satisficing" is a term coined by economist Herbert Simon, who argues that most decision-making behavior takes not an optimizing but "a 'satisficing' path, a path that will permit satisfaction at some specified level of all its [relevant] needs." Herbert A. Simon, "Rational Choice and the Structure of the Environment," 138. Cf. Schwartz, *Paradox of Choice*, ch. 4.
40. Cf. Firer Hinze, *Glass Ceilings, Dirt Floors*, ch. 4.
41. Hillquit and Ryan, *Socialism*, 248–49.
42. Broderick, *Right Reverend New Dealer*, 110–11.
43. For more on "radical-transformationist" ethical and practical approaches, see Firer Hinze, "Christian Feminists, James Luther Adams, and the Search for a Radically Transformative Ethics."
44. See the oft-cited later works of Martin Luther King Jr., e.g., *Where Do We Go from Here.*
45. Maritain puts this theologically: "Through temporal activity, the Christian does not aim to make of this world itself the final kingdom, but to make of this world "according to the historical ideal required by different ages, and . . . by the *moltings* of this ideal, the place of a truly and fully human earthly life, that is, one which is full of defects, but is also full of love, whose social structures have as their measure justice, the dignity of the human person, and fraternal love." *Integral Humanism*, 111.
46. This is a repeated theme in Francis, *Laudato si'*.
47. Baum, "Class Struggle and the Magisterium," calls this "partial solidarity."
48. On solidarity in risk, see Perrot, "Le risque au coeur de l'éthique financière." Matthew Desmond appeals to risk solidarity by proposing to lower or eliminate mortgage interest deductions in order to fund affordable housing for all families. Desmond, "How Homeownership Became the Engine of American Inequality," *New York Times Magazine*, May 9, 2017, https://www.nytimes.com/2017/05/09/magazine/how-homeownership-became-the-engine-of-american-inequality.html.
49. Traina, "'This is the Year,'" 15–16.
50. Traina, 16; My own, radical-transformationist position resonates with Traina's argument for a "liberationist" versus "liberal" perspective on structural evil and social transformation.
51. See challenging, research-based criticisms of white liberals' class- and race-based bias and blindness in Goldberg, "White Saviors."
52. See Bogle, *Enough*, 46; Simon, "Rational Choice;" Schwartz, *Paradox of Choice*.
53. Francis, *Laudato si'*, §§222, 223.
54. On Sen, see Cloutier, *Vice of Luxury*, 112–14.
55. Barrera, "Degrees of Unmet Needs," 464, 467.
56. Barrera, 470.
57. Barrera, 471.
58. Raworth, *Doughnut Economics*; cf. Barrera, "Degrees of Unmet Needs," 470; Herman Daly, "Three Limits to Growth," Center for the Advancement of the Steady State Economy, September 4, 2014, https://steadystate.org/three-limits-to-growth/.

59. Francis, Address to Bishops Taking Part in the World Meeting of Families, Philadelphia, September 27, 2015, https://www.vatican.va/content/francesco/en/speeches/2015/september/documents/papa-francesco_20150927_usa-vescovi-festa-famiglie.html. Cf. Nicolás, "Depth, Universality, and Learned Ministry."

60. See Julie Hanlon Rubio's work on families' important roles in forming change-seeking communities; e.g., *Family Ethics*, ch. 2.

61. Marilynne Robinson, "Imagination and Community: What Holds Us Together," *Commonweal*, February 27, 2012, https://www.commonwealmagazine.org/imagination-community.

62. Tina Beattie, "How to Theologise at Times Like These?" *Tablet*, August 1, 2018, https://www.thetablet.co.uk/features/2/14066/how-to-theologise-at-times-like-these.

63. Nancy Fraser, "Capitalism's Crisis of Care," interview by Sarah Leonard, *Dissent*, Fall 2016, https://www.dissentmagazine.org/article/nancy-fraser-interview-capitalism-crisis-of-care.

64. Fraser.

65. US Bureau of Labor Statitstics, News Release, "Economic Characteristics of Families Summary," April 21, 2020, https://www.bls.gov/news.release/famee.nr0.htm; Nancy Folbre, "The Future of the Gender Bend," *Economix* (blog), *New York Times*, April 1, 2013, https://economix.blogs.nytimes.com/2013/04/01/the-future-of-the-gender-bend/; Silbaugh, "Women's Place."

66. Folbre, "Future of the Gender Bend."

67. Fraser, "Capitalism's Crisis of Care"; Williams, *Unbending Gender*, 4.

68. Folbre, *Who Pays for the Kids*, 103.

69. Folbre, ed., *For Love or Money*, xvi.

70. David Cloutier, "The Paid Family Leave Impasse: How Catholic Social Teaching Can Help," *Commonweal*, September 16, 2019, https://www.commonwealmagazine.org/paid-family-leave-impasse.

71. Folbre, ed., *For Love or Money*, xvi. Chapter 8 summarizes research and recommends policies.

72. See Osborne, "Migrant Domestic Careworkers"; Weir, "Global Universal Caregiver"; Weir, "Global Care Chains." See also "Human Rights in Supply Chains: A Call for a Binding Global Standard on Due Diligence," Human Rights Watch, May 30, 2016, https://www.hrw.org/report/2016/05/30/human-rights-supply-chains/call-binding-global-standard-due-diligence.

73. Draut, *Understanding the Working Class*, 5. Cf. Henry and Fredericksen, *Equity in the Balance*; Weller, *Working-Class Families*.

74. The greatest race-based disparities in 2014 working-class family incomes were between white and nonwhite two-parent, two-child families. Draut, 5; see also also Henry and Fredericksen, *Equity in the Balance*.

75. Draut, *Understanding the Working Class*, 8.

76. Draut, 10, table 2.

77. Ross, *Cultural Contestation in Ethnic Conflict*, chs. 1, 2.

78. Lani Guinier, "Race and Reality in a Front-Porch Encounter," *Chronicle of Higher Education*, July 30, 2009, https://www.chronicle.com/article/RaceReality-in-a/47509/.

79. Guinier, "Race and Reality"; also Guinier, "From Racial Liberalism to Literacy"; Leondar-Wright, *Class Matters*. On implicit bias, see Payne, *Broken Ladder*, 171; also

Bertram Gawronski and B. Keith Payne, "History of Implicit Social Cognition"; but cf. Davis, "Implicit Bias of Implicit Bias Theory."

80. Walter Benn Michaels, Charles W. Mills, Linda Hirshman, and Carla Murphy, "What Is the Left Without Identity Politics?" *Nation*, December 16, 2016, https://www.thenation.com/article/what-is-the-left-without-identity-politics/. Emphasis added.

81. Joseph A. McCartin, "Bargaining for the Common Good," *Dissent*, Spring 2016, https://www.dissentmagazine.org/article/bargaining-common-good-community-union-alignment; and "WCP: Bargaining for the Common Good comes of Age," Georgetown University Kalmanovitz Initiative for Labor and the Working Poor, March 14, 2019, https://lwp.georgetown.edu/2019/03/14/wcp-bargaining-for-the-common-good-comes-of-age/.

82. All quotes from McCartin, "Bargaining for the Common Good."

83. Zweig, "Rethinking Class," 18.

84. On past US reparations programs, see Adeel Hassan and Jack Healy, "America Has Tried Reparations Before. Here Is How It Went," *New York Times*, June 19, 2019, https://www.nytimes.com/2019/06/19/us/reparations-slavery.html/.

85. Marc Parry furnishes historical background and illumines the contentious, current status of Georgetown's process in "A New Path to Atonement," *Chronicle of Higher Education*, January 20, 2019, https://www.chronicle.com/article/A-New-Path-to-Atonement/245511. Cf. Georgetown University Slavery Project, "Georgetown University: Slavery, Memory, Reconciliation," http://slavery.georgetown.edu/.

86. In 2019, Democratic presidential candidates Senator Elizabeth Warren and former South Bend, Indiana, mayor Pete Buttigieg each proffered plans to address "the aftereffects of generations of racist inequality."

87. See Cyndi Suarez, "How Black Reparations Differs from a New Economic Rights Project," *Nonprofit Quarterly*, April 16, 2019, https://nonprofitquarterly.org/how-black-reparations-differs-from-a-new-economic-rights-project/.

88. Luke 3:3–4, 10–14.

89. E.g., Christine Firer Hinze, "Labor and Trade," *Blackwell Companion to Christian Ethics*.

90. Francis, address to the Participants in the World Meeting of Popular Movements, October 28, 2014, http://www.vatican.va/content/francesco/en/speeches/2014/october/documents/papa-francesco_20141028_incontro-mondiale-movimenti-popolari.html.

91. Francis, address to Centesimus Annus Pro Pontifice Foundation, May 25, 2013, http://www.vatican.va/content/francesco/en/speeches/2013/may/documents/papa-francesco_20130525_centesimus-annus-pro-pontifice.html.

92. Ryan, *Distributive Justice*, 355–56; Arendt, *Human Condition*, 236–47.

93. Cooper, *Raising the Federal Minimum Wage*.

94. See e.g., Neumark, "Living Wages"; and responses to Neumark in Pollin, Brenner, Wicks-Lim, and Luce, *Measure of Fairness*, part 5.

95. Matthew Desmond, "How Homeownership Became the Engine of American Inequality," *New York Times Magazine*, May 9, 2017, https://www.nytimes.com/2017/05/09/magazine/how-homeownership-became-the-engine-of-american-inequality.html; cf. Desmond, *Evicted*.

96. Cohen, *Financial Crisis in American Households*, 180.

97. Squires, "Social Insecurity," 290.

98. Cohen, *Financial Crisis in American Households*, 177.

99. Cohen, 21.

100. Dorling, *Better Politics*, 100–101. See also Seccareccia, "Basic Income, Full Employment"; Seccareccia, "Dualism and Economic Stagnation," 16.
101. Most proposals include income caps (usually quite high) beyond which the UBI would be rescinded.
102. Van Parijs and Vanderborght, *Basic Income*.
103. Van Parijs and Vanderborght, 103.
104. Van Parijs and Vanderborght, 106.
105. Seccareccia, "Basic Income, Full Employment"; Seccareccia, "Dualism and Economic Stagnation."
106. Cass, *Once and Future Worker*, 2.
107. Cass, 164.
108. Cass, 166, 171.
109. "Business Culture Has Shifted," B Corporation Certification Program, https://bcorporation.net/news/business-culture-has-shifted.
110. Alperovitz, *What Then Must We Do*, ch. 7, discusses B Corps and other forms of "quiet democratization" of business and economy. See also Heerad Sabeti, "The For-Benefit Enterprise," *Harvard Business Review*, November 2011, https://hbr.org/2011/11/the-for-benefit-enterprise; Alana Semuels, "A New Business Strategy: Treating Employees Well," *Atlantic*, November 2014, https://www.theatlantic.com/business/archive/2014/11/a-new-business-strategy-treating-employees-well/383192/.
111. Ryan, *Social Reconstruction*, 176; cf. *Declining Liberty*, 225–38.
112. Other examples are John Fullerton, *Regenerative Capitalism*, report, Capital Institute, April 20, 2015, www.CapitalInstitute.org/Regenerative-Capitalism; Dorrien, "Case for Economic Democracy." Arguably, Catholic social agendas for economic livelihood also fall in this spectrum. Alperovitz and Dubb, "The Possibility of a Pluralist Commonwealth," 8.
113. Alperovitz and Dubb, 9–10.
114. Alperovitz and Dubb, 12.
115. Gar Alperovitz, "'Community,' Why is Community Important to the Pluralist Commonwealth?" The Next System Project, May 15, 2017, https://thenextsystem.org/community.
116. Alperovitz, *What Must We Do*, 3. "There are currently more than 5.8 million employer firms in the United States; those which employ more than 5000 people account for a mere one-third of one percent of this total."
117. Gar Alperovitz, "Why is the Pluralist Commonwealth an American System?" The Next System Project, May 15, 2017, https://thenextsystem.org/america.
118. Gar Alperovitz and Keane Bhatt, "What Then Can I Do? Ten Ways to Democratize the Economy," Gar Alperovitz website, September 2013, https://www.garalperovitz.com/what-then-can-i-do/.
119. The new employee-owned businesses include a solar power company, an industrial laundry, and a city-center hydroponic farm growing lettuces and basil. Andy Beckett, "The New Left Economics: How a Network of Thinkers Is Transforming Capitalism," *Guardian*, June 25, 2019, https://www.theguardian.com/news/2019/jun/25/the-new-left-economics-how-a-network-of-thinkers-is-transforming-capitalism.
120. In 2019 CommunityWealth.org listed efforts in more than twenty cities.
121. Beckett, "New Left Economics."
122. See, e.g., Tara García Matthewson, "US Sisters' Ability to Connect Social, Environmental Justice Offers a Path Forward," *Global Sisters Report*, November 9, 2015, https://www.globalsistersreport.org/news/environment/us-sisters-ability-connect-social

-environmental-justice-offers-path-forward-33491; InterFaith Power and Light, "Mission and History," https://www.interfaithpowerandlight.org/about/mission-history/; Taylor, *Green Sisters*.

123. Dorrien, "Case for Economic Democracy."
124. Alperovitz and Bhatt, "What Then Can I Do?"
125. Paul VI, *Octogesima adveniens* (1971), and Benedict XVI, *Caritas in veritate* (2009), both encourage diverse experiments with power-sharing market and political arrangements.
126. Dorrien, "Economic Democracy."
127. Unlike "business unionism," social movement unionism: (1) is locally focused and based; (2) experiments with collective actions that go beyond strikes or workplace-located activities; (3) builds alliances and coalitions within the community and beyond; and (4) embraces emancipatory politics, framing demands politically and formulating transformative visions. Peter Fairbrother, "Social Movement Unionism," 213–14, citing Lopez, *Reorganizing the Rust Belt*, 1.
128. Francis, Address at the Second World Meeting of Popular Movements, Santa Cruz de la Sierra, Bolivia, July 9, 2015, http://w2.vatican.va/content/francesco/en/speeches/2015/july/documents/papa-francesco_20150709_bolivia-movimenti-popolari.html.
129. Levine, *Get Up, Stand Up*, 140–45, 161–65.
130. Chris Crass, "Organizing Lessons from Civil Rights Leader Ella Baker," anarkismo.net, March 3, 2008, https://www.anarkismo.net/article/7645; Mueller, "Ella Baker and the Origins of 'Participatory Democracy.'"
131. Marshall Ganz, https://marshallganz.com/; also Hoggan, *I'm Right*.
132. Hoggan, *I'm Right*, loc. 2909.
133. Ganz, "Leading Change," 10–11.
134. Marshall Ganz, "Staying Connected to Our Moral Sources," *TPM Café* (blog), *Talking Points Memo*, March 29, 2007, http://marshallganz.usmblogs.com/files/2012/08/Staying-Connected-to-Our-Moral-Sources.pdf. Cf. Ganz, *Why David Sometimes Wins*.
135. Ganz, "Leading Change," 9.
136. Ganz, 10–11.
137. Stout, *Blessed Are the Organized*.
138. Ganz, "Leading Change," 11. Stout notes that non-elites' apathy, inaction, and ineptitude are a boon to elites who benefit from the status quo. *Blessed Are the Organized*, 278. Cf. Aronowitz, *How Class Works*, 174; also, Welch, *Feminist Ethic of Risk*, 158–61, on Martin Luther King Jr.'s "beloved community" as the matrix for a justice-seeking "ethic of risk."
139. "The IAF partners with religious congregations and civic organizations at the local level to build broad-based organizing projects, which create new capacity in a community for leadership development, citizen-led action and relationships across the lines that often divide our communities." Industrial Areas Foundation, "Who We Are," http://www.industrialareasfoundation.org/. Ryan Lizza, "The Agitator: Barack Obama's Unlikely Political Education," *New Republic*, March 19, 2007, https://newrepublic.com/article/61068/the-agitator-barack-obamas-unlikely-political-education.
140. Samuel G. Freedman, "Edward Chambers, Community Organizing's Unforgiving Hero," *New Yorker*, May 6, 2015, https://www.newyorker.com/news/news-desk/edward-chambers-community-organizings-unforgiving-hero.
141. See *IAF: 50 Years of Organizing*, 7; see also Lynch, "Industrial Areas Foundation."
142. *IAF: 50 Years of Organizing*, cf. Lynch, "Industrial Areas Foundation."

143. Freedman, "Edward Chambers"; "Living Wages," West/Southwest Industrial Areas Foundation website, https://www.swiaf.org/living_wages; also Lynch, "Industrial Areas Foundation," 575–78; Hoggan, *I'm Right*, loc. 176.

144. Stout, *Blessed Are the Organized*, ch. 2, 168–69 (Christine Stephens and Maribeth Larkin); Schultz, "Labor Movement" (Sweeney and Durango). George E. Schultze, "The Labor Movement, Teachers' Unions, and Catholic Social Teaching," *Catholic World Report*, August 31, 2014, https://www.catholicworldreport.com/2014/08/31/the-labor-movement-teachers-unions-and-catholic-social-teaching/.

145. Hinze, *Prophetic Obedience*, chs 1, 2, and 6, explores local congregation- and community-organizing and coalitions in the Bronx, New York, educing lessons and resources for a dialogical, "prophetically obedient" reenvisioning of Catholic church identity and practice.

146. Stout, *Blessed Are the Organized*, chs. 13–16, narrates examples of collaborations between faith communities and grassroots community organizations in various US cities.

147. Henry and Frederickson, *Equity in the Balance*; Cooper, *Raising the Federal Minimum Wage*.

148. "Collective action frames are action-oriented sets of beliefs and meanings that inspire and legitimate the activities and campaigns of a social movement." Benford and Snow, "Framing Processes and Social Movements," 614.

149. Benford and Snow, 614.

150. Snarr, *All You That Labor*.

151. Snarr, "Religion, Race, and Bridge Building," 77.

152. Snarr, "Religion, Race, and Bridge Building"; also Snarr, *All You That Labor*, 73–77.

153. Snarr, "Religion, Race, and Bridge Building," 80.

154. Snarr, 80.

155. Snarr, 74, 78.

156. Snarr, 74, 81.

157. Snarr, "Religion, Race, and Bridge Building," 78; Snarr, *All You That Labor*, 10–11, 68.

158. Snarr, "Religion, Race, and Bridge Building," 84. Religious congregations' internal polity, and the extent to which lay leadership is cultivated and exercised, makes a significant difference. Here, Catholic parishes often fall short. In working-class and lower income communities, "the general correlation of Protestantism with African-American membership and Latinos with Catholicism . . . means that blacks attain a bigger boost politically from their involvement in congregational life," 86.

159. Mich, "Living Wage Movement," 241–42.

160. Gertner, "What Is a Living Wage?" *New York Times Magazine*, January 15, 2006, https://www.nytimes.com/2006/01/15/magazine/what-is-a-living-wage-627275.html.

161. On framing and living wage campaigns, see also David Howell, "Reframing the Minimum Wage Debate," *American Prospect*, Summer 2016, https://prospect.org/article/reframing-minimum-wage-debate. David Howell, Kea Fiedler, and Stephanie Luce offer evidence-based arguments for dethroning "no job loss" as an absolute criterion and contend that a vigorous "minimum living wage" agenda at the federal level would yield enough positive outcomes to offset the harm that potential (not certain) job losses would inflict. Howell, Fiedler, and Luce, *What's the Right Minimum Wage*.

162. Mariya Strauss, "In Search of New Frames: Q & A with the Authors of *Producers, Parasites, Patriots*," Political Research Associates, May 13, 2019, https://www.politicalresearch.org/2019/05/13/search-new-frames.

163. Rorty quoted in Conor Friedersdorf, "The Book That Predicted Trump's Rise Offers the Left a Roadmap for Defeating Him," *Atlantic*, July 6, 2017, https://www.theatlantic.com /politics/archive/2017/07/advice-for-the-left-on-achieving-a-more-perfect-union /531054/.

164. Romero, *Violence of Love*, 182–83.

BIBLIOGRAPHY

Abela, Andrew V. "The Price of Freedom: Consumerism and Liberty in Secular Research and Catholic Teaching." *Journal of Markets and Morality* 10, no. 1 (Spring 2007): 7–25.

Adams, David Wallace. *Education for Extinction: American Indians and the Boarding School Experience, 1875–1928.* Lawrence: University Press of Kansas, 1995.

Adams, James Truslow. *The Epic of America.* New Brunswick, NJ: Transaction, 2012.

Albrecht, Gloria. "Forget Your Right to Work: Detroit and the Demise of Workers' Rights." *Journal of the Society of Christian Ethics* 37, no. 1 (Spring/Summer 2017): 119–39.

———. *Hitting Home: Feminist Ethics, Women's Work, and the Betrayal of 'Family Values.'* New York: Bloomsbury Academic, 2002.

Alexander, Michelle. *The New Jim Crow; Mass Incarceration in the Age of Colorblindness.* New York: The New Press, 2012.

Alexander, Patricia, and Sally Baden. *Glossary on Macroeconomics from a Gender Perspective.* Bridge Institute of Development Studies, 2000. https://www.bridge.ids.ac.uk/reports/re48c.pdf.

Allen, Theodore. *The Invention of the White Race.* Vol. 1, *Racial Oppression and Social Control.* New York: Verso, 1994.

———. *The Invention of the White Race.* Vol. 2, *The Origin of Racial Oppression in Anglo-America.* New York: Verso, 1997.

Allman, Mark. Introduction to *The Almighty Dollar: Reflections on "EJA" Twenty-Five Years Later.* Winona, MN: Anselm Academic, 2012.

Aldred, Jonathan. *The Skeptical Economist: Revealing the Ethics inside Economics.* London: Earthscan, 2009.

Alperovitz, Gar. *What Then Must We Do? Straight Talk About the Next American Revolution.* White River Junction, VT: Chelsea Green, 2013.

Alperovitz, Gar, and Steve Dubb. "The Possibility of a Pluralist Commonwealth and a Community-Sustaining Economy." *Good Society* 22, no. 1 (2013): 1–25.

Anderson, Carol. *White Rage: The Unspoken Truth of Our Racial Divide.* New York: Bloomsbury, 2016.

Andolsen, Barbara Hilkert. *"Daughters of Jefferson, Daughters of Bootblacks": Racism and American Feminism.* Macon, GA: Mercer University Press, 1986.

———. *The New Job Contract: Economic Justice in an Age of Insecurity.* Cleveland: Pilgrim Press, 1998.

Ansley, Frances Lee. "Stirring the Ashes: Race, Class and the Future of Civil Rights Scholarship." *Cornell Law Review* 74, no. 6 (1989): 993–1077.

Antonopoulos, Rania. "The Unpaid Care Work-Paid Work Connection." International Labor Office. Policy Integrations and Statistics Department. Working Paper no. 86. Geneva: International Labor Organization, 2009.

Antonopoulos, Rania, Thomas Masterson, and Ajit Zacharais. *The Interlocking of Time and Income Deficits: Revisiting Poverty Measurement, Informing Policy Responses.* Undoing Knots, Innovating for Change 3. New York: United Nations Development Program, 2012.

Aquino, María Pilar. *Our Cry for Life: Feminist Theology from Latin America.* Maryknoll, NY: Orbis Books, 1993.

Arbo, Matthew. *Political Vanity: Adam Ferguson on the Moral Tensions of Early Capitalism.* Minneapolis: Fortress, 2014.

Arendt, Hannah. *The Human Condition.* 2nd ed. Chicago: University of Chicago Press, 2013.

———. *The Life of the Mind.* New York: Harcourt Brace Jovanovich, 1978.

———. *The Origins of Totalitarianism.* New York: Harcourt, Brace and World, 1968.

Aronowitz, Stanley. *How Class Works: Power and Social Movement.* New Haven, CT: Yale University Press, 2005.

Arts, Herwig. "The Spirituality of John A. Ryan." In *Religion and Public Life: The Legacy of Monsignor John A. Ryan,* ed. Robert G. Kennedy. Lanham, MD: University Press of America, 2001.

Asante-Muhammad, Dedrick, Chuck Collins, Josh Hoxie, and Emanuel Nieves. *The Road to Zero Wealth: How the Racial Wealth Divide Is Hollowing out America's Middle Class.* Washington, DC: Institute for Policy Studies, 2017. https://prosperitynow.org/sites/default/files/PDFs/road_to_zero_wealth.pdf.

Atkin, Nicolas, and Frank Tallett. *Priests, Prelates and People: A History of European Catholicism since 1750.* New York: Oxford University Press, 2003.

Attfield, Sarah. "Rejecting Respectability: On Being Unapologetically Working Class." *Journal of Working-Class Studies* 1, no. 1 (December 2016): 45–56.

Austin, Algernon. "Native Americans and Jobs: The Challenge and the Promise." Briefing Paper 370, Economic Policy Institute, December 17, 2013. https://www.epi.org/files/2013/NATIVE-AMERICANS-AND-JOBS-The-Challenge-and-the-Promise.pdf.

Autor, David H., Lawrence F. Katz, and Melissa S. Kearney. "The Polarization of the U.S. Labor Market." *American Economic Review* 96, no. 2 (2006): 189–94.

Avila, Francisco de. *Tratado de los Evangelios.* London: Forgotten Books, 2016.

Baldwin, James. "White Man's Guilt." In *The Price of the Ticket: Collected Non-Fiction, 1948–1985.* New York: St. Martin's, 1985.

Balkin, J. M. *Cultural Software: A Theory of Ideology.* New Haven, CT: Yale University Press, 1998.

Bailey, James P. *Rethinking Poverty: Income, Assets, and the Catholic Social Justice Tradition.* Notre Dame, IN: University of Notre Dame Press, 2010.

Bair, Jennifer. "On Difference and Capital: Gender and the Globalization of Production." *Signs: Journal of Women in Culture and Society* 36, no. 1 (2010): 203–26.

Banks, Nina. "Uplifting the Race through Domesticity: Capitalism, African-American Migration, and the Household Economy in the Great Migration Era of 1916–1930." *Feminist Economics* 12, no. 4 (2006): 599–624.

Barnum, Gertrude. "Story of a Fall River Mill Girl." *Independent* 58 (1905): 241–43.

Barrera, Albino. "Degrees of Unmet Needs and the Superfluous Income Criterion." *Review of Social Economy* 55, no. 4 (Winter 1997): 464–86.

Baum, Gregory. "Class Struggle and the Magisterium: A New Note." *Theological Studies* 45, no. 4: 690–701.

———. "The Meaning of Ideology." *Proceedings of the Catholic Theological Society of America* 34 (1979): 171–75.

———. *The Priority of Labor: A Commentary on* Laborem exercens, *Encyclical Letter of Pope John Paul II*. New York: Paulist, 1982.

———. "The Social Economy: An Alternative Model of Economic Development." *Journal of Catholic Social Thought* 6, no. 1 (2009): 253–62.

———. "Structures of Sin." In *The Logic of Solidarity: Commentaries on Pope John Paul II's Encyclical "On Social Concern,"* edited by Gregory Baum and Robert Ellsberg. Maryknoll, NY: Orbis Books, 1989.

Beabout, Gregory, and Eduardo Echeverria. "The Culture of Consumerism: A Catholic and Personalist Critique." *Journal of Markets and Morality* 5, no. 2 (2002): 339–83.

Beaudoin, Thomas M. *Consuming Faith: Integrating Who We Are with What We Buy*. Lanham, MD: Rowman and Littlefield, 2007.

Beck, Ulrich. *Risk Society: Towards a New Modernity*. London: Sage Publications, 1992.

Beckley, Harlan. "The Legacy of John A. Ryan's Theory of Justice." *American Journal of Jurisprudence* 33, no. 1 (1988): 61–98.

———. "Love, Human Dignity, and Justice; Some Legacies from Protestant and Catholic Ethics." *Notre Dame Law Review* 66, no. 4 (1991): 1053–73.

———. *Passion for Justice: Retrieving the Legacies of Walter Rauschenbusch, John A. Ryan, and Reinhold Niebuhr*. Louisville, KY: Westminster John Knox, 1992.

Beder, Sharon. "Consumerism—An Historical Perspective." *Pacific Ecologist* 9 (Spring 2004): 42–48. http://www.pacificecologist.org/archive/consumerhistory.html.

———. *Selling the Work Ethic: From Puritan to Pulpit to Corporate PR*. Melbourne, AUS: Scribe, 2000.

Bell, Daniel. *Work and Its Discontents*. Boston: Beacon Press, 1956.

Benedict XVI. *Caritas in veritate*. June 29, 2009.

Benford, Robert D., and David A. Snow. "Framing Processes and Social Movements: An Overview and Assessment." *Annual Review of Sociology* 26 (2000): 611–39.

Benjamin, Rich. *Searching for Whitopia: An Improbable Journey into the Heart of White America*. New York: Hyperion, 2009.

Berendt, Emil B. "A Mathematical Note on Msgr. John A. Ryan's Thought on the Minimum Wage." *Review of Social Economy* 65, no. 4 (2007): 459–73.

Berger, Bethany R. "Red: Racism and the American Indian." *UCLA Law Review* 56, no. 3 (2009): 591–656.

Beyer, Gerald J. "The Continuing Relevance of *Brothers and Sisters to Us* in Confronting White Privilege." *Josephinum Journal of Theology* 19, no. 2 (2012): 235–64.

Bhabha, Homi K. "The Other Question: The Stereotype and Colonial Discourse." In *The Location of Culture*, ed. Homi K. Bhabha, 94–120. Oxford: Routledge, 2004.

Bilgrien, Marie Vianney. *Solidarity: A Principle, an Attitude, a Duty? Or the Virtue for an Interdependent World?* New York: Peter Lang, 1989.

Bivens, Josh, Elise Gould, Lawrence Mishel, and Heidi Shierholz. "Raising America's Pay: Why It's Our Central Economic Policy Challenge." Briefing Paper 378, Economic Policy Institute, June 4, 2014. https://www.epi.org/files/pdf/65287.pdf.

Blanchflower, David, and Richard B. Freeman. "Going Different Ways: Unionism in the U.S. and Other Advanced O.E.C.D. Countries." Working Paper 3342. National Bureau of Economic Research. April 1990.

Bogle, John C. *Enough: True Measures of Money, Business, and Life.* Hoboken, NJ: John Wiley, 2009.

Bonilla-Silva, Eduardo. *Racism without Racists: Color-Blind Racism and the Persistence of Racial Inequality in the United States.* Lanham, MD: Rowman & Littlefield, 2006.

Borowski, Oden. *Every Living Thing: Daily Use of Animals in Ancient Israel.* Walnut Creek, CA: Altamira, 1998.

Boucher, Joanne. "Betty Friedan and the Radical Past of Liberal Feminism." *New Politics* 9, no. 3 (Summer 2003). http://nova.wpunj.edu/newpolitics/issue35/boucher35.htm.

Bourdieu, Pierre. *The Logic of Practice.* Stanford, CA: Stanford University Press, 1990.

———. *Outline of a Theory of Practice.* Translated by Richard Nice. Cambridge: Cambridge University Press, 1977.

Braxton, Edward. "The Catholic Church and the Black Lives Matter Movement: The Racial Divide in the United States Revisited." Pastoral letter, February 26, 2016. https://www .diobelle.org/documents/diocese/bishop/290-racial-divide-revisited/file.

Broderick, Francis L. *Right Reverend New Dealer.* New York: Macmillan, 1963.

Burggraf, Shirley P. *The Feminine Economy and Economic Man: Reviving the Role of Family in the Post-Industrial Age.* Reading, MA: Addison-Wesley, 1997.

Burke, Kenneth. *A Rhetoric of Motives.* New York: Prentice-Hall, 1950.

Caldecott, Leonie. "Sincere Gift: The Pope's 'New Feminism.'" In *Readings in Moral Theology* §10: *John Paul II and Moral Theology,* edited by Charles E. Curran and Richard A. McCormick. New York: Paulist, 1998.

Callahan, Sidney. "Homosexuality, Moral Theology, and Scientific Evidence." In *Sexual Diversity and Catholicism,* edited by Patricia Beattie Jung and Joseph Andrew Coray. 201–15. Collegeville, MN: Liturgical Press, 2001.

Calo, Zachary R. "'True Economic Liberalism' and the Development of American Catholic Social Thought, 1920–1940." *Journal of Catholic Social Thought* 5, no. 2 (2008): 285–314.

Carbado, Devon W., and Mitu Gulati. "The Law and Economics of Critical Race Theory." Review of *Crossroads, Directions, and a New Critical Race Theory,* edited by Francisco Valdes, Jerome McCristal Culp, and Angela P. Harris. *Yale Law Review* 112 (2003): 1751–828.

Carlson, Allan C. *From Cottage to Work Station: The Family's Search for Social Harmony in the Industrial Age.* San Francisco: Ignatius Press, 1993.

Cass, Oren. *The Once and Future Worker: A Vision for the Renewal of Work in America.* New York: Encounter Books, 2018.

Cassidy, Laurie M., and Alex Mikulich. *Interrupting White Privilege: Catholic Theologians Break the Silence.* Maryknoll, NY: Orbis Books, 2007.

Catechism of the Catholic Church. 2nd ed. New York: Doubleday, 2003.

Center on Poverty and Inequality. *Bare Minimum: Why We Need to Raise Wages for America's Lowest-Paid Families.* Washington, DC: Leadership Conference Education Fund, 2018. http://civilrightsdocs.info/pdf/reports/Bare-Minimum.pdf.

Chappel, James. *Catholic Modern: The Challenge of Totalitarianism and the Remaking of the Church.* Cambridge, MA: Harvard University Press, 2018.

Cherrington, David J. *The Work Ethics: Working Values and Values that Work.* New York: AMACOM, 1980.

Chinoy, Ely. *Automobile Workers and the American Dream.* 2nd ed. Urbana: University of Illinois Press, 1992.

Clapp, Rodney, ed. *The Consuming Passion: Christianity and The Consumer Culture.* Downers Grove, IL: InterVarsity Pres, 1998.

Clark, Charles M. A. "Wealth as Abundance and Scarcity: Perspectives from Catholic Social Thought and Economic Theory." In *Rediscovering Abundance: Interdisciplinary Essays on Wealth, Income, and Their Distribution in the Catholic Social Tradition*. Edited by Helen Alford, Charles M. A. Clark, S. A. Cortright, Michael J. Naughton, 28–56. Notre Dame, IN: University of Notre Dame Press, 2006.

Clark-Lewis, Elizabeth. *Living In, Living Out: African American Domestics in Washington, D.C., 1900–1940*. Washington, DC: Smithsonian Institution Press, 1994.

Clarkson, Gavin. "Tribal Bondage: Statutory Shackles and Regulatory Restraints on Tribal Economic Development." University of Michigan Law School. John Olin Center for Law and Economics Working Paper Series 2003–2009, no. 63 (2006): 1–54.

Clawson, Dan, and Mary Ann Clawson. "What Happened to the U.S. Labor Movement? Union Decline and Renewal." *Annual Review of Sociology* 25 (1999): 99–113.

Cloutier, David. "American Lifestyles and Structures of Sin: The Practical Implications of Pope Benedict XVI's Ecological Vision for the American Church." In *Environmental Justice and Climate Change: Assessing Pope Benedict XVI's Ecological Vision for the Catholic Church in the United States*, edited by Jame Schaefer and Tobias Winright, 215–37. Lanham, MD: Rowman and Littlefield, 2013.

———. "Exclusion, Fragmentation, and Theft: A Survey and Synthesis of Moral Approaches to Economic Inequality." *Journal of Moral Theology* 7, no. 1 (2018): 141–72.

———. *The Vice of Luxury: Economic Excess in a Consumer Age*. Washington, DC: Georgetown University Press, 2015.

Cobble, Dorothy Sue. *The Other Women's Movement: Workplace Justice and Social Rights in Modern America*. Princeton, NJ: Princeton University Press, 2005.

Cohen, Joseph Nathan. *Financial Crisis in American Households: The Basic Expenses That Bankrupt the Middle Class*. New York: Praeger, 2017.

Coleman, John A. *An American Strategic Theology*. Eugene, OR: Wipf and Stock, 2005.

Congressional Budget Office. *Trends in Family Wealth, 1989 to 2013*. Washington, DC: August 2016. https://www.cbo.gov/sites/default/files/114th-congress-2015-2016/reports/51846-familywealth.pdf.

Coontz, Stephanie. *The Way We Never Were: American Families and the Nostalgia Trap*. New York: Basic Books, 1992.

Cooper, Betsy, Daniel Cox, Rachel Lienesch, and Robert P. Jones. *The Divide over America's Future: 1950 or 2050? Findings from the 2016 American Values Survey*. Washington, DC: Public Religion Research Institute, 2016. https://www.prri.org/wp-content/uploads/2016/10/PRRI-2016-American-Values-Survey.pdf.

Cooper, David. *Raising the Federal Minimum Wage to $15 by 2024 Would Lift Pay for Nearly 40 Million Workers*. Washington, DC: Economic Policy Institute, 2019. https://www.epi.org/files/pdf/160909.pdf.

Copeland, M. Shawn. *Enfleshing Freedom: Body, Race, and Being*. Minneapolis: Fortress, 2009.

———. *A Genetic Study of the Idea of the Human Good in the Thought of Bernard Lonergan*. PhD diss., Boston College, 1991.

Coser, Lewis A. *Masters of Sociological Thought: Ideas in Historical and Social Context*. 2nd ed. New York: Harcourt Brace Jovanovich, 1977.

Cott, Nancy F. *The Bonds of Womanhood: "Women's Sphere" in New England, 1780–1835*. 2nd ed. New Haven, CT: Yale University Press, 1997.

Couture, Pamela D. *Blessed Are the Poor? Women's Poverty, Family Policy, and Practical Theology*. Nashville: Abingdon, 1991.

Cox, Daniel, Juhem Navarro-Rivera, and Robert P. Jones. *Economic Insecurity, Rising Inequality, and Doubts about the Future: Findings from the 2014 American Values Survey.* Washington, DC: Public Religion Research Institute, 2014. https://www.prri.org/wp-content/uploads/2014/09/PRRI-AVS-with-Transparancy-Edits.pdf.

Crain, Marion, and Kenneth Matheny. "Beyond Unions, Notwithstanding Labor Law." *University of California Irvine Journal of Labor Law* 4, no. 2 (2015): 461–607.

Crenshaw, Kimberlé. "Demarginalizing the Intersection of Race and Sex: A Black Feminist Critique of Antidiscrimination Doctrine, Feminist Theory and Antiracist Politics." *University of Chicago Legal Forum* 1989, no. 1 (1989). http://chicagounbound.uchicago.edu/uclf/vol1989/iss1/.

Cressler, Matthew J. *Authentically Black and Truly Catholic: The Rise of Black Catholicism in the Great Migration.* New York: New York University Press, 2017.

Cronin, John F., and Harry W. Flannery. *The Church and the Workingman.* New York: Hawthorn Books, 1965.

Cross, Gary. *An All-Consuming Century: Why Commercialism Won in Modern America.* New York: Columbia University Press, 2000.

———. *Time and Money.* London: Routledge, 1993.

Crowe, F. E., ed. *Collection of Papers by Bernard Lonergan.* New York: Herder and Herder, 1967.

Curran, Charles E. *American Catholic Social Ethics: Twentieth-Century Approaches.* Notre Dame, IN: University of Notre Dame Press, 1982.

———. *Catholic Social Teaching: 1891–Present.* Washington, DC: Georgetown University Press, 2002.

———. "Reception of Catholic Social and Economic Teaching in the United States." In *Modern Catholic Social Teaching: Commentaries and Interpretations,* edited by Kenneth R. Himes, 469–92. Washington, DC: Georgetown University Press, 2004.

Damaske, Sarah. *For the Family? How Class and Gender Shape Women's Work.* New York: Oxford University Press, 2011.

Dávila. María Teresa. "The Role of the Social Sciences in Catholic Social Thought: Being Able to 'See' in the Rubric 'See, Judge, Act' and the Preferential Option for the Poor." Plenary Paper at the Catholic Social Teaching Global Poverty Conference. Villanova University. March 2011.

Davis, Cyprian. *The History of Black Catholics in the United States.* New York: Crossroad, 1994.

Davis, John B., and Edward J. O'Boyle, eds. *The Social Economics of Human Material Need.* Carbondale: Southern Illinois University Press, 1994.

Davis, Tryon P. "The Implicit Bias of Implicit Bias Theory." *Drexel Law Review* 10, no. 632 (2018): 631–72.

Dean, Jodi. *Solidarity of Strangers: Feminism after Identity Politics.* Berkeley: University of California Press, 2018.

Denike, Margaret. "Scapegoat Racism and the Sacrificial Politics of 'Security.'" *Journal of International Political Theory* 11, no. 1 (2015): 111–27.

Deslippe, Dennis. "For Faith and Free Markets: The Lay Commission and Conservative Catholics in the 1980s." *Journal of Policy History* 28, no. 4 (2016): 597–623.

Desmond, Matthew. *Evicted: Poverty and Profit in the American City.* New York: Penguin Random House, 2017.

Desmond, Matthew, and Nathan Wilmers. "Do the Poor Pay More for Housing? Exploitation, Profit, and Risk in Rental Markets." *American Journal of Sociology.* 124, no. 4 (January 2019): 1090–124. https://doi.org/10.1086/701697.

Detweiler, Frederick G. "The Anglo-Saxon Myth in the United States." *American Sociological Review* 3, no. 2 (1938): 183–89.

De Vries, Jan. "The Industrial Revolution and the Industrious Revolution." *Journal of Economic History* 54, no. 2 (June 1994): 249–70.

———. *The Industrious Revolution: Consumer Behavior and the Household Economy, 1650 to the Present.* Cambridge: Cambridge University Press, 2008.

Dimand, Robert W., Evelyn L. Forget, and Chris Nyland. "Retrospectives: Gender in Classical Economics." *Journal of Economic Perspectives* 18, no. 1 (Winter 2004): 229–40.

Dolan, Jay. *The American Catholic Experience: A History from Colonial Times to the Present.* Notre Dame, IN: University of Notre Dame Press, 1992.

Dorling, Danny. *A Better Politics: How Government Can Help Make Us Happier.* London: London Publishing Partnership, 2016. http://www.dannydorling.org/books/betterpolitics /dorling-betterpolitics.pdf.

———. *The Equality Effect: Improving Life for Everyone.* Oxford: New Internationalist Publications, 2017.

Dorr, Donal. *Option for the Poor and for the Earth.* Maryknoll, NY: Orbis Books, 2012.

———. "Solidarity and Integral Human Development." In *The Logic of Solidarity: Commentaries on Pope John Paul II's Encyclical "On Social Concern"*, edited by Gregory Baum and Robert Ellsberg, 143–54. Maryknoll, NY: Orbis Books, 1989.

Dorrien, Gary J. "A Case for Economic Democracy." *Tikkun* 24, no. 3 (May/June 2009): 34–37.

———. *Reconstructing the Common Good: Theology and the Social Order.* Maryknoll, NY: Orbis Books, 1990.

Douglas, Kelly Brown. *Stand Your Ground: Black Bodies and the Justice of God.* Maryknoll, NY: Orbis Books, 2015. Kindle.

Draut, Tamara. *Understanding the Working Class.* New York: Demos, 2018. https://www .demos.org/sites/default/files/publications/WorkingClass_Explainer_Final.pdf.

Draut, Tamara, Jennifer Wheary, and Thomas M. Shapiro. *By a Thread: The New Experience of America's Middle Class.* New York: Demos, 2007. http://www.demos.org/sites/default /files/publications/ByAThread_MiddleClass_Demos.pdf.

Dresser, Laura, Mary C. King, and Raahi Reddy. *Oregon's Care Economy: The Case for Public Care Investment, February 2017.* Madison: COWS, University of Wisconsin, 2017. https://www.cows.org/_data/documents/1832.pdf.

Drucker, Peter F. "The Age of Social Transformation." *Atlantic*, September 2004, 53–80.

Dubofsky, Melvyn. *The State and Labor in Modern America.* Chapel Hill: University of North Carolina Press, 1994.

Du Bois, W. E. B. *Black Reconstruction in the United States, 1860–1880.* New York, 1977.

———. *The Souls of Black Folk.* 3rd ed. Chicago: A.C. McClurg, 1903.

Duis, Perry R. *Challenging Chicago: Coping with Everyday Life, 1847–1920.* Urbana: University of Illinois Press, 2006.

Ehrenreich, Barbara. *Nickel and Dimed: On (Not) Getting by in America.* New York: Holt, 2008.

Ellul, Jacques. *Propaganda: The Formation of Men's Attitudes.* New York: Vintage Books, 1973.

Elshtain, Jean Bethke. *Augustine and the Limits of Politics.* Notre Dame, IN: University of Notre Dame Press, 1995.

Evans, Sarah, and Harry C. Boyte. *Free Spaces: The Sources of Democratic Change in America.* Chicago: University of Chicago Press, 1986.

Ewen, Stuart. *Captains of Consciousness: Advertising and the Social Roots of the Consumer Culture.* New York: McGraw-Hill, 2001.

Fairbrother, Peter. "Social Movement Unionism or Trade Unions as Social Movements." *Employer Responsibilities and Rights Journal* 20, no. 3 (2008): 213–20.

Farrelly, Maura Jane. "American Slavery, American Freedom, American Catholicism." *Early American Studies* 10, no. 1 (Winter 2012): 69–100.

Ferrer-i-Carbonell, Ada, and Xavier Ramos. "Inequality and Happiness: A Survey." GINI Discussion Paper 38. Amsterdam: AIAS, 2012.

———. "Inequality and Happiness." *Journal of Economic Surveys* 28, no. 5 (2014): 1016–27.

Fields, Karen E., and Barbara J. Fields. *Racecraft: The Soul of Inequality in American Life*. London: Verso, 2014.

Figart, Deborah. "Social Responsibility for Living Standards: Presidential Address, Association for Social Economics, 2007." *Review of Social Economy* 65, no. 4 (December 2007): 391–405.

Finn, Daniel K. *Christian Economic Ethics: History and Implications*. Minneapolis: Fortress Press, 2014.

———. *Consumer Ethics in a Global Economy*. Washington, DC: Georgetown University Press, 2020.

———. *The Moral Ecology of Markets: Assessing Claims about Markets and Justice*. New York: Cambridge University Press, 2006.

———. "Power and Public Presence in Catholic Social Thought, the Church, and the CTSA." *Proceedings of the Catholic Theological Society of America* 62 (2007): 62–77.

———. "What Is a Sinful Social Structure?" *Theological Studies* 77, no. 1 (2016): 136–64.

Firer Hinze, Christine. "Bridge Discourse on Wage Justice: Roman Catholic and Feminist Perspectives on the Family Living Wage." In *Feminist Ethics and the Catholic Moral Tradition*, edited by Charles E. Curran, Margaret A. Farley, and Richard McCormick, 511–40. Mahwah, NJ: Paulist Press, 1996.

———. "Christian Feminists, James Luther Adams, and the Search for a Radically Transformative Ethics." *Journal of Religious Ethics* 21, no. 2 (Fall, 1993): 275–302.

———. *Comprehending Power in Christian Social Ethics*. Oxford: Oxford University Press, 1995.

———. "Dirt and Economic Inequality: A Christian-Ethical Peek Under the Rug." *Annual of the Society of Christian Ethics* 21 (2001): 45–62.

———. "The Drama of Social Sin and the (Im)Possibility of Solidarity: Reinhold Niebuhr and Modern Catholic Social Teaching." *Society for the Study of Christian Ethics* 22, no. 4 (2009): 442–60.

———. *Glass Ceilings, Dirt Floors: Women, Work, and the Global Economy*. Mahwah, NJ: Paulist, 2015.

———. "Labor and Trade." In *Blackwell Companion to Christian Ethics*, edited by William Schweiker. 3rd ed. In press.

———. "John A. Ryan: Theological Ethics and Political Engagement." *Proceedings of the Catholic Theological Society of America* 50 (1995): 174–91.

———. "Over, Under, Around, and Through: Ethics, Solidarity, and the Saints." *Proceedings of the Catholic Theological Society of America* 66 (2011): 33–60.

———. "A Response to Michael Baxter." *Proceedings of the Catholic Theological Society of America* 59 (2012): 46–49.

———. "U.S. Catholic Social Thought, Gender, and Economic Livelihood." *Theological Studies* 66, no. 3 (September 2005): 568–91.

———. "Women, Families, and the Legacy of *Laborem Exercens*: An Unfinished Agenda." *Journal of Catholic Social Thought* 6, no. 1 (2009): 63–92.

Firer Hinze, Christine, and J. Patrick Hornbeck II, eds. *More than a Monologue: Sexual Diversity and the Catholic Church*. Vol. 1, *Voices of Our Times*. New York: Fordham University Press, 2014.

Fitch, Robert. *Solidarity for Sale: How Corruption Destroyed the Labor Movement and Undermined America's Promise*. New York: Public Affairs, 2006.

Fletcher, Bill, Jr. "How Race Enters Class in the United States." In *What's Class Got to Do with It? American Society in the Twenty-First Century*, edited by Michael Zweig, 35–44. Ithaca, NY: Cornell University Press, 2004.

Fletcher, Bill, and Fernando Gapasin. *Solidarity Divided: The Crisis in Organized Labor and a New Path toward Social Justice*. Berkeley: University of California Press, 2009.

Folbre, Nancy, ed. *For Love or Money: Care Provision in the United States*. New York: Russell Sage, 2000.

———. "Measuring Care: Gender, Empowerment, and the Care Economy." *Journal of Human Development* 7, no. 2 (July 2006): 184–99.

———. "The Unproductive Housewife: Her Evolution in Nineteenth-Century Economic Thought." *Signs* 16, no. 3 (Spring 1991): 463–84.

———. *Who Pays for the Kids? Gender and the Structures of Constraint*. Hoboken, NJ: Taylor and Francis, 2004.

Folbre, Nancy, Janet C. Gornick, Helen Connolly, and Teresa Munzi. "Women's Unemployment, Unpaid Work, and Economic Inequality." *Income Inequality: Economic Disparities and the Middle Class in Affluent Countries*, edited by Janet C. Gornick and Markus Jäntti, 234–60. Stanford, CA: Stanford University Press, 2013.

Folbre, Nancy, and Julie Nelson. "For Love or Money—Or Both?" *Journal of Economic Perspectives* 14, no. 4 (Fall 2000): 123–40.

Foner, Eric, and Joshua Brown. *Forever Free: The Story of Emancipation and Reconstruction*. New York: Doubleday, 2013.

Forbath, William E. "Caste, Class, and Equal Citizenship." *Michigan Law Review* 98, no. 1 (1999): 1–91.

Ford, S. Dennis. *Sins of Omission: A Primer on Moral Indifference*. Minneapolis: Fortress, 1990.

Foucault, Michel. *Power/Knowledge: Selected Interview & Other Writings, 1972–1977*. Edited by Colin Gordon. New York: Harvester, 1980.

Francis. *Evangelii gaudium*. Apostolic exhortation, 2013. http://w2.vatican.va/content/francesco/en/apost_exhortations/documents/papa-francesco_esortazione-ap_20131124_evangelii-gaudium.html.

———. *Laudato si'*. Encyclical letter, 2015. http://w2.vatican.va/content/francesco/en/encyclicals/documents/papa-francesco_20150524_enciclica-laudato-si.html.

Francis, Megan Ming. *Civil Rights and the Making of the Modern American State*. New York: Cambridge University Press, 2014.

Frank, Robert. *Choosing the Right Pond*. New York: Oxford University Press, 1985.

———. *The Darwin Economy: Liberty, Competition, and the Common Good*. Princeton, NJ: Princeton University Press, 2011.

———. *Falling Behind: How Rising Inequality Harms the Middle Class*. Berkeley: University of California Press, 2013.

———. *Luxury Fever: Why Money Fails to Satisfy in an Era of Excess*. Princeton, NJ: Princeton University Press, 1999.

Fraser, Nancy. *Fortunes of Feminism: From State-Managed Capitalism to Neoliberal Crisis*. Brooklyn: Verso Books, 2013.

Fraser, Steve. *The Limousine Liberal: How an Incendiary Image United the Right and Fractured America*. New York: Basic Books, 2016.

Freeden, Michael. *Ideologies and Political Theory: A Conceptual Approach*. New York: Clarendon, 1996.

Friedman, Samantha, and Emily Rosenbaum. "Does Suburban Residence Mean Better Neighborhood Conditions for All Households? Assessing the Influence of Nativity Status and Race/Ethnicity." *Social Science Research* 36, no. 1 (March 2007): 286–312.

Frye, Marilyn. *The Politics of Reality: Essays in Feminist History*. Berkeley, CA: Crossing Press, 2007.

Fukuda-Parr, Sakiko, James Heintz, and Stephanie Seguino. "Critical Perspectives on Financial and Economic Crises: Heterodox Macroeconomics Meets Feminist Economics." *Feminist Economics* 19, no. 3 (2013): 4–31.

Gaillardetz, Richard R. "John A. Ryan: An Early Revisionist?" *Journal of Religious Ethics* 18, no. 2 (Fall 1990): 107–22.

Ganz, Marshall. "Leading Change: Leadership, Organization, and Social Movements." In *Handbook of Leadership Theory and Practice: A Harvard Centennial Colloquium*, edited by Nitin Nohria and Rakesh Khurana. Boston: Harvard Business School Publishing, 2010.

———. *Why David Sometimes Wins: Leadership, Organization, and Strategy in the California Farm Worker Movement*. New York: Oxford, 2010.

Gates, Henry Louis, Jr. *Life upon These Shores: Looking at African American History, 1513–2008*. New York: Alfred Knopf, 2011.

Gaudium et spes. Documents of Vatican II, 1965. http://www.vatican.va/archive/hist_councils /ii_vatican_council/documents/vat-ii_const_19651207_gaudium-et-spes_en.html.

Gawronski, Bertram, and B. Keith Payne. "A History of Implicit Social Cognition." In *Handbook of Implicit Social Cognition: Measurement, Theory, and Applications*. New York: Guilford, 2010.

Gearty, Patrick W. *The Economic Thought of Monsignor John A. Ryan*. Washington, DC: Catholic University of America Press, 1953.

Gest, Justin. *The New Minority: White Working Class Politics in an Age of Immigration and Inequality*. New York: Oxford University Press, 2016.

———. "The White Working-Class Minority: A Counter-Narrative." *Politics, Groups, and Identities* 4, no. 1 (2016): 126–43.

Giddens, Anthony. *Central Problems in Social Theory: Action, Structure, and Contradiction in Social Analysis*. Berkeley: University of California Press, 1979.

———. *The Constitution of Society: Outline of the Theory of Structuration*. Berkeley: University of California Press, 1984.

Gilens, Martin. *Why Americans Hate Welfare: Race, Media, and the Politics of Antipoverty Policy*. Chicago: University of Chicago Press, 1999.

Gilkes, Cheryl Townsend. "The Storm and the Light: Church, Family, Work, and Social Crisis in the African-American Experience." In *Work, Family, and Religion in Contemporary Society*, edited by Nancy Tatom Ammerman and Wade Clark Roof, 177–98. New York: Routledge, 1995.

Glazer, Nona Y. *Women's Paid and Unpaid Labor: The Work Transfer in Health Care and Retailing*. Philadelphia: Temple University Press, 1993.

Glenn, Evelyn Nakano. *Forced to Care: Coercion and Caregiving in America*. Cambridge, MA: Harvard University Press, 2012.

———. "From Servitude to Service Work: Historical Continuities in the Racial Division of Paid Reproductive Labor." *Signs* 18, no. 1 (Autumn 1992): 1–43.

———. "Racial Ethnic Women's Labor: The Intersection of Race, Gender, and Class Oppression." *Review of Radical Political Economics* 17, no. 3 (1985): 86–108.

———. *Unequal Freedom: How Race and Gender Shaped American Citizenship and Labor.* Cambridge, MA: Harvard University Press, 2004.

Glickman, Lawrence B. *A Living Wage: American Workers and the Making of Consumer Society.* Ithaca, NY: Cornell University Press, 1997.

Goldin, Claudia Dale. "The Quiet Revolution that Transformed Women's Employment, Education and Family." *American Economic Review* 96, no. 2 (2006): 1–21.

Goldin, Claudia Dale, and Lawrence F. Katz. "Long-Run Changes in the Wage Structure: Narrowing, Widening, Polarizing." *Brookings Papers on Economic Activity* 2 (2007): 135–65.

Gompers, Samuel. "A Minimum Living Wage." *American Federationist* 5 (April 1898): 26.

Graham, Jesse, Jonathan Haidt, Sena Koleva, Matt Motyl, Ravi Iyer, Sean P. Wojcik, and Peter H. Ditto. "Moral Foundations Theory: The Pragmatic Validity of Moral Pluralism." *Advances in Experimental Social Psychology* 47, no. 1 (2013): 55–130.

Greeley, Andrew M. *The Catholic Imagination.* Berkeley: University of California Press, 2000.

———. *The Catholic Myth: The Behavior and Beliefs of American Catholics.* New York: Simon & Schuster, 1997.

———. *The Church and the Suburbs.* New York: Sheed and Ward, 1959.

Greenberg, Stanley B. *Middle Class Dreams: The Politics and Power of the New American Majority, Revised and Updated Edition.* Revised, Updated edition. New Haven: Yale University Press, 1996.

Guinier, Lani. "From Racial Liberalism to Racial Literacy: *Brown v. Board of Education* and the Interest-Divergence Dilemma." *Journal of American History* 19, no. 1 (June 2004): 92–118.

Haidt, Jonathan. *The Righteous Mind: Why Good People Are Divided by Politics and Religion.* New York: Vintage, 2013.

Hamilton, Darrick, William Darity Jr., Anne E. Price, Vishnu Sridharan, and Rebecca Tippett. *Umbrellas Don't Make It Rain: Why Studying and Working Hard Isn't Enough for Black Americans.* Oakland, CA: Insight Center for Community Economic Development, 2015. http://www.insightcced.org/wp-content/uploads/2015/08/Umbrellas_Dont_Make_It_Rain_Final.pdf.

Harkness, Susan. "Women's Employment and Household Income Inequality." In *Income Inequality: Economic Disparities and the Middle Class in Affluent Countries,* edited by Janet C. Gornick and Markus Jäntti, 207–33. Stanford, CA: Stanford University Press, 2013.

Harris, Cheryl I. "Whiteness as Property." *Harvard Law Review* 106, no. 8 (1993): 1707–91.

Hatton, Erin. *The Temp Economy: From Kelly Girls to Permatemps in Postwar America.* Philadelphia: Temple University Press, 2011.

Heath, Julia, David H. Ciscel, and David C. Sharp. "The Work of Families: The Provision of Market and Household Labor and the Role of Public Policy." *Review of Social Economy* 56, no. 4 (1998): 501–21.

Heineman, Kenneth J. "A Catholic New Deal: Religion and Labor in 1930s Pittsburgh." *Pennsylvania Magazine of History and Biography* 118, no. 4 (October 1994): 363–94.

Henry, Ben, and Allyson Fredericksen. *Equity in the Balance: How a Living Wage Would Help Women and People of Color Make Ends Meet.* Job Gap: Economic Prosperity Series. Alliance for a Just Society, November 2014. https://jobgap2013.files.wordpress.com/2014/11/2014jobgapequity1.pdf.

Hernandez, Donald J. "Changes in the Demographics of Families over the Course of American History." In *Unfinished Work: Building Equality and Democracy in an Era of Working Families*, edited by Jody Heymann and Christopher Beem, 13–35. New York: New Press, 2005.

Hewlett, Sylvia. *A Lesser Life: The Myth of Women's Liberation in America*. New York: William Morrow, 1986.

———. *When the Bough Breaks: The Cost of Neglecting Our Children*. New York: Basic Books, 1991.

Heymann, Jody. *Forgotten Families: Ending the Growing Crisis Confronting Children and Working Parents in the Global Economy*. New York: Oxford University Press, 2006.

Heymann, Jody, and Magda Barrera. *Addressing Poverty in a Globalized Economy*. London: Progressive Economy, 2008.

Heymann, Jody, Aron Fischer, and Michael Engleman. "Labor Conditions and the Health of Children, Elderly and Disabled Family Members." In *Global Inequalities at Work: Work's Impact on the Health of Individuals, Families, and Societies*, edited by Jody Heymann, 75–105. New York: Oxford, 2003.

Hill Fletcher, Jeannine. *The Sin of White Supremacy: Christianity, Racism, and Religious Diversity in America*. Maryknoll, NY: Orbis Books, 2017.

Hillquit, Morris, and John A. Ryan. *Socialism: Promise or Menace?* New York: Macmillan, 1914.

Himes, Kenneth. "Catholic Social Teaching, Economic Inequality, and American Society." *Journal of Religious Ethics* 47, no. 2 (2019): 283–310.

———. "Consumerism and Christian Ethics." *Theological Studies* 68, no. 1 (February 2007): 132–53.

———, ed. *Modern Catholic Social Teaching: Commentaries and Interpretations*. Washington, DC: Georgetown University Press, 2004.

Hinze, Bradford E. *Prophetic Obedience: Ecclesiology for a Dialogical Church*. Maryknoll, NY: Orbis Books, 2016.

Hirsch, Fred. *The Social Limits to Growth*. Cambridge, MA: Harvard University Press, 1976.

Hirschfeld, Mary. "Rethinking Economic Inequality: A Theological Perspective." *Journal of Religious Ethics* 47, no. 2 (2019): 259–82.

Hochschild, Arlie Russell. *The Second Shift: Working Families and the Revolution at Home*. With Anne Machung. Rev. ed. New York: Penguin Books, 2012.

———. *Strangers in Their Own Land: Anger and Mourning on the American Right*. New York: New Press, 2016.

———. *The Time Bind: When Work Becomes Home and Home Becomes Work*. New York: Metropolitan Books, 1997.

Hochschild, Jennifer. *Facing Up to the American Dream: Race, Class, and the Soul of the Nation*. Princeton, NJ: Princeton University Press, 1996.

Hochschild, Jennifer L., and Brenna Marea Powell. "Racial Reorganization and the United States Census, 1850–1930: Mulattoes, Half-Breeds, Mixed Parentage, Hindoos, and the Mexican Race." *Studies in American Political Development* 22, no. 1 (2008): 59–96.

Hoggan, James. *I'm Right and You're an Idiot: The Toxic State of Public Discourse and How to Clean it Up*. 2nd ed. Gabriola, BC, Canada: New Society, 2019. Kindle.

Holland, Joe. "The Crisis of Family and Unions in Late Modern Global Capitalism." *Journal of Catholic Social Thought* 9, no. 1 (Winter 2012): 43–58.

Hollenbach, David. *Claims in Conflict: Retrieving and Renewing the Catholic Human Rights Tradition.* New York: Paulist, 1979.

———. "Globalization, Solidarity, and Justice." *East Asian Pastoral Review* 43, no. 1 (2006).

Hooker, Juliet. *Race and the Politics of Solidarity.* New York: Oxford University Press, 2009.

hooks, bell. *Where We Stand: Class Matters.* New York: Routledge, 2000.

Horowitz, Daniel. *The Morality of Spending: Attitudes toward the Consumer Society in America, 1875–1940.* Baltimore: Johns Hopkins University Press, 1985.

Horsman, Reginald. *Race and Manifest Destiny: The Origins of American Racial Anglo-Saxonism.* Cambridge, MA: Harvard University Press, 2009.

Hosang, Daniel Martinez, and Joseph E. Lowndes. *Producers, Parasites, Patriots: Race and the New Right-Wing Politics of Precarity.* Minneapolis: University of Minnesota Press, 2019.

Hossain, Naomi. "Exports, Equity, and Empowerment: The Effects of Readymade Garments Manufacturing Employment on Gender Equality in Bangladesh." Background paper, World Development Report 2012: Gender Equality and Development, 2011. http:// siteresources.worldbank.org/INTWDR2012/Resources/7778105-1299699968583 /7786210-1322671773271/Hossain-Export-Equity-employment.pdf.

Howell, David R., Kea Fiedler, and Stephanie Luce. *What's the Right Minimum Wage? Reframing the Debate from "No Job Loss" to a "Minimum Living Wage."* Washington, DC: Washington Center for Equitable Growth, 2016. http://equitablegrowth.org/wp-content/uploads /2016/06/howell-fiedler-luce-right-minwage-revised1.pdf.

Hoy, Suellen. *Chasing Dirt: The American Pursuit of Cleanliness.* New York: Oxford University Press, 1995.

Hsu, Hua. "White Plight?" *New Yorker,* July 25, 2016.

Hudson, Kenneth. "The New Labor Market Segmentation: Labor Market Dualism in the New Economy." *Social Science Research* 36, no. 1 (2007): 286–312.

Hunnicutt, Benjamin K. "Monsignor John A. Ryan and the Shorter Hours of Labor: A Forgotten Vision of 'Genuine' Progress." *Catholic Historical Review* 69, no. 3 (1983): 384–402.

———. *Work without End: Abandoning Shorter Hours for the Right to Work.* Philadelphia: Temple University Press, 1988.

Hustinx, Lesley, and Frans Lammertyn. "Solidarity and Volunteering under a Reflexive-Modern Sign: Towards a New Conceptual Framework." Working paper, Catholic University Leuven, Belgium, 2000. https://cdn.ymaws.com/www.istr.org/resource/resmgr /working_papers_dublin/hustinx.pdf.

Imperatori-Lee, Natalia. *Cuéntame: Narrative in the Ecclesial Present.* Maryknoll, NY: Orbis Press, 2018.

Industrial Areas Foundation. *IAF: 50 Years of Organizing for Change.* Franklin Square, NY: Industrial Areas Foundation, 1990.

International Labour Office. *ABC of Women Workers' Rights and Gender Equality.* 2nd ed. 2007. http://www.ilo.org/wcmsp5/groups/public/---dgreports/---gender/documents /publication/wcms_087314.pdf.

Isasi-Díaz, Ada María. *En la Lucha / In the Struggle: Elaborating a Mujerista Theology.* 2nd ed. Minneapolis: Fortress, 2004.

Isenberg. Nancy. *White Trash: The 400-Year Untold History of Class in America.* New York: Viking, 2016.

Jacobsen, Dennis A. *Doing Justice: Congregations and Community Organizing.* Minneapolis: Fortress, 2017.

Jacobson, Matthew Frye. *Roots Too: White Ethnic Revival in Post–Civil Rights America*. Cambridge, MA: Harvard University Press, 2006.

———. *Whiteness of a Different Color: European Immigrants and the Alchemy of Race*. Cambridge, MA: Harvard University Press, 1998.

Jensen, Barbara. "Becoming Versus Belonging: Psychology, Speech, and Social Class." Paper presented at the Youngstown Working Class Studies Conference, June 1997. http://www.classmatters.org/2004_04/becoming_vs_belonging.php.

———. Cover copy. *Reading Classes: On Culture and Classism in America*. Ithaca, NY: Cornell University Press, 2012.

Jensen, David. *Responsive Labor: A Theology of Work*. Louisville, KY: Westminster/John Knox, 2006.

John XXIII. *Mater et magistra*, May 15, 1961.

———. *Pacem in terris*, April 11, 1963.

John Paul II. *Centesimus annus*, May 1, 1991.

———. *Evangelium vitae*, May 25, 1995.

———. *Laborem exercens*, September 14, 1981.

———. *Letter to Women*. June 29, 1995.

———. *Mulieris dignitatem*. August 15, 1988.

———. *Reconciliatio et paenitentia*, December 2, 1984.

———. *Sollicitudo rei socialis*. December 30, 1987.

Johnson, Elizabeth A. *Ask the Beasts: Darwin and the God of Love*. London: Bloomsbury, 2014.

Jones, Christopher D., and Conor Kelly. "Sloth: America's Ironic Structural Vice." *Journal of the Society of Christian Ethics* 37, no. 2 (2017): 117–34.

Jones, Jacqueline. *Labor of Love, Labor of Sorrow: Black Women, Work, and the Family, from Slavery to the Present*. 2nd ed. New York: Basic Books, 2010.

Jung, Patricia Beattie, and Joseph Andrew Coray, eds. *Sexual Diversity and Catholicism*. Collegeville, MN: Liturgical Press, 2001.

Kasper, Walter. "The Power of Christian Love to Transform the World." In *Faith and the Future*. New York: Crossroad, 1982.

Kaztauskis, Antanas. "Life Story of a Lithuanian." In *Life Stories of Undistinguished Americans*, edited by Hamilton Holt, 2nd ed., 6–20. New York: Routledge, 1990.

Katzman, David M., and William M. Tuttle, Jr., eds. *Plain Folk: The Life and Stories of Undistinguished Americans*. Urbana: University of Illinois Press, 1982.

Kavanaugh, John F. *Following Christ in a Consumer Society: The Spirituality of Cultural Resistance*. 2nd ed. Maryknoll, NY: Orbis Books, 1991.

———. *Following Christ in a Consumer Society: The Spirituality of Cultural Resistance*. 25th anniversary ed. Maryknoll, NY: Orbis Books, 2006.

Kazin, Michael. *The Populist Persuasion: An American History*. Ithaca, NY: Cornell University Press, 2017.

Keister, Lisa A. "Upward Wealth Mobility: Exploring the Roman Catholic Advantage." *Social Forces* 85, no. 3 (March 2007): 1–31.

Kelly, Conor M. "The Nature and Operation of Structural Sin: Additional Insights from Theology and Moral Psychology." *Theological Studies* 80, no. 2 (2019): 293–327.

Kendi, Ibram X. *How to Be an Antiracist*. New York: Penguin, 2019.

Kerber, Linda K. *No Constitutional Right to be Ladies: Women and the Obligations of Citizenship*. New York: Hill and Wang, 1998.

———. "Separate Spheres, Female Worlds: The Rhetoric of Women's History." *Journal of American History* 75, no. 1 (June 1988): 9–39.

Kessler-Harris, Alice. *Out to Work: A History of America's Wage-Earning Women.* New York: Oxford University Press, 1982.

———. *A Woman's Wage: Historical Meanings and Social Consequences.* Lexington: University of Kentucky Press, 2015.

King, Anthony. "The Accidental Derogation of the Lay Actor: A Critique of Giddens's Concept of Structure." *Philosophy of the Social Sciences* 30, no. 3 (2000): 362–83.

King, Martin Luther, Jr. *Where Do We Go from Here: Chaos or Community?* Boston: Beacon Press, 1968.

Kittay, Eva Feder. "The Global Heart Transplant and Caring across Boundaries." *Southern Journal of Philosophy* 46, no. S1 (2008): 138–65.

Kittay, Eva Feder, and Ellen K. Feder, eds. *The Subject of Care: Feminist Perspectives on Dependency.* Lanham, MD: Rowman and Littlefield, 2003.

Kittay, Eva Feder, Bruce Jennings, and Angela A. Wasunna. "Dependency, Difference and the Global Ethic of Longterm Care." *Journal of Political Philosophy* 13, no. 4 (2005): 443–69.

Kochan, Thomas A. "Building a New Social Contract at Work: A Moral and Economic Imperative." *Journal of Catholic Social Thought* 9, no. 1 (Winter 2012): 7–22.

Kroløkke, Charlotte, and Anne Scott Sørensen. *Gender Communication Theories and Analyses: From Silence to Performance.* Thousand Oaks, CA: Sage, 2006.

Kruse, Kevin M. *One Nation under God: How Corporate America Invented Christian America.* New York: Basic Books, 2016.

Kurdek, Lawrence A. "The Allocation of Household Labor by Partners in Gay and Lesbian Couples." *Journal of Family Issues* 28, no. 1 (January 2007): 132–48.

Kusnet, David, Lawrence Mishel, and Ruy Teixeira. *Talking Past Each Other: What Everyday Americans Really Think (And Elites Don't Get) About the Economy.* Washington, DC: Economic Policy Institute, 2006.

Kyrk, Hazel. *A Theory of Consumption.* New York: Arno, 1976.

Lambert, Jennifer R. "Beyond the 'Goods Life': Mass Consumerism, Conflict, and the Latchkey-Kid." *Human Architecture: Journal of Sociology of Self Knowledge* 3, no. 1 (2004): 103–8. https://www.okcir.com/Articles%20III%201&2/HAfall04sp05p103-108.pdf.

Lamont, Michèle. *The Dignity of Working Men: Morality and the Boundaries of Race, Class, and Immigration.* Cambridge, MA: Harvard University Press, 2000.

Lane, Robert E. *The Market Experience.* Cambridge: Cambridge University Press, 1991.

Lasch, Christopher. *The Culture of Narcissism.* New York: W. W. Norton, 1979.

Lebacqz, Karen. "Love Your Enemy: Sex, Power, and Christian Ethics." *Annual of the Society of Christian Ethics* 10 (1990): 3–23.

Lee, Frederic. "Heterodox Economics." In *New Palgrave Dictionary of Economics*, edited by L. F. Blume and S. Durlauf, 2720–24. London: Palgrave Macmillan, 2008.

Lemann, Nicholas. *The Promised Land: The Great Black Migration and How It Changed America.* New York: Knopf, 1991.

Leo XIII. *Quod apostolici muneris*, December 29, 1878.

———. *Rerum novarum*, May 15, 1891.

Leondar-Wright, Betsy. *Class Matters: Cross-Class Alliance Building for Middle-Class Activists.* Gabriola Island, BC, Canada: New Society, 2005.

———. *Missing Class: Strengthening Social Movement Groups by Seeing Class Cultures.* Ithaca, NY: Cornell University Press, 2014.

Levanon, Asaf, Paula England, and Paul Allison. "Occupational Feminization and Pay: Assessing Causal Dynamics Using 1950–2000 U.S. Census Data." *Social Forces* 88, no. 2 (2009): 865–91.

Levine, Bruce E. *Get Up, Stand Up: Uniting Populists, Energizing the Defeated, and Battling the Corporate Elite.* White River Junction, VT: Chelsea Green, 2011.

Lipset, Seymour Martin. "Radicalism or Reformism: The Sources of Working-Class Politics." *American Political Science Review* 77, no. 1 (1983): 1–18.

Lipset, Seymour Martin, and R. Bendix. *Social Mobility in Industrial Society.* Berkeley: University of California Press, 1959.

Lipsitz, George. *The Possessive Investment in Whiteness: How White People Profit from Identity Politics.* Philadelphia: Temple University Press, 1998.

Littleton, Christine. "Reconstructing Sexual Equality." In *Living with Contradictions: Controversies in Feminist Ethics*, edited by Allison Jaggar, 28–33. Boulder, CO: Westview, 1994.

Logan, James. *Good Punishment? Christian Moral Practice and U.S. Imprisonment.* Grand Rapids, MI: Eerdmans, 2008.

Lonergan, Bernard, J. F. *Insight: A Study in Human Understanding.* 3rd ed. New York: Philosophical Library, 1970.

Lopez, Steven H. *Reorganizing the Rust Belt: An Inside Story of the American Labor Movement.* Berkeley: University of California, 2004.

Lustig, R. Jeffrey. "The Tangled Knot of Race and Class in America." In *What's Class Got to Do with It? American Society in the Twenty-First Century*, edited by Micahel Zweig, 45–60. Ithaca, NY: Cornell University Press, 2004.

Lutz, Mark A. "An Essay on the Nature and Significance of Social Economics." In *Social Economics: Retrospect and Prospect*, edited by Mark A. Lutz, 407–42. Boston: Kluwer Academic, 1990.

———. "Social Economics in the Humanistic Tradition." In *Social Economics: Retrospect and Prospect*, edited by Mark A. Lutz, 235–67. Dordrecht: Springer, 1990.

Lynch, Helena. "Industrial Areas Foundation." *New York Law School Law Review* 50 (2005–2006): 571–78.

MacIntyre, Alasdair C. *Dependent Rational Animals: Why Human Beings Need the Virtues.* Chicago: Open Court, 2006.

Mainardi, Pat. "The Politics of Housework." In *Sisterhood is Powerful: An Anthology of Writings from the Women's Liberation Movement*, edited by Robin Morgan, 447–53. New York: Random House, 1970.

Maldonado, Laurie Chisholm. "Doing Better for Single-Parent Families: Poverty and Policy Across 45 Countries." PhD diss., University of California, Los Angeles, 2017. https://escholarship.org/uc/item/49w2b8gg#author.

Marchand, Roland. *Advertising the American Dream: Making Way for Modernity, 1920–1940.* Berkeley: University of California Press, 1985.

Maritain, Jacques. *Integral Humanism: Temporal and Spiritual Problems of a New Christendom.* Translated by Joseph Evans. New York: Charles Scribner, 1968.

———. *True Humanism.* Translated by M. R. Adamson. London: Geoffrey Bles, 1938.

Massingale, Bryan N. "James Cone and Recent Catholic Episcopal Teaching on Racism." *Theological Studies* 61, no. 4 (2000): 700–730.

———. *Racial Justice and the Catholic Church.* Maryknoll, NY: Orbis Books, 2010.

Matheny, Ken. "The Disappearance of Labor Unions and Social Encyclicals of Popes John Paul II and Benedict XVI." *Southern California Interdisciplinary Law Journal* 23, no. 1 (2014): 1–35.

Matovina, Timothy. *Latino Catholicism: Transformation in America's Largest Church.* Princeton, NJ: Princeton University Press, 2012.

May, Martha. "Bread before Roses: American Workingmen, Labor Unions and the Family Wage." In *Women, Work, and Protest: A Century of US Women's Labor History,* edited by Ruth Milkman, 1–21. London: Routledge, 2016.

Mazzenga, Maria. "One Hundred Years of American Catholics and Organized Labor, 1870s–1970s." *Journal of Catholic Social Thought* 9, no. 1 (Winter 2012): 23–42.

McCann, Dennis. "Catholic Social Teaching in an Era of Economic Globalization: A Resource for Business Ethics." *Business Ethics Quarterly* 7, no. 2 (March 1997): 57–70.

McCarraher, Eugene D. "The Saint in the Gray Flannel Suit: The Professional-Managerial Class, 'The Layman,' and American-Catholic Religious Culture, 1945–1965." *U.S. Catholic Historian* 15, no. 3 (Summer 1997): 99–118.

McCarthy, David Matzko. *The Good Life: Genuine Christianity for the Middle Class.* Grand Rapids, MI: Brazos, 2004.

McCartin, Joseph A. *Collision Course: Ronald Reagan, the Air Traffic Controllers, and the Strike That Changed America.* New York: Oxford University, 2011.

———. "Fire the Hell Out of Them: Sanitation Workers' Struggles and the Normalization of the Striker Replacement Strategy in the 1970s." *Labor: Studies in Working-Class History of the Americas* 2, no. 3 (2005): 67–92.

McConahay, John B., Betty B. Hardee, Valerie Batts. "Has Racism Declined in America? It Depends on Who Is Asking and What Is Asked." *Journal of Conflict Resolution* 25, no. 4 (December 1981): 563–79.

McGreevy, John T. *Catholicism and American Freedom: A History.* New York: W. W. Norton, 2004.

———. *Parish Boundaries: The Catholic Encounter with Race in the Twentieth-Century Urban North.* Chicago: University of Chicago Press, 1997.

McRorie, Christina G. "Adam Smith, Ethicist: A Case for Reading Political Economy as Moral Anthropology." *Journal of Religious Ethics* 43, no. 4 (December 2015): 674–96.

———. "Heterodox Economics, Social Ethics, and Inequalities: New Tools for Thinking Critically about Markets and Economic Injustices." *Journal of Religious Ethics* 47, no. 2 (2019): 232–58.

McShane, Joseph. *"Sufficiently Radical": Catholicism, Progressivism, and the Bishops' Program of 1919.* Washington, DC: Catholic University of America Press, 1986.

Memmi, Albert. *Dominated Man: Notes Toward a Portrait.* Boston: Beacon, 1969.

———. *Racism.* Minneapolis: University of Minnesota Press, 2000.

Metzgar, Jack. "Politics and the American Class Vernacular." *WorkingUSA* 7, no. 1 (2003): 49–80. https://onlinelibrary.wiley.com/doi/epdf/10.1111/j.1743-4580.2003.00003.x-i1.

Mich, Marvin Krier. *Catholic Social Teaching and Movements.* Mystic, CT: Twenty-Third, 1998.

———. "The Living Wage Movement and Catholic Social Teaching." *Journal of Catholic Social Thought* 6, no. 1 (2009): 231–52.

Miller, Daniel. "Consumption as the Vanguard of History: A Polemic by Way of an Introduction." In *Acknowledging Consumption: A Review of New Studies,* edited by Daniel Miller, 1–52. London: Routledge, 1995.

Miller, Jean Baker. *Toward a New Psychology of Women*. Boston: Beacon, 1986.

Miller, Vincent J. *Consuming Religion: Christian Faith and Practice in a Consumer Culture*. New York: Continuum, 2004.

———. "Taking Consumer Culture Seriously." *Horizons* 27, no. 2 (2000) 276–95.

Mills, Charles. *The Racial Contract*. Ithaca, NY: Cornell University Press, 1997.

Mink, Gwendolyn. *The Wages of Motherhood, Inequality in the Welfare State, 1917–1942*. Ithaca, NY: Hill and Wang, 1998.

Mishel, Lawrence, Jared Bernstein, and Sylvia Allegretto. *The State of Working America, 2006–07*. Washington, DC, and Ithaca, NY: Economic Policy Institute and Cornell University Press, 2007.

Mishel, Lawrence, Elise Gould, and Josh Bivens. *Wage Stagnation in Nine Charts*. Washington, DC: Economic Policy Institute, 2015. https://www.epi.org/files/2013/wage-stagnation-in-nine-charts.pdf.

Misner, Paul. *Social Catholicism in Europe: From the Onset of Industrialization to the First World War*. New York: Crossroad, 1991.

Molony, John. *The Worker Question: A New Historical Perspective on "Rerum Novarum."* Dublin: Gill and Macmillan, 1991.

Monkkonen, Eric H. *America Becomes Urban: The Development of U.S. Cities and Towns, 1780–1980*. Berkeley: University of California Press, 1988.

Moore, Joan. "The Social Fabric of the Hispanic Community since 1965." In *Hispanic Catholic Culture in the U.S.: Issues and Concerns*, edited by Jay P. Dolan and Allan Figueroa Deck, 6–49. Notre Dame, IN: University of Notre Dame Press, 1994.

Mosco, Vincent. *The Political Economy of Communication*. Los Angeles: Sage, 2010.

Moyn, Samuel. *Not Enough: Human Rights in an Unequal World*. Cambridge, MA: Harvard University Press, 2018.

Mueller, Carol. "Ella Baker and the Origins of 'Participatory Democracy.'" In *The Black Studies Reader*, edited by Jacqueline Bobo, Cynthia Hudley, and Claudine Michel, 79–90. New York: Routledge, 2004.

Muhammad, Khalil Gibran. *The Condemnation of Blackness: Race, Crime, and the Making of Modern Urban America*. Cambridge, MA: Harvard University Press, 2011.

Mullainthan, Sendhil, and Eldar Shafir. *Scarcity: Why Having Too Little Means So Much*. New York: Times Books, Henry Holt and Company, 2013.

Muller, Jerry Z. "Capitalism and Inequality: What the Right and the Left Get Wrong." *Foreign Affairs* 92, no. 2 (2013): 30–51.

Murphy, Laura. "An 'Indestructible Right': John Ryan and the Catholic Origins of the U.S. Living Wage Movement, 1906–1938." *Labor: Studies in Working-Class History of the Americas* 6, no. 1 (Spring 2009): 57–86.

Murray, Charles. *Coming Apart: The State of White America, 1960–2010*. New York: Crown Forum, 2013.

Myrdal, Gunnar. *An American Dilemma: The Negro Problem and Modern Democracy*. New York: Harper, 1944.

National Catholic Welfare Council. "Bishops Program of Social Reconstruction." 1919. https://cuomeka.wrlc.org/items/show/825.

National Opinion Research Center at the University of Chicago. *Trends in Public Evaluations of Economic Well-Being, 1972–2014*. General Social Survey Final Report, April 2015. http://www.norc.org/PDFs/GSS%20Reports/GSS_EconomicWellBeing15_final_formatted.pdf.

Nelson, Julie. *Economics for Humans*. Chicago: University of Chicago Press, 2006.

Neubeck, Kenneth J., and Noel A. Cazenave. *Welfare Racism: Playing the Race Card against America's Poor*. New York: Routledge, 2001.

Neumark, David. "Living Wages: Protection for or Protection from Low-Wage Workers?" *Industrial and Labor Relations Review* 58 (2004): 27–51.

Newman, Katherine. *No Shame in My Game: The Working Poor in the Inner City*. New York: Vintage Books and Russell Sage Foundation, 2009.

Newman, Katherine, and Victor Tan Chen. *The Missing Class: Portraits of the Near Poor in America*. Boston: Beacon, 2007.

Nicolás, Adolfo. "Depth, Universality, and Learned Ministry: Challenges to Jesuit Higher Education Today." Remarks for "Networking Jesuit Higher Education: Shaping the Future for a Humane, Just, Sustainable Globe," Mexico City, April 23, 2010. http://www.sjweb.info /documents/ansj/100423_Mexico%20City_Higher%20Education%20Today_ENG .pdf.

Nixon, Mark G. "The Economic Foundations of Modern Catholic Social Teaching, Past, and Prospect." PhD diss., Fordham University, 2015.

———. "Satisfaction for Whom? Freedom for What? Theology and Economic Theory of the Consumer." *Journal of Business Ethics* 70, no. 1 (2007): 39–60.

Novak, Michael, Michael Joyce, and the Lay Commission on Catholic Social Teaching. *Toward the Future: Catholic Social Thought and the U.S. Economy*. Washington, DC: Catholic University of America Press, 1985.

Oats, Mary J. "Catholic Laywomen in the Labor Force, 1850–1950." In *American Catholic Women*, edited by K. Kennelly, 81–124. New York: Macmillan, 1989.

O'Boyle, Edward J. "Origins of the Association for Social Economics." *Forum for Social Economics* 43, no. 1 (2014): 104–6.

O'Brien, David J. *American Catholics and Social Reform: The New Deal Years*. New York: Oxford University Press, 1968.

———. *Public Catholicism*. 2nd ed. Maryknoll, NY: Orbis Books, 1996.

O'Connell, Maureen. *If These Walls Could Talk: Community Muralism and the Beauty of Justice*. Collegeville, MN: Liturgical Press, 2012.

O'Neill, William L. *Feminism in America: A History*. 2nd rev. ed. London: Routledge, 2017.

Organisation for Economic Co-operation and Development (OECD). *Income Inequality Remains High in the Face of Weak Recovery*. Income Inequality Update, November 2016. http://www.oecd.org/social/OECD2016-Income-Inequality-Update.pdf.

Orsi, Robert. *The Madonna of 115th Street: Faith and Community in Italian Harlem, 1880–1950*. 3rd ed. New Haven, CT: Yale University Press, 2010.

Ortiz, Isabel, and Matthew Cummins. "Global Inequality: Beyond the Bottom Billion—A Rapid Review of Income Distribution in 141 Countries." Working Paper. United Nations Children's Fund (UNICEF), New York, April 2011.

Osborne, Catherine R. "Migrant Domestic Careworkers: Between the Public and the Private in Catholic Social Teaching." *Journal of Religious Ethics* 40, no. 1 (2012): 1–25.

Packard, Vance. *The Status Seekers: An Exploration of Class Behaviour in America*. Harmondsworth, Middlesex: Penguin, 1961.

Palmer, Phyllis. *Domesticity and Dirt: Housewives and Domestic Servants in the United States, 1920–1945*. Philadelphia: Temple University Press, 1989.

Parreñas, Rhacel Salazar. *Servants of Globalization: Women, Migration, and Domestic Work*. Stanford, CA: Stanford University Press, 2001.

Parsons, Talcott. "The Sociology and Economics of Class Conflict in the Light of Recent Sociological Theory." *American Economic Review* 39, no. 3 (May 1949): 16–26.

Paul VI. *Octogesima adveniens*, May 14, 1971.

———. *Populorum progressio*, March 26, 1967.

Payne, Keith. *The Broken Ladder: How Inequality Affects the Way We Think, Live, and Die.* New York: Penguin Books, 2018.

Pehl, Matthew. *The Making of Working-Class Religion.* Urbana: University of Illinois Press, 2016. Kindle.

Peiss, Kathy. "Gender Relations and Working-Class Leisure: New York City, 1880–1920." In *"To Toil the Livelong Day": America's Women at Work, 1780–1980,* edited by Carol Groneman and Mary Beth Norton, 98–111. Ithaca, NY: Cornell University Press, 1987.

Perrot, Étienne. "Le risque au coeur de l'éthique financière." *Finance & Bien Commun* 2–3, no. 31–32 (2008): 119–28. https://www.cairn.info/revue-finance-et-bien-commun-2008 -2-page-119.htm#.

Philipps, Lisa. "Silent Partners: The Role of Unpaid Market Labor in Families." *Feminist Economics* 14, no. 2 (April 2008): 37–57.

Piketty, Thomas. *Capital in the Twenty-First Century.* Translated by Arthur Goldhammer. Cambridge, MA: Harvard University Press, 2013.

Pius XI. *Quadragesimo anno*, May 15, 1931.

Pollin, Robert, Mark Brenner, Jeannette Wicks-Lim, and Stephanie Luce. *A Measure of Fairness: The Economics of Living Wages and Minimum Wages in the United States.* Ithaca, NY: Cornell University Press, 2008.

Pontifical Commission for Justice and Peace. *Compendium of the Social Doctrine of the Catholic Church.* Vatican City: Libreria Editrice Vaticana, 2004.

Pope, Stephen J. "The Magisterium's Arguments against 'Same-Sex Marriage': An Ethical Analysis and Critique." *Theological Studies* 65, no. 3 (September 2004): 530–65.

———. "Scientific and Natural Law Assessments of Homosexuality." *Journal of Religious Ethics* 25, no. 1 (Spring 1997): 89–126.

Power, Marilyn. "Social Provisioning as a Starting Point for Feminist Economics." *Feminist Economics* 10, no. 3 (November 2004): 3–19.

Prentiss, Craig R. *Debating God's Economy: Social Justice in America on the Eve of Vatican II.* University Park, PA: Pennsylvania State University Press, 2008.

Putnam, Robert D. *Bowling Alone: The Collapse and Revival of American Community.* New York: Simon & Schuster, 2000.

———. "E Pluribus Unum: Diversity and Community in the Twenty-First Century: The 2006 Johan Skytte Prize Lecture." *Scandinavian Political Studies* 30, no. 2 (2007): 137–74.

———. *Our Kids: The American Dream in Crisis.* New York: Simon & Schuster, 2015.

Quadagno, Jill. *One Nation, Uninsured: Why the U.S. Has No National Health Insurance.* Oxford: Oxford University Press, 2005.

Raines, John, and Donna C. Day-Lower. *Modern Work and Human Meaning.* Philadelphia: Westminster, 1986.

Rapp, Rayna. "Family and Class in America: Notes Toward an Understanding of Ideology." In *American Families: A Multicultural Reader,* edited by Stephanie Coontz with Maya Parson and Gabrielle Raley, 180–96. New York: Routledge, 1999.

Rathbone, Eleanor. *The Disinherited Family: A Plea for the Endowment of the Family.* London: Arnold, 1924.

Ratzinger, Joseph. "Letter to the Bishops of the Catholic Church on the Collaboration of Men and Women in the Church and in the World." July 31, 2004. Congregation of the Doctrine of the Faith. https://www.ewtn.com/catholicism/library/on-collaboration-of-men-and-women-in-the-church-and-in-the-world-2106.

Raworth, Kate. *Doughnut Economics: 7 Ways to Think Like a 21st Century Economist*. White River Junction, VT: Chelsea Green, 2017.

Reeves, Richard, Elizabeth Kneebone, and Edward Rodrigue. *Five Evils: Multidimensional Poverty and Race in America*. Washington, DC: Brookings Institution, 2016. https://www.brookings.edu/wp-content/uploads/2016/06/ReevesKneeboneRodrigue_MultidimensionalPoverty_FullPaper.pdf.

Reich, Robert. *The Work of Nations: Preparing Ourselves for 21st Century Capitalism*. New York: Vintage Books, 1992.

Reid, Lesley Williams, and Beth A. Rubin. "Integrating Economic Dualism and Labor Market Segmentation: The Effects of Race, Gender, and Structural Location on Earnings, 1974–2000. *Sociology Quarterly* 44, no. 3 (2003): 405–32.

Reimer-Barry, Emily. Review of *The Vice of Luxury: Economic Excess in a Consumer Age*, by David Cloutier. *Journal of the Society of Christian Ethics* 36, no. 2 (2016): 211–13.

Rice, Lincoln. *Healing the Racial Divide, A Catholic Interracial Framework Inspired by Dr. Arthur Falls*. Eugene, OR: Pickwick, 2014.

Roediger, David. *Colored White: Transcending the Racial Past*. Berkeley: University of California Press, 2002.

———. *The Wages of Whiteness: Race and the Making of the American Working Class*. Rev. ed. London: Verso, 2007.

———. *Working toward Whiteness: How America's Immigrants Became White: The Strange Journey from Ellis Island to the Suburbs*. London: Basic Books, 2018.

Romero, Oscar H. *The Violence of Love*. Compiled and translated by James Brockman. Farmington, PA: Plough, 2007.

Rose, Stephen K. *The Growing Size and Income of the Upper Middle Class*. Washington, DC: Urban Institute, 2016. http://www.urban.org/research/publication/growing-size-and-incomes-upper-middle-class/view/full_report.

Rosenfeld, Jake. "Economic Determinants of Voting in an Era of Union Decline." *Social Science Quarterly* 91, no. 2 (June 2010): 379–96.

Rosenfeld, Jake, Patrick Denice, and Jennifer Laird. *Union Decline Lowers Wages of Nonunion Workers*. Washington, DC: Economic Policy Institute, 2016. https://www.epi.org/files/pdf/112811.pdf.

Ross, Marc Howard. *Cultural Contestation in Ethnic Conflict*. Cambridge: Cambridge University Press, 2017.

Rothman, Adam. "Reckoning with Slavery at Georgetown." *American Association of Colleges and Universities* 21, no. 3 (Summer 2018). https://www.aacu.org/diversitydemocracy/2018/summer/rothman.

Rubin, Lillian B. *Families on the Fault Line: America's Working Class Speaks about the Family, the Economy, Race, and Ethnicity*. New York: HarperCollins, 1994.

———. *Worlds of Pain: Life in the Working Class Family*. New York: Basic Books, 1993.

Rubio, Julie Hanlon. *Family Ethics: Practices for Christians*. Washington, DC: Georgetown University Press, 2010.

Ryan, John A. *A Better Economic Order*. New York: Harper, 1935.

———. *The Catholic Church and the Citizen*. New York: Macmillan, 1928.

———. *The Church and Socialism, and other Essays*. London: BiblioLife, 2009.

———. *Declining Liberty and Other Papers*. New York: Macmillan, 1927.

———. *Distributive Justice*. 1916. Rev. ed. New York: Macmillan, 1927, 1942.

———. "The Experts Look at Unemployment: II. A Shorter Work Period." *Commonweal* 10 (1929): 636–38.

———. *Family Limitation and the Church and Birth Control*. New York: Paulist, 1921.

———. *A Living Wage: Its Ethical and Economic Aspects*. New York: Macmillan, 1912.

———. *The Norm of Morality: Defined and Applied to Particular Actions*. Washington, DC: National Welfare Conference, 1944.

———. *Questions of the Day*. Boston: Stratford, 1931.

———. *Social Doctrine in Action: A Personal History*. New York: Harper & Brothers, 1941.

———. *Social Reconstruction*. New York: Macmillan, 1920.

———. "Two Objectives for Catholic Economists." *Review of Social Economy* 1, no. 1 (1942): 1–5.

Sandel, Michael. *Democracy's Discontent: America in Search of a Public Philosophy*. Cambridge, MA: Belknap Press of Harvard University Press, 1996.

Schiltz, Elizabeth Rose. "Motherhood and the Mission: What Catholic Law Schools Could Learn from Harvard about Women." *Catholic University Law Review* 56 (2007): 405–50.

Schneebaum, Alyssa. "The Economics of Same-Sex Couples: Essays on Work, Wages, and Poverty." PhD diss., University of Massachusetts, Amherst, 1993.

Scholz, Sally J. *Political Solidarity*. University Park, PA: Penn State University Press, 2012.

Schor, Juliet. *Born to Buy: The Commercialized Child and the New Consumer Culture*. New York: Scribner, 2004.

———. *The Overspent American: Why We Want What We Don't Need*. New York: HarperPerennial, 1998.

———. *The Overworked American: The Unexpected Decline of Leisure*. New York: Basic Books, 1992.

Schuck, Michael J. *That They May Be One: The Social Teaching of the Papal Encyclicals, 1740–1989*. Washington, DC: Georgetown University Press, 1991.

Schwartz, Barry. *The Paradox of Choice: Why More Is Less*. 2nd ed. San Francisco: HarperCollins, 2016.

Seaton, Douglas P. *Catholics and Radicals: The Association of Catholic Trade Unionists and the American Labor Movement, from the Depression to the Cold War*. Lewisburg, PA: Bucknell University Press, 1981.

Seccareccia, Mario. "Basic Income, Full Employment, and Social Provisioning: Some Polanyian/Keynesian Insights." *Journal of Economic Issues* 49, no. 2 (2015): 397–404.

———. "Dualism and Economic Stagnation: Can a Policy of Guaranteed Basic Income Return Mature Market Economies to *les Trente Glorieuses*?" Conference Paper, Institute for New Economic Thinking, October 23, 2017. https://www.ineteconomics.org/uploads/papers/Seccareccia-INET-Dualism-GI-01.pdf.

Sennett, Richard, and Jonathan Cobb. *The Hidden Injuries of Class*. New York: W. W. Norton, 1972.

Shadle, Matthew. *Interrupting Capitalism: Catholic Social Thought and the Economy*. New York: Oxford University Press, 2018.

Shands, Harley C., and James D. Meltzer. *Language and Psychiatry*. The Hague: Mouton, 1973.

Siegel, Reva B. "Home as Work: The First Woman's Rights Claims Concerning Wives' Household Labor, 1850–1880." *Yale Law Journal* 103 (1994): 1073–217.

Silbaugh, Katharine B. "Women's Place: Urban Planning, Housing Design, and Work-Family Balance." *Fordham Law Review* 76, no. 3 (2007): 1797–1852.

Silverblatt, Irene. *Modern Inquisitions: Peru and the Colonial Origins of the Civilized World.* Durham, NC: Duke University Press, 2005.

Simon, Herbert A. "Rational Choice and the Structure of the Environment," *Psychological Review* 63, no. 2 (1956): 129–38.

Sinclair, Upton. *The Jungle.* New York: Doubleday and Jabber, 1906.

Skocpol, Theda. "Civic Transformation and Inequality in the Contemporary United States." In *Social Inequality*, edited by Kathryn M. Neckerman, 729–67. New York: Russell Sage Foundation, 2004.

Smith, Gregory, et al. "America's Changing Religious Landscape." Report. Pew Research Center, May 12, 2015, chapter 3, "Demographic Profiles of Religious Groups." https://www.pewforum.org/2015/05/12/chapter-3-demographic-profiles-of-religious-groups/.

Smith, Tom W. "The Emerging 21st Century Family." Gerner Social Survey Social Change Report No. 42, National Opinion Research Center at the University of Chicago, April 1999. https://gss.norc.org/Documents/reports/social-change-reports/SC42.pdf.

Snarr, C. Melissa. *All You That Labor: Religion and Ethics in the Living Wage Movement.* New York: New York University Press, 2011.

———. "Religion, Race, and Bridge Building in Economic Justice Coalitions." *WorkingUSA* 12, no. 1 (March 2009): 73–95.

Snow, David A. "Framing and Social Movements." *Wiley-Blackwell Encyclopedia of Social and Political Movements*, January 14, 2013. https://doi.org/10.1002/9780470674871.wbespm434.

Snow, Richard. *"I Invented the Modern Age": The Rise of Henry Ford.* New York: Scribners, 2013.

Soelle, Dorothee. *To Work and to Love: A Theology of Creation.* With Shirley A. Cloyes. Philadelphia: Fortress, 1984.

Squires, Gregory D. *The Fight for Fair Housing: Causes, Consequences, and Future Implications of the 1968 Federal Fair Housing Act.* New York: Routledge, 2018.

———. "Social Insecurity: The Roller Coaster Ride of America's Middle Class." *Notre Dame Journal of Law, Ethics, and Public Policy* 24, no. 2 (2010): 285–91.

Stabile, Susan J. "Othering and the Law." *University of St. Thomas Law Journal* 12, no. 2 (2016): 381–410.

Starr, Martha. "Consumption, Work Hours, and Values in the Writings of John A. Ryan: Is It Possible to Return to the Road Not Taken?" *Review of Social Economy* 66, no. 1 (2008): 7–24.

Statistical Abstract of the United States. Washington, DC: Government Printing Office, 1929.

Stevens, Krista. "Challenging the Catholic Church: Constructing a Social Ethics of Racial Solidarity." PhD diss., Fordham University, 2015.

Stiglitz, Joseph E. *The Price of Inequality: How Today's Divided Society Endangers Our Future.* New York: W. W. Norton, 2012. Kindle.

Stone, Pamela. *Opting Out? Why Women Really Quit Careers and Head Home.* Berkeley: University of California Press, 2007.

Stout, Jeffrey. *Blessed Are the Organized: Grassroots Democracy in America.* Princeton, NJ: Princeton University Press, 2010.

Streib, Jessi, Miryea Ayala, and Colleen Wixted. "Benign Inequality: Frames of Poverty and Social Class Inequality in Children's Movies." *Journal of Poverty* 21, no. 1 (2017): 1–19.

Sugrue, Thomas. *Origins of the Urban Crisis*. Princeton, NJ: Princeton University Press, 2005.

Sullivan-Dunbar, Sandra. "The Care Economy as Alternative Economy." In *Working Alternatives: American and Catholic Experiments in Work and Economy*, edited by John C. Seitz and Christine Firer Hinze. New York: Fordham University Press, 2020.

———. *Human Dependency and Christian Ethics*. Cambridge: Cambridge University Press, 2017.

Tanner, Michael D. *The Inclusive Economy: How to Bring Wealth to America's Poor*. New York: Cato Institute, 2018.

Taylor, Charles. "Modern Social Imaginaries." *Public Culture*, 14, no. 1 (2002): 91–124.

Taylor, Sarah McFarland. *Green Sisters: A Spiritual Ecology*. Cambridge, MA: Harvard University Press, 2009.

Teixeira, Ruy, and Joel Rogers. *America's Forgotten Majority: Why the White Working Class Still Matters*. New York: Basic Books, 2000.

Temin, Peter. *The Vanishing Middle Class: Prejudice and Power in a Dual Economy*. Boston: MIT Press, 2017.

Tentler, Leslie Woodcock. *Catholics and Contraception: An American History*. Ithaca, NY: Cornell University Press, 2009.

———. *Wage-Earning Women: Industrial Work and Family Life in the United States, 1900–1930*. New York: Oxford University, 1979.

Terborg-Penn, Rosalyn. "Survival Strategies among African-American Women Workers: A Continuing Process." In *Women, Work, and Protest: A Century of U.S. Women's Labor History*, edited by Ruth Milkman, 139–55. London: Routledge, 2016.

Tesler, Michael. *Post-Racial or Most-Racial: Race and Politics in the Obama Era*. Chicago: University of Chicago Press, 2016.

Tocqueville, Alexis, de. *Democracy in America and Two Essays*. London: Penguin, 2003.

Thornton, Timothy, and Bernard Taithe, eds. *Propaganda: Political Rhetoric and Identity, 1300–2000*. Gloucestershire: Sutton, 1999.

Todres, Jonathan. "Law, Otherness, and Human Trafficking." *Santa Clara Law Review* 49, no. 3 (2009): 605–72.

Tracy, David. *The Analogical Imagination: Christian Theology and the Culture of Pluralism*. New York: Continuum, 1998.

Traina, Cristina L. H. "'This Is the Year': Narratives of Structural Evil." *Journal of the Society of Christian Ethics* 37, no. 2 (2017): 3–17.

Trotter, Joe W. *From a Raw Deal to a New Deal? African Americans, 1929–1945*. New York: Oxford University Press, 1995.

———. "Perspectives on Black Working-Class History and the Labor Movement Today." Seattle: Center for Labor Studies, 1996. http://www.forschungsnetzwerk.at/downloadpub/Trotter_Perspectives.pdf.

Troy, Leo. "Is the U.S. Unique in the Decline of Private Sector Unionism?" *Journal of Labor Research* 11, no. 2 (Spring 1990): 111–43.

———. "The Rise and Fall of American Trade Unions: The Labor Movement from FDR to RR." In *Unions in Transition: Entering the Second Century*, edited by Seymour Martin Lipset, 72–87. San Francisco: Institute for Contemporary Studies, 1986.

Tusser, Thomas. *Five Hundred Pointes of Good Husbandrie*. Edited by W. Payne and J. Herrtage. London: Tufner, 1887. First published 1570.

Twomey, Gerald S. "Pope John Paul II and the 'Preferential Option for the Poor.'" *Journal of Catholic Legal Studies* 45, no. 2 (2006): 321–68.

United Nations. *Progress of the World's Women, 2015–2016: Transforming Economies, Realizing Rights.* New York: UN Women, 2015. https://progress.unwomen.org/en/2015/pdf/UNW_progressreport.pdf.

United Nations Development Fund for Women. *Who Answers to Women? Gender & Accountability: Progress of the World's Women 2008/2009.* 2008. https://www.un.org/ruleoflaw/files/POWW08_Report_Full_Text.pdf.

United Nations Development Programme. *Humanity Divided: Confronting Inequality in Developing Countries.* November 2013.

United Press International Dispatch. "Dr. King Calls Vietnam Negotiation Essential." *Los Angeles Times,* July 3, 1965.

Urbina, Martin Guevera, and Sofia Espinoza Alvarez, eds. *Ethnicity and Criminal Justice in the Era of Mass Incarceration: A Critical Reader on the Latino Experience.* Springfield, IL: Charles C. Thomas, 2017.

US Catholic Bishops. *Brothers and Sisters to Us.* Pastoral letter, 1979. http://www.usccb.org/issues-and-action/cultural-diversity/african-american/brothers-and-sisters-to-us.cfm.

———. *Economic Justice for All: Pastoral Letter on Catholic Social Teaching and the U.S. Economy.* Washington, DC: United States Conference of Catholic Bishops, 2009. First published 1986. http://www.usccb.org/upload/economic_justice_for_all.pdf.

———. *Open Wide Our Hearts: The Enduring Call to Love; a Pastoral Letter against Racism.* Washington, DC: US Catholic Conference, 2018.

———. *Program of Social Reconstruction: A General Review of the Problems and Survey of the Remedies.* Washington, DC: National Catholic Welfare Conference, 1919. https://cuomeka.wrlc.org/files/original/370054457647c656264d6eb9bfdbc3aa.pdf.

Van Parijs, Philippe, and Yanick Vanderborght. *Basic Income: A Radical Proposal for a Free Society and a Sane Economy.* Cambridge, MA: Harvard University Press, 2017.

Vandenberg, Kathleen M. "René Girard and the Rhetoric of Consumption." *Contagion: Journal of Violence, Mimesis, and Culture* 12, no. 1 (2006): 259–72.

Verba, Sidney, Kay Lehman Schlozman, and Henry Brady. *Voice and Equality: Civic Voluntarism in American Politics.* Cambridge, MA: Harvard University Press, 1995.

Wachter, Michael L. "Labor Unions: A Corporatist Institution in a Competitive World." *University of Pennsylvania Law Review* 155, no. 3 (2007): 581–634.

Wallace, Catherine M. *Selling Ourselves Short: Why We Struggle to Earn a Living and Have a Life.* Grand Rapids, MI: Brazos, 2003.

Wallis, Jim. *America's Original Sin: Racism, White Privilege and the Bridge to a New America.* Grand Rapids, MI: Brazos, 2016.

Ward, Kate, and Kenneth R. Himes. "'Growing Apart': The Rise of Inequality." *Theological Studies* 75 (2014): 118–32.

Weir, Allison. "Global Care Chains: Freedom, Responsibility, and Solidarity." *Southern Journal of Philosophy* 46, no. S1 (2008): 166–75.

———. "The Global Universal Caregiver: Imagining Women's Liberation in the New Millennium." *Constellations* 12, no. 3 (2005): 308–30.

Weiss, Richard. *The American Myth of Success: From Horatio Alger to Norman Vincent Peale.* Urbana: University of Illinois Press, 1969.

Weisshaar, Katherine. "Earnings Equality and Relationship Stability for Same-Sex and Heterosexual Couples." *Social Forces* 93, no. 1 (2014): 92–123.

Welch, Sharon D. *A Feminist Ethic of Risk.* Minneapolis, MN: Fortress, 1990, 2000.

Weller, Christian E. *Working-Class Families Are Getting Hit from All Sides.* Washington, DC: Center for American Progress, 2018. https://cdn.americanprogress.org/content/uploads/2018/07/25091808/GettingHitOnAllSides-brief2.pdf.

West, Cornel. *Prophesy Deliverance! An Afro-American Revolutionary Christianity.* Louisville, KY: Westminster John Knox, 2002.

Western, Bruce, and Jake Rosenfeld. "Unions, Norms, and the Rise in US Wage Inequality." *American Sociological Review* 76, no. 4 (2011): 513–37.

Wheary, Jennifer, and Thomas M. Shapiro. *The Downslide before the Downturn: Declining Economic Security among Middle Class African Americans and Latinos, 2000–2006.* New York: Demos, 2009. https://www.demos.org/sites/default/files/publications/Downslide Downturn_Demos.pdf.

Wick, Ingeborg. *Women Working in the Shadows: The Informal Economy and Export Processing Zones.* Siegburg/Munich: Südwind e.V. Institut für Ökonomie und Ökumene, 2010.

Wilber, Charles. "The Ethics of Consumption: A Roman Catholic View." In *Ethics of Consumption: The Good Life, Justice, and Global Stewardship,* edited by David Crocker and Toby Linden, 403–16. Lanham, MD: Rowman and Littlefield, 1998.

Wilkinson, Richard, and Kate Pickett. *The Spirit Level: Why Greater Equality Makes Societies Stronger.* London: Bloomsbury, 2009. Kindle.

Williams, Joan C. *Reshaping the Work-Family Debate: Why Men and Class Matter.* Cambridge, MA: Harvard University Press, 2010.

———. *Unbending Gender: Why Family and Work Conflict and What to Do about It.* New York: Oxford University Press, 2000.

———. *White Working Class: Overcoming Class Cluelessness in America.* Boston, MA: Harvard Business Review, 2017.

Williams, Joan, and Heather Boushey. *The Three Faces of Work-Family Conflict: The Poor, the Professionals, and the Missing Middle Class.* Washington, DC: Center for American Progress, 2010. https://cdn.americanprogress.org/wp-content/uploads/issues/2010/01/pdf/threefaces.pdf.

Wilson, Midge, and Kathy Russell. *Divided Sisters: Bridging the Gap between Black Women and White Women.* New York: Anchor Books, 1996.

Wilson, Valerie. "People of Color Will Be a Majority of the Working Class in 2032." Economic Policy Institute, June 9, 2016. https://www.epi.org/files/pdf/108254.pdf.

Wilson, William Julius, and Richard Taub. *There Goes the Neighborhood: Racial, Ethnic, and Class Tensions in Four Chicago Neighborhoods and Their Meaning for America.* New York: Vintage Books, 2006.

Winant, Howard. *The New Politics of Race: Globalization, Difference, Justice.* Minneapolis: University of Minnesota Press, 2004.

Wise, Tim. *Between Barack and a Hard Place: Racism and White Denial in the Age of Obama.* San Francisco: City Lights Books, 2009.

Wolcott, Victoria. *Remaking Respectability: African American Women in Interwar Detroit.* Chapel Hill, NC: University of North Carolina Press, 2001.

World Synod of Catholic Bishops. *Justicia in mundo.* 1971.

Wright, Danaya C. "Theorizing History: Separate Spheres, the Public/Private Binary and a New Analytic for Family Law History." *Australia & New Zealand Law & History E-Journal.* Refereed Paper No. 2. (2012): 44–77. http://classic.austlii.edu.au/au/journals/ANZLawHisteJl/2012/2.html.

Wrong, Dennis H. *Power: Its Forms, Bases and Uses*. New York: Routledge, 2017.

Wuthnow, Robert. *American Misfits and the Making of Middle-Class Respectability*. Princeton, NJ: Princeton University Press, 2017.

Young, Iris Marion. "The Ideal of Community and the Politics of Difference." *Social Theory and Practice* 12, no. 1 (1986): 1–26.

———. *Justice and the Politics of Difference*. Princeton, NJ: Princeton University Press, 2011.

Yuengert, Andrew. "Free Markets and the Culture of Consumption." In *Catholic Social Teaching and the Market Economy*, edited by Philip Booth, 145–63. London: Institute of Economic Affairs, 2007.

Zunz, Oliver. *The Changing Faces of Inequality: Urbanization, Industrial Development, and Immigrants in Detroit, 1880–1920*. Chicago: University of Chicago Press, 1982.

Zweig, Michael. "Rethinking Class and Contemporary Working Class Studies." *Journal of Working-Class Studies* 1, no. 1 (December 2016): 14–22.

———, ed. *What's Class Got to Do with It? American Society in the Twenty-First Century*. Ithaca, NY: Cornell University Press, 2004.

———. *The Working Class Majority: America's Best Kept Secret*. 2nd ed. Ithaca, NY: ILR Press, an imprint of Cornell University Press, 2012.

INDEX

ABOUT THE AUTHOR

CHRISTINE FIRER HINZE is a professor of theological ethics and former director of the Curran Center for American Catholic Studies at Fordham University. She is the author of *Comprehending Power in Christian Social Ethics* and *Glass Ceilings and Dirt Floors: Women, Work, and the Global Economy*. She is also the coeditor of *More Than a Monologue: Sexual Diversity and the Catholic Church: Voices of Our Times* with J. Patrick Hornbeck, II, and of *Working Alternatives: American and Catholic Experiments in Work and Economy* with John C. Seitz.

CPSIA information can be obtained
at www.ICGtesting.com
Printed in the USA
JSHW021442200722
28295JS00001BA/12